821.8
0

The OXFORD book of eighteenth century verse,
chosen by David Nichol Smith.   Oxford Univ.
Pr., 1926. 727p.   9.75

1. English poetry - 18th cent.
Smith, David Nichol, 1875-   , ed.

The
Oxford Book
Of Eighteenth Century
Verse

The Oxford Book Of Eighteenth Century Verse

Chosen by

David Nichol Smith

Oxford

At the Clarendon Press

Oxford University Press, Ely House, London W. 1

GLASGOW NEW YORK TORONTO MELBOURNE WELLINGTON
CAPE TOWN SALISBURY IBADAN NAIROBI DAR ES SALAAM LUSAKA ADDIS ABABA
BOMBAY CALCUTTA MADRAS KARACHI LAHORE DACCA
KUALA LUMPUR SINGAPORE HONG KONG TOKYO

FIRST EDITION 1926
REPRINTED 1936, 1942, 1946, 1951, 1958, 1963, 1965
1966, 1971

PRINTED IN GREAT BRITAIN

PREFACE

THIS book takes 'the eighteenth century' in its simplest meaning, and endeavours to represent the poetry that was written in this country during the hundred years from 1700 to 1800. It happens to cover the period from the death of Dryden to the death of Cowper, but neither births nor deaths of poets, nor poetical fashions and reputations, have fixed its limits; nor has it been made with the purpose of illustrating any particular view of what this period stands for in the history of our literature. It opens fittingly with Pomfret's *Choice*, of which Johnson said that 'perhaps no composition in our language has been more often perused'; and in the pieces which immediately follow we find the variety in subject, and note, and spirit, which is to increase as the century proceeds. Nothing is given that is known to have been printed before 1700, though written by men who made their name after that date. But the book cannot be so easily rounded in its conclusion. With the publication of *Lyrical Ballads* in September 1798 the flood-gates are opened. It has therefore been thought best to omit *The Ancient Mariner* and *Tintern Abbey*, though these are both eighteenth-century poems.

PREFACE

Probably every man who makes an anthology finds that at some stage it begins to take its own shape, and that the final form was not foreseen. His own favourites are his first choice. He has then to consider the favourites of the public, for he must not forget the pronouncement of the wisest of eighteenth-century critics that ' by the common sense of readers, uncorrupted with literary prejudices, after all the refinements of subtilty and the dogmatism of learning, must be finally decided all claim to poetical honours '. Friends, or Chance, may direct him to pieces that he has missed, or open his eyes to beauties that he has not seen. So far his only standard of choice may be intrinsic merit. But in time other claims demand a hearing. A piece may have an historical interest, or popular associations ; another may be quoted in a famous work, or one of its lines may be widely familiar ; another, though nowhere excelling, may be representative. Once these claims are conceded, the collection ceases to be strictly an anthology. The florist has begun to develop, or to degenerate, into the botanist. When the field from which he gathers is limited, the change may be desirable, if not inevitable. All will be well so long as he does not become a curator of dried specimens.

As in other Oxford Books, the arrangement is in the main chronological, and all the poems by the same author are printed together; but the authors are not placed in the order of their birth, nor—as in Campbell's *Specimens*—of their death. By the one method Cowper would come before Chatterton; by the other, Churchill before Young. They are placed by a central date in their career, or by the date of their most important work—Pope by his *Iliad*, Young by his *Night Thoughts*, Cowper by *The Task*. But even this method has its faults; while it aims at a truer chronology, it permits and invites the exercise of no little whim, and occasionally—but rarely it is hoped—it may fail of its purpose. There may be whim, for instance, in the wide separation of the brothers Warton, though it can be defended, for Joseph, who was born earlier and died later, wrote his best poems as a young man in his twenties, and Thomas, who was only six years his junior, did not come to his full power till middle age; but if Pope is rightly placed before Young, we can only regret that their *Characters of Women* cannot be given in their proper sequence. The insurmountable difficulty in chronological arrangement is that a book requires contemporaries who moved abreast to find their place in single file. When the order in this collection appears to be unsatisfactory, a corrective will be found in the brief note appended to each poem giving the date of first publication, or of composition, and sometimes of the earliest print known to the editor. The text of the poem is often taken from a later and revised edition.

Our attitude to the century is still in process of readjustment. We do not now feel the need of a new point of view for earlier periods. We may have, we must have, our personal likes or dislikes of the Elizabethans and Carolines, but from the judgement which has been passed on them as a whole there is no demand for an appeal. No such judgement has yet been given on the poetry of the eighteenth century. The verdict of the nineteenth century is now before the twentieth for revision. The critics speak as counsel engaged on one side or the other, or show a conscious air of impartiality. Of the friendly critics, the most judicial find some misunderstanding to correct, or some prejudice to combat; all tend to assume an attitude of defence. What is reasonably certain is that a new verdict, favourable or unfavourable, will be given by the twentieth century, and that in time we ourselves, or more probably our successors, will speak of the eighteenth century with as little sense of contention as we now speak of the seventeenth and the age of Elizabeth.

When that time comes we shall have ceased to look upon the poetry of this century as the battle-ground of forces ranged somehow

under the standards of the ' classical ' and the
' romantic ', and shall have little use for the
flimsy mottoes with which both standards are
marked. If we are disposed to search in this
volume for the explanation of such catchwords
as ' the poetry of the Town ', ' the tyranny of
Pope ', ' the domination of the heroic couplet ',
we are likely to be disappointed. The intro-
duction into English criticism, from French
and German criticism, of the terms ' classical '
and ' romantic ' has not helped us to a truer
appreciation of our literature. Sooner or later
we have to enlarge or qualify the meaning
which we attach to them if they are to fit all
the facts ; they tempt us to manipulate the facts
to fit our definitions, and they ask us to find
distinction where separation may not be natural
or even possible. We should do well to forget
them when we consider the poetry of the
eighteenth century. So long as we continue to
employ them we must think of the century as,
from one point of view, a period of decadence,
and, from another, a period of preparation. It
was much more. It was a period of definite
achievement.

The nature of this achievement does not
concern us here. The whole duty of an antho-
logist is to select and arrange. But the evidence
from which we can come to our own just con-
clusions is provided in this volume, if it is as

representative as the editor has tried to make it. Those who are interested in poetic movements and fashions may find in it what they want; others, too, who prefer to think of this century, as they may of every century, as an age of transition. Its poetry is rich in conscious echoes; but it is richer in anticipations. Who was it that wrote these lines?—

> O ye Northumbrian shades, which overlook
> The rocky pavement and the mossy falls
> Of solitary Wensbeck's limpid stream;
> How gladly I recall your well-known seats
> Belov'd of old, and that delightful time
> When all alone, for many a summer's day,
> I wander'd through your calm recesses, led
> In silence by some powerful hand unseen.
>   Nor will I e'er forget you: nor shall e'er
> The graver tasks of manhood, or the advice
> Of vulgar wisdom, move me to disclaim
> These studies which possess'd me in the dawn
> Of life, and fix'd the colour of my mind
> For every future year.

Not Wordsworth, but Akenside; who elsewhere in his clean-cut phrasing sometimes reminds us of Landor. Or again, who wrote these lines describing a forsaken woman who has lost her reason?—

> When thirst and hunger griev'd her most,
>   If any food she took,
> It was the berry from the thorn,
>   The water from the brook.

x

From every hedge a flower she pluck'd,
   And moss from every stone,
To make a garland for her Love,
   Yet left it still undone.

Still, as she rambled, was she wont
   To trill a plaintive song,
'Twas wild, and full of fancies vain,
   Yet suited well her wrong.

Oft too a smile, but not of joy,
   Play'd on her brow o'ercast ;
It was the faint cold smile of Spring,
   Ere Winter yet is past.

Not a Lake poet with views on the language of poetry, but a young Fellow of an Oxford college, who spent his short life between Oxford and Winchester. The spirit and the note of Byron are to be found best, not in the satirists of whom he was a professed disciple, but in a poet whom he appears not to have known—the author of the *Duke of Benevento*. Sometimes we are reminded of more recent verse. Much of the satire and many of the descriptions might have been written to-day. But anticipations and movements are, it is hoped, only an incidental matter of interest in a volume which of design takes the poets individually and tries to see them in their best work. The greater men are masters in the final art of self-expression, and give us what we cannot find elsewhere.

PREFACE

The editor has made this book at the invitation of the officials of the Clarendon Press, and he now offers his thanks to them—who habitually remain nameless—for many valuable suggestions, especially when the book was printing. At an early stage he had the support of Mr. H. V. Elwin's company through several volumes of Chalmers's *English Poets*, and at the last stage he had the skilled and unremitting assistance of Mr. F. Page and Mr. C. Williams.

D. N. S.

Merton College, Oxford.

JOHN POMFRET

1667–1702

I

The Choice

IF Heav'n the Grateful Liberty wou'd give,
That I might Chuse my Method how to Live,
And all those Hours, propitious Fate should lend,
In blissful Ease, and Satisfaction spend :
  Near some fair Town, I'd have a private Seat,
Built Uniform, not Little, nor too Great :
Better, if on a Rising Ground it stood ;
Fields on this side, on that a Neighbouring Wood.
It shou'd within no other Things contain,
But what were Useful, Necessary, Plain :
Methinks 'tis Nauseous, and I'd ne'er endure
The needless Pomp of Gaudy Furniture.
A little Garden, Grateful to the Eye,
And a Cool Rivulet run murm'ring by :
On whose delicious Banks a stately Row
Of Shady Limes, or Sycamores, shou'd grow :
At th' End of which a silent Study plac'd,
Shou'd be with all the Noblest Authors Grac'd :
Horace, and *Virgil*, in whose Mighty Lines
Immortal Wit, and Solid Learning shines :
Sharp *Juvenal*, and Am'rous *Ovid* too,
Who all the Turns of Love's soft Passion knew ;
He that with Judgment reads his charming Lines,
In which strong Art, with stronger Nature joyns,
Must grant his Fancy does the best Excel,
His Thoughts so tender, and Exprest so well ;
With all those Moderns, Men of steady Sense,
Esteem'd for Learning, and for Eloquence.

In some of these, as Fancy shou'd Advise,
I'd always take my Morning Exercise:
For sure no Minutes bring us more Content,
Than those in Pleasing, Useful Studies spent.

    I'd have a Clear, and Competent Estate,
That I might Live Gentilely, but not Great:
As much as I cou'd moderately spend,
A little more, sometimes t' Oblige a Friend.
Nor shou'd the Sons of Poverty Repine
Too much at Fortune, they shou'd Taste of mine;
And all, that Objects of true Pitty were,
Shou'd be Reliev'd with what my Wants cou'd spare
For what, our Maker has too largely giv'n,
Shou'd be return'd, in Gratitude, to Heav'n.
A frugal Plenty shou'd my Table spread;
With Healthy, not Luxurious Dishes Fed:
Enough to Satisfy, and something more
To Feed the Stranger, and the Neighb'ring Poor.
Strong Meat Indulges Vice, and pampering Food
Creates Diseases, and Inflames the Blood.
But what's sufficient to make Nature strong,
And the bright Lamp of Life continue long,
I'd freely take, and as I did Possess,
The Bounteous Author of my Plenty Bless.

    I'd have a little Vault, but always stor'd
With the Best Wines, each Vintage cou'd afford.
Wine whets the Wit, improves its Native force,
And gives a pleasant Flavour to Discourse;
By making all our Spirits Debonair,
Throws off the Lees, the Sediment of Care.
But as the greatest Blessing, Heaven lends,
May be Debauch'd, and serve Ignoble Ends:

2

So, but too oft, the Grape's refreshing Juice
Does many Mischievous Effects produce.
My House shou'd no such rude Disorders know,
As from high Drinking consequently flow.
Nor wou'd I use, what was so kindly giv'n,
To the Dishonour of Indulgent Heav'n.
If any Neighbour came, he shou'd be Free,
Us'd with Respect, and not uneasy be,
In my Retreat, or to himself, or me.
What Freedom, Prudence, and right Reason give,
All Men may with Impunity receive :
But the least swerving from their Rule's too much :
For, what's forbidden us, 'tis Death to touch.

That Life might be more Comfortable yet,
And all my Joys Refin'd, Sincere, and Great ;
I'd Chuse two Friends, whose Company wou'd be
A great Advance to my Felicity :
Well Born, of Humours suited to my own,
Discreet, and Men, as well as Books, have known ;
Brave, Gen'rous, Witty, and exactly Free
From loose Behaviour, or Formality ;
Airy, and Prudent, Merry, but not Light,
Quick in Discerning, and in Judging right.
Secret they shou'd be, Faithful to their Trust ;
In Reas'ning Cool, Strong, Temperate, and Just ;
Obliging, Open, without Huffing Brave,
Brisk in Gay Talking, and in Sober, Grave ;
Close in Dispute, but not Tenacious, try'd
By Solid Reason, and let that Decide ;
Not prone to Lust, Revenge, or Envious Hate,
Nor busy Medlers with Intreagues of State ;
Strangers to Slander, and sworn Foes to Spight,

Not Quarrelsome, but Stout enough to Fight;
Loyal, and Pious, Friends to *Cæsar* true.
As Dying Martyrs to their Maker too;
In their Society, I cou'd not miss
A Permanent, Sincere, Substantial Bliss.

   Wou'd Bounteous Heav'n once more Indulge. I'd choose,
(For who wou'd so much Satisfaction lose,
As Witty Nymphs, in Conversation, give,)
Near some Obliging, Modest Fair to live;
For there's that Sweetness in a Female Mind,
Which in a Man's we cannot hope to find:
That by a Secret, but a Pow'rful, Art
Winds up the Springs of Life, and does impart
Fresh Vital Heat to the Transported Heart.

   I'd have her Reason all her Passions sway;
Easy in Company, in Private Gay:
Coy to a Fop, to the Deserving Free,
Still Constant to her self, and Just to me.
A Soul she shou'd have, for Great Actions fit;
Prudence, and Wisdom to direct her Wit:
Courage to look bold Danger in the Face,
No Fear, but only to be Proud, or Base:
Quick to Advise, by an Emergence prest,
To give good Counsel, or to take the best.
I'd have th' Expression of her Thoughts be such,
She might not seem Reserv'd, nor talk too much;
That shews a want of Judgment and of Sense:
More than Enough is but Impertinence:
Her Conduct Regular, her Mirth Refin'd,
Civil to Strangers, to her Neighbours kind:
Averse to Vanity, Revenge, and Pride,
In all the Methods of Deceit untry'd:

So Faithful to her Friend, and Good to all,
No Censure might upon her Actions fall:
Then wou'd e'en Envy be compell'd to say,
She goes the least of Woman-kind Astray

   To this Fair Creature I'd sometimes Retire;
Her Conversation wou'd new Joys inspire;
Give Life an Edge so keen, no surly Care
Would venture to Assault my Soul, or dare
Near my Retreat to hide one secret Snare.
But so Divine, so Noble a Repast,
I'd seldom, and with Moderation, taste.
For Highest Cordials all their Virtue lose,
By a too frequent, and too bold an Use:
And what wou'd Cheer the Spirits in Distress,
Ruines our Health, when taken to Excess.

   I'd be concern'd in no Litigious Jar,
Belov'd by all, not vainly Popular.
What e're Assistance I had Pow'r to bring
T' Oblige my Country, or to Serve my King,
When e're they Call'd, I'd readily afford
My Tongue, my Pen, my Counsel, or my Sword.
Law Suits I'd shun, with as much studious Care,
As I wou'd Dens where hungry Lyons are:
And rather put up Injuries, than be
A Plague to him who'd be a Plague to me.
I value Quiet at a Price too great,
To give for my Revenge so dear a Rate:
For what do we, by all our Bustle, gain,
But Counterfeit Delight, for real Pain?

   If Heav'n a Date of many Years wou'd give,
Thus I'd in Pleasure, Ease, and Plenty live.
And as I near approach'd the Verge of Life,

Some kind Relation, (for I'd have no Wife)
Shou'd take upon him all my Worldly Care,
While I did for a better State prepare.
Then I'd not be with any Trouble vex'd,
Nor have the Ev'ning of my days perplex'd;
But by a silent, and a peaceful Death,
Without a Sigh, resign my Aged Breath:
And when committed to the Dust, I'd have
Few Tears, but Friendly, dropt into my Grave.
Then wou'd my Exit so propitious be,
All Men wou'd wish to Live, and Dye like me.

The Choice, 1700

DANIEL DEFOE

1661–1731

2

The English Race

THE *Romans* first with *Julius Cæsar* came,
Including all the Nations of that Name,
Gauls, *Greeks*, and *Lombards*; and by Computation,
Auxiliaries or Slaves of ev'ry Nation.
With *Hengist*, *Saxons*; *Danes* with *Sueno* came,
In search of Plunder, not in search of Fame.
Scots, *Picts*, and *Irish* from th' *Hibernian* Shore:
And Conqu'ring *William* brought the *Normans* o're.

All these their Barb'rous Offspring left behind,
The Dregs of Armies, they of all Mankind;
Blended with *Britains* who before were here,
Of whom the *Welsh* ha' blest the Character.

DANIEL DEFOE

From this Amphibious Ill-born Mob began
That vain ill-natur'd thing, an Englishman.
The Customs, Sirnames, Languages, and Manners,
Of all these Nations are their own Explainers:
Whose Relicks are so lasting and so strong,
They ha' left a *Shiboleth* upon our Tongue;
By which with easy search you may distinguish
Your *Roman-Saxon-Danish-Norman* English.

The great Invading *Norman* let us know
What Conquerors in After-Times might do.
To ev'ry *Musqueteer he brought to *Town*,   * *Or* Archer.
He gave the Lands which never were his own.
When first the *English* Crown he did obtain,
He did not send his *Dutchmen* home again.
No Reassumptions in his Reign were known,
Davenant might there ha' let his Book alone.
No Parliament his Army cou'd disband;
He rais'd no Money, for he paid in Land.
He gave his Legions their Eternal Station,
And made them all Freeholders of the Nation.
He canton'd out the Country to his Men,
And ev'ry Soldier was a Denizen.
The Rascals thus enrich'd, he call'd them *Lords,*
To please their Upstart Pride with new-made Words;
And *Doomsday Book* his Tyranny Records.

And here begins the Ancient Pedigree
That so exalts our Poor Nobility:
'Tis that from some *French* Trooper they derive,
Who with the *Norman* Bastard did arrive:
The Trophies of the Families appear;
Some show the Sword, the Bow, and some the Spear,
Which their Great Ancestor, *forsooth*, did wear.

7

These in the Heralds Register remain,
Their Noble mean Extraction to explain.
Yet who the Hero was, no Man can tell,
Whether a Drummer or a Colonel:
The silent Record blushes to reveal
Their Undescended Dark Original.

But grant the best, How came the Change to pass;
A *True-Born Englishman* of *Norman* Race?
A *Turkish* Horse can show more History,
To prove his Well-descended Family.
Conquest, as by the Moderns 'tis exprest,
May give a Title to the Lands possest:
But that the Longest Sword shou'd be so Civil,
To make a *Frenchman English,* that's the Devil.

These are the Heroes who despise the *Dutch,*
And rail at new-come Foreigners so much;
Forgetting that themselves are all deriv'd
From the most Scoundrel Race that ever liv'd,
A horrid Crowd of Rambling Thieves and Drones,
Who ransack'd Kingdoms, and dispeopled Towns:
The *Pict* and Painted *Britain,* Treach'rous *Scot,*
By Hunger, Theft, and Rapine, hither brought;
Norwegian Pirates, Buccaneering *Danes,*
Whose Red-hair'd Offspring ev'ry where remains;
Who join'd with *Norman-French* compound the Breed
From whence your *True-Born Englishmen* proceed.

The True-Born Englishman, 1701

JOHN PHILIPS

1676–1709

3 *The Thirsty Poet*

SO pass my Days. But when Nocturnal Shades
  This World invelop, and th' inclement Air
Persuades Men to repel benumming Frosts
With pleasant Wines, and crackling Blaze of Wood;
Me lonely sitting, nor the glimmering Light
Of Make-weight Candle, nor the joyous Talk
Of loving Friend delights; distress'd, forlorn,
Amidst the Horrors of the tedious Night,
Darkling I sigh, and feed with dismal Thoughts
My anxious Mind; or sometimes mournful Verse
Indite, and sing of Groves and Myrtle Shades,
Or desperate Lady near a purling Stream,
Or Lover pendent on a Willow-Tree:
Mean while, I labour with eternal Drought,
And restless wish, and rave; my parched Throat
Finds no Relief, nor heavy Eyes Repose:
But if a Slumber haply does invade
My weary Limbs, my Fancy, still awake,
Thoughtful of Drink, and eager, in a Dream
Tipples imaginary Pots of Ale:
In vain; awake I find the settled Thirst
Still gnawing, and the pleasant Phantom curse.
  Thus do I live from Pleasure quite debarr'd,
Nor taste the Fruits that the Sun's genial Rays
Mature, *John-Apple*, nor the downy *Peach*,
Nor *Walnut* in rough-furrow'd Coat secure,
Nor *Medlar*, Fruit delicious in Decay.

The Splendid Shilling; 1701

1663–1708

Song

4

O F all the Torments, all the Cares,
   With which our Lives are curst;
Of all the Plagues a Lover bears,
   Sure Rivals are the worst!
By Partners, in each other kind,
   Afflictions easier grow;
In Love alone we hate to find
   Companions of our Woe.

Sylvia, for all the Pangs you see,
   Are lab'ring in my Breast;
I beg not you would favour me,
   Would you but slight the rest!
How great so e'er your Rigours are,
   With them alone I'll cope;
I can endure my own Despair,
   But not another's Hope.

               Poetical Miscellanies, v, 1704

The Despairing Lover

5

D ISTRACTED with Care,
   For *Phillis* the Fair;
Since nothing cou'd move her,
Poor *Damon,* her Lover,
Resolves in Despair
No longer to languish,
Nor bear so much Anguish;

10

WILLIAM WALSH

But, mad with his Love,
To a Precipice goes;
Where, a Leap from above
Wou'd soon finish his Woes.

When in Rage he came there,
Beholding how steep
The Sides did appear,
And the Bottom how deep;
His Torments projecting,
And sadly reflecting,
That a Lover forsaken
A new Love may get;
But a Neck, when once broken,
Can never be set:
And, that he cou'd die
Whenever he wou'd;
But, that he cou'd live
But as long as he cou'd:
How grievous soever
The Torment might grow,
He scorn'd to endeavour
To finish it so.
But Bold, Unconcern'd
At Thoughts of the Pain,
He calmly return'd
To his Cottage again.

Poetical Miscellanies, **v**, 1704

MARY LEE, LADY CHUDLEIGH

1656–1710

6

The Resolve

FOR what the World admires I'll wish no more,
  Nor court that airy nothing of a Name:
Such flitting Shadows let the Proud adore,
  Let them be Suppliants for an empty Fame.

If Reason rules within, and keeps the Throne,
  While the inferior Faculties obey,
And all her Laws without Reluctance own,
  Accounting none more fit, more just than they:

If Virtue my free Soul unsully'd keeps,
  Exempting it from Passion and from Stain:
If no black guilty Thoughts disturb my Sleeps,
  And no past Crimes my vext Remembrance pain:

If, tho' I Pleasure find in living here,
  I yet can look on Death without Surprise:
If I've a Soul above the Reach of Fear,
  And which will nothing mean or sordid prize:

A Soul, which cannot be depress'd by Grief,
  Nor too much rais'd by the sublimest Joy;
Which can, when troubled, give it self Relief,
  And to Advantage all its Thoughts employ:

Then am I happy in my humble State,
  Altho' not crown'd with Glory nor with Bays:
A Mind, that triumphs over Vice and Fate,
  Esteems it mean to court the World for Praise.

Poems on Several Occasions, 1703

WILLIAM CONGREVE

1670–1729

7

Song

AH stay! ah turn! ah whither would you fly,
　　Too charming, too relentless Maid?
I follow not to Conquer, but to Die;
　　You of the fearful are afraid.

In vain I call; for she like fleeting Air,
　　When prest by some tempestuous Wind,
Flies swifter from the Voice of my Despair,
　　Nor casts one pitying Look behind.
　　　　　　　　　　　The Fair Penitent, Act ii, 1703

8

A Hue and Cry after Fair Amoret

FAIR *Amoret* is gone astray;
　　Pursue and seek her, ev'ry Lover;
I'll tell the Signs, by which you may
　　The wand'ring Shepherdess discover.

Coquet and Coy at once her Air,
　　Both study'd, tho' both seem neglected;
Careless she is with artful Care,
　　Affecting to seem unaffected.

With Skill her Eyes dart ev'ry Glance,
　　Yet change so soon you'd ne'er suspect 'em;
For she'd persuade they wound by chance,
　　Tho' certain Aim and Art direct 'em.

She likes her self, yet others hates
   For that which in her self she prizes;
And while she Laughs at them, forgets
   She is the Thing that she despises.

Poetical Miscellanies, v, 1704

9   *Song*

FALSE though she be to me and Love,
   I'll ne'er pursue Revenge;
For still the Charmer I approve,
   Tho' I deplore her Change.

In Hours of Bliss we oft have met,
   They could not always last;
And though the present I regret,
   I'm grateful for the past.

Works, iii, 1710

10   *Nil Admirari*

COME, see thy Friend, retir'd without Regret,
   Forgetting Care, or striving to forget;
In easy Contemplation soothing Time
With Morals much, and now and then with Rhime,
Not so robust in Body, as in Mind,
And always undejected, tho' declin'd;
Not wond'ring at the World's new wicked Ways,
Compar'd with those of our Fore-fathers Days,
For Virtue now is neither more nor less,
And Vice is only vary'd in the Dress:
Believe it, *Men* have ever been the *same*,
And *Ovid*'s GOLDEN AGE, is but a *Dream*.

Of Improving the present Time, 1729

MATTHEW PRIOR

1664–1721

11

An English Padlock

MISS DANAE, when Fair and Young
(As HORACE has divinely sung)
Could not be kept from JOVE's Embrace
By Doors of Steel, and Walls of Brass.
The Reason of the Thing is clear;
(Would JOVE the naked Truth aver:)
CUPID was with Him of the Party;
And show'd himself sincere and hearty:
For, give That Whipster but his Errand,
He takes my Lord Chief Justice' Warrant:
Dauntless as Death away He walks;
Breaks the Doors open; snaps the Locks;
Searches the Parlour, Chamber, Study;
Nor stops, 'till He has CULPRIT's Body.

Since This has been Authentick Truth,
By Age deliver'd down to Youth;
Tell us, mistaken Husband, tell us,
Why so Mysterious, why so Jealous?
Does the Restraint, the Bolt, the Bar
Make Us less Curious, Her less Fair?
The Spy, which does this Treasure keep,
Does She ne'er say her Pray'rs, nor sleep?
Does She to no Excess incline?
Does She fly Musick, Mirth, and Wine?
Or have not Gold and Flatt'ry Pow'r,
To purchase One unguarded Hour?

Your Care does further yet extend:
That Spy is guarded by your Friend.——
But has This Friend nor Eye, nor Heart?
May He not feel the cruel Dart,
Which, soon or late, all Mortals feel?
May He not, with too tender Zeal,
Give the Fair Pris'ner Cause to see,
How much He wishes, She were free?
May He not craftily infer
The Rules of Friendship too severe,
Which chain Him to a hated Trust;
Which make Him Wretched, to be Just?
And may not She, this Darling She,

Youthful and healthy, Flesh and Blood,
Easie with Him, ill-us'd by Thee,

Allow this Logic to be good?

Sir, Will your Questions never end?
I trust to neither Spy nor Friend.
In short, I keep Her from the Sight
Of ev'ry Human Face.——She'll write.——
From Pen and Paper She's debarr'd.——
Has She a Bodkin and a Card?
She'll prick her Mind.——She will, You say:
But how shall She That Mind convey?
I keep Her in one Room: I lock it:
The Key (look here!) is in this Pocket.
The Key-hole, is That left? Most certain.
She'll thrust her Letter thro'——Sir MARTIN.

Dear angry Friend, what must be done?
Is there no Way?——There is but One.

Send Her abroad; and let Her see,
That all this mingl'd Mass, which She
Being forbidden longs to know,
Is a dull Farce, an empty Show,
Powder, and Pocket-Glass, and Beau;
A Staple of Romance and Lies,
False Tears, and real Perjuries;
Where Sighs and Looks are bought and sold;
And Love is made but to be told:
Where the fat Bawd, and lavish Heir
The Spoils of ruin'd Beauty share:
And Youth seduc'd from Friends and Fame,
Must give up Age to Want and Shame.
Let Her behold the Frantick Scene,
The Women wretched, false the Men:
And when, these certain Ills to shun,
She would to Thy Embraces run;
Receive Her with extended Arms:
Seem more delighted with her Charms:
Wait on Her to the Park and Play:
Put on good Humour; make Her gay:
Be to her Virtues very kind:
Be to her Faults a little blind:
Let all her Ways be unconfin'd:
And clap your PADLOCK——on her Mind.

First printed 1705

12 *To a Child of Quality Five Years Old*

The Author Forty

LORDS, Knights, and Squires, the num'rous Band
　That wear the Fair Miss *Mary*'s Fetters,
Were summon'd, by her high Command,
　To show their Passion by their Letters.

My Pen amongst the rest I took,
　Least those bright Eyes that cannot read
Shou'd dart their kindling Fires, and look
　The Pow'r they have to be obey'd.

Nor Quality, nor Reputation,
　Forbid me yet my Flame to tell,
Dear Five Years old befriends my Passion,
　And I may Write 'till she can Spell.

For while she makes her Silk-worms Beds
　With all the tender things I swear,
Whilst all the House my Passion reads,
　In Papers round her Baby's Hair,

She may receive and own my Flame,
　For tho' the strictest *Prudes* shou'd know it,
She'll pass for a most virtuous Dame,
　And I for an unhappy Poet.

Then too, alas, when she shall tear
　The Lines some younger Rival sends,
She'll give me leave to Write, I fear,
　And we shall still continue Friends.

For as our diff'rent Ages move,
'Tis so ordain'd, wou'd Fate but mend it,
That I shall be past making Love,
When she begins to comprehend it.

Poetical Miscellanies, **v, 1704**

13 *A Letter to the Honourable Lady Miss*
      Margaret-Cavendish-Holles-Harley

MY noble, lovely, little PEGGY,
  Let this, my FIRST-EPISTLE, beg ye,
At dawn of morn, and close of even,
To lift your heart and hands to heaven:
In double beauty say your pray'r,
Our father first, then *notre père*;
And, dearest CHILD, along the day,
In ev'ry thing you do and say,
Obey and please my LORD and LADY,
So GOD shall love, and ANGELS aid, Ye.

If to these PRECEPTS You attend,
No SECOND-LETTER need I send,
And so I rest Your constant Friend,

M. P.
Miscellaneous Works, **1740**

14 *Written in the Beginning of Mezeray's*
      History of France

WHATE'ER thy Countrymen have done,
  By Law and Wit, by Sword and Gun,
In Thee is faithfully recited:
And all the Living World, that view
Thy Work, give Thee the Praises due:
At once Instructed and Delighted.

Yet for the Fame of all these Deeds,
What Beggar in the *Invalides*,
   With Lameness broke, with Blindness smitten,
Wished ever decently to die,
To have been either *Mezeray*,
   Or any Monarch He has written?

It strange, dear Author, yet it true is,
That down from *Pharamond* to *Loüis*,
   All covet Life, yet call it Pain;
All feel the Ill, yet shun the Cure:
Can Sense this Paradox endure?
   Resolve me, *Cambray*, or *Fontaine*.

The Man in graver Tragic known,
Tho' his best Part long since was done,
   Still on the Stage desires to tarry:
And He who play'd the *Harlequin*,
After the Jest still loads the Scene,
   Unwilling to retire, tho' Weary.

Poems on Several Occasions, 1709

15   *An Epitaph*

INTERR'D beneath this Marble Stone,
  Lie Saunt'ring JACK, and Idle JOAN.
While rolling Threescore Years and One
Did round this Globe their Courses run;
If Human Things went Ill or Well;
If changing Empires rose or fell;
The Morning past, the Evening came,
And found this Couple still the same.

20

They Walk'd and Eat, good Folks: What then?
Why then They Walk'd and Eat again:
They soundly slept the Night away:
They did just Nothing all the Day:
And having bury'd Children Four,
Wou'd not take Pains to try for more.
Nor Sister either had, nor Brother:
They seem'd just Tally'd for each other

   Their Moral and Oeconomy
Most perfectly They made agree:
Each Virtue kept it's proper Bound,
Nor Trespass'd on the other's Ground.
Nor Fame, nor Censure They regarded:
They neither Punish'd, nor Rewarded.
He car'd not what the Footmen did:
Her Maids She neither prais'd, nor chid:
So ev'ry Servant took his Course;
And bad at First, They all grew worse.
Slothful Disorder fill'd His Stable;
And sluttish Plenty deck'd Her Table.
Their Beer was strong; Their Wine was *Port*;
Their Meal was large; Their Grace was short.
They gave the Poor the Remnant-meat,
Just when it grew not fit to eat.

   They paid the Church and Parish-Rate;
And took, but read not the Receit:
For which They claim'd their *Sunday*'s Due,
Of slumb'ring in an upper Pew.

   No Man's Defects sought They to know;
So never made Themselves a Foe.
No Man's good Deeds did They commend;
So never rais'd Themselves a Friend.

Nor cherish'd They Relations poor:
That might decrease Their present Store:
Nor Barn nor House did they repair:
That might oblige Their future Heir.

  They neither Added, nor Confounded:
They neither Wanted, nor Abounded.
Each *Christmas* They Accompts did clear;
And wound their Bottom round the Year.
Nor Tear, nor Smile did They imploy
At News of Public Grief, or Joy.
When Bells were Rung, and Bonfires made;
If ask'd, They ne'er deny'd their Aid:
Their Jugg was to the Ringers carry'd;
Who ever either Dy'd, or Marry'd.
Their Billet at the Fire was found;
Who ever was Depos'd, or Crown'd.

  Nor Good, nor Bad, nor Fools, nor Wise;
They wou'd not learn, nor cou'd advise:
Without Love, Hatred, Joy, or Fear,
They led——a kind of——as it were:
Nor Wish'd, nor Car'd, nor Laugh'd, nor Cry'd:
And so They liv'd; and so They dy'd.

Poems on Several Occasions, 1718

16   *Answer to Cloe Jealous*

DEAR CLOE, how blubber'd is that pretty Face?
   Thy Cheek all on Fire, and Thy Hair all uncurl'd
Pr'ythee quit this Caprice; and (as old FALSTAF says)
  Let Us e'en talk a little like Folks of this World.

Bottom] skein.

How can'st Thou presume, Thou hast leave to destroy
    The Beauties, which Venus but lent to Thy keeping?
Those Looks were design'd to inspire Love and Joy:
    More ord'nary Eyes may serve People for weeping.

To be vext at a Trifle or two that I writ,
    Your Judgment at once, and my Passion You wrong:
You take that for Fact, which will scarce be found Wit:
    Od's Life! must one swear to the Truth of a Song?

What I speak, my fair Cloe, and what I write, shows
    The Diff'rence there is betwixt Nature and Art:
I court others in Verse; but I love Thee in Prose:
    And They have my Whimsies; but Thou hast my Heart.

The God of us Verse-men (You know Child) the Sun,
    How after his Journeys He sets up his Rest:
If at Morning o'er Earth 'tis his Fancy to run,
    At Night he reclines on his Thetis's Breast.

So when I am weary'd with wand'ring all Day,
    To Thee my Delight in the Evening I come:
No Matter what Beauties I saw in my Way:
    They were but my Visits; but Thou art my Home.

Then finish, Dear Cloe, this Pastoral War;
    And let us like Horace and Lydia agree:
For Thou art a Girl as much brighter than Her,
    As He was a Poet sublimer than Me.

Poems on Several Occasions, 1718

17   *Love and Reason*

GREAT Heav'n! how frail thy Creature Man is made!
    How by Himself insensibly betray'd!
In our own Strength unhappily secure,
Too little cautious of the adverse Pow'r,

And by the Blast of Self-opinion mov'd,
We wish to charm, and seek to be belov'd.
On Pleasure's flowing Brink We idly stray,
Masters as yet of our returning Way:
Seeing no Danger, We disarm our Mind,
And give our Conduct to the Waves and Wind:
Then in the flow'ry Mead, or verdant Shade,
To wanton Dalliance negligently laid,
We weave the Chaplet, and We crown the Bowl,
And smiling see the nearer Waters roll;
'Till the strong Gusts of raging Passion rise;
'Till the dire Tempest mingles Earth and Skies;
And swift into the boundless Ocean born,
Our foolish Confidence too late We mourn:
Round our devoted Heads the Billows beat;
And from our troubl'd View the lessen'd Lands retreat.

O mighty Love! from thy unbounded Pow'r
How shall the human Bosom rest secure?
How shall our Thought avoid the various Snare?
Or Wisdom to our caution'd Soul declare
The diff'rent Shapes, Thou pleasest to imploy,
When bent to hurt, and certain to destroy?

The haughty Nymph in open Beauty drest,
To-Day encounters our unguarded Breast:
She looks with Majesty, and moves with State:
Unbent her Soul, and in Misfortune great,
She scorns the World, and dares the Rage of Fate.

Here whilst we take stern Manhood for our Guide,
And guard our Conduct with becoming Pride,
Charm'd with the Courage in her Action shown,
We praise her Mind, the Image of our own.

She that can please, is certain to perswade:
To-day belov'd, To-morrow is obey'd.
We think we see thro' Reason's Optics right;
Nor find, how Beauty's Rays elude our Sight:
Struck with her Eye whilst We applaud her Mind;
And when We speak Her great, We wish Her kind.

To-morrow, cruel Pow'r, Thou arm'st the Fair
With flowing Sorrow, and dishevel'd Hair:
Sad her Complaint, and humble is her Tale,
Her Sighs explaining where her Accents fail.
Here gen'rous Softness warms the honest Breast:
We raise the sad, and succour the distress'd:
And whilst our Wish prepares the kind Relief,
Whilst Pity mitigates her rising Grief,
We sicken soon from her contagious Care,
Grieve for her Sorrows, groan for her Despair;
And against Love too late those Bosoms arm,
Which Tears can soften, and which Sighs can warm.

Against this nearest cruelest of Foes,
What shall Wit meditate, or Force oppose?
Whence, feeble Nature, shall We summon Aid,
If by our Pity, and our Pride betray'd?
External Remedy shall We hope to find,
When the close Fiend has gain'd our treach'rous Mind,
Insulting there does Reason's Pow'r deride,
And blind Himself, conducts the dazl'd Guide?

Solomon, Book ii—*Poems on Several Occasions*, 1718

For My own Monument

AS DOCTORS give physic by way of prevention,
  MATT alive and in health, of his TOMB-STONE took care,
For delays are unsafe, and his pious intention
  May haply be never fulfill'd by his Heir.

Then take MATT's word for it, the SCULPTOR is paid,
  That the FIGURE is fine, pray believe your own eye,
Yet credit but lightly what more may be said,
  For we flatter our selves, and teach marble to lye.

Yet counting as far as to FIFTY his years,
  His virtues and vices were as other men's are,
High hopes he conceiv'd, and he smother'd great fears,
  In a life party-colour'd, half pleasure, half care.

Nor to business a drudge, nor to faction a slave,
  He strove to make int'rest and freedom agree,
In public employments industrious and grave,
  And alone with his friends, Lord how merry was he.

Now in equipage stately, now humbly on foot,
  Both fortunes he try'd, but to neither would trust,
And whirl'd in the round, as the wheel turn'd about,
  He found riches had wings, and knew man was but dust.

This verse little polish'd, tho' mighty sincere,
  Sets neither his titles nor merit to view;
It says that his relics collected lie here,
  And no mortal yet knows too if this may be true.

Fierce robbers there are that infest the highway,
  So MATT may be kill'd, and his bones never found;
False witness at court, and fierce tempests at sea,
  So MATT may yet chance to be hang'd, or be drown'd.

If his bones lie in earth, roll in sea, fly in air,
  To Fate we must yield, and the thing is the same;
And if passing thou giv'st him a smile, or a tear,
  He cares not—yet pr'ythee be kind to his FAME.

Miscellaneous Works, 1740

19   *Jinny the Just*

RELEAS'D from the noise of the Butcher and Baker
  Who, my old Friends be thanked, did seldom forsake her,
And from the soft Duns of my Landlord the Quaker,

From chiding the Footmen and watching the Lasses,
From Nell that burn'd Milk, and Tom that broke Glasses
(Sad mischiefs thro which a good housekeeper passes!)

From some real Care but more fancy'd vexation,
From a life party Colour'd half reason half passion,
Here lies after all the best Wench in the Nation.

From the Rhine to the Po, from the Thames to the Rhone,
Joanna or Janneton, Jinny or Joan,
Twas all one to her by what name She was known.

For the Idiom of words very little She heeded,
Provided the Matter She drove at succeeded,
She took and gave Languages just as She needed.

So for Kitching and Market, for bargain and Sale,
She paid English or Dutch or French down on the Nail,
But in telling a Story she sometimes did fail;

Then begging Excuse as She happen'd to Stammer,
With respect to her betters but none to her Grammer,
Her blush helpt her out and her Jargon became her.

27

Her Habit and Mein she endeavor'd to frame
To the different Gout of the place where She came;
Her outside stil chang'd, but her inside the same:

At the Hague in her Slippers and hair as the Mode is,
At Paris all Falbalow'd fine as a Goddess,
And at censuring London in smock sleeves and Bodice.

She order'd Affairs that few People cou'd tell
In what part about her that mixture did dwell
Of Vrough, or Mistress, or Medemoiselle.

For her Sirname and race let the Heraults e'en Answer;
Her own proper worth was enough to advance her,
And he who lik'd her, little valu'd her Grandsire.

But from what House so ever her lineage may come
I wish my own Jinny but out of her Tomb,
Tho all her Relations were there in her Room.

Of such terrible beauty She never cou'd boast
As with absolute Sway o'er all hearts rules the roast
When J— bawls out to the Chair for a Toast;

But of good Household Features her Person was made,
Nor by Faction cry'd up nor of Censure afraid,
And her beauty was rather for Use than Parade.

Her Blood so well mix't and flesh so well Pasted
That tho her Youth faded her Comliness lasted;
The blew was wore off, but the Plum was well tasted.

Less smooth than her Skin and less white than her breast
Was this pollisht stone beneath which she lyes prest:
Stop, Reader, and Sigh while thou thinkst on the rest.

With a just trim of Virtue her Soul was endu'd,
Not affectedly Pious nor secretly lewd
She cut even between the Cocquet and the Prude.

Her Will with her Duty so equally stood
That seldom oppos'd She was commonly good,
And did pritty well, doing just what she wou'd.

Declining all Pow'r she found means to perswade,
Was then most regarded when most she Obey'd,
The Mistress in truth when she seem'd but the Maid.

Such care of her own proper Actions She took
That on other folks lives She had no time to look,
So Censure and Praise were struck out of her Book.

Her thought stil confin'd to its own little Sphere,
She minded not who did Excell or did Err
But just as the matter related to her.

Then too when her Private Tribunal was rear'd
Her Mercy so mix'd with her judgment appear'd
That her Foes were condemn'd and her friends always clear'd.

Her Religion so well with her learning did suite
That in Practice sincere, and in Controverse Mute,
She shew'd She knew better to live than dispute.

Some parts of the Bible by heart She recited,
And much in historical Chapters delighted,
But in points about Faith She was something short sighted;

So Notions and modes She refer'd to the Schools,
And in matters of Conscience adher'd to Two Rules,
To advise with no Biggots, and jest with no Fools.

And scrupling but little, enough she believ'd,
By Charity ample smal sins She retriev'd,
And when she had New Cloaths She always receiv'd.

Thus stil whilst her Morning unseen fled away
In ord'ring the Linnen and making the Tea
That she scarce cou'd have time for the Psalms of the Day;

And while after Dinner the Night came so soon
That half she propos'd very seldom was done;
With twenty God bless Me's how this day is gone;

While she read and accounted and payd and abated,
Eat and drank, play'd and work't, laught and cry'd, lov'd
    and hated,
As answer'd the end of her being Created:

In the midst of her Age came a cruel Desease
Which neither her Julips nor recepts cou'd appease;
So down dropt her Clay, may her Soul be at peace.

Retire from this Sepulchre all the Prophane,
You that love for Debauch, or that marry for gain,
Retire least Ye trouble the Manes of J——

But Thou that know'st Love above Intrest or Lust,
Strew the Myrtle and Rose on this once belov'd Dust,
And shed one pious tear upon Jinny the Just.

Tread soft on her Grave, and do right to her honor,
Let neither rude hand nor ill Tongue light upon her,
Do all the smal Favors that now can be done her.

And when what Thou lik't shal return to her Clay,
For so I'm perswaded she must do one Day
What ever fantastic J.... Asgil may say,

30

When as I have done now, thou shalt set up a Stone
For something however distinguisht or known,
May some Pious Friend the Misfortune bemoan,
And make thy Concern by reflexion his own.

First printed 1907

RICHARD STEELE

1672–1729

20   *Song*

ME Cupid made a Happy Slave,
      A merry wretched Man,
I slight the Nymphs I cannot have,
      Nor Doat on those I can.

This constant Maxim still I hold,
      To baffle all Despair;
The Absent Ugly are and Old,
      The Present Young and Fair.

The Muses Mercury, February 1707

JOSEPH ADDISON

1672–1719

21   *Italy and Britain*

HOW has kind Heav'n adorn'd the happy Land,
      And scatter'd Blessings with a wastful Hand!
But what avail her unexhausted Stores,
Her blooming Mountains and her sunny Shores,
With all the Gifts that Heav'n and Earth impart,
The Smiles of Nature, and the Charms of Art,
While proud Oppression in her Vallies reigns,
And Tyranny usurps her happy Plains?

The poor Inhabitant beholds in vain
The red'ning Orange and the swelling Grain:
Joyless he sees the growing Oils and Wines,
And in the Myrtle's fragrant Shade repines:
Starves in the midst of Nature's Bounty curst,
And in the loaden Vine-yard dies for Thirst.

Oh *Liberty*, thou *Goddess* Heav'nly bright,
Profuse of Bliss, and pregnant with Delight,
Eternal Pleasures in thy Presence reign,
And smiling Plenty leads thy wanton Train!
Eas'd of her load Subjection grows more light,
And Poverty looks cheerful in thy sight;
Thou mak'st the gloomy Face of Nature gay,
Giv'st Beauty to the Sun, and Pleasure to the Day.

Thee, *Goddess*, Thee, *Britannia*'s Isle adores;
How has she oft exhausted all her Stores,
How oft in Fields of Death thy Presence sought?
Nor thinks the mighty Prize too dearly bought:
On Foreign Mountains may the Sun refine
The Grape's soft Juice, and mellow it to Wine,
With Citron Groves adorn a distant Soil,
And the fat Olive swell with floods of Oil:
We envy not the warmer Clime that lies
In ten Degrees of more indulgent Skies,
Nor at the Courseness of our Heav'n repine,
Tho' o're our Heads the frozen *Pleiads* shine:
'Tis Liberty that Crowns *Britannia*'s Isle,
And makes her barren Rocks and her bleak Mountains smile.

A Letter from Italy, 1701

22 *Blenheim*

BUT O, my Muse, what Numbers wilt thou find
To sing the furious Troops in Battel join'd!
Methinks I hear the Drum's tumultuous Sound
The Victor's Shouts and Dying Groans confound,
The dreadful Burst of Cannon rend the Skies,
And all the Thunder of the Battel rise.
'Twas then Great MARLBRO's mighty Soul was prov'd,
That, in the Shock of Charging Hosts unmov'd,
Amidst Confusion, Horror, and Despair,
Examin'd all the Dreadful Scenes of war;
In peaceful Thought the Field of Death survey'd,
To fainting Squadrons sent the timely Aid,
Inspir'd repuls'd Battalions to engage,
And taught the doubtful Battel where to rage.
So when an Angel by Divine Command
With rising Tempests shakes a guilty Land,
Such as of late o'er pale *Britannia* past,
Calm and Serene he drives the furious Blast;
And, pleas'd th' Almighty's Orders to perform,
Rides in the Whirl-wind, and directs the Storm.

But see the haughty Houshold-Troops advance!
The Dread of *Europe*, and the Pride of *France*.
The War's whole Art each private Soldier knows,
And with a Gen'ral's Love of Conquest glows;
Proudly He Marches on, and void of Fear
Laughs at the shaking of the *British* spear:
Vain Insolence! with Native Freedom brave
The meanest *Briton* scorns the highest Slave;
Contempt and Fury fire their Souls by turns,
Each Nation's Glory in each Warriour burns,

Each fights, as in his Arm th' important Day
And all the Fate of his great Monarch lay:
A Thousand glorious Actions, that might claim
Triumphant Laurels, and Immortal Fame,
Confus'd in Crouds of glorious Actions lye,
And Troops of Heroes undistinguish'd die.
O *Dormer*, how can I behold thy Fate,
And not the Wonders of thy Youth relate!
How can I see the Gay, the Brave, the Young,
Fall in the Cloud of War, and lye unsung!
In Joys of Conquest he resigns his Breath,
And, fill'd with *England*'s Glory, smiles in Death.

The Campaign, 1705

23   *Pastoral Hymn*

THE Lord my Pasture shall prepare,
   And feed me with a Shepherd's Care:
His Presence shall my wants supply,
And guard me with a watchful Eye;
My Noon-day Walks he shall attend,
And all my midnight Hours defend.

When in the sultry Glebe I faint,
Or on the thirsty Mountain pant,
To fertile Vales and dewy Meads
My weary wand'ring Steps he leads;
Where peaceful Rivers, soft and slow,
Amid the verdant Landskip flow.

Tho' in the Paths of Death I tread,
With gloomy Horrors over-spread;

My steadfast Heart shall fear no Ill,
For thou, O Lord, art with me still;
Thy friendly Crook shall give me Aid,
And guide me through the dreadful Shade.

Tho' in a bare and rugged Way,
Through devious lonely Wilds I stray,
Thy Bounty shall my Pains beguile:
The barren Wilderness shall smile
With sudden Greens and Herbage crown'd,
And Streams shall murmur all around.

The Spectator, July 26, 1712

24 *Hymn*

WHEN all thy Mercies, O my God,
My rising Soul surveys;
Transported with the View, I'm lost
In Wonder, Love, and Praise.

O how shall Words with equal Warmth
The Gratitude declare
That glows within my Ravish'd Heart!
But thou canst read it there.

Thy Providence my Life sustain'd
And all my Wants redrest,
When in the silent Womb I lay,
And hung upon the Breast.

To all my weak Complaints and Cries
Thy Mercy lent an Ear,
Ere yet my feeble Thoughts had learnt
To form themselves in Pray'r.

35

JOSEPH ADDISON

Unnumber'd Comforts to my Soul
    Thy tender Care bestow'd,
Before my Infant Heart conceiv'd
    From whom those Comforts flow'd.

When in the slipp'ry Paths of Youth
    With heedless Steps I ran,
Thine Arm unseen convey'd me safe
    And led me up to Man;

Through hidden Dangers, Toils, and Deaths
    It gently clear'd my Way,
And through the pleasing Snares of Vice,
    More to be fear'd than they.

When worn with Sickness, oft hast thou
    With Health renew'd my Face,
And when in Sins and Sorrows sunk,
    Revived my Soul with Grace.

Thy bounteous Hand with worldly Bliss
    Has made my Cup run o'er,
And in a kind and faithful Friend
    Has doubled all my Store.

Ten thousand thousand precious Gifts
    My Daily Thanks employ,
Nor is the least a chearful Heart,
    That tastes those Gifts with Joy.

Through ev'ry Period of my Life
    Thy Goodness I'll pursue,
And after Death in distant Worlds
    The glorious Theme renew.

JOSEPH ADDISON

When Nature fails, and Day and Night
   Divide thy Works no more,
My Ever-grateful Heart, O Lord,
   Thy Mercy shall adore.

Through all Eternity to Thee
   A joyful Song I'll raise,
For oh! Eternity 's too short
   To utter all thy Praise.

The Spectator, August 9, 1712

25 *Ode*

THE Spacious Firmament on high,
   With all the blue Etherial Sky,
And spangled Heav'ns, a Shining Frame,
Their great Original proclaim:
Th' unwearied Sun, from Day to Day,
Does his Creator's Power display,
And publishes to every Land
The Work of an Almighty Hand.

Soon as the Evening Shades prevail,
The Moon takes up the wondrous Tale,
And nightly to the listning Earth
Repeats the Story of her Birth:
Whilst all the Stars that round her burn,
And all the Planets, in their turn,
Confirm the Tidings as they rowl,
And spread the Truth from Pole to Pole.

What though, in solemn Silence, all
Move round the dark terrestrial Ball?

What tho' nor real Voice nor Sound
Amid their radiant Orbs be found?
In Reason's Ear they all rejoice,
And utter forth a glorious Voice,
For ever singing, as they shine,
' The Hand that made us is Divine.'

The Spectator, August 23; 1712

26 *Ode*

HOW are thy Servants blest, O Lord!
    How sure is their Defence!
Eternal Wisdom is their Guide,
    Their Help Omnipotence.

In foreign Realms, and Lands remote,
    Supported by Thy Care,
Through burning Climes I pass'd unhurt,
    And breath'd in tainted Air.

Thy Mercy sweetned ev'ry Soil,
    Made ev'ry Region please;
The hoary *Alpine* Hills it warm'd,
    And smooth'd the *Tyrrhene* Seas:

Think, O my Soul, devoutly think,
    How with affrighted Eyes
Thou saw'st the wide extended Deep
    In all its Horrors rise!

Confusion dwelt in ev'ry Face,
    And Fear in ev'ry Heart;
When Waves on Waves, and Gulphs in Gulphs,
    O'ercame the Pilot's Art.

Yet then from all my Griefs, O Lord,
  Thy Mercy set me free,
Whilst in the Confidence of Pray'r
  My Soul took Hold on Thee;

For tho' in dreadful Whirles we hung
  High on the broken Wave,
I knew Thou wert not slow to hear,
  Nor Impotent to save.

The Storm was laid, the Winds retir'd,
  Obedient to Thy Will;
The Sea, that roar'd at Thy Command,
  At Thy Command was still.

In Midst of Dangers, Fears and Death,
  Thy Goodness I'll adore,
And praise Thee for Thy Mercies past;
  And humbly hope for more.

My Life, if Thou preserv'st my Life,
  Thy Sacrifice shall be;
And Death, if Death must be my Doom,
  Shall join my Soul to Thee!

The Spectator, September 20, 1712

ANNE FINCH, COUNTESS OF WINCHILSEA
1661–1720

27   *The Portrait*

DEEP Lines of Honour all can hit,
  Or mark out a superior Wit;
Consummate Goodness all can show,
And where such Graces shine below:
But the more tender Strokes to trace,
T' express the Promise of a Face,

When but the Dawnings of the Mind
We from an Air unripen'd find;
Which alt'ring, as new Moments rise,
The Pen or Pencil's Art defies;
When Flesh and Blood in Youth appears,
Polish'd like what our Marble wears;
Fresh as that Shade of op'ning Green,
Which first upon our Groves is seen;
Enliven'd by a harmless Fire,
And brighten'd by each gay Desire;
These nicer Touches wou'd demand
A *Cowley*'s or a *Waller*'s Hand,
T' explain, with undisputed Art,
What 'tis affects th' enlighten'd Heart,
When ev'ry darker Thought gives way,
Whilst blooming Beauty we survey.

The Birthday of Catharine Tufton.
Miscellany Poems, 1713

28   *The Petition for an Absolute Retreat*

GIVE me, O indulgent Fate!
Give me, yet, before I Dye,
A sweet, but absolute Retreat,
'Mongst Paths so lost, and Trees so high,
That the World may ne'er invade,
Through such Windings and such Shade,
My unshaken Liberty.

No Intruders thither come!
Who visit, but to be from home;
None who their vain Moments pass,
Only studious of their Glass;

News, that charm to listning Ears,
That false Alarm to Hopes and Fears,
That common Theme for every Fop,
From the Statesman to the Shop,
In those Coverts ne'er be spread;
Of who's Deceas'd, or who's to Wed,
Be no Tidings thither brought,
But Silent, as a Midnight Thought,
Where the World may ne'er invade,
Be those Windings, and that Shade.
   Courteous Fate! afford me there
A *Table* spread without my Care,
With what the neighb'ring Fields impart,
Whose Cleanliness be all it's Art,
When, of old, the Calf was drest,
(Tho' to make an Angel's Feast)
In the plain, unstudied Sauce
Nor *Treufle*, nor *Morillia* was;
Nor cou'd the mighty Patriarch's Board
One far-fetch'd *Ortolane* afford.
Courteous Fate, then give me there
Only plain and wholesome Fare.
Fruits indeed (wou'd Heaven bestow)
All, that did in *Eden* grow,
All, but the *Forbidden Tree*,
Wou'd be coveted by me;
Grapes, with Juice so crouded up,
As breaking thro' the native Cup;
Figs (yet growing) candy'd o'er,
By the Sun's attracting Pow'r;
Cherries, with the downy Peach,
All within my easie Reach

Whilst creeping near the humble Ground,
Shou'd the Strawberry be found
Springing wheresoe'er I stray'd,
Thro' those Windings and that Shade. . . .

Give me there (since Heaven has shown
It was not Good to be alone)
A Partner suited to my Mind,
Solitary, pleas'd and kind;
Who, partially, may something see
Preferr'd to all the World in me;
Slighting, by my humble Side,
Fame and Splendor, Wealth and Pride.
When but Two the Earth possest,
'Twas their happiest Days, and best;
They by Bus'ness, nor by Wars,
They by no Domestick Cares,
From each other e'er were drawn,
But in some Grove, or flow'ry Lawn.
Spent the swiftly flying Time,
Spent their own, and Nature's Prime,
In Love; that only Passion given
To perfect Man, whilst Friends with Heaven
Rage, and Jealousie, and Hate.
Transports of his fallen State,
(When by *Satan*'s Wiles betray'd)
Fly those Windings, and that Shade! . . .

Let me then, indulgent Fate!
Let me still, in my Retreat.
From all roving Thoughts be freed,
Or Aims, that may Contention breed:
Nor be my Endeavours led
By Goods, that perish with the Dead!

ANNE, COUNTESS OF WINCHILSEA

Fitly might the Life of Man
Be indeed esteem'd a Span,
If the present Moment were
Of Delight his only Share;
If no other Joys he knew
Than what round about him grew:
But as those, who Stars wou'd trace
From a subterranean Place,
Through some Engine lift their Eyes
To the outward, glorious Skies;
So th' immortal Spirit may,
When descended to our Clay,
From a rightly govern'd Frame
View the Height, from whence she came;
To her Paradise be caught,
And Things unutterable taught.
Give me then, in that Retreat,
Give me, O indulgent Fate!
For all Pleasures left behind,
Contemplations of the Mind.
Let the Fair, the Gay, the Vain
Courtship and Applause obtain;
Let th' Ambitious rule the Earth;
Let the giddy Fool have Mirth;
Give the Epicure his Dish,
Ev'ry one their sev'ral Wish;
Whilst my Transports I employ
On that more extensive Joy,
When all Heaven shall be survey'd
From those Windings and that Shade.

Miscellany Poems, 1713

29 *The Tree*

FAIR *Tree!* for thy delightful Shade
'Tis just that some Return be made:
Sure, some Return is due from me
To thy cool Shadows, and to thee.
When thou to *Birds* do'st Shelter give,
Thou Musick do'st from them receive;
If *Travellers* beneath thee stay,
'Till Storms have worn themselves away,
That Time in praising thee they spend,
And thy protecting Pow'r commend:
The *Shepherd* here, from Scorching freed,
Tunes to thy dancing Leaves his Reed;
Whilst his lov'd Nymph, in Thanks, bestows
Her flow'ry Chaplets on thy Boughs.
Shall I then only Silent be,
And no Return be made by me?
No; let this Wish upon thee wait,
And still to flourish be thy Fate,
To future Ages may'st thou stand
Untouch'd by the rash Workman's hand;
'Till that large Stock of Sap is spent,
Which gives thy Summer's Ornament;
'Till the fierce Winds, that vainly strive
To shock thy Greatness whilst alive,
Shall on thy lifeless Hour attend,
Prevent the Axe, and grace thy End;
Their scatter'd Strength together call,
And to the Clouds proclaim thy Fall;

Who then their Ev'ning-Dews may spare,
When thou no longer art their Care;
But shalt, like ancient Heroes, burn,
And some bright Hearth be made thy Urn.

Miscellany Poems, 1713

30   *A Nocturnal Reverie*

IN such a *Night*, when every louder Wind
 Is to its distant Cavern safe confin'd;
And only gentle *Zephyr* fans his Wings,
And lonely *Philomel*, still waking, sings;
Or from some Tree, fam'd for the *Owl*'s delight,
She, hollowing clear, directs the Wand'rer right:
In such a *Night*, when passing Clouds give place,
Or thinly vail the Heav'ns mysterious Face;
When in some River, overhung with Green,
The waving Moon and trembling Leaves are seen;
When freshen'd Grass now bears it self upright,
And makes cool Banks to pleasing Rest invite,
Whence springs the *Woodbind*, and the *Bramble*-Rose,
And where the sleepy *Cowslip* shelter'd grows;
Whilst now a paler Hue the *Foxglove* takes,
Yet checquers still with Red the dusky brakes:
When scatter'd *Glow-worms*, but in Twilight fine,
Shew trivial Beauties, watch their Hour to shine;
Whilst *Salisb'ry* stands the Test of every Light,
In perfect Charms, and perfect Virtue bright:
When Odours, which declin'd repelling Day,
Thro' temp'rate Air uninterrupted stray;
When darken'd Groves their softest Shadows wear,
And falling Waters we distinctly hear;

45

ANNE, COUNTESS OF WINCHILSEA

When thro' the Gloom more venerable shows
Some ancient Fabrick, awful in Repose,
While Sunburnt Hills their swarthy Looks conceal,
And swelling Haycocks thicken up the Vale:
When the loos'd *Horse* now, as his Pasture leads,
Comes slowly grazing thro' th' adjoining Meads,
Whose stealing Pace, and lengthen'd Shade we fear,
Till torn up Forage in his Teeth we hear:
When nibbling *Sheep* at large pursue their Food,
And unmolested Kine rechew the Cud;
When *Curlews* cry beneath the Village-walls,
And to her straggling Brood the *Partridge* calls;
Their shortliv'd Jubilee the Creatures keep,
Which but endures, whilst Tyrant-*Man* do's sleep;
When a sedate Content the Spirit feels,
And no fierce Light disturbs, whilst it reveals;
But silent Musings urge the Mind to seek
Something, too high for Syllables to speak;
Till the free Soul to a compos'dness charm'd,
Finding the Elements of Rage disarm'd,
O'er all below a solemn Quiet grown,
Joys in th' inferiour World, and thinks it like her Own:
In such a *Night* let Me abroad remain,
Till Morning breaks, and All's confus'd again;
Our Cares, our Toils, our Clamours are renew'd,
Or Pleasures, seldom reach'd, again pursu'd.

Miscellany Poems, 1713

ISAAC WATTS

31   *The Day of Judgment*

An Ode

Attempted in English Sapphick

WHEN the fierce Northwind with his airy Forces
   Rears up the *Baltick* to a foaming Fury;
And the red Lightning with a Storm of Hail comes
            Rushing amain down,

How the poor Sailors stand amaz'd and tremble!
While the hoarse Thunder like a bloody Trumpet
Roars a loud Onset to the gaping Waters
            Quick to devour them.

Such shall the Noise be, and the wild Disorder,
(If things Eternal may be like these Earthly)
Such the dire Terror when the great Archangel
            Shakes the Creation;

Tears the strong Pillars of the Vault of Heaven,
Breaks up old Marble the Repose of Princes;
See the Graves open, and the Bones arising,
            Flames all around 'em.

Hark the shrill Outcries of the guilty Wretches!
Lively bright Horror and amazing Anguish
Stare thro' their Eye-lids, while the living Worm lies
            Gnawing within them.

Thoughts like old Vultures prey upon their Heartstrings,
And the Smart twinges, when their Eye beholds the
Lofty Judge frowning, and a Flood of Vengeance
                                        Rolling afore him

Hopeless Immortals! how they scream and shiver
While Devils push them to the Pit wide yawning
Hideous and gloomy, to receive them headlong
                                        Down to the Centre.

Stop here my Fancy: (all away ye horrid
Doleful Ideas) come arise to *Jesus*,
How he sits God-like! and the Saints around him
                                        Thron'd, yet adoring!

O may I sit there when he comes Triumphant
Dooming the Nations: then ascend to Glory,
While our *Hosannahs* all along the Passage
                                        Shout the Redeemer.
                                        Horæ Lyricæ, 1706

32   *God's Dominion and Decrees*

KEEP Silence, all created Things,
    And wait your Maker's Nod:
The Muse stands trembling while she sings
    The Honours of her God.

Life, Death, and Hell, and Worlds unknown
    Hang on his firm Decree:
He sits on no precarious Throne,
    Nor borrows Leave to Be.

Th' Almighty Voice bid ancient Night
    Her endless Realms resign,
And lo, ten thousand Globes of Light
    In Fields of Azure shine.

Now Wisdom with superior Sway
    Guides the vast moving Frame,
Whilst all the Ranks of Being pay
    Deep Rev'rence to his Name.

He spake; The Sun obedient stood,
    And held the falling Day:
Old *Jordan* backward drives his Flood,
    And disappoints the Sea.

Lord of the Armies of the Sky,
    He marshals all the Stars;
Red Comets lift their Banners high,
    And wide proclaim his Wars.

Chain'd to his Throne a Volume lies
    With all the Fates of Men,
With every Angel's Form and Size
    Drawn by th' eternal Pen.

His Providence unfolds the Book,
    And makes his Counsels shine:
Each opening Leaf and every Stroke
    Fulfils some deep Design.

Here he exalts neglected Worms
    To Scepters and a Crown;
Anon the following Page he turns,
    And treads the Monarchs down.

Not *Gabriel* asks the Reason why,
 Nor God the Reason gives,
Nor dares the Favourite-Angel pry
 Between the folded Leaves.

My God, I never long'd to see
 My Fate with curious Eyes,
What gloomy Lines are writ for me,
 Or what bright Scenes shall rise.

In thy fair Book of Life and Grace
 May I but find my Name
Recorded in some humble Place
 Beneath my Lord the Lamb.

Horæ Lyricæ, 1709

33   *True Riches*

I AM not concern'd to know
What to morrow Fate will do:
'Tis enough that I can say
I've possest my self to day:
Then if haply Midnight-Death
Seize my Flesh and stop my Breath,
Yet to morrow I shall be
Heir to the best Part of Me.
 Glittering Stones and Golden things,
Wealth and Honours that have Wings,
Ever fluttering to be gone
I could never call my own:
Riches that the World bestows
She can take and I can lose;

But the Treasures that are mine
Lie afar beyond her Line.
When I view my spacious Soul,
And survey my self awhole,
And injoy my self alone,
I'm a Kingdom of my own.

I've a mighty Part within
That the World hath never seen,
Rich as *Eden*'s happy Ground,
And with choicer Plenty crown'd.
Here on all the shining Boughs
Knowledge fair and useful grows;
On the same young flow'ry Tree
All the Seasons you may see;
Notions in the Bloom of Light,
Just disclosing to the Sight;
Here are Thoughts of larger **Growth,**
Rip'ning into solid Truth;
Fruits refin'd, of noble Taste;
Seraphs feed on such Repast.
Here in a green and shady Grove
Streams of Pleasure mix with Love:
There beneath the smiling Skies
Hills of Contemplation rise;
Now upon some shining Top
Angels light, and call me up;
I rejoyce to raise my Feet,
Both rejoyce when there we meet.

There are endless Beauties more
Earth hath no Resemblance for;
Nothing like them round the Pole,
Nothing can describe the Soul:

ISAAC WATTS

'Tis a Region half unknown,
That has Treasures of its own,
More remote from publick View
Than the Bowels of *Peru*;
Broader 'tis and brighter far
Than the Golden *Indies* are;
Ships that trace the watry Stage
Cannot coast it in an Age;
Harts or Horses, strong and fleet,
Had they Wings to help their Feet,
Could not run it half way o'er
In ten thousand Days and more.

Yet the silly wandring Mind
Loath to be too much confin'd
Roves and takes her dayly Tours,
Coasting round the narrow Shores,
Narrow Shores of Flesh and Sense,
Picking Shells and Pebbles thence:
Or she sits at Fancy's Door,
Calling Shapes and Shadows to her,
Foreign Visits still receiving,
And t' her self a Stranger living.
Never, never would she buy
Indian Dust or *Tyrian* Dye,
Never trade abroad for more
If she saw her native Store,
If her inward Worth were known
She might ever live alone.

Horæ Lyricæ, 1709

34 *Crucifixion to the World by the Cross of Christ*

WHEN I survey the wond'rous Cross
  On which the Prince of Glory dy'd,
My richest Gain I count but Loss,
And pour Contempt on all my Pride.

Forbid it, Lord, that I should boast
Save in the Death of *Christ* my God;
All the vain things that charm me most,
I sacrifice them to his Blood.

See from his Head, his Hands, his Feet,
Sorrow and Love flow mingled down;
Did e'er such Love and Sorrow meet?
Or Thorns compose so rich a Crown?

His dying Crimson like a Robe
Spreads o'er his Body on the Tree,
Then am I dead to all the Globe,
And all the Globe is dead to me.

Were the whole Realm of Nature mine,
That were a Present far too small;
Love so amazing, so divine
Demands my Soul, my Life, my All.

Hymns and Spiritual Songs, 1707

35 *A Prospect of Heaven makes Death easy*

THERE is a Land of pure Delight
  Where Saints Immortal reign;
Infinite Day excludes the Night,
  And Pleasures banish Pain.

There everlasting Spring abides,
    And never-withering Flowers:
Death like a narrow Sea divides
    This Heav'nly Land from ours.

Sweet Fields beyond the Swelling Flood
    Stand drest in living Green:
So to the *Jews* old *Canaan* stood,
    While *Jordan* roll'd between

But timorous Mortals start and shrink
    To cross this narrow Sea,
And linger shivering on the Brink,
    And fear to lanch away.

O could we make our Doubts remove,
    These gloomy Doubts that rise,
And see the *Canaan* that we love,
    With unbeclouded Eyes.

Could we but climb where *Moses* stood,
    And view the Landskip o're,
Not *Jordan*'s Stream, nor Death's cold Flood,
    Should fright us from the Shore.

Hymns and Spiritual Songs, 1707

36   *Man Frail, and God Eternal*

OUR God, our Help in Ages past,
    Our Hope for Years to come,
Our Shelter from the Stormy Blast,
    And our eternal Home.

ISAAC WATTS

Under the Shadow of thy Throne
  Thy Saints have dwelt secure;
Sufficient is thine Arm alone,
  And our Defence is sure.

Before the Hills in order stood,
  Or Earth receiv'd her Frame,
From everlasting Thou art God,
  To endless Years the same.

Thy Word commands our Flesh to Dust,
  Return, ye Sons of Men :
All Nations rose from Earth at first,
  And turn to Earth again.

A thousand Ages in thy Sight
  Are like an Evening gone;
Short as the Watch that ends the Night
  Before the rising Sun.

The busy Tribes of Flesh and Blood
  With all their Lives and Cares
Are carried downwards by thy Flood,
  And lost in following Years.

Time like an ever-rolling Stream
  Bears all its Sons away;
They fly forgotten as a Dream
  Dies at the opening Day.

Like flow'ry Fields the Nations stand
  Pleas'd with the Morning-light;
The Flowers beneath the Mower's Hand
  Ly withering e'er 'tis Night.

Our God, our Help in Ages past,
　　Our Hope for Years to come,
Be thou our Guard while Troubles last,
　　And our eternal Home.

The Psalms of David Imitated, 1719

37　　*Against Quarrelling and Fighting*

LET Dogs delight to bark and bite,
　　For God hath made them so;
Let Bears and Lions growl and fight,
　　For 'tis their Nature too.

But, Children, you should never let
　　Such angry Passions rise;
Your little Hands were never made
　　To tear each other's Eyes.

Let Love thro' all your Actions run,
　　And all your Words be mild;
Live like the blessed Virgin's Son,
　　That sweet and lovely Child.

His Soul was gentle as a Lamb;
　　And as his Stature grew,
He grew in Favour both with Man,
　　And God his Father too.

Now, Lord of all, he reigns above,
　　And from his heav'nly Throne
He sees what Children dwell in Love,
　　And marks them for his own.

Divine Songs, for the use of Children, 1720

38   *Against Idleness and Mischief*

HOW doth the little busy Bee
    Improve each shining Hour,
And gather Honey all the Day
    From ev'ry op'ning Flow'r!

How skilfully she builds her Cell!
    How neat she spreads the Wax!
And labours hard to store it well
    With the sweet Food she makes.

In Works of Labour or of Skill
    I would be busy too:
For *Satan* finds some Mischief still
    For idle Hands to do.

In Books, or Work, or healthful Play,
    Let my first Years be past,
That I may give for every Day
    Some good Account at last.

Divine Songs, 1720

39   *The Sluggard*

'TIS the Voice of the Sluggard; I heard him complain,
    ' You have wak'd me too soon, I must slumber again.'
As the Door on its Hinges, so he on his Bed,
Turns his Sides and his Shoulders and his heavy Head.

' A little more Sleep, and a little more Slumber;'
Thus he wastes half his Days and his Hours without Number;
And when he gets up, he sits folding his Hands,
Or walks about sauntring, or trifling he stands.

I pass'd by his Garden, and saw the wild Brier,
The Thorn and the Thistle grow broader and higher;
The Clothes that hang on him are turning to Rags;
And his Money still wastes, till he starves or he begs.

I made him a Visit, still hoping to find
He had took better Care for improving his Mind:
He told me his Dreams, talk'd of Eating and Drinking;
But he scarce reads his Bible, and never loves Thinking.

Said I then to my Heart, ' Here 's a Lesson for me; '
That Man 's but a Picture of what I might be:
But thanks to my Friends for their Care in my Breeding,
Who taught me betimes to love Working and Reading.

Divine Songs, 1720

40 *A Cradle Hymn*

HUSH! my Dear, lie still and slumber,
　　Holy Angels guard thy Bed!
Heavenly Blessings without Number
　　Gently falling on thy Head.

Sleep, my Babe; thy Food and Raiment,
　　House and Home thy Friends provide;
All without thy Care or Payment,
　　All thy Wants are well supply'd.

How much better thou'rt attended
　　Than the SON of GOD could be,
When from Heaven he descended,
　　And became a Child like thee?

58

ISAAC WATTS

Soft and easy is thy Cradle:
  Coarse and hard thy Saviour lay;
When his Birth-place was a Stable,
  And his softest Bed was Hay.

Blessed Babe! what glorious Features,
  Spotless fair, divinely bright!
Must he dwell with brutal Creatures?
  How could Angels bear the Sight?

Was there nothing but a Manger
  Cursed Sinners could afford,
To receive the Heav'nly Stranger?
  Did they thus affront their LORD?

Soft, my Child; I did not chide thee,
  Tho' my Song might sound too hard;
'Tis thy $\left\{\begin{array}{l}\text{* Mother}\\\text{Nurse that}\end{array}\right\}$ sits beside thee,
  And her Arms shall be thy Guard.

Yet to read the shameful Story,
  How the Jews abus'd their King,
How they serv'd the LORD of Glory,
  Makes me angry while I sing.

See the kinder Shepherds round him,
  Telling Wonders from the Sky;
There they sought him, there they found him,
  With his Virgin-Mother by.

* Here you may use the words, *Brother, Sister, Neighbour, Friend*, &c.

ISAAC WATTS

See the lovely Babe a dressing;
  Lovely Infant, how he smil'd!
When he wept, the Mother's Blessing
  Sooth'd and hush'd the holy Child.

Lo, he slumbers in his Manger,
  Where the horned Oxen fed;
Peace, my Darling, here's no Danger,
  Here's no Ox a-near thy Bed.

'Twas to save thee, Child, from dying,
  Save my Dear from burning Flame,
Bitter Grones and endless Crying,
  That thy blest Redeemer came.

May'st thou live to know and fear Him,
  Trust and love Him all thy Days;
Then go dwell for ever near Him,
  See his Face, and sing his Praise!

I could give thee thousand Kisses,
  Hoping what I most desire;
Not a Mother's fondest Wishes,
  Can to greater Joys aspire.

Divine Songs, 1720

CHARLES MORDAUNT, EARL OF PETERBOROUGH

1658–1735

41   *Chloe*

I SAID to my Heart, between sleeping and waking,
  Thou wild Thing, that ever art leaping or aching,
For the Black, for the Fair: In what Clime, in what Nation,
Hast thou not felt a Fit of Pitapatation?

60

Thus accus'd, the wild Thing gave this serious Reply;
See the Heart without Motion, tho' *Celia* pass by;
Not the Beauty she has, nor the Wit that she borrows,
Gives the Eye any Joys, or the Heart any Sorrows.

When our *Sappho* appears, whose Wit's so refined,
I am forced to admire with the rest of Mankind:
Whatever she says is with Spirit and Fire;
Every Word I attend, but I only admire.

Prudentia, as vainly too, puts in her Claim;
Ever gazing on Heaven, tho' Man is her Aim.
'Tis Love, not Devotion, that turns up her Eyes:
Those Stars of the World are too good for the Skies.

But my *Chloe*, so lovely, so easy, so fair;
Her Wit so genteel, without Art, without Care;
When she comes in my Way, Oh! the Motion and Pain,
The Leapings and Achings, they return all again.

Thou wonderful Creature! A Woman of Reason!
Never grave out of Pride, never gay out of Season!
When so easy to guess, who this Angel should be,
Would one think that my *Chloe* ne'er thought it was she.

The Universal Journal, January 1, 1723/4

JONATHAN SWIFT

1667–1745

42   *Baucis and Philemon*

IN Ancient Times, as Story tells,
The Saints would often leave their Cells,
And strole about, but hide their Quality,
To try good People's Hospitality.

It happen'd on a Winter Night,
As Authors of the Legend write,
Two Brother Hermits, Saints by Trade,
Taking their *Tour* in Masquerade,
Disguis'd in tatter'd Habits, went
To a small Village down in *Kent*;
Where, in the Strolers canting Strain,
They begg'd from Door to Door in vain;
Try'd ev'ry Tone might Pity win,
But not a Soul would let them in.

Our wand'ring Saints in woful State,
Treated at this ungodly Rate,
Having thro' all the Village pass'd,
To a small Cottage came at last;
Where dwelt a good honest old Yeoman,
Call'd in the Neighbourhood, *Philemon*.
Who kindly did these Saints invite
In his poor Hut to pass the Night:
And then the hospitable Sire
Bid Goody *Baucis* mend the Fire;
While he from out the Chimney took
A Flitch of Bacon off the Hook;
And freely from the fattest Side
Cut out large Slices to be fry'd:
Then stept aside to fetch 'em Drink,
Fill'd a large Jug up to the Brink;
And saw it fairly twice go round:
Yet (what is wonderful) they found
'Twas still replenish'd to the Top,
As if they ne'er had touch'd a Drop.
The good old Couple was amaz'd,
And often on each other gaz'd:

For both were frighted to the Heart,
And just began to cry,——What art!
Then softly turn'd aside to view,
Whether the Lights were burning blue.
The gentle *Pilgrims* soon aware on't,
Told 'em their Calling, and their Errant:
Good Folks, you need not be afraid,
We are but *Saints*, the Hermits said:
No Hurt shall come to You, or Yours;
But, for that Pack of churlish Boors,
Not fit to live on Christian Ground,
They and their Houses shall be drown'd:
Whilst you shall see your Cottage rise,
And grow a Church before your Eyes.

They scarce had spoke; when fair and soft,
The Roof began to mount aloft;
Aloft rose ev'ry Beam and Rafter,
The heavy Wall climb'd slowly after.

The Chimney widen'd, and grew higher,
Became a Steeple with a Spire.

The Kettle to the Top was hoist,
And there stood fast'ned to a Joist;
But with the Upside down, to show
Its Inclination for below:
In vain; for a superior Force
Apply'd at Bottom, stops its Course,
Doom'd ever in Suspence to dwell,
'Tis now no Kettle, but a Bell.

A wooden Jack, which had almost
Lost, by Disuse, the Art to Roast,
A sudden Alteration feels,
Increas'd by new Intestine Wheels:

And, what exalts the Wonder more,
The Number made the Motion slow'r.
The Flyer, tho't had Leaden Feet,
Turn'd round so quick, you scarce could see't;
But slacken'd by some secret Power,
Now hardly moves an Inch an Hour.
The Jack and Chimney near ally'd,
Had never left each other's Side;
The Chimney to a Steeple grown,
The Jack would not be left alone,
But up against the Steeple rear'd,
Became a Clock, and still adher'd:
And still its Love to Houshold Cares
By a shrill Voice at Noon declares,
Warning the Cook-maid, not to burn
That Roast-meat which it cannot turn.

The groaning Chair began to crawl
Like an huge Snail along the Wall;
There stuck aloft, in publick View,
And with small change, a Pulpit grew.

The Porringers, that in a Row
Hung high, and made a glitt'ring Show,
To a less noble Substance chang'd,
Were now but Leathern Buckets rang'd.

The Ballads pasted on the Wall,
Of *Joan* of *France*, and *English Moll*,
Fair *Rosamond*, and *Robin Hood*,
The *Little Children in the Wood*,
Now seem'd to look abundance better,
Improv'd in Picture, Size, and Letter
And high in Order plac'd, describe
The Heraldry of ev'ry Tribe.

JONATHAN SWIFT

A Bedstead of the Antique Mode,
Compact of Timber many a Load,
Such as our Ancestors did use,
Was Metamorphos'd into Pews;
Which still their ancient Nature keep,
By lodging Folks dispos'd to Sleep.

The Cottage, by such Feats as these,
Grown to a Church by just Degrees,
The Hermits then desir'd their Host
To ask for what he fancy'd most.
Philemon, having paus'd awhile,
Return'd 'em Thanks in homely Style;
Then said, My House is grown so fine,
Methinks I still would call it mine:
I'm old, and fain would live at Ease,
Make me the *Parson*, if you please.

He spoke, and presently he feels
His Grazier's Coat fall down his Heels;
He sees, yet hardly can believe,
About each Arm a Pudding-sleeve;
His Wastcoat to a Cassock grew,
And both assum'd a sable Hue;
But being Old, continu'd just
As Thread-bare, and as full of Dust.
His Talk was now of *Tythes* and *Dues*;
He smok'd his Pipe, and read the News;
Knew how to preach old Sermons next,
Vamp'd in the Preface and the Text;
At Christ'nings well could act his Part,
And had the Service all by Heart;
Wish'd Women might have Children fast,
And thought whose Sow had farrow'd last:

Against *Dissenters* would repine,
And stood up firm for *Right Divine*:
Found his Head fill'd with many a System,
But Classick Authors,—he ne'er miss'd 'em.

   Thus having furbish'd up a Parson,
Dame *Baucis* next they play'd their Farce on:
Instead of Home-spun Coifs were seen
Good Pinners edg'd with Colberteen:
Her Petticoat transform'd apace,
Became black Sattin flounc'd with Lace.
Plain *Goody* would no longer down,
'Twas *Madam*, in her Grogram Gown.
Philemon was in great Surprize,
And hardly could believe his Eyes,
Amaz'd to see her look so prim;
And she admir'd as much as Him.

   Thus, happy in their Change of Life,
Were several Years this Man and Wife:
When on a Day, which prov'd their last,
Discoursing o'er old Stories past,
They went by chance, amidst their Talk,
To the Church-yard to take a Walk;
When *Baucis* hastily cry'd out,
My Dear, I see your Forehead sprout!
Sprout, quoth the Man, What's this you tell us?
I hope you don't believe me Jealous:
But yet, methinks, I feel it true;
And really, Yours is budding too—
Nay,—now I cannot stir my Foot:
It feels as if 'twere taking Root.

   Description would but tire my Muse:
In short, they both were turn'd to *Yews*.

JONATHAN SWIFT

Old Goodman *Dobson* of the Green
Remembers he the Trees has seen;
He'll talk of them from Noon to Night,
And goes with Folks to shew the Sight:
On *Sundays*, after Evening Prayer,
He gathers all the Parish there;
Points out the Place of either *Yew*;
Here *Baucis*, there *Philemon* grew :
Till once, a Parson of our Town,
To mend his Barn, cut *Baucis* down;
At which, 'tis hard to be believ'd,
How much the other Tree was griev'd,
Grew scrubby, dy'd a-top, was stunted:
So, the next Parson stubb'd and burnt it.

Written 1706; *Poetical Miscellanies*, vi, 1709

43   *In Sickness*

Written soon after the Author's coming to live in Ireland,
upon the Queen's Death, October 1714

'TIS true,—then why should I repine,
To see my Life so fast decline?
But, why obscurely here alone?
Where I am neither lov'd nor known.
My State of Health none care to learn;
My Life is here no Soul's Concern.
And those with whom I now converse,
Without a Tear will tend my Herse.
Remov'd from kind *Arbuthnot*'s Aid,
Who knows his Art, but not the Trade;
Preferring his Regard for me
Before his Credit, or his Fee.

Some formal Visits, Looks, and Words,
What meer Humanity affords,
I meet perhaps from three or four,
From whom I once expected more:
Which those who tend the Sick for Pay
Can act as decently as they :
But no obliging tender Friend
To help at my approaching End.
My Life is now a Burden grown
To others, e'er it be my own.

Ye formal Weepers for the Sick,
In your last Offices be quick :
And spare my absent Friends the Grief
To hear, yet give me no Relief;
Expir'd To-day, entomb'd To-morrow,
When known, will save a double Sorrow.

Miscellanies, v, 1735

44
Stella's Birth-Day

March 13. 1726/7

THIS Day, whate'er the Fates decree,
  Shall still be kept with Joy by me:
This Day then, let us not be told,
That you are sick, and I grown old,
Nor think on our approaching Ills,
And talk of Spectacles and Pills;
To morrow will be Time enough
To hear such mortifying Stuff.
Yet, since from Reason may be brought
A better and more pleasing Thought,
Which can, in spite of all Decays,
Support a few remaining Days:

From not the gravest of Divines,
Accept for once some serious Lines.

Although we now can form no more
Long Schemes of Life, as heretofore;
Yet you, while Time is running fast,
Can look with Joy on what is past.

Were future Happiness and Pain
A mere Contrivance of the Brain,
As Atheists argue, to entice,
And fit their Proselytes for Vice;
(The only Comfort they propose,
To have Companions in their Woes)
Grant this the Case, yet sure 'tis hard,
That Virtue, stil'd its own Reward,
And by all Sages understood
To be the chief of human Good,
Should acting, die, nor leave behind
Some lasting Pleasure in the Mind,
Which by Remembrance will assuage,
Grief, Sickness, Poverty, and Age;
And strongly shoot a radiant Dart,
To shine through Life's declining Part.

Say, *Stella*, feel you no Content,
Reflecting on a Life well spent?
Your skilful Hand employ'd to save
Despairing Wretches from the Grave;
And then supporting, with your Store,
Those whom you dragg'd from Death before:
(So Providence on Mortals waits,
Preserving what it first creates)
Your gen'rous Boldness to defend
An innocent and absent Friend:

That Courage which can make you just
To Merit humbled in the Dust:
The Detestation you express
For Vice in all its glitt'ring Dress:
That Patience under tort'ring Pain,
Where stubborn Stoicks would complain.

Must these like empty Shadows pass,
Or Forms reflected from a Glass?
Or mere Chimæra's in the Mind,
That fly and leave no Marks behind?
Does not the Body thrive and grow
By Food of twenty Years ago?
And, had it not been still supply'd,
It must a thousand Times have dy'd.
Then, who with Reason can maintain,
That no Effects of Food remain?
And, is not Virtue in Mankind
The Nutriment that feeds the Mind?
Upheld by each good Action past,
And still continued by the last:
Then, who with Reason can pretend,
That all Effects of Virtue end?

Believe me *Stella*, when you show
That true Contempt for Things below,
Nor prize your Life for other Ends
Than merely to oblige your Friends;
Your former Actions claim their Part,
And join to fortify your Heart.
For Virtue in her daily Race,
Like *Janus*, bears a double Face;
Looks back with Joy where she has gone,
And therefore goes with Courage on.

She at your sickly Couch will wait,
And guide you to a better State.

O then, whatever Heav'n intends,
Take Pity on your pitying Friends;
Nor let your Ills affect your Mind,
To fancy they can be unkind.
Me, surely me, you ought to spare,
Who gladly would your Suff'rings share;
Or give my Scrap of Life to you,
And think it far beneath your Due;
You, to whose Care so oft I owe,
That I'm alive to tell you so.

Miscellanies, iii, 1728

45   *A Soldier and a Scholar*
      Or the Lady's Judgment upon those two Characters

THUS spoke to my Lady the Knight full of Care,
Let me have your Advice in a weighty Affair:
This *Hamilton*'s Bawn, while it sticks on my Hand,
I lose by the House, what I get by the Land;
But how to dispose of it to the best Bidder,
For a Barrack or Malt-house, we now must consider:
First, let me suppose, I make it a Malt-house,
Here, I have computed the Profit will fall t'us;
There's Nine hundred Pounds for Labour and Grain;
I increase it to Twelve; so Three hundred remain;
A handsome Addition for Wine and good Cheer,
Three Dishes a Day, and Three hundred a Year,
With a Dozen large Vessels my Vaults shall be stor'd,
No little scrub Joint shall come on my Board;
And you, and the Dean, no more shall combine,
To stint me at Night to one Bottle of Wine;

Nor shall I, for his Humours, permit you shou'd purloin
A Stone and a half of Beef from my Surloin.
If I make it a Barrack, the Crown is my Tenant:
My Dear, I have ponder'd again, and again on't,
In Poundage and Drawback, I lose half my Rent,
And, whatever they give me, I must be content,
Or joyn with the Court in every Debate;
And rather than that, I would lose my Estate.

Thus ended the Knight: Thus began the meek Wife:
It must, and it shall be a Barrack, my Life:
I am grown a mere Mopes, no Company comes,
But a Rabble of Tenants, and rusty dull Rums;
With Parsons, what Lady can keep herself clean?
I am all over dawb'd, when I sit by the Dean;
But if you will give us a Barrack, my Dear,
The Captain, I'm sure, will always come here.
I then shall not value his Deanship a Straw;
For the Captain, I'll warrant, will keep him in Awe.
Or should he pretend to be brisk and alert,
We'll tell him that Chaplains should not be so pert;
That Men of his Coat should be minding their Prayers,
And not among Ladies, to give themselves Airs.

Thus argu'd my Lady, but argu'd in vain;
The Knight his Opinion resolv'd to maintain.
But *Hannah*, who listen'd to all that was past,
And could not endure so vulgar a Taste,
As soon as her Ladyship call'd to be drest,
Cry'd, Madam, why sure, my Master's possest;
Sir *Arthur* the Malster! how fine it would sound?
I'd rather the Bawn were sunk under Ground:
But, Madam, I guess'd, there would never come Good,
When I saw him so often with *Darby* and *Wood*.

And now my Dream's out; for I was a-dream'd,
That I saw a huge Rat; O dear, how I scream'd!
And after, methought, I lost my new Shoes,
And *Molly*, she said, I should hear some ill News.
Dear Madam, had you but the Spirit to teaze,
You might have a Barrack, whenever you please,
And, Madam, I always believ'd you so stout,
That for twenty Denials, you would not give out.
If I had a Husband like him, I protest,
'Till he gave me my Will, I would give him no Rest,
And rather than come in the same Pair of Sheets
With such a cross Man, I would lie in the Streets.
But, Madam, I beg, you'll contrive and invent,
And worry him out, till he gives his Consent.
Dear Madam, whene'er on a Barrack I think,
An I were to be hang'd, I can't sleep a Wink,
For if a new Crotchet comes into my Brain,
I can't get it out tho' I'd never so fain.
I fancy already a Barrack contriv'd
At *Hamilton*'s Bawn, and the Troop is arriv'd:
Of this, to be sure, Sir *Arthur* has Warning,
And waits on the Captain, betimes in the Morning.
Now see when they meet, how their Honours behave—
Noble Captain, your Servant—Sir *Arthur*, your Slave.
You honour me much—The Honour is mine.
'Twas a sad rainy Night—But the Morning is fine.
Pray how does my Lady?—My Wife's at your Service.
I think I have seen her Picture at *Jervais*'.
Good morrow, good Captain—I'll wait on you down.
You shan't stir a Foot—You'll think me a Clown.
For all the World, Captain, not half an Inch farther—
You must be obey'd; your Servant, Sir *Arthur*;

My humble Respects to my Lady, unknown—
I hope you will use my House as your own.
    —Go bring me my Smock, and leave off your Prate,
Thou hast certainly gotten a Cup in thy Pate.
Pray, Madam; be quiet, what was it I said?
You had like to have put it quite out of my Head.
Next Day, to be sure, the Captain will come,
At the Head of his Troop, with his Trumpet and Drum:
Now, Madam, observe, how he marches in State,
The Man with the Kettle-drum enters the Gate,
Dub, dub, a dub dub; the Trumpeters follow,
Tantara, Tantara; while all the Boys halloo.
See, now comes the Captain, all dawb'd with Gold Lace:
O law! the sweet Gentleman, look in his Face,
And see how he rides like a Lord of the Land,
With the fine Flaming-Sword he holds in his Hand;
And his Horse, the dear Creature, it prances and rears,
With Ribbands in Knots, at his Tail and his Ears.
At last comes the Troop, at the Word of Command,
Drawn up in our Court, till the Captain cries, Stand.
Your Ladyship lifts up the Sash to be seen,
For sure I had dizen'd you out like a Queen;
The Captain, to shew he was proud of the Favour,
Looks up to the Window, and cocks up his Beaver.
His Beaver is cockt, pray, Madam, mind that;
For a Captain of Horse never takes off his Hat;
Because he has never a Hand that is idle,
For the Right holds the Sword, and the Left holds the Bridle.
Then flourishing twice his Sword in the Air,
As a Compliment due to a Lady so fair:
How I tremble to think of the Blood it has spilt!
Then he lowers the Point; then he kisses the Hilt.

Your Ladyship smiles, and then you begin:
Pray, Captain, be pleas'd to alight, and walk in.
The Captain salutes you, with Congee profound;
And your Ladyship curtsies half-way to the Ground.
Kit, run to your Master, and bid him come to us;
I'm sure he'll be proud of the Honour you do us:
And, Captain, you'll do us the Favour to stay
And take a short Dinner here with us To-day;
You're heartily welcome; but as for good Cheer,
You came in the very worst Time of the Year.
Had I but expected so worthy a Guest—
Lord, Madam, your Ladyship sure is in Jest:
You banter me, Madam; the Kingdom must grant—
You Officers, Captain, are so complaisant.
Hist, Hussy, I think I hear Somebody coming.
No, Madam, 'tis only Sir *Arthur* a-humming.
To shorten my Tale, for I hate a long Story,
The Captain, at Dinner, appears in his Glory.
The Dean and the Doctor have humbled their Pride;
For the Captain's intreated to sit by their Side.
And because he's their Betters, you carve for him first;
The Parsons, for Envy, are ready to burst.
The Servants, amaz'd, are scarce ever able
To keep off their Eyes, as he sits at the Table.
And *Molly* and I do thrust in our Nose,
To peep at the Captain, in all his fine Cloaths.
Dear, Madam, 'be sure, he's a fine-spoken Man;
Do but hear, on the Clergy, how glib his Tongue ran.

    And, Madam, said he, if such Dinners you give,
You'll never want Parsons as long as you live:
I ne'er knew a Parson without a good Nose;
But the Devil's as welcome, where-ever he goes.

G— d— me, they bid us reform and repent;
But, Zounds, by their Looks, they never keep Lent.
Mr. Curate, for all your grave Looks, I'm afraid,
You cast a Sheep's Eye on her Ladyship's Maid:
I wish she would lend you her lilly-white Hand,
In mending your Gown, and smoothing your Band.
For the Dean was so shabby, and look'd like a Ninny,
That the Captain suppos'd he was Curate to *Jenny*.
Whenever you see a Cassock and Gown,
An hundred to one, but it covers a Clown.
Observe how a Parson comes into a Room:
G— d— me, he hobbles as bad as my Groom.
A Scholard, when just from the College broke loose,
Can hardly tell how to cry Bo to a Goose.
Your *Novids*, and *Bludurks*, and *Omers*, and Stuff;
By G—d, they don't signify this Pinch of Snuff.
To give a young Gentleman right Education,
The Army's the very best School in the Nation.
My School-master call'd me a Dunce and a Fool;
But at Cuffs, I was always the Cock of the School.
I never could take to my Books for the Blood o'me;
And the Puppy confest, he expected no Good o'me.
Now, Madam, you'll think it a strange thing to say,
But the Sight of a Book makes me sick to this Day.

  Never since I was born, did I hear so much Wit;
And, Madam, I laugh'd, till I thought I should split.
So then you look'd scornful, and snuff'd at the Dean:
As who should say, Now am I skinny and lean?
And he durst not so much as open his Lips.
And the Dean, he was plaguily down in the Hips.

  Thus merciless *Hannah* run on in her Talk,

Novids, and *Bludurks*] *Ovids* and *Plutarchs*

Till she heard the Dean call, Will your Ladyship walk.
Her Ladyship answers—I'm just coming down.
Then turning to *Hannah*, and forcing a Frown:
Altho' it was plain, in her Heart she was glad;
Cry'd, Hussy, why sure, the Wench is gone mad:
How could these Chimera's get into your Brains?
Come hither, and take this old Gown for your Pains.
But if ever this Secret should reach the Dean's Ears,
He ne'er will have done with his Jibes and his Jeers.
For your Life, not a Word of this Matter, I charge you.
Give me but a Barrack, a Fig for the Clergy.

A Soldier and a Scholar, 1732

46   *Critics*

*H*OBBES clearly proves that every Creature
    Lives in a State of War by Nature.
The Greater for the Smallest watch,
But meddle seldom with their Match.
A Whale of moderate Size will draw
A Shole of Herrings down his Maw.
A Fox with Geese his Belly crams;
A Wolf destroys a thousand Lambs.
But search among the rhiming Race,
The Brave are worried by the Base.
If on *Parnassus*' Top you sit,
You rarely bite, are always bit:
Each Poet of inferior Size
On you shall rail and criticize;
And strive to tear you Limb from Limb,
While others do as much for him.
    The Vermin only teaze and pinch
Their Foes superior by an Inch.

So, Nat'ralists observe, a Flea
Hath smaller Fleas that on him prey,
And these have smaller Fleas to bite 'em,
And so proceed *ad infinitum*:
Thus ev'ry Poet in his Kind
Is bit by him that comes behind;
Who, tho' too little to be seen,
Can teaze, and gall, and give the Spleen;
Call Dunces, Fools, and Sons of Whores,
Lay *Grubstreet* at each others Doors:
Extol the *Greek* and *Roman* Masters,
And curse our modern Poetasters.
Complain, as many an ancient Bard did,
How Genius is no more rewarded;
How wrong a Taste prevails among us;
How much our Ancestors out-sung us;
Can personate an awkward Scorn
For those who are not Poets born:
And all their Brother Dunces lash,
Who crowd the Press with hourly Trash.

On Poetry : A Rhapsody, 1733

47   *Verses on the Death of Dr. Swift*
       Written by Himself: Nov. 1731

THE time is not remote, when I
Must by the course of nature die;
When, I foresee, my special friends
Will try to find their private ends:
And though 'tis hardly understood
Which way my death can do them good,
Yet thus, methinks, I hear them speak:
' See, how the Dean begins to break!

'Poor gentleman, he droops apace!
'You plainly find it in his face.
'That old vertigo in his head
'Will never leave him, till he's dead.
'Besides, his memory decays:
'He recollects not what he says;
'He cannot call his friends to mind;
'Forgets the place where last he din'd;
'Plies you with stories o'er and o'er;
'He told them fifty times before.
'How does he fancy we can sit
'To hear his out-of-fashion wit?
'But he takes up with younger folks,
'Who for his wine will bear his jokes.
'Faith! he must make his stories shorter,
'Or change his comrades once a quarter:
'In half the time he talks them round,
'There must another set be found.

  'For poetry, he's past his prime:
'He takes an hour to find a rhyme;
'His fire is out, his wit decay'd,
'His fancy sunk, his Muse a jade.
'I'd have him throw away his pen;—
'But there's no talking to some men!'
  And then their tenderness appears
By adding largely to my years:
'He's older than he would be reckon'd,
'And well remembers *Charles* the Second.
'He hardly drinks a pint of wine;
'And that, I doubt, is no good sign.
'His stomach too begins to fail:
'Last year we thought him strong and hale:

' But now he 's quite another thing:
' I wish he may hold out till spring!'
They hug themselves, and reason thus:
' It is not yet so bad with us!'
    In such a case, they talk in tropes,
And by their fears express their hopes.
Some great misfortune to portend,
No enemy can match a friend.
With all the kindness they profess,
The merit of a lucky guess
(When daily *Howd'y's* come of course,
And servants answer ' Worse and worse!')
Would please them better, than to tell,
That, ' God be prais'd, the Dean is well.'
Then he, who prophesied the best,
Approves his foresight to the rest:
' You know I always fear'd the worst,
' And often told you so at first.'
He'd rather choose that I should die,
Than his predictions prove a lie.
Not one foretells I shall recover;
But all agree to give me over.

   .   .   .   .

    Behold the fatal day arrive!
' How is the Dean? '—' He 's just alive.'
Now the departing prayer is read;
' He hardly breathes '—' The Dean is dead.'
    Before the passing-bell begun,
The news through half the town is run.
' O! may we all for death prepare!
' What has he left? and who 's his heir?

' I know no more than what the news is;
' 'Tis all bequeath'd to publick uses.
　To publick uses! there 's a whim!
' What had the publick done for him?
' Mere envy, avarice, and pride:
' He gave it all—but first he died.
' And had the Dean, in all the nation,
' No worthy friend, no poor relation?
' So ready to do strangers good,
' Forgetting his own flesh and blood! '

　　Now Grubstreet wits are all employ'd;
With elegies the town is cloy'd:
Some paragraph in every paper,
To *curse* the *Dean*, or *bless* the *Drapier*.

　　The doctors, tender of their fame,
Wisely on me lay all the blame.
' We must confess, his case was nice;
' But he would never take advice.
' Had he been rul'd, for aught appears,
' He might have liv'd these twenty years:
' For, when we open'd him, we found,
' That all his vital parts were sound.'

　　From *Dublin* soon to *London* spread,
'Tis told at court, ' The Dean is dead.'
And Lady *Suffolk* in the spleen
Runs laughing up to tell the Queen.
The Queen, so gracious, mild, and good,
Cries ' Is he gone ! 'tis time he should.
' He 's dead, you say ; then let him rot ;
' I'm glad the medals were forgot.
' I promis'd him, I own ; but when ?
' I only was the Princess then :

' But now, as Consort of the King,
' You know, 'tis quite another thing ' . . .

Now *Curll* his shop from rubbish drains :
Three genuine tomes of *Swift*'s remains !
And then, to make them pass the glibber,
Revis'd by *Tibbalds, Moore,* and *Cibber.*
He'll treat me as he does my betters,
Publish my Will, my Life, my Letters ;
Revive the libels born to die ;
Which *Pope* must bear, as well as I.

Here shift the scene, to represent
How those I love my death lament.
Poor *Pope* will grieve a month, and *Gay*
A week, and *Arbuthnot* a day.

St. John himself will scarce forbear
To bite his pen, and drop a tear.
The rest will give a shrug, and cry,
' I'm sorry, but we all must die ! '

Indifference, clad in Wisdom's guise,
All fortitude of mind supplies:
For how can stony bowels melt
In those who never pity felt !
When we are lash'd, they kiss the rod,
Resigning to the will of God.

The fools, my juniors by a year,
Are tortur'd with suspense and fear;
Who wisely thought my age a screen,
When death approach'd, to stand between:
The screen remov'd, their hearts are trembling;
They mourn for me without dissembling.

My female friends, whose tender hearts
Have better learn'd to act their parts,

Receive the news in doleful dumps:
' The Dean is dead: (Pray what is trumps?)
' Then, Lord have mercy on his soul!
' (Ladies, I'll venture for the vole.)
' Six deans, they say, must bear the pall:
' (I wish I knew what king to call)
' Madam, your husband will attend
' The funeral of so good a friend.
' No, madam, 'tis a shocking sight;
' And he 's engag'd to-morrow night:
' My lady Club will take it ill,
' If he should fail her at quadrille.
' He lov'd the Dean (I lead a heart)
' But dearest friends, they say, must part.
' His time was come; he ran his race;
' We hope he 's in a better place.'

Why do we grieve that friends should die?
No loss more easy to supply.
One year is past; a different scene!
No farther mention of the Dean;
Who now, alas, no more is miss'd,
Than if he never did exist.
Where 's now the favourite of *Apollo*?
Departed:—*And his Works must follow*:
Must undergo the common fate;
His kind of wit is out of date.

Some country squire to *Lintot* goes,
Inquires for *Swift* in verse and prose.
Says *Lintot*, ' I have heard the name;
' He died a year ago.'—' The same.'
He searches all the shop in vain.
' Sir, you may find them in *Duck Lane*:

' I sent them, with a load of books,
' Last Monday to the pastry-cook's.
' To fancy, they could live a year!
' I find you're but a stranger here.
' The Dean was famous in his time,
' And had a kind of knack at rhyme.
' His way of writing now is past:
' The town has got a better taste.
' I keep no antiquated stuff,
' But spick and span I have enough.
' Pray, do but give me leave to shew 'em:
' Here's *Colley Cibber*'s birthday poem.

. . . .

Suppose me dead; and then suppose
A club assembled at the Rose;
Where, from Discourse of this and that,
I grow the Subject of their Chat.
And while they toss my name about,
With favour some, and some without;
One, quite indifferent in the cause,
My character impartial draws:

' The Dean, if we believe report,
' Was never ill-received at court.
' As for his works in verse and prose,
' I own myself no judge of those:
' Nor can I tell what criticks thought 'em;
' But this I know, all people bought 'em;
' As with a moral view design'd
' To cure the vices of mankind:
' His vein, ironically grave,
' Expos'd the fool, and lash'd the knave;

the Rose] a tavern adjoining Drury Lane Theatre

' To steal a hint was never known,
' But what he writ was all his own.
    ' He never thought an honour done him,
' Because a duke was proud to own him;
' Would rather slip aside, and choose
' To talk with wits in dirty shoes;
' Despis'd the fools with stars and garters,
' So often seen caressing *Chartres*.
' He never courted men in station,
' Nor persons held in admiration;
' Of no man's greatness was afraid,
' Because he sought for no man's aid.
' Though trusted long in great affairs,
' He gave himself no haughty airs:
' Without regarding private ends,
' Spent all his credit for his friends:
' And only chose the wise and good;
' No flatterers; no allies in blood:
' But succour'd virtue in distress,
' And seldom fail'd of good success;
' As numbers in their hearts must own,
' Who, but for him, had been unknown.
    ' He kept with princes due decorum;
' Yet never stood in awe before 'em.
' He follow'd *David*'s lesson just,
' In princes never put thy trust:
' And, would you make him truly sour,
' Provoke him with a slave in power.
' The Irish senate if you nam'd,
' With what impatience he declaim'd!
' Fair LIBERTY was all his cry;
' For her he stood prepar'd to die;

85

' For her he boldly stood alone
' For her he oft' expos'd his own.
' Two kingdoms, just as faction led,
' Had set a price upon his head;
' But not a traitor could be found,
' To sell him for six hundred pound.
  ' Had he but spar'd his tongue and pen,
' He might have rose like other men:
' But power was never in his thought,
' And wealth he valu'd not a groat:
' Ingratitude he often found,
' And pitied those who meant the wound:
' But kept the tenour of his mind,
' To merit well of humankind:
' Nor made a sacrifice of those
' Who still were true, to please his foes.
' He labour'd many a fruitless hour,
' To reconcile his friends in power;
' Saw mischief by a faction brewing,
' While they pursu'd each other's ruin.
' But finding vain was all his care,
' He left the court in mere despair.
  ' And, oh! how short are human schemes!
' Here ended all our golden dreams.
' What *St. John*'s skill in state affairs,
' What *Ormond*'s valour, *Oxford*'s cares,
' To save their sinking country lent,
' Was all destroy'd by one event.
' Too soon that precious life was ended,
' On which alone our weal depended.

    .   .   .   .

JONATHAN SWIFT

‘ Perhaps I may allow the Dean
‘ Had too much satire in his vein;
‘ And seem'd determin'd not to starve it,
‘ Because no age could more deserve it.
‘ Yet malice never was his aim;
‘ He lash'd the vice, but spar'd the name.
‘ No individual could resent,
‘ Where thousands equally were meant;
‘ His satire points at no defect,
‘ But what all mortals may correct;
‘ For he abhorr'd that senseless tribe
‘ Who call it humour when they gibe:
‘ He spar'd a hump, or crooked nose,
‘ Whose owners set not up for beaux.
‘ True genuine dulness mov'd his pity,
‘ Unless it offer'd to be witty.
‘ Those who their ignorance confest,
‘ He ne'er offended with a jest;
‘ But laugh'd to hear an idiot quote
‘ A verse from *Horace* learn'd by rote.

  ‘ He knew a hundred pleasing stories,
‘ With all the turns of Whigs and Tories:
‘ Was cheerful to his dying day;
‘ And friends would let him have his way.

  ‘ He gave the little wealth he had
‘ To build a house for fools and mad;
‘ And shewed, by one satirick touch,
‘ No nation wanted it so much.
‘ That kingdom he hath left his debtor,
‘ I wish it soon may have a better.'

Verses on the Death of Doctor Swift, 1739
               (Faulkner's text)

ALEXANDER POPE

48 *Ode on Solitude*

HAPPY the man, whose wish and care
  A few paternal acres bound,
Content to breathe his native air,
              In his own ground.

Whose herds with milk, whose fields with bread,
  Whose flocks supply him with attire,
Whose trees in summer yield him shade,
              In winter fire.

Blest, who can unconcern'dly find
  Hours, days, and years slide soft away,
In health of body, peace of mind,
              Quiet by day,

Sound sleep by night; study and ease,
  Together mixt; sweet recreation;
And innocence, which most does please
              With meditation.

Thus let me live, unseen, unknown,
  Thus unlamented let me die,
Steal from the world, and not a stone
              Tell where I lie.

                    Written about 1700 ; *Works*, 1735

49 *Paraphrase on Thomas à Kempis*

SPEAK, Gracious Lord, oh speak; thy Servant hears :
  For I'm thy Servant, and I'll still be so :
Speak words of Comfort in my willing Ears ;
  And since my Tongue is in thy praises slow,
And since that thine all Rhetorick exceeds ;
Speak Thou in words, but let me speak in deeds !

88

Nor speak alone, but give me grace to hear
   What thy celestial Sweetness does impart;
Let it not stop when entred at the Ear,
   But sink, and take deep rooting in my Heart.
As the parch'd Earth drinks Rain (but grace afford)
With such a Gust will I receive thy word.

Nor with the Israelites shall I desire
   Thy heav'nly word by Moses to receive,
Lest I should die: but Thou who didst inspire
   Moses himself, speak Thou, that I may live.
Rather with Samuel I beseech with tears,
Speak, gracious Lord, oh speak; thy Servant hears.

Moses indeed may say the words, but Thou
   Must give the Spirit, and the Life inspire;
Our Love to thee his fervent Breath may blow,
   But 'tis thyself alone can give the fire:
Thou without them may'st speak and profit too;
But without thee, what could the Prophets do?

They preach the Doctrine, but Thou mak'st us do't;
   They teach the misteries thou dost open lay;
The trees they water, but Thou giv'st the fruit;
   They to Salvation show the arduous way,
But none but you can give us Strength to walk;
You give the Practice, they but give the Talk.

Let them be Silent then; and Thou alone
   (My God) speak comfort to my ravish'd ears;
Light of my eyes, my Consolation,
   Speak when Thou wilt, for still thy Servant hears.
What-ere thou speak'st, let this be understood:
Thy greater Glory, and my greater Good!

                      Written about 1700 ; first published 1854

50 *A little Learning*

A LITTLE Learning is a dang'rous thing;
    Drink deep, or taste not the *Pierian* spring:
There shallow draughts intoxicate the brain,
And drinking largely sobers us again.
Fir'd at first sight with what the Muse imparts,
In fearless youth we tempt the heights of Arts,
While from the bounded level of our mind,
Short views we take, nor see the lengths behind;
But more advanc'd, behold with strange surprize
New distant scenes of endless science rise!
So pleas'd at first the tow'ring *Alps* we try,
Mount o'er the vales, and seem to tread the sky,
Th' eternal snows appear already past,
And the first clouds and mountains seem the last:
But those attain'd, we tremble to survey
The growing labours of the lengthen'd way,
Th' increasing prospect tires our wandring eyes,
Hills peep o'er hills, and *Alps* on *Alps* arise!

An Essay on Criticism, **1711**

51 *Poetical Numbers*

B UT most by Numbers judge a Poet's song,
    And smooth or rough, with them, is right or wrong;
In the bright Muse tho' thousand charms conspire,
Her Voice is all these tuneful fools admire;
Who haunt *Parnassus* but to please their ear,
Not mend their minds; as some to Church repair,
Not for the doctrine, but the music there.
These equal syllables alone require,
Tho' oft' the ear the open vowels tire;

90

While expletives their feeble aid do join;
And ten low words oft' creep in one dull line;
While they ring round the same unvary'd chimes,
With sure returns of still-expected rhymes.
Where-e'er you find *the cooling western breeze,*
In the next line, it *whispers thro' the trees*;
If crystal streams *with pleasing murmurs creep,*
The reader's threaten'd (not in vain) with *sleep.*
Then, at the last, and only couplet fraught
With some unmeaning thing they call a Thought,
A needless *Alexandrine* ends the song,
That like a wounded snake, drags its slow length along.
Leave such to tune their own dull rhimes, and know
What's roundly smooth, or languishingly slow;
And praise the easy vigor of a line,
Where *Denham's* strength, and *Waller's* sweetness join.
True ease in writing comes from art, not chance,
As those move easiest who have learn'd to dance.
'Tis not enough no harshness gives offence,
The sound must seem an echo to the sense.
Soft is the strain when *Zephyr* gently blows,
And the smooth stream in smoother numbers flows;
But when loud surges lash the sounding shore,
The hoarse, rough verse should like the torrent roar.
When *Ajax* strives, some rock's vast weight to throw,
The line too labours, and the words move slow;
Not so, when swift *Camilla* scours the plain,
Flies o'er th' unbending corn, and skims along the main.
Hear how *Timotheus'* various lays surprize,
And bid alternate passions fall and rise!
While, at each change, the son of *Lybian Jove*
Now burns with glory, and then melts with love:

Now his fierce eyes with sparkling fury glow,
Now sighs steal out, and tears begin to flow:
Persians and *Greeks* like turns of nature found,
And the World's victor stood subdu'd by Sound!
The pow'r of Music all our hearts allow;
And what *Timotheus* was, is *Dryden* now.

An Essay on Criticism, 1711

52   *Windsor Forest*

THE groves of *Eden*, vanish'd now so long,
Live in description, and look green in song:
These, were my breast inspir'd with equal flame,
Like them in beauty, should be like in fame.
Here hills and vales, the woodland and the plain,
Here earth and water seem to strive again,
Not *Chaos*-like together crush'd and bruis'd,
But as the world, harmoniously confus'd:
Where order in variety we see,
And where, tho' all things differ, all agree.
Here waving groves a checquer'd scene display,
And part admit, and part exclude the day;
As some coy nymph her lover's warm address
Nor quite indulges, nor can quite repress.
There, interspers'd in lawns and opening glades,
Thin trees arise that shun each others shades.
Here in full light the russet plains extend;
There wrapt in clouds the blueish hills ascend:
Ev'n the wild heath displays her purple dyes,
And 'midst the desert fruitful fields arise,
That crown'd with tufted trees and springing corn,
Like verdant isles the sable waste adorn.

Let *India* boast her plants, nor envy we
The weeping amber or the balmy tree,
While by our Oaks the precious loads are born,
And realms commanded which those trees adorn.
Not proud *Olympus* yields a nobler sight,
Tho' Gods assembled grace his tow'ring height,
Than what more humble mountains offer here,
Where, in their blessings, all those Gods appear.
See *Pan* with flocks, with fruits *Pomona* crown'd,
Here blushing *Flora* paints th' enamel'd ground,
Here *Ceres'* gifts in waving prospect stand,
And nodding tempt the joyful reaper's hand,
Rich Industry sits smiling on the plains,
And Peace and Plenty tell, a *Stuart* reigns.

Windsor Forest, 1713.

53 *Field Sports*

WHEN milder autumn summer's heat succeeds,
And in the new-shorn field the Partridge feeds,
Before his Lord the ready Spaniel bounds,
Panting with hope, he tries the furrow'd grounds,
But when the tainted gales the game betray,
Couch'd close he lies, and meditates the prey;
Secure they trust th' unfaithful field, beset,
Till hov'ring o'er 'em sweeps the swelling net.
See! from the brake the whirring Pheasant springs,
And mounts exulting on triumphant wings.
Short is his joy; he feels the fiery wound,
Flutters in blood, and panting beats the ground.
Ah! what avail his glossy, varying dyes,
His purple crest, and scarlet-circled eyes,

The vivid green his shining plumes unfold,
His painted wings, and breast that flames with gold?
  Nor yet, when moist *Arcturus* clouds the sky,
The woods and fields their pleasing toils deny.
To plains with well-breath'd beagles we repair,
And trace the mazes of the circling hare.
(Beasts, urg'd by us, their fellow beasts pursue,
And learn of man each other to undo.)
With slaught'ring guns th' unweary'd fowler roves,
When frosts have whiten'd all the naked groves;
Where doves in flocks the leafless trees o'ershade,
And lonely woodcocks haunt the wat'ry glade.
He lifts the tube, and levels with his eye;
Strait a short thunder breaks the frozen sky.
Oft', as in airy rings they skim the heath,
The clam'rous Lapwings feel the leaden death:
Oft', as the mounting Larks their notes prepare,
They fall, and leave their little lives in air.

Windsor Forest, 1713

54 *The Toilet*

AND now, unveil'd, the Toilet stands display'd,
  Each silver Vase in mystic order laid.
First, rob'd in white, the nymph intent adores
With head uncover'd, the cosmetic pow'rs.
A heav'nly Image in the glass appears,
To that she bends, to that her eyes she rears;
Th' inferior Priestess, at her altar's side,
Trembling, begins the sacred rites of Pride.
Unnumber'd treasures ope at once, and here
The various off'rings of the world appear;

From each she nicely culls with curious toil,
And decks the Goddess with the glitt'ring spoil.
This casket *India*'s glowing gems unlocks,
And all *Arabia* breaths from yonder box.
The Tortoise here and Elephant unite,
Transform'd to Combs, the speckled, and the white.
Here files of Pins extend their shining rows,
Puffs, Powders, Patches, Bibles, Billet-doux.
Now awful Beauty puts on all its arms;
The fair each moment rises in her charms,
Repairs her smiles, awakens ev'ry grace,
And calls forth all the wonders of her face;
Sees by degrees a purer blush arise,
And keener lightnings quicken in her eyes.
The busy *Sylphs* surround their darling care,
These set the head, and those divide the hair,
Some fold the sleeve, while others plait the gown;
And *Betty*'s prais'd for labours not her own.

The Rape of the Lock, i, 1714

55   *Ombre at Hampton Court*

CLOSE by those meads, for ever crown'd with flow'rs,
   Where *Thames* with pride surveys his rising tow'rs,
There stands a structure of majestic frame,
Which from the neighb'ring *Hampton* takes its name.
Here *Britain*'s statesmen oft' the fall foredoom
Of foreign tyrants, and of nymphs at home;
Here thou, great *Anna !* whom three realms obey,
Dost sometimes counsel take—and sometimes Tea.
   Hither the heroes and the nymphs resort,
To taste a while the pleasures of a Court;

In various talk th' instructive hours they past,
Who gave the ball, or paid the visit last:
One speaks the glory of the *British* Queen,
And one describes a charming *Indian* screen;
A third interprets motions, looks, and eyes;
At ev'ry word a reputation dies.
Snuff, or the fan, supply each pause of chat,
With singing, laughing, ogling, and all that.

Mean while declining from the noon of day,
The sun obliquely shoots his burning ray;
The hungry Judges soon the sentence sign,
And wretches hang that Jury-men may dine;
The merchant from th' *Exchange* returns in peace,
And the long labours of the Toilet cease.—
Belinda now, whom thirst of fame invites,
Burns to encounter two adventrous Knights,
At *Ombre* singly to decide their doom;
And swells her breast with conquests yet to come.
Strait the three bands prepare in arms to join,
Each band the number of the sacred nine.
Soon as she spreads her hand, th' aerial guard
Descend, and sit on each important card:
First *Ariel* perch'd upon a Matadore,
Then each, according to the rank they bore;
For *Sylphs*, yet mindful of their ancient race,
Are, as when women, wondrous fond of place.

Behold, four Kings in majesty rever'd,
With hoary whiskers and a forky beard:
And four fair Queens whose hands sustain a flow'r,
Th' expressive emblem of their softer pow'r;
Four Knaves in garbs succinct, a trusty band,
Caps on their heads, and halberds in their hand

And particolour'd troops, a shining train,
Draw forth to combat on the velvet plain.

The skilful nymph reviews her force with care;
Let Spades be trumps, she said, and trumps they were.

Now move to war her sable Matadores,
In show like leaders of the swarthy Moors.
Spadillio first, unconquerable Lord!
Led off two captive trumps, and swept the board.
As many more *Manillio* forc'd to yield,
And march'd a victor from the verdant field.
Him *Basto* follow'd, but his fate more hard
Gain'd but one trump and one *Plebeian* card.
With his broad sabre next, a chief in years,
The hoary Majesty of Spades appears;
Puts forth one manly leg, to sight reveal'd;
The rest, his many-colour'd robe conceal'd.
The rebel-Knave, who dares his prince engage,
Proves the just victim of his royal rage.
Ev'n mighty *Pam* that Kings and Queens o'erthrew,
And mow'd down armies in the fights of *Lu*,
Sad chance of war! now, destitute of aid,
Falls undistinguish'd by the victor Spade!

Thus far both armies to *Belinda* yield;
Now to the Baron fate inclines the field.
His warlike *Amazon* her host invades,
Th' imperial consort of the crown of Spades.
The Club's black Tyrant first her victim dy'd,
Spite of his haughty mien, and barb'rous pride:
What boots the regal circle on his head,
His giant limbs, in state unwieldy spread;
That long behind he trails his pompous robe,
And, of all monarchs, only grasps the globe?

ALEXANDER POPE

The Baron now his Diamonds pours apace;
Th' embroider'd King who shows but half his face,
And his refulgent Queen, with pow'rs combin'd,
Of broken troops an easy conquest find.
Clubs, Diamonds, Hearts, in wild disorder seen,
With throngs promiscuous strow the level green.
Thus when dispers'd a routed army runs,
Of *Asia*'s troops, and *Afric*'s sable sons,
With like confusion different nations fly,
In various habits, and of various dye,
The pierc'd battalions dis-united fall,
In heaps on heaps; one fate o'erwhelms them all.

The Knave of Diamonds tries his wily arts,
And wins (oh shameful chance) the Queen of Hearts.
At this, the blood the virgin's cheek forsook,
A livid paleness spreads o'er all her look;
She sees, and trembles at th' approaching ill,
Just in the jaws of ruin, and *Codille*.
And now, (as oft' in some distemper'd state)
On one nice Trick depends the gen'ral fate.
An Ace of Hearts steps forth: The King unseen
Lurk'd in her hand, and mourn'd his captive Queen:
He springs to vengeance with an eager pace,
And falls like thunder on the prostrate Ace.
The nymph exulting fills with shouts the sky,
The walls, the woods, and long canals reply.

Oh thoughtless mortals! ever blind to fate,
Too soon dejected, and too soon elate!
Sudden, these honours shall be snatch'd away,
And curs'd for ever this victorious day.

The Rape of the Lock, iii, 1714

To a Young Lady

On her leaving the Town after the Coronation

AS some fond virgin, whom her mother's care
  Drags from the town to wholsom country air,
Just when she learns to roll a melting eye,
And hear a spark, yet think no danger nigh;
From the dear man unwilling she must sever,
Yet takes one kiss before she parts for ever.
Thus from the world fair *Zephalinda* flew,
Saw others happy, and with sighs withdrew;
Not that their pleasures caus'd her discontent,
She sigh'd not that They stay'd, but that She went.

  She went, to plain-work and to purling brooks,
Old-fashion'd halls, dull aunts, and croaking rooks,
She went from Op'ra, park, assembly, play,
To morning walks, and pray'rs three hours a day:
To part her time 'twixt reading and Bohea,
To muse, and spill her solitary Tea,
Or o'er cold coffee trifle with the spoon,
Count the slow clock, and dine exact at noon;
Divert her eyes with pictures in the fire,
Hum half a tune, tell stories to the squire;
Up to her godly garret after sev'n,
There starve and pray, for that's the way to heav'n.

  Some Squire, perhaps, you take delight to rack;
Whose game is Whisk, whose treat a toast in sack,
Who visits with a gun, presents you birds,
Then gives a smacking buss, and cries—No words!
Or with his hound comes hollowing from the stable,
Makes love with nods, and knees beneath a table;

Whose laughs are hearty, tho' his jests are coarse,
And loves you best of all things—but his horse.

    In some fair evening, on your elbow laid,
You dream of triumphs in the rural shade;
In pensive thought recall the fancy'd scene,
See Coronations rise on ev'ry green,
Before you pass th' imaginary sights
Of Lords, and Earls, and Dukes, and garter'd Knights;
While the spread Fan o'ershades your closing eyes;
Then give one flirt, and all the vision flies.
Thus vanish sceptres, coronets, and balls,
And leave you in lone woods, or empty walls.

    So when your slave, at some dear, idle time,
(Not plagu'd with headachs, or the want of rhime)
Stands in the streets, abstracted from the crew,
And while he seems to study, thinks of you:
Just when his fancy points your sprightly eyes,
Or sees the blush of *Parthenissa* rise,
Gay pats my shoulder, and you vanish quite;
Streets, chairs, and coxcombs, rush upon my sight;
Vext to be still in town, I knit my brow,
Look sow'r, and hum a song—as you may now.

Works, 1717

57   *Honest Fame*

WHAT could thus high thy rash ambition raise?
    Art thou, fond youth, a candidate for praise?
    'Tis true, said I, not void of hopes I came,
For who so fond as youthful bards of fame?
But few, alas! the casual blessing boast,
So hard to gain, so easy to be lost:

How vain that second life in others breath,
Th' estate which wits inherit after death!
Ease, health, and life, for this we must resign,
(Unsure the tenour, but how vast the fine!)
The great man's curse, without the gains, endure,
Be envy'd, wretched, and be flatter'd, poor;
All luckless wits our enemies profest,
And all successful, jealous friends at best.
Nor Fame I slight, nor for her favours call;
She comes unlook'd for, if she comes at all.
But if the purchase costs so dear a price,
As soothing folly, or exalting vice:
Oh! if the Muse must flatter lawless sway,
And follow still where fortune leads the way;
Or if no basis bear my rising name,
But the fal'n ruins of another's fame:
Then teach me, Heav'n! to scorn the guilty bays;
Drive from my breast that wretched lust of praise;
Unblemish'd let me live, or die unknown;
Oh grant an honest fame, or grant me none!

The Temple of Fame, 1715.

58 To Mr. Jervas, with Fresnoy's Art of Painting, Translated by Mr. Dryden

THIS verse be thine, my friend, nor thou refuse
This, from no venal or ungrateful Muse.
Whether thy hand strike out some free design,
Where life awakes, and dawns at ev'ry line;
Or blend in beauteous tints the colour'd mass,
And from the canvas call the mimic face:

ALEXANDER POPE

Read these instructive leaves, in which conspire
Fresnoy's close art, and *Dryden*'s native fire:
And reading wish, like theirs, our fate and fame,
So mix'd our studies, and so join'd our name,
Like them to shine thro' long succeeding age,
So just thy skill, so regular my rage.

    Smit with the love of Sister-arts we came,
And met congenial, mingling flame with flame;
Like friendly colours found our arts unite,
And each from each contract new strength and light.
How oft' in pleasing tasks we wear the day,
While summer suns roll unperceiv'd away?
How oft' our slowly-growing works impart,
While images reflect from art to art?
How oft' review; each finding like a friend
Something to blame, and something to commend?

    What flatt'ring scenes our wand'ring fancy wrought,
Rome's pompous glories rising to our thought!
Together o'er the *Alps* methinks we fly,
Fir'd with ideas of fair *Italy*.
With thee, on *Raphael*'s Monument I mourn,
Or wait inspiring dreams at *Maro*'s Urn:
With thee repose, where *Tully* once was laid,
Or seek some ruin's formidable shade;
While fancy brings the vanish'd piles to view,
And builds imaginary *Rome* a-new.
Here thy well-study'd Marbles fix our eye;
A fading Fresco here demands a sigh:
Each heav'nly piece unweary'd we compare,
Match *Raphael*'s grace, with thy lov'd *Guido*'s air,
Caracci's strength, *Correggio*'s softer line,
Paulo's free stroke, and *Titian*'s warmth divine.

How finish'd with illustrious toil appears
This small, well-polish'd gem, the work of years!
Yet still how faint by precept is exprest
The living image in the Painter's breast?
Thence endless streams of fair ideas flow,
Strike in the sketch, or in the picture glow;
Thence beauty, waking all her forms, supplies
An Angel's sweetness, or *Bridgwater*'s eyes.

Muse! at that name thy sacred sorrows shed,
Those tears eternal, that embalm the dead:
Call round her tomb each object of desire,
Each purer frame inform'd with purer fire:
Bid her be all that chears or softens life,
The tender sister, daughter, friend and wife;
Bid her be all that makes mankind adore;
Then view this marble, and be vain no more!

Yet still her charms in breathing paint engage
Her modest cheek shall warm a future age.
Beauty, frail flow'r that ev'ry season fears,
Blooms in thy colours for a thousand years.
Thus *Churchill*'s race shall other hearts surprize,
And other Beauties envy *Wortley*'s eyes,
Each pleasing *Blount* shall endless smiles bestow,
And soft *Belinda*'s blush for ever glow.

Oh lasting as those colours may they shine,
Free as thy stroke, yet faultless as thy line!
New graces yearly, like thy works, display;
Soft without weakness, without glaring gay;
Led by some rule, that guides, but not constrains;
And finish'd more thro' happiness than pains!
The kindred arts shall in their praise conspire,
One dip the pencil, and one string the lyre.

Yet should the Graces all thy figures place,
And breathe an air divine on ev'ry face;
Yet should the Muses bid my numbers roll,
Strong as their charms, and gentle as their soul;
With *Zeuxis' Helen* thy *Bridgwater* vie,
And these be sung till *Granville*'s *Myra* die;
Alas! how little from the grave we claim?
Thou but preserv'st a Form, and I a Name.

Du Fresnoy's Art of Painting (ed. 2), 1716

59 *Elegy to the Memory of an Unfortunate Lady*

WHAT beck'ning ghost, along the moonlight shade
Invites my steps, and points to yonder glade?
'Tis she!—but why that bleeding bosom gor'd,
Why dimly gleams the visionary sword?
Oh ever beauteous, ever friendly! tell,
Is it, in heav'n, a crime to love too well?
To bear too tender, or too firm a heart,
To act a Lover's or a *Roman*'s part?
Is there no bright reversion in the sky,
For those who greatly think, or bravely die?

Why bade ye else, ye Pow'rs! her soul aspire
Above the vulgar flight of low desire?
Ambition first sprung from your blest abodes;
The glorious fault of Angels and of Gods:
Thence to their Images on earth it flows,
And in the breasts of Kings and Heroes glows!
Most souls, 'tis true, but peep out once an age,
Dull sullen pris'ners in the body's cage:
Dim lights of life that burn a length of years,
Useless, unseen, as lamps in sepulchres;

Like Eastern Kings a lazy state they keep,
And close confin'd in their own palace sleep.

　From these perhaps (e'er nature bade her die)
Fate snatch'd her early to the pitying sky.
As into air the purer spirits flow,
And sep'rate from their kindred dregs below;
So flew the soul to its congenial place,
Nor left one virtue to redeem her Race.

　But thou, false guardian of a charge too good,
Thou, mean deserter of thy brother's blood!
See on these ruby lips the trembling breath,
These cheeks, now fading at the blast of death:
Cold is that breast which warm'd the world before,
And those love-darting eyes must roll no more.
Thus, if eternal justice rules the ball,
Thus shall your wives, and thus your children fall:
On all the line a sudden vengeance waits,
And frequent herses shall besiege your gates.
There passengers shall stand, and pointing say,
(While the long fun'rals blacken all the way)
Lo these were they, whose souls the Furies steel'd,
And curs'd with hearts unknowing how to yield.
Thus unlamented pass the proud away,
The gaze of fools, and pageant of a day!
So perish all, whose breast ne'er learn'd to glow
For others good, or melt at others woe.

　What can atone (oh ever-injur'd shade!)
Thy fate unpity'd, and thy rites unpaid?
No friend's complaint, no kind domestic tear
Pleas'd thy pale ghost, or grac'd thy mournful bier;
By foreign hands thy dying eyes were clos'd,
By foreign hands thy decent limbs compos'd,

ALEXANDER POPE

By foreign hands thy humble grave adorn'd,
By strangers honour'd, and by strangers mourn'd!
What tho' no friends in sable weeds appear,
Grieve for an hour, perhaps, then mourn a year,
And bear about the mockery of woe
To midnight dances, and the publick show?
What tho' no weeping Loves thy ashes grace,
Nor polish'd marble emulate thy face?
What tho' no sacred earth allow thee room,
Nor hallow'd dirge be mutter'd o'er thy tomb?
Yet shall thy grave with rising flow'rs be drest,
And the green turf lie lightly on thy breast:
There shall the morn her earliest tears bestow,
There the first roses of the year shall blow;
While Angels with their silver wings o'ershade
The ground, now sacred by thy reliques made.

So peaceful rests, without a stone, a name,
What once had beauty, titles, wealth, and fame.
How lov'd, how honour'd once, avails thee not,
To whom related, or by whom begot;
A heap of dust alone remains of thee;
'Tis all thou art, and all the proud shall be!

Poets themselves must fall, like those they sung;
Deaf the prais'd ear, and mute the tuneful tongue.
Ev'n he, whose soul now melts in mournful lays,
Shall shortly want the gen'rous tear he pays;
Then from his closing eyes thy form shall part,
And the last pang shall tear thee from his heart,
Life's idle business at one gasp be o'er,
The Muse forgot, and thou belov'd no more!

Works, 1717

60 *Eloisa*

HOW happy is the blameless Vestal's lot?
    The world forgetting, by the world forgot.
Eternal sun-shine of the spotless mind!
Each pray'r accepted, and each wish resign'd;
Labour and rest, that equal periods keep;
' Obedient slumbers that can wake and weep';
Desires compos'd, affections ever even,
Tears that delight, and sighs that waft to heav'n.
Grace shines around her with serenest beams,
And whisp'ring Angels prompt her golden dreams.
For her the Spouse prepares the bridal ring,
For her white virgins *Hymenæals* sing;
For her th' unfading rose of *Eden* blooms,
And wings of Seraphs shed divine perfumes;
To sounds of heav'nly harps, she dies away,
And melts in visions of eternal day.
    Far other dreams my erring soul employ,
Far other raptures, of unholy joy:
When at the close of each sad, sorrowing day,
Fancy restores what vengeance snatch'd away,
Then conscience sleeps, and leaving nature free,
All my loose soul unbounded springs to thee.
O curst, dear horrors of all-conscious night!
How glowing guilt exalts the keen delight!
Provoking Dæmons all restraint remove,
And stir within me ev'ry source of love.
I hear thee, view thee, gaze o'er all thy charms,
And round thy phantom glue my clasping arms.
I wake—no more I hear, no more I view,
The phantom flies me, as unkind as you.

I call aloud; it hears not what I say;
I stretch my empty arms; it glides away:
To dream once more I close my willing eyes;
Ye soft illusions, dear deceits, arise!
Alas no more!—methinks we wandring go
Thro' dreary wastes, and weep each other's woe;
Where round some mould'ring tow'r pale ivy creeps,
And low-brow'd rocks hang nodding o'er the deeps.
Sudden you mount! you becken from the skies;
Clouds interpose, waves roar, and winds arise.
I shriek, start up, the same sad prospect find,
And wake to all the griefs I left behind.

For thee the fates, severely kind, ordain
A cool suspense from pleasure and from pain;
Thy life a long, dead calm of fix'd repose;
No pulse that riots, and no blood that glows.
Still as the sea, e'er winds were taught to blow,
Or moving spirit bade the waters flow;
Soft as the slumbers of a saint forgiv'n,
And mild as opening gleams of promis'd heav'n.

Come *Abelard!* for what hast thou to dread?
The torch of *Venus* burns not for the dead;
Cut from the root my perish'd joys I see,
And love's warm tyde for ever stopt in thee.
Nature stands check'd; Religion disapproves;
Ev'n thou art cold—yet *Eloisa* loves.
Ah hopeless, lasting flames! like those that burn
To light the dead, and warm th' unfruitful urn.

What scenes appear where-e'er I turn my view,
The dear Ideas, where I fly, pursue,
Rise in the grove, before the altar rise,
Stain all my soul, and wanton in my eyes!

I waste the Matin lamp in sighs for thee,
Thy image steals between my God and me,
Thy voice I seem in ev'ry hymn to hear,
With ev'ry bead I drop too soft a tear.
When from the Censer clouds of fragrance roll,
And swelling organs lift the rising soul;
One thought of thee puts all the pomp to flight,
Priests, Tapers, Temples, swim before my sight:
In seas of flame my plunging soul is drown'd,
While Altars blaze, and Angels tremble round.

While prostrate here in humble grief I lie,
Kind, virtuous drops just gath'ring in my eye,
While praying, trembling, in the dust I roll,
And dawning grace is opening on my soul:
Come, if thou dar'st, all charming as thou art!
Oppose thy self to heav'n; dispute my heart;
Come, with one glance of those deluding eyes
Blot out each bright Idea of the skies;
Take back that grace, those sorrows, and those tears,
Take back my fruitless penitence and pray'rs,
Snatch me, just mounting, from the blest abode,
Assist the Fiends and tear me from my God!

No, fly me, fly me! far as Pole from Pole;
Rise *Alps* between us! and whole oceans roll!
Ah come not, write not, think not once of me,
Nor share one pang of all I felt for thee.
Thy oaths I quit, thy memory resign,
Forget, renounce me, hate whate'er was mine.
Fair eyes, and tempting looks (which yet I view!)
Long lov'd, ador'd ideas! all adieu!
O grace serene! oh virtue heav'nly fair!
Divine oblivion of low-thoughted care!

Fresh blooming hope, gay daughter of the sky!
And faith, our early immortality!
Enter each mild, each amicable guest;
Receive, and wrap me in eternal rest!

Eloisa to Abelard.—Works, 1717

61   Hector and Andromache

YET while my *Hector* still survives, I see
My Father, Mother, Brethren, all, in thee.
Alas! my Parents, Brothers, Kindred, all,
Once more will perish if my *Hector* fall.
Thy Wife, thy Infant, in thy Danger share:
Oh prove a Husband's and a Father's Care!
That Quarter most the skillful *Greeks* annoy,
Where yon' wild Fig-Trees join the Wall of *Troy*:
Thou, from this Tow'r defend th' important Post;
There *Agamemnon* points his dreadful Host,
That Pass *Tydides*, *Ajax* strive to gain,
And there the vengeful *Spartan* fires his Train.
Thrice our bold Foes the fierce Attack have giv'n,
Or led by Hopes, or dictated from Heav'n.
Let others in the Field their Arms employ,
But stay my *Hector* here, and guard his *Troy*.

The Chief reply'd: That Post shall be my Care,
Nor that alone, but all the Works of War.
How would the Sons of *Troy*, in Arms renown'd,
And *Troy*'s proud Dames whose Garments sweep the Ground,
Attaint the Lustre of my former Name,
Should *Hector* basely quit the Field of Fame?
My early Youth was bred to martial Pains,
My Soul impells me to th' embattel'd Plains;

110

Let me be foremost to defend the Throne,
And guard my Father's Glories, and my own.

    Yet come it will, the Day decreed by Fates;
(How my Heart trembles while my Tongue relates!)
The Day when thou, Imperial *Troy!* must bend,
And see thy Warriors fall, thy Glories end.
And yet no dire Presage so wounds my Mind,
My Mother's Death, the Ruin of my Kind,
Not *Priam*'s hoary Hairs defil'd with Gore,
Not all my Brothers gasping on the Shore;
As thine, *Andromache!* thy Griefs I dread;
I see thee trembling, weeping, Captive led!
In *Argive* Looms our Battels to design,
And Woes, of which so large a Part was thine!
To bear the Victor's hard Commands, or bring
The Weight of Waters from *Hyperia*'s Spring.
There, while you groan beneath the Load of Life,
They cry, Behold the mighty *Hector*'s Wife!
Some haughty *Greek* who lives thy Tears to see,
Embitters all thy Woes, by naming me.
The Thoughts of Glory past, and present Shame,
A thousand Griefs shall waken at the Name!
May I lie cold before that dreadful Day,
Press'd with a Load of Monumental Clay!
Thy *Hector* wrapt in everlasting Sleep,
Shall neither hear thee sigh, nor see thee weep.

    Thus having spoke, th' illustrious Chief of *Troy*
Stretch'd his fond Arms to clasp the lovely Boy.
The Babe clung crying to his Nurse's Breast,
Scar'd at the dazling Helm, and nodding Crest.
With secret Pleasure each fond Parent smil'd,
And *Hector* hasted to relieve his Child,

The glitt'ring Terrors from his Brows unbound,
And plac'd the beaming Helmet on the Ground.
Then kist the Child, and lifting high in Air,
Thus to the Gods prefer'd a Father's Pray'r.

O Thou! whose Glory fills th' Ætherial Throne,
And all ye deathless Pow'rs! protect my Son!
Grant him, like me, to purchase just Renown,
To guard the *Trojans*, to defend the Crown,
Against his Country's Foes the War to wage,
And rise the *Hector* of the future Age!
So when triumphant from successful Toils,
Of Heroes slain he bears the reeking Spoils,
Whole Hosts may hail him with deserv'd Acclaim,
And say, This Chief transcends his Father's Fame:
While pleas'd amidst the gen'ral Shouts of *Troy*,
His Mother's conscious Heart o'erflows with Joy.

He spoke, and fondly gazing on her Charms
Restor'd the pleasing Burden to her Arms;
Soft on her fragrant Breast the Babe she laid,
Hush'd to Repose, and with a Smile survey'd
The troubled Pleasure soon chastis'd by Fear,
She mingled with the Smile a tender Tear.
The soften'd Chief with kind Compassion view'd,
And dry'd the falling Drops, and thus pursu'd.

Andromache! my Soul's far better Part,
Why with untimely Sorrows heaves thy Heart?
No hostile Hand can antedate my Doom,
Till Fate condemns me to the silent Tomb.
Fix'd is the Term to all the Race of Earth,
And such the hard Condition of our Birth.
No Force can then resist, no Flight can save,
All sink alike, the Fearful and the Brave.

No more—but hasten to thy Tasks at home,
There guide the Spindle, and direct the Loom:
Me Glory summons to the martial Scene,
The Field of Combate is the Sphere for Men.
Where Heroes war, the foremost Place I claim,
The first in Danger as the first in Fame.

The Iliad, vi, 1716

62 *The Pyre of Patroclus*

THUS while he spoke, each Eye grew big with Tears:
And now the rosy-finger'd Morn appears,
Shews every mournful Face with Tears o'erspread,
And glares on the pale Visage of the Dead.
But *Agamemnon,* as the Rites demand,
With Mules and Waggons sends a chosen Band
To load the Timber and the Pile to rear,
A Charge consign'd to *Merion*'s faithful Care.
With proper Instruments they take the Road,
Axes to cut, and Ropes to sling the Load.
First march the heavy Mules, securely slow,
O'er Hills, o'er Dales, o'er Crags, o'er Rocks, they go:
Jumping high o'er the Shrubs of the rough Ground,
Rattle the clatt'ring Cars, and the shockt Axles bound.
But when arriv'd at *Ida*'s spreading Woods,
(Fair *Ida,* water'd with descending Floods)
Loud sounds the Axe, redoubling Strokes on Strokes;
On all sides round the Forest hurles her Oaks
Headlong. Deep-echoing groan the Thickets brown;
Then rustling, crackling, crashing, thunder down.
The Wood the *Grecians* cleave, prepar'd to burn;
And the slow Mules the same rough Road return.

The sturdy Woodmen equal Burthens bore
(Such charge was giv'n 'em) to the sandy Shore;
There on the Spot which great *Achilles* show'd,
They eas'd their Shoulders, and dispos'd the Load;
Circling around the Place, where Times to come
Shall view *Patroclus*' and *Achilles*' Tomb.

The Iliad, xxiii, 1720

63 *Priam and Achilles*

AS when a Wretch, (who conscious of his Crime
Pursu'd for Murder, flies his native Clime)
Just gains some Frontier, breathless, pale! amaz'd!
All gaze, all wonder: Thus *Achilles* gaz'd:
Thus stood th' Attendants stupid with Surprize;
All mute, yet seem'd to question with their Eyes:
Each look'd on other, none the Silence broke,
Till thus at last the Kingly Suppliant spoke.

Ah think, thou favour'd of the Pow'rs Divine!
Think of thy Father's Age, and pity mine!
In me, that Father's rev'rend Image trace,
Those silver Hairs, that venerable Face;
His trembling Limbs, his helpless Person, see!
In all my Equal, but in Misery!
Yet now, perhaps, some Turn of human Fate
Expells him helpless from his peaceful State;
Think from some pow'rful Foe thou see'st him fly,
And beg Protection with a Feeble Cry.
Yet still one Comfort in his Soul may rise;
He hears his Son still lives to glad his Eyes;
And hearing still may hope, a better Day
May send him thee to chase that Foe away.
No Comfort to my Griefs, no Hopes remain,

114

The best, the bravest of my Sons are slain!
Yet what a Race! e'er *Greece* to *Ilion* came,
The Pledge of many a lov'd, and loving Dame;
Nineteen one Mother bore—Dead, all are dead!
How oft, alas! has wretched *Priam* bled?
Still One was left, their Loss to recompense;
His Father's Hope, his Country's last Defence.
Him too thy Rage has slain! beneath thy Steel
Unhappy, in his Country's Cause he fell!

   For him, thro' hostile Camps I bent my way,
For him thus prostrate at thy Feet I lay;
Large Gifts, proportion'd to thy Wrath, I bear;
Oh hear the Wretched, and the Gods revere!

   Think of thy Father, and this Face behold!
See him in me, as helpless and as old!
Tho' not so wretched: There he yields to me,
The First of Men in sov'reign Misery.
Thus forc'd to kneel, thus grov'ling to embrace
The Scourge and Ruin of my Realm and Race;
Suppliant my Childrens Murd'rer to implore,
And kiss those Hands yet reeking with their Gore!

   These Words soft Pity in the Chief inspire,
Touch'd with the dear Remembrance of his Sire.

The Iliad, xxiv, 1720

64   *Ulysses and his Dog*

THUS, near the gates conferring as they drew,
  Argus, the Dog, his antient master knew;
He, not unconscious of the voice, and tread,
Lifts to the sound his ear, and rears his head.
Bred by *Ulysses*, nourish'd at his board,
But ah! not fated long to please his Lord!

To him, his swiftness and his strength were vain;
The voice of Glory call'd him o'er the main.
'Till then in ev'ry sylvan chace renown'd,
With *Argus*, *Argus*, rung the woods around;
With him the youth pursu'd the goat or fawn,
Or trac'd the mazy leveret o'er the lawn.
Now left to man's ingratitude he lay,
Un-hous'd, neglected, in the publick way;
And where on heaps the rich manure was spread,
Obscene with reptiles, took his sordid bed.

He knew his Lord; he knew, and strove to meet,
In vain he strove, to crawl, and kiss his feet;
Yet (all he could) his tail, his ears, his eyes
Salute his master, and confess his joys.
Soft pity touch'd the mighty master's soul;
Adown his cheek a tear unbidden stole,
Stole unperceiv'd; he turn'd his head, and dry'd
The drop humane: then thus impassion'd cry'd.

What noble beast in this abandon'd state
Lies here all helpless at *Ulysses'* gate?
His bulk and beauty speak no vulgar praise;
If, as he seems, he *was* in better days,
Some care his Age deserves: Or was he priz'd
For worthless beauty? therefore now despis'd?
Such dogs, and men there are, meer things of state,
And always cherish'd by their friends, the Great.

Not *Argus* so, (*Eumæus* thus rejoin'd)
But serv'd a master of a nobler kind,
Who never, never shall behold him more!
Long, long since perish'd on a distant shore!
Oh had you seen him, vig'rous, bold and young,
Swift as a stag, and as a lion strong,

Him no fell Savage on the plain withstood,
None 'scap'd him, bosom'd in the gloomy wood;
His eye how piercing, and his scent how true,
To winde the vapour in the tainted dew?
Such, when *Ulysses* left his natal coast;
Now years un-nerve him, and his lord is lost!
The women keep the gen'rous creature bare,
A sleek and idle race is all their care:
The master gone, the servants what restrains?
Or dwells humanity where riot reigns?
Jove fix'd it certain, that whatever day
Makes man a slave, takes half his worth away.

This said, the honest herdsman strode before:
The musing Monarch pauses at the door:
The Dog whom Fate had granted to behold
His Lord, when twenty tedious years had roll'd,
Takes a last look, and having seen him, dies;
So clos'd for ever faithful *Argus*' eyes!

The Odyssey, xvii, 1726

65 To Robert Earl of Oxford and Earl Mortimer
Dedication of Parnell's Poems

SUCH were the Notes, thy once-lov'd Poet sung,
'Till Death untimely stop'd his tuneful Tongue.
Oh just beheld, and lost! admir'd, and mourn'd!
With softest Manners, gentlest Arts, adorn'd!
Blest in each Science, blest in ev'ry Strain!
Dear to the Muse, to HARLEY dear—in vain!

For him, thou oft hast bid the World attend,
Fond to forget the Statesman in the Friend;
For *Swift* and him, despis'd the Farce of State,
The sober Follies of the Wise and Great;

Dextrous, the craving, fawning Crowd to quit,
And pleas'd to 'scape from Flattery to Wit.

   Absent or dead, still let a Friend be dear,
(A Sigh the Absent claims, the Dead a Tear)
Recall those Nights that clos'd thy toilsom Days,
Still hear thy *Parnell* in his living Lays:
Who careless, now, of Int'rest, Fame, or Fate,
Perhaps forgets that OXFORD e'er was Great;
Or deeming meanest what we greatest call,
Beholds thee glorious only in thy Fall.

   And sure if ought below the Seats Divine
Can touch Immortals, 'tis a Soul like thine:
A Soul supreme, in each hard Instance try'd,
Above all Pain, all Passion, and all Pride,
The Rage of Pow'r, the Blast of publick Breath,
The Lust of Lucre, and the Dread of Death.

   In vain to Desarts thy Retreat is made;
The Muse attends thee to the silent Shade:
'Tis hers, the brave Man's latest Steps to trace,
Re-judge his Acts, and dignify Disgrace.
When Int'rest calls off all her sneaking Train,
When all th' Oblig'd desert, and all the Vain;
She waits, or to the Scaffold, or the Cell,
When the last ling'ring Friend has bid farewel.
Ev'n now she shades thy Evening Walk with Bays,
(No Hireling she, no Prostitute to Praise)
Ev'n now, observant of the parting Ray,
Eyes the calm Sun-set of thy Various Day,
Thro' Fortune's Cloud One truly Great can see,
Nor fears to tell, that MORTIMER is He.

Parnell's Poems on Several Occasions, 1722

66   *To Mrs. M. B. on her Birth-Day*

OH, be thou blest with all that Heav'n can send!
   Long Health, long Youth, long Pleasure, and **a Friend**:
Not with those Toys the Female Race admire,
Riches that *vex*, and Vanities that *tire*;
Not as the World its pretty Slaves rewards,
A Youth of Frolicks, an Old-Age of Cards;
Fair to no Purpose, artful to no End,
Young without Lovers, old without a Friend;
A Fop their Passion, but their Prize a Sot;
Alive, ridiculous; and dead, forgot!

   Let Joy, or Ease, let Affluence, or Content,
And the gay Conscience of a Life well spent,
Calm ev'ry Thought, inspirit ev'ry Grace,
Glow in thy Heart, and smile upon thy Face:
Let Day improve on Day, and Year on Year,
Without a *Pain*, a *Trouble*, or a *Fear* :
Till Death unfelt that tender Frame destroy,
In some soft Dream, or Extasy of Joy,
Peaceful sleep out the Sabbath of the Tomb,
And wake to Raptures in a Life to come!
   The British Journal, 14 November **1724**; *Miscellanies*, iii, **1727**

67   *On a Certain Lady at Court*

I KNOW the thing that's most uncommon;
   (Envy be silent and attend!)
I know a Reasonable Woman,
   Handsome and witty, yet a Friend.

Not warp'd by Passion, aw'd by Rumour,
   Not grave thro' Pride, or gay thro' Folly,
An equal Mixture of good Humour,
   And sensible soft Melancholy.

' Has she no Faults then (Envy says) Sir ? '
  Yes she has one, I must aver :
When all the World conspires to praise her,
  The Woman's deaf, and does not hear.

Miscellanies, iii, 1732

68　　　　*Hope springs eternal*

HEAV'N from all creatures hides the book of Fate,
  All but the page prescrib'd, their present state,
From brutes what men, from men what spirits know,
Or who could suffer Being here below?
The lamb thy riot dooms to bleed to-day,
Had he thy Reason, would he skip and play?
Pleas'd to the last, he crops the flow'ry food,
And licks the hand just rais'd to shed his blood.
Oh blindness to the future! kindly giv'n,
That each may fill the circle mark'd by Heav'n:
Who sees with equal eye, as God of all,
A hero perish, or a sparrow fall,
Atoms or systems into ruin hurl'd,
And now a bubble burst, and now a world.

　　Hope humbly then; with trembling pinions soar;
Wait the great teacher, Death; and God adore!
What future bliss, he gives not thee to know,
But gives that *Hope* to be thy blessing now,
Hope springs eternal in the human breast;
Man never *is*, but always *to be* blest:
The soul uneasy, and confin'd at home,
Rests, and expatiates, in a life to come.

　　Lo! the poor Indian, whose untutor'd mind
Sees God in clouds, or hears him in the wind;

His soul, proud Science never taught to stray
Far as the solar walk, or milky way;
Yet simple Nature to his Hope has giv'n,
Behind the cloud-topt hill, an humbler heav'n;
Some safer world in depth of woods embrac'd,
Some happier island in the watry waste,
Where slaves once more their native land behold,
No fiends torment, no Christians thirst for gold.
To *be*, contents his natural desire,
He asks no Angel's wing, no Seraph's fire;
But thinks, admitted to that equal sky,
His faithful dog shall bear him company.

An Essay on Man, i, 1733

69   *Whatever is, is Right*

CEASE then, nor ORDER *Imperfection* name:
  Our proper bliss depends on what we blame.
Know thy own *Point*: This kind, this due degree
Of blindness, weakness, Heav'n bestows on thee.
Submit—in this, or any other Sphere,
Secure to be as blest as thou canst bear:
Safe in the hand of one disposing Pow'r,
Or in the natal, or the mortal Hour.
All Nature is but Art, unknown to thee;
All Chance, Direction which thou canst not see;
All Discord, Harmony not understood;
All partial Evil, universal Good:
And spite of Pride, in erring Reason's spite,
One truth is clear, WHATEVER IS, is RIGHT.

An Essay on Man, i, 1733

70

Know then thyself

KNOW then thyself, presume not God to scan;
The proper study of Mankind is *Man*.
Plac'd on this Isthmus of a middle state,
A Being darkly wise, and rudely great:
With too much knowledge for the Sceptic side,
With too much weakness for the Stoic's pride,
He hangs between; in doubt to act, or rest;
In doubt to deem himself a God, or Beast;
In doubt his Mind or Body to prefer;
Born but to die, and reas'ning but to err;
Alike in ignorance, his Reason such,
Whether he thinks too little, or too much:
Chaos of Thought and Passion, all confus'd;
Still by himself abus'd, or dis-abus'd;
Created half to rise, and half to fall;
Great Lord of all things, yet a Prey to all;
Sole Judge of Truth, in endless Error hurl'd:
The Glory, Jest, and Riddle of the world!

An Essay on Man, ii, 1733

71

Life's poor play

SEE! some strange Comfort ev'ry *state* attend,
And Pride bestow'd on all, a common friend;
See! some fit Passion ev'ry *age* supply,
Hope travels thro', nor quits us when we die.
    Behold the child, by Nature's kindly law,
Pleas'd with a rattle, tickled with a straw:
Some livelier play-thing gives his youth delight,
A little louder, but as empty quite:

Scarfs, garters, gold, amuse his riper stage,
And beads and pray'r-books are the toys of age:
Pleas'd with this bauble still, as that before;
'Till tir'd he sleeps, and Life's poor play is o'er.

An Essay on Man, ii, 1733, 1743

72   *Charity*

FOR Forms of Government let fools contest;
    Whate'er is best administer'd, is best:
For Modes of Faith let graceless zealots fight;
His can't be wrong whose life is in the right:
In Faith and Hope the world will disagree,
But all Mankind's concern is Charity:
All must be false that thwart this One great End;
And all of God, that bless Mankind, or mend.

An Essay on Man, iii, 1733, 1743

73   *Henry St. John, Viscount Bolingbroke*

COME then, my Friend! my Genius come along;
    Oh master of the poet, and the song!
And while the Muse now stoops, or now ascends,
To Man's low passions, or their glorious ends,
Teach me like thee, in various nature wise,
To fall with dignity, with temper rise;
Form'd by thy converse, happily to steer
From grave to gay, from lively to severe,
Correct with spirit, eloquent with ease,
Intent to reason, or polite to please.
O! while along the stream of Time thy name
Expanded flies, and gathers all its fame,
Say, shall my little bark attendant sail,
Pursue the triumph, and partake the gale?

When Statesmen, Heroes, Kings, in dust repose,
Whose sons shall blush their fathers were thy foes,
Shall then this verse to future age pretend
Thou wert my Guide, Philosopher, and Friend?
That urg'd by thee, I turn'd the tuneful art
From sounds to things, from Fancy to the Heart;
For Wit's false mirror held up Nature's light;
Shew'd erring Pride, WHATEVER IS, is RIGHT;
That REASON, PASSION, answer one great aim;
That true SELF-LOVE and SOCIAL are the same;
That VIRTUE only makes our Bliss below;
And all our Knowledge is, OURSELVES TO KNOW.

An Essay on Man, iv, 1734

74　　*The Duke of Buckingham*

IN the worst inn's worst room, with mat half-hung,
The floors of plaister, and the walls of dung,
On once a flockbed, but repair'd with straw,
With tape-ty'd curtains, never meant to draw,
The George and Garter dangling from that bed
Where tawdry yellow strove with dirty red,
Great *Villers* lies—alas! how chang'd from him,
That life of pleasure, and that soul of whim!
Gallant and gay, in *Cliveden's* proud alcove,
The bow'r of wanton *Shrewsbury* and Love;
Or just as gay, at Council, in a ring
Of mimick'd Statesmen, and their merry King.
No Wit to flatter, left of all his store!
No Fool to laugh at, which he valu'd more.
There, Victor of his health, of fortune, friends,
And fame, this lord of useless thousands ends.

Of the Use of Riches, 1732

Timon's Villa

AT *Timon*'s Villa let us pass a day,
　　Where all cry out, ' What sums are thrown away ! '
So proud, so grand; of that stupendous air,
Soft and *Agreeable* come never there.
Greatness, with *Timon*, dwells in such a draught
As brings all *Brobdignag* before your thought.
To compass this, his building is a Town,
His pond an Ocean, his parterre a Down:
Who but must laugh, the Master when he sees,
A puny insect, shiv'ring at a breeze!
Lo! what huge heaps of littleness around!
The whole, a labour'd Quarry above ground.
Two *Cupids* squirt before: a Lake behind
Improves the keenness of the Northern wind.
His Gardens next your admiration call,
On ev'ry side you look, behold the Wall!
No pleasing Intricacies intervene,
No artful wildness to perplex the scene;
Grove nods at grove, each Alley has a brother,
And half the platform just reflects the other.
The suff'ring eye inverted Nature sees,
Trees cut to Statues, Statues thick as trees,
With here a Fountain, never to be play'd,
And there a Summer-house, that knows no shade.
Here *Amphitrite* sails thro' myrtle bow'rs;
There *Gladiators* fight, or die in flow'rs;
Un-water'd see the drooping sea-horse mourn,
And swallows roost in *Nilus*' dusty Urn.
　　My Lord advances with majestic mien,
Smit with the mighty pleasure, to be seen:

But soft—by regular approach—not yet—
First thro' the length of yon hot Terrace sweat;
And when up ten steep slopes you've dragg'd your thighs,
Just at his Study-door he'll bless your eyes.

His *Study*? with what Authors is it stor'd?
In Books, not Authors, curious is my Lord;
To all their *dated Backs* he turns you round:
These *Aldus* printed, those *Du Suëil* has bound.
Lo some are *Vellom*, and the rest as good
For all his Lordship knows, but they are Wood.
For *Locke* or *Milton* 'tis in vain to look,
These shelves admit not any modern book.

And now the Chappel's silver bell you hear,
That summons you to all the Pride of Pray'r:
Light quirks of Musick, broken and uneven,
Make the soul dance upon a Jig to Heav'n.
On painted Cielings you devoutly stare,
Where sprawl the Saints of *Verrio*, or *Laguerre*,
On gilded clouds in fair expansion lie,
And bring all Paradise before your eye.
To rest, the Cushion and soft Dean invite,
Who never mentions Hell to ears polite.

But hark! the chiming Clocks to dinner call;
A hundred footsteps scrape the marble Hall:
The rich Buffet well-colour'd *Serpents* grace,
And gaping *Tritons* spew to wash your face.
Is this a dinner? this a Genial room?
No, 'tis a Temple, and a Hecatomb;
A solemn Sacrifice, perform'd in state,
You drink by measure, and to minutes eat.
So quick retires each flying course, you'd swear
Sancho's dread Doctor and his Wand were there.

Between each Act the trembling salvers ring,
From soup to sweetwine, and *God bless the King*.
In plenty starving, tantaliz'd in state,
And complaisantly help'd to all I hate,
Treated, caress'd, and tir'd, I take my leave,
Sick of his civil Pride from Morn to Eve;
I curse such lavish cost, and little skill,
And swear no Day was ever past so ill.

Yet hence the *Poor* are cloath'd, the *Hungry* fed;
Health to himself, and to his Infants bread
The Lab'rer bears: What his hard Heart denies,
His charitable Vanity supplies.

Of Taste, 1731, 1735

76   *The Gem and the Flower*

'TIS from high Life high Characters are drawn;
A Saint in Crape is twice a Saint in Lawn;
A Judge is just, a Chanc'lor juster still;
A Gownman, learn'd; a Bishop, what you will;
Wise, if a Minister; but if a King,
More wise, more learn'd, more just, more ev'ry thing.
Court-virtues bear, like Gems, the highest rate,
Born where Heav'n's influence scarce can penetrate:
In life's low vale, the soil the Virtues like,
They please as beauties, here as wonders strike.
Tho' the same Sun with all-diffusive rays
Blush in the Rose, and in the Di'mond blaze,
We prize the stronger effort of his pow'r,
And justly set the Gem above the Flow'r.

Of the Characters of Men, 1733

77 *Characters of Women*
Flavia, Atossa, and Cloe

FLAVIA'S a Wit, has too much sense to *pray*;
 To *toast* our wants and wishes, is her way;
Nor asks of God, but of her Stars, to give
The mighty blessing, ' while we live, to live.'
Then all for Death, that Opiate of the soul!
Lucretia's dagger, *Rosamonda*'s bowl.
Say, what can cause such impotence of mind?
A Spark too fickle, or a Spouse too kind.
Wise Wretch! with Pleasures too refin'd to please,
With too much Spirit to be e'er at ease,
With too much Quickness ever to be taught,
With too much Thinking to have common Thought:
You purchase Pain with all that Joy can give,
And die of nothing but a Rage to live.
 Turn then from Wits; and look on *Simo*'s Mate,
No Ass so meek, no Ass so obstinate:
Or her, that owns her Faults, but never mends,
Because she's honest, and the best of Friends:
Or her, whose life the Church and Scandal share,
For ever in a Passion, or a Pray'r:
Or her, who laughs at Hell, but (like her Grace)
Cries, ' Oh how charming if there's no such place!'
Or who in sweet vicissitude appears
Of Mirth and Opium, Ratafie and Tears,
The daily Anodyne, and nightly Draught,
To kill those foes to Fair ones, Time and Thought

Woman and Fool are *two* hard things to hit;
For true No-meaning puzzles more than Wit.
  But what are these to great *Atossa*'s mind?
Scarce once herself, by turns all Womankind!
Who, with herself, or others, from her birth
Finds all her life one warfare upon earth:
Shines in exposing Knaves, and painting Fools,
Yet is, whate'er she hates and ridicules.
No Thought advances, but her Eddy Brain
Whisks it about, and down it goes again.
Full sixty years the World has been her Trade,
The wisest Fool much Time has ever made:
From loveless youth to unrespected age,
No Passion gratify'd except her Rage.
So much the Fury still out-ran the Wit,
The Pleasure miss'd her, and the Scandal hit.
Who breaks with her, provokes Revenge from Hell,
But he's a bolder man who dares be well.
Her ev'ry turn with Violence pursu'd,
Nor more a storm her Hate than Gratitude:
To that each Passion turns, or soon or late;
Love, if it makes her yield, must make her hate
Superiors? death! and Equals? what a curse!
But an Inferior not dependant? worse.
Offend her, and she knows not to forgive;
Oblige her, and she'll hate you while you live:
But die, and she'll adore you—Then the Bust
And Temple rise—then fall again to dust.
Last night, her Lord was all that's good and great;
A Knave this morning, and his Will a Cheat.
Strange! by the Means defeated of the Ends,
By Spirit robb'd of Pow'r, by Warmth of Friends,

By Wealth of Follow'rs! without one distress
Sick of herself thro' very selfishness!
Atossa, curs'd with ev'ry granted pray'r,
Childless with all her Children, wants an Heir.
To Heirs unknown descends th' unguarded store,
Or wanders, Heav'n-directed, to the Poor.

Pictures like these, dear Madam, to design,
Asks no firm hand, and no unerring line;
Some wand'ring touches, some reflected light,
Some flying stroke, alone can hit them right:
For how should equal colours do the knack?
Chameleons who can paint in white and black?

' Yet *Cloe* sure was form'd without a spot '—
Nature in her then err'd not, but forgot.
' With ev'ry pleasing, ev'ry prudent part,
' Say, what can *Cloe* want? '—She wants a Heart.
She speaks, behaves, and acts just as she ought;
But never, never, reach'd one gen'rous Thought.
Virtue she finds too painful an endeavour,
Content to dwell in Decencies for ever;
So very reasonable, so unmov'd,
As never yet to love, or to be lov'd.
She, while her Lover pants upon her breast,
Can mark the figures on an Indian chest;
And when she sees her Friend in deep despair,
Observes how much a Chintz exceeds Mohair.
Forbid it Heav'n, a Favour or a Debt
She e'er should cancel—but she may forget.
Safe is your Secret still in *Cloe*'s ear;
But none of *Cloe*'s shall you ever hear.
Of all her Dears she never slander'd one,
But cares not if a thousand are undone.

130

Would *Cloe* know if you're alive or dead?
She bids her Footman put it in her head.
Cloe is prudent—Would you too be wise?
Then never break your heart when *Cloe* dies.
Of the Characters of Women, 1735, 1746, 1751

78   *Woman's Ruling Passions*

BUT grant, in Public, Men sometimes are shown,
A Woman's seen in Private life alone:
Our bolder Talents in full light display'd,
Your Virtues open fairest in the shade.
Bred to disguise, in Publick 'tis you hide;
There, none distinguish 'twixt your Shame or Pride,
Weakness or Delicacy; all so nice,
That each may seem a Virtue, or a Vice.

In Men, we various Ruling Passions find;
In Women, two almost divide the kind;
Those, only fix'd, they first or last obey,
The Love of Pleasure, and the Love of Sway.
That, Nature gives; and where the lesson taught
Is but to please, can Pleasure seem a fault?
Experience, this; by Man's oppression curst,
They seek the second not to lose the first.
Of the Characters of Women, 1735, &c.

79   *Heaven's last best Work*

OH! blest with Temper, whose unclouded ray
Can make to-morrow chearful as to-day;
She, who can love a Sister's charms, or hear
Sighs for a Daughter with unwounded ear;
She, who ne'er answers till a Husband cools,
Or, if she rules him, never shows she rules;

131

Charms by accepting, by submitting sways,
Yet has her humour most, when she obeys;
Let Fops or Fortune fly which way they will,
Disdains all loss of Tickets, or Codille;
Spleen, Vapours, or Small-pox, above them all,
And Mistress of herself, tho' China fall.

And yet, believe me, good as well as ill,
Woman's at best a Contradiction still.
Heav'n, when it strives to polish all it can
Its last best work, but forms a softer Man;
Picks from each sex, to make the Fav'rite blest,
Your love of Pleasure, our desire of Rest;
Blends, in exception to all gen'ral rules,
Your Taste of Follies, with our Scorn of Fools,
Reserve with Frankness, Art with Truth ally'd,
Courage with Softness, Modesty with Pride,
Fix'd Principles, with Fancy ever new;
Shakes all together, and produces—You.

Of the Characters of Women, 1735, &c.

80   *Why did I write ?*

OF all mad creatures, if the learn'd are right,
It is the slaver kills, and not the bite.
A fool quite angry is quite innocent:
Alas! 'tis ten times worse when they *repent.*

One dedicates in high heroic prose,
And ridicules beyond a hundred foes;
One from all *Grub-street* will my fame defend,
And, more abusive, calls himself my friend.
This prints my *Letters,* that expects a bribe,
And others roar aloud, ' Subscribe, subscribe.'

There are, who to my Person pay their court:

132

ALEXANDER POPE

I cough like *Horace*, and, tho' lean, am short,
Ammon's great son one shoulder had too high,
Such *Ovid*'s nose, and ' Sir! you have an *Eye* '—
Go on, obliging creatures, make me see
All that disgrac'd my Betters, met in me :
Say for my comfort, languishing in bed,
' Just so immortal *Maro* held his head: '
And when I die, be sure you let me know
Great *Homer* dy'd three thousand years ago.

Why did I write? what sin to me unknown
Dipt me in Ink, my parents, or my own?
As yet a child, nor yet a fool to fame,
I lisp'd in numbers, for the numbers came.
I left no calling for this idle trade,
No duty broke, no father disobey'd.
The Muse but serv'd to ease some friend, not Wife,
To help me thro' this long disease, my Life,
To second, ARBUTHNOT! thy Art and Care,
And teach, the Being you preserv'd, to bear.

But why then publish? *Granville* the polite,
And knowing *Walsh*, would tell me I could write;
Well-natur'd *Garth* inflam'd with early praise,
And *Congreve* lov'd, and *Swift* endur'd my lays;
The courtly *Talbot, Somers, Sheffield* read,
Ev'n mitred *Rochester* would nod the head,
And *St. John*'s self (great *Dryden*'s friends before)
With open arms receiv'd one Poet more.
Happy my Studies, when by these approv'd!
Happier their Author, when by these belov'd!
From these the world will judge of Men and Books,
Not from the *Burnets, Oldmixons*, and *Cooks*.

Epistle to Dr. Arbuthnot, 1734

81   *Verbal Critics*

PAINS, reading, study, are their just pretence,
   And all they want is spirit, taste, and sense.
Comma's and points they set exactly right,
And 'twere a sin to rob them of their mite.
Yet ne'er one sprig of laurel grac'd these ribalds,
From slashing *Bentley* down to pidling *Tibalds.*
Each Wight who reads not, and but scans and spells,
Each Word-catcher that lives on syllables,
Ev'n such small Critics some regard may claim,
Preserv'd in *Milton*'s or in *Shakespear*'s name.
Pretty! in amber to observe the forms
Of hairs, or straws, or dirt, or grubs, or worms!
The things, we know, are neither rich nor rare,
But wonder how the devil they got there.

                              Epistle to Dr. Arbuthnot, 1734

82   *Atticus*

PEACE to all such! but were there One whose fires
   True Genius kindles, and fair Fame inspires,
Blest with each Talent and each Art to please,
And born to write, converse, and live with ease:
Shou'd such a man, too fond to rule alone,
Bear, like the *Turk,* no brother near the throne,
View him with scornful, yet with jealous eyes,
And hate for Arts that caus'd himself to rise;
Damn with faint praise, assent with civil leer,
And without sneering, teach the rest to sneer;
Willing to wound, and yet afraid to strike,
Just hint a fault, and hesitate dislike;

Alike reserv'd to blame, or to commend,
A tim'rous foe, and a suspicious friend,
Dreading ev'n fools, by Flatterers besieg'd,
And so obliging that he ne'er oblig'd;
Like *Cato*, give his little Senate laws,
And sit attentive to his own applause;
While Wits and Templers ev'ry sentence raise,
And wonder with a foolish face of praise.
Who but must laugh, if such a man there be?
Who would not weep, if *Atticus* were he!

Written 1715; *Epistle to Dr. Arbuthnot*, 1734

83 *Bufo*

PROUD as *Apollo* on his forked hill,
Sate full-blown *Bufo*, puff'd by ev'ry quill;
Fed with soft Dedication all day long,
Horace and he went hand in hand in song.
His Library (where Busts of Poets dead
And a true *Pindar* stood without a head)
Receiv'd of Wits an undistinguish'd race,
Who first his Judgment ask'd, and then a Place:
Much they extoll'd his Pictures, much his Seat,
And flatter'd ev'ry day, and some days eat:
Till grown more frugal in his riper days,
He paid some Bards with Port, and some with Praise,
To some a dry Rehearsal was assign'd,
And others (harder still) he paid in kind.
Dryden alone (what wonder?) came not nigh,
Dryden alone escap'd this judging eye:
But still the *Great* have kindness in reserve,
He help'd to bury whom he help'd to starve.

eat = ate, *then rhyming with* seat, great.

135

May some choice Patron bless each gray goose quill!
May ev'ry *Bavius* have his *Bufo* still!
So, when a Statesman wants a Day's defence,
Or Envy holds a whole Week's war with Sense,
Or simple Pride for Flatt'ry makes demands,
May dunce by dunce be whistled off my hands!
Blest be the *Great!* for those they take away,
And those they leave me; for they left me GAY;
Left me to see neglected Genius bloom,
Neglected die! and tell it on his Tomb:
Of all thy blameless Life the sole return
My Verse, and QUEENSB'RY weeping o'er thy Urn!

Epistle to Dr. Arbuthnot, 1734

84   *The Court of Charles II*

IN Days of Ease, when now the weary Sword
  Was sheath'd, and *Luxury* with *Charles* restor'd;
In ev'ry Taste of foreign Courts improv'd,
' All, by the King's Example, liv'd and lov'd.'
Then Peers grew proud in Horsemanship t'excell,
New-market's Glory rose, as Britain's fell;
The Soldier breath'd the Gallantries of France,
And ev'ry flow'ry Courtier writ Romance.
Then Marble, soften'd into life, grew warm,
And yielding Metal flow'd to human form:
Lely on animated Canvas stole
The sleepy Eye, that spoke the melting Soul.
No wonder then, when all was Love and Sport,
The willing Muses were debauch'd at Court.

Epistle to Augustus, 1737

85 *The Poet's Use*

OF little use the Man you may suppose,
    Who says in verse what others say in prose;
Yet let me show, a Poet's of some weight,
And (tho' no Soldier) useful to the State.
What will a Child learn sooner than a song?
What better teach a Foreigner the tongue?
What's long or short, each accent where to place,
And speak in publick with some sort of grace?
I scarce can think him such a worthless thing,
Unless he praise some monster of a King,
Or Virtue, or Religion turn to sport,
To please a lewd, or unbelieving Court.
Unhappy Dryden!—In all Charles's days,
Roscommon only boasts unspotted Bays;
And in our own (excuse some Courtly stains)
No whiter page than Addison remains.
He, from the taste obscene reclaims our Youth,
And sets the Passions on the side of Truth;
Forms the soft bosom with the gentlest art,
And pours each human Virtue in the heart.
Let Ireland tell, how Wit upheld her cause,
Her Trade supported, and supply'd her Laws;
And leave on SWIFT this grateful verse ingrav'd,
The Rights a Court attack'd, a Poet sav'd.
Behold the hand that wrought a Nation's cure,
Stretch'd to relieve the Idiot and the Poor,
Proud Vice to brand, or injur'd Worth adorn,
And stretch the Ray to Ages yet unborn.
Not but there are, who merit other palms;
Hopkins and Sternhold glad the heart with Psalms:

The Boys and Girls whom Charity maintains,
Implore your help in these pathetic strains:
How could Devotion touch the country pews,
Unless the Gods bestow'd a proper Muse?
Verse chears their leisure, Verse assists their work,
Verse prays for Peace, or sings down Pope and Turk.
The silenc'd Preacher yields to potent strain,
And feels that grace his pray'r besought in vain;
The blessing thrills thro' all the lab'ring throng,
And Heav'n is won by violence of Song.

Epistle to Augustus, 1737

86   *Satire*

ASK you what Provocation I have had?
The strong Antipathy of Good to Bad.
When Truth or Virtue an Affront endures,
Th'Affront is mine, my Friend, and should be yours.
Mine, as a Foe profess'd to false Pretence,
Who think a Coxcomb's Honour like his Sense;
Mine, as a Friend to ev'ry worthy mind;
And mine as Man, who feel for all mankind.
    Friend. You're strangely proud.

                    Poet. So proud, I am no Slave:
So impudent, I own myself no Knave:
So odd, my Country's Ruin makes me grave.
Yes, I am proud; I must be proud to see
Men not afraid of God, afraid of me:
Safe from the Bar, the Pulpit, and the Throne,
Yet touch'd and sham'd by *Ridicule* alone.

    O sacred Weapon! left for Truth's defence,
Sole Dread of Folly, Vice, and Insolence!
    138

To all but Heav'n-directed hands deny'd,
The Muse may give thee, but the Gods must guide.
Rev'rent I touch thee! but with honest zeal;
To rouse the Watchmen of the Publick Weal,
To Virtue's Work provoke the tardy Hall,
And goad the Prelate slumb'ring in his Stall.

Ye tinsel Insects! whom a Court maintains,
That counts your Beauties only by your Stains,
Spin all your Cobwebs o'er the Eye of Day!
The Muse's wing shall brush you all away:
All his Grace preaches, all his Lordship sings,
All that makes Saints of Queens, and Gods of Kings,
All, all but Truth, drops dead-born from the Press,
Like the last Gazette, or the last Address.

One Thousand Seven Hundred and Thirty Eight,
Dialogue ii, 1738

87 *The Triumph of Dulness*

O MUSE! relate (for you can tell alone,
Wits have short Memories, and Dunces none)
Relate, who first, who last resign'd to rest;
Whose Heads she partly, whose completely blest;
What Charms could Faction, what Ambition lull,
The Venal quiet, and intrance the Dull;
'Till drown'd was Sense, and Shame, and Right, and Wrong—
O sing, and hush the Nations with thy Song!

*　　*　　*　　*　　*　　*

In vain, in vain,—the all-composing Hour
Resistless falls: The Muse obeys the Pow'r.
She comes! she comes! the sable Throne behold
Of *Night* Primæval, and of *Chaos* old!

ALEXANDER POPE

Before her, *Fancy*'s gilded clouds decay,
And all its varying Rain-bows die away.
Wit shoots in vain its momentary fires,
The meteor drops, and in a flash expires.
As one by one, at dread Medea's strain,
The sick'ning stars fade off th'ethereal plain;
As Argus' eyes, by Hermes' wand opprest,
Clos'd one by one to everlasting rest;
Thus at her felt approach, and secret might,
Art after *Art* goes out, and all is Night.
See skulking *Truth* to her old Cavern fled,
Mountains of Casuistry heap'd o'er her head!
Philosophy, that lean'd on Heav'n before,
Shrinks to her second cause, and is no more.
Physic of *Metaphysic* begs defence,
And *Metaphysic* calls for aid on *Sense !*
See *Mystery* to *Mathematics* fly !
In vain! they gaze, turn giddy, rave, and die.
Religion blushing veils her sacred fires,
And unawares *Morality* expires.
Nor *public* Flame, nor *private*, dares to shine;
Nor *human* Spark is left, nor Glimpse *divine !*
Lo! thy dread Empire, CHAOS! is restor'd;
Light dies before thy uncreating word:
Thy hand, great Anarch! lets the curtain fall;
And Universal Darkness buries All.

The Dunciad, iv, 1728, 1742

1675–1749

88   *Pastoral Landscape*

Geron.   Hobbinol.   Lanquet

Geron.

HOW still the Sea! behold; how calm the Sky!
    And how, in sportive Chase, the Swallows fly!
My Goats, secure from Harm, no Tendance need,
While high on yonder hanging Rock they feed:
And here below, the banky Shore along,
Your Heifers graze: And I to hear your Song
Dispos'd. As eldest, *Hobbinol*, begin;
And *Lanquet*'s Under-Song by Turns come in.

    .   .   .   .

Hobbinol.

In vain the Seasons of the Moon I know,
The Force of healing Herbs, and where they grow;
There is no Herb, no Season, may remove
From my fond Heart the racking Pains of Love.

Lanquet.

What profits me, that I in Charms have Skill,
And Ghosts and Goblins order as I will;
Yet have, with all my Charms, no Pow'r to lay
The Sprite, that breaks my Quiet Night and Day.

Hobbinol.

O that like *Colin* I had Skill in Rhymes:
To purchase Credit with succeeding Times!
Sweet *Colin Clout*! who never yet had Peer,
Who sung thro' all the Seasons of the Year.

141

Lanquet.

Let me like *Wrenock* sing; his Voice had Pow'r
To free the clipsing Moon at Midnight Hour:
And, as he sung, the Fairies, with their Queen,
In Mantles blue came tripping o'er the Green.

Geron.

Here end your pleasing Strife. Both Victors are;
And both with *Colin* may in Rhyme compare.
A Boxen Haut-Boy, loud, and sweet of Sound,
All varnish'd, and with brazen Ringlets bound,
To both I give. A mizling Mist descends
Adown that steepy Rock: And this way tends
Yon distant Rain. Shore-ward the Vessels strive;
And, see, the Boys their Flocks to Shelter drive.

Pastorals, vi.—*Poetical Miscellanies*, vi, 1709

89   *A Winter-Piece*

To the Earl of Dorset

Copenhagen, March 9, 1709

FROM Frozen Climes, and Endless Tracks of Snow,
From Streams that Northern Winds forbid to flow;
What Present shall the Muse to *Dorset* bring;
Or how, so near the Pole, attempt to sing?
The hoary Winter here conceals from Sight
All pleasing Objects that to Verse invite.
The Hills and Dales, and the Delightful Woods,
The Flowry Plains, and Silver Streaming Floods,
By Snow disguis'd, in bright Confusion lye,
And with one dazling Waste fatigue the Eye.

142

AMBROSE PHILIPS

No gentle breathing Breeze prepares the Spring,
No Birds within the Desart Region sing.
The Ships unmov'd the boist'rous Winds defy,
While rattling Chariots o'er the Ocean fly.
The vast *Leviathan* wants Room to play,
And spout his Waters in the Face of Day.
The starving Wolves along the main Sea prowl,
And to the Moon in Icy Valleys howl.
For many a shining League the level Main
Here spreads it self into a Glassy Plain:
There solid Billows of enormous Size,
Alpes of green Ice, in wild Disorder rise.

And yet but lately have I seen, e'en here,
The Winter in a lovely Dress appear.
E'er yet the Clouds let fall the treasur'd Snow,
Or Winds begun thro' hazy Skies to blow.
At Ev'ning a keen Eastern Breeze arose;
And the descending Rain unsullied froze.
Soon as the silent Shades of Night withdrew,
The ruddy Morn disclos'd at once to View
The Face of Nature in a rich Disguise,
And brighten'd ev'ry Object to my Eyes.
For ev'ry Shrub, and ev'ry Blade of Grass,
And ev'ry pointed Thorn, seem'd wrought in Glass.
In Pearls and Rubies rich the Hawthorns show,
While thro' the Ice the Crimson Berries glow.
The thick-sprung Reeds the watry Marshes yield,
Seem polish'd Lances in a hostile Field.
The Stag in limpid Currents with Surprize
Sees Chrystal Branches on his Forehead rise.
The spreading Oak, the Beech, and tow'ring Pine,
Glaz'd over, in the freezing Æther shine.

The frighted Birds the rattling Branches shun,
That wave and glitter in the distant Sun.
　　When if a sudden Gust of Wind arise,
The brittle Forrest into Atoms flies:
The crackling Wood beneath the Tempest bends,
And in a spangled Show'r the Prospect ends.
Or if a Southern Gale the Region warm,
And by Degrees unbind the Wintry Charm;
The Traveller a miry Country sees,
And Journeys sad beneath the dropping Trees.
　　Like some deluded Peasant, *Merlin* leads
Thro' fragrant Bow'rs, and thro' delicious Meads;
While here inchanted Gardens to him rise,
And airy Fabricks there attract his Eyes,
His wand'ring Feet the Magick Paths pursue;
And while he thinks the fair Illusion true,
The trackless Scenes disperse in fluid Air,
And Woods and Wilds, and thorny Ways appear:
A tedious Road the weary Wretch returns,
And, as He goes, the transient Vision mourns.

The Tatler, May 5–7, 1709

90　　　　*Fragment of Sappho*

BLEST as th' Immortal Gods is he,
The Youth who fondly sits by thee,
And hears and sees thee all the while
Softly speak and sweetly smile.

'Twas this depriv'd my Soul of Rest,
And rais'd such Tumults in my Breast;
For while I gaz'd, in Transport tost,
My Breath was gone, my Voice was lost:

My Bosom glow'd; the subtle Flame
Ran quick thro' all my vital Frame;
O'er my dim Eyes a Darkness hung;
My Ears with hollow Murmurs rung:

In dewy Damps my Limbs were chill'd;
My Blood with gentle Horrours thrill'd;
My feeble Pulse forgot to play;
I fainted, sunk, and dy'd away.

The Spectator, November 22, 1711

91   *To Miss Charlotte Pulteney
in her Mother's Arms*

May 1, 1724

TIMELY blossom, infant fair,
   Fondling of a happy pair,
Every morn, and every night,
Their solicitous delight,
Sleeping, waking, still at ease,
Pleasing, without skill to please,
Little gossip, blithe and hale,
Tatling many a broken tale,
Singing many a tuneless song,
Lavish of a heedless tongue,
Simple maiden, void of art,
Babbling out the very heart,
Yet abandon'd to thy will,
Yet imagining no ill,
Yet too innocent to blush,
Like the linlet in the bush,
To the Mother-linnet's note
Moduling her slender throat,

Chirping forth thy petty joys,
Wanton in the change of toys,
Like the linnet green, in *May*,
Flitting to each bloomy spray,
Wearied then, and glad of rest,
Like the linlet in the nest.
This thy present happy lot,
This, in time, will be forgot:
Other pleasures, other cares,
Ever-busy time prepares;
And thou shalt in thy daughter see,
This picture, once, resembled thee.

Poems (Dublin), 1725

92   *To Signora Cuzzoni*

May 25, 1724

LITTLE *Siren* of the stage,
   Charmer of an idle age,
Empty warbler, breathing lyre,
Wanton gale of fond desire,
Bane of every manly art,
Sweet enfeebler of the heart,
O, too pleasing in thy strain,
Hence, to southern climes again;
Tuneful mischief, vocal spell,
To this island bid farewel;
Leave us as we ought to be,
Leave the *Britons* rough and free.

The Hive, iii, 1725

1674–1718

93 *Colin's Complaint*

DESPAIRING beside a clear Stream,
   A Shepherd forsaken was laid;
And while a false Nymph was his Theme,
   A Willow supported his Head.
The Wind that blew over the Plain,
   To his Sighs with a Sigh did reply;
And the Brook, in return to his Pain,
   Ran mournfully murmuring by.

Alas, silly Swain that I was!
   Thus sadly complaining he cry'd,
When first I beheld that fair Face,
   'Twere better by far I had dy'd.
She talk'd, and I bless'd the dear Tongue;
   When she smil'd, 'twas a Pleasure too great.
I listen'd, and cry'd, when she sung,
   Was Nightingale ever so sweet?

How foolish I was to believe
   She could doat on so lowly a Clown,
Or that her fond Heart would not grieve
   To forsake the fine Folk of the Town?
To think that a Beauty so gay,
   So kind and so constant would prove;
Or go clad like our Maidens in Grey,
   Or live in a Cottage on Love?

What tho' I have Skill to complain,
   Tho' the Muses my Temples have crown'd;
What tho' when they hear my soft Strain,
   The Virgins sit weeping around.

NICHOLAS ROWE

Ah, *Colin*, thy Hopes are in vain,
  Thy Pipe and thy Lawrel resign;
Thy false one inclines to a Swain,
  Whose Musick is sweeter than thine.

And you, my Companions so dear,
  Who sorrow to see me betray'd,
Whatever I suffer, forbear,
  Forbear to accuse the false Maid.
Tho' thro' the wide World I should range,
  'Tis in vain from my Fortune to fly,
'Twas hers to be false and to change,
  'Tis mine to be constant and die.

If while my hard Fate I sustain,
  In her Breast any Pity is found,
Let her come with the Nymphs of the Plain,
  And see me laid low in the Ground.
The last humble Boon that I crave,
  Is to shade me with Cypress and Yew;
And when she looks down on my Grave,
  Let her own that her Shepherd was true.

Then to her new Love let her go,
  And deck her in Golden Array,
Be finest at ev'ry fine Show,
  And frolick it all the long Day;
While *Colin*, forgotten and gone,
  No more shall be talk'd of, or seen,
Unless when beneath the pale Moon
  His Ghost shall glide over the Green.

                    Written about 1712 ; broadside of about 1714

94 *Cato's Address to his Troops in Lybia*

FELLOWS in Arms! whose Bliss, whose chiefest Good
Is *Rome*'s Defence, and Freedom bought with Blood;
You, who, to die with Liberty, from far
Have follow'd *Cato* in this fatal War,
Be now for Virtue's noblest Task prepar'd,
For Labours many, perillous, and hard.
Think thro' what burning Climes, what Wilds we go,
No leafie Shades the naked Desarts know,
Nor silver Streams thro' flowry Meadows flow;
But Horrors there and various Deaths abound,
And Serpents guard th' unhospitable Ground.
Hard is the Way; but thus our Fate demands;
Rome and her Laws we seek amidst these Sands.
Let those who, glowing with their Country's Love,
Resolve with me these dreadful Plains to prove,
Nor of Return nor Safety once debate,
But only dare to go, and leave the rest to Fate.
Think not I mean the Dangers to disguise,
Or hide 'em from the cheated Vulgar's Eyes:
Those, only those, shall in my Fate partake,
Who love the Daring for the Danger's sake;
Those who can suffer all that worst can come,
And think it what they owe themselves and *Rome*.
If any yet shall doubt, or yet shall fear;
If Life be, more than Liberty, his Care;
Here, e'er we journey further, let him stay,
Inglorious let him, like a Slave, obey,
And seek a Master in some safer Way.

Foremost, behold, I lead you to the Toil,
My Feet shall foremost print the dusty Soil:
Strike me the first, thou flaming God of Day,
First let me feel thy fierce, thy scorching Ray;
Ye living Poisons all, ye snaky Train,
Meet me the first upon the fatal Plain.
In ev'ry Pain, which you my Warriors fear,
Let me be first, and teach you how to bear.
Who sees me pant for Drought, or fainting first,
Let him upbraid me, and complain of Thirst.
If e'er for Shelter to the Shades I fly,
Me let him curse, me, for the sultry Sky.
If while the weary Soldier marches on,
Your Leader by distinguish'd Ease be known,
Forsake my Cause, and leave me there alone.
The Sands, the Serpents, Thirst, and burning Heat,
Are dear to Patience, and to Virtue sweet;
Virtue, that scorns on Cowards Terms to please,
Or cheaply to be bought, or won with Ease;
But then She joys, then smiles upon her State,
Then fairest to her self, then most compleat,
When glorious Danger makes her truly great.
So *Lybia*'s Plains alone shall wipe away
The foul Dishonours of *Pharsalia*'s Day;
So shall your Courage now, transcend that Fear:
You fled with Glory there, to Conquer here.

He said; and hardy Love of Toil inspir'd;
And ev'ry Breast with Godlike Ardor fir'd.
Strait, careless of Return, without delay
Thro' the wide Waste he took his pathless Way.
Lybia, ordain'd to be his last Retreat,
Receives the Hero, fearless of his Fate;

Here the good Gods his last of Labours doom,
Here shall his Bones and sacred Dust find room,
And his great Head be hid, within an humble Tomb.

Lucan's Pharsalia, ix.—Poetical Miscellanies, vi, 1709

95   *Pompey and Cornelia*

OH who can speak, what Numbers can reveal
  The Tenderness, which pious Lovers feel?
Who can their secret Pangs and Sorrows tell,
With all the croud of Cares that in their Bosoms dwell?
See what new Passions now the Hero knows,
Now first he doubts Success, and fears his Foes;
Rome, and the World he hazards in the Strife,
And gives up all to Fortune, but his Wife.
Oft' he prepares to speak, but knows not how,
Knows they must part, but cannot bid her go;
Deferrs the killing News with fond Delay,
And ling'ring, puts off Fate from Day to Day.
The fleeting Shades began to leave the Sky,
And Slumber soft forsook the drooping Eye;
When, with fond Arms, the fair *Cornelia* prest
Her Lord, reluctant, to her snowy Breast:
Wond'ring, she found he shunn'd her just Embrace,
And felt warm Tears upon his manly Face.
Heart-wounded with the sudden Woe, she griev'd,
And scarce the weeping Warrior yet believ'd.
When, with a Groan, thus he: My truest Wife,
To say how much I love thee more than Life,
Poorly expresses what my Heart wou'd show,
Since Life, alas! is grown my Burthen now.

That long, too long delay'd, that dreadful Doom,
That cruel parting Hour at length is come.
Fierce, haughty, and collected in his Might,
Advancing *Cæsar* calls me to the Fight.
Haste then, my gentle Love, from War retreat;
The *Lesbian* Isle attends thy peaceful Seat:
Nor seek, oh! seek not to increase my Cares,
Seek not to change my Purpose with thy Pray'rs;
My self, in vain, the fruitless Suit have try'd,
And my own pleading Heart has been deny'd.
Shun thou the Crush of my impending Fate,
Nor let it fall on thee with all its Weight.
Then if the Gods my Overthrow ordain,
And the fierce Victor chace me o'er the Plain,
Thou shalt be left me still, my better Part,
To sooth my Cares, and heal my broken Heart;
Thy open Arms I shall be sure to meet,
And fly with Pleasure to the dear Retreat.

Stunn'd and astonish'd at the deadly Stroke,
All Sense, at first, the Matron sad forsook.
Motion, and Life, and Speech at length returns,
And thus in Words of heaviest Woe she mourns
No, *Pompey!* 'tis not that my Lord is dead,
'Tis not the Hand of Fate has robb'd my Bed;
But like some base *Plebeian* I am curs'd,
And by my cruel Husband stand divorc'd.
But *Cæsar* bids us part! thy Father comes!
And we must yield to what that Tyrant dooms!
Is thy *Cornelia*'s Faith so poorly known,
That thou should'st think her safer whilst alone?
Are not our Loves, our Lives, our Fortunes one?
Canst thou, Inhuman, drive me from thy Side,

And bid my single Head the coming Storm abide?
Do I not read thy Purpose in thy Eye?
Dost thou not hope, and wish, ev'n now to die?
And can I then be safe? Yet Death is free,
That last Relief is not deny'd to me;
Tho' banish'd by thy harsh Command I go,
Yet I will join thee in the Realms below.
Thou bidst me with the Pangs of Absence strive,
And, 'till I hear thy certain Loss, survive.
My vow'd Obedience, what it can, shall bear;
But, oh! my Heart's a Woman, and I fear.
If the good Gods, indulgent to my Pray'r,
Shou'd make the Laws of *Rome*, and thee, their Care;
In distant Climes I may prolong my Woe,
And be the last thy Victory to know.
On some bleak Rock, that frowns upon the Deep,
A constant Watch thy weeping Wife shall keep;
There from each Sail Misfortune shall I guess,
And dread the Bark that brings me thy Success.
Nor shall those happier Tidings end my Fear,
The vanquish'd Foe may bring new Danger near;
Defenceless I may still be made a Prize,
And *Cæsar* snatch me with him, as he flies:
With Ease my known Retreat he shall explore,
While thy great Name distinguishes the Shore:
Soon shall the *Lesbian* Exile stand reveal'd,
The Wife of *Pompey* cannot live conceal'd.
But if th' o'er-ruling Pow'rs thy Cause forsake,
Grant me this only last Request I make;
When thou shalt be of Troops and Friends bereft,
And wretched Flight is all thy Safety left;
Oh! follow not the Dictates of thy Heart,

But chuse a Refuge in some distant Part
Where-e'er thy unauspicious Bark shall steer,
Thy sad *Cornelia*'s fatal Shore forbear,
Since *Cæsar* will be sure to seek thee there.

Lucan's Pharsalia, v, 1718

THOMAS PARNELL

1679–1718

96   *A Hymn to Contentment*

LOVELY, lasting Peace of Mind!
    Sweet Delight of human kind!
Heavenly born, and bred on high,
To crown the Fav'rites of the Sky
With more of Happiness below,
Than Victors in a Triumph know!
Whither, O whither art thou fled,
To lay thy meek, contented Head?
What happy Region dost thou please
To make the Seat of Calms and Ease?

    Ambition searches all its Sphere
Of Pomp and State, to meet thee there.
Encreasing Avarice would find
Thy Presence in its Gold enshrin'd.
The bold Advent'rer ploughs his way,
Thro' Rocks amidst the foaming Sea,
To gain thy Love; and then perceives
Thou wert not in the Rocks and Waves.
The silent Heart which Grief assails,
Treads soft and lonesome o'er the Vales,
Sees Daisies open, Rivers run,
And seeks (as I have vainly done)

Amusing Thought; but learns to know
That Solitude's the Nurse of Woe.
No real Happiness is found
In trailing Purple o'er the Ground:
Or in a Soul exalted high,
To range the Circuit of the Sky,
Converse with Stars above, and know
All Nature in its Forms below;
The Rest it seeks, in seeking dies,
And Doubts at last for Knowledge rise.

Lovely, lasting Peace appear!
This World it self, if thou art here,
Is once again with *Eden* bless'd,
And Man contains it in his Breast.

'Twas thus, as under Shade I stood,
I sung my Wishes to the Wood,
And lost in Thought, no more perceiv'd
The Branches whisper as they wav'd:
It seem'd, as all the quiet Place
Confess'd the Presence of the Grace,
When thus she spoke—Go rule thy Will,
Bid thy wild Passions all be still,
Know God—and bring thy Heart to know
The Joys which from Religion flow:
Then ev'ry Grace shall prove its Guest,
And I'll be there to crown the rest.

Oh! by yonder Mossy Seat,
In my Hours of sweet Retreat,
Might I thus my Soul employ,
With sense of Gratitude and Joy:
Rais'd as antient Prophets were,
In heavenly Vision, Praise, and Pray'r;

Pleasing all Men, hurting none,
Pleas'd and bless'd with God alone:
Then while the Gardens take my Sight,
With all the Colours of Delight;
While silver Waters glide along,
To please my Ear, and court my Song:
I'll lift my Voice, and tune my String,
And thee, great *Source* of *Nature*, sing.

The Sun that walks his airy Way,
To light the World, and give the Day;
The Moon that shines with borrow'd Light;
The Stars that gild the gloomy Night;
The Seas that roll unnumber'd Waves;
The Wood that spreads its shady Leaves;
The Field whose Ears conceal the Grain,
The yellow Treasure of the Plain;
All of these, and all I see,
Shou'd be sung, and sung by me:
They speak their Maker as they can,
But want and ask the Tongue of Man.

Go search among your idle Dreams,
Your *busy*, or your *vain* Extreams;
And find a Life of equal Bliss,
Or own the *next* begun in *This*.

Steele's *Poetical Miscellanies*, 1714

97   *Song*

WHEN thy Beauty appears
In its Graces and Airs,
All bright as an Angel new dropt from the Sky;
At distance I gaze, and am aw'd by my Fears,
So strangely you dazzle my Eye!

But when without Art,
Your kind Thoughts you impart,
When your Love runs in Blushes thro' ev'ry Vein;
When it darts from your Eyes, when it pants in your
Heart,
Then I know you're a Woman again.

There's a Passion and Pride
In our Sex, (she reply'd,)
And thus (might I gratify both) I wou'd do:
Still an Angel appear to each Lover beside,
But still be a Woman to you.

Poems on Several Occasions, 1722

98 *A Night-Piece on Death*

BY the blue Taper's trembling Light,
No more I waste the wakeful Night,
Intent with endless view to pore
The Schoolmen and the Sages o'er:
Their Books from Wisdom widely stray,
Or point at best the longest Way.
I'll seek a readier Path, and go
Where Wisdom's surely taught *below*.

How deep yon Azure dies the Sky!
Where Orbs of Gold unnumber'd lye,
While thro' their Ranks in silver pride
The nether Crescent seems to glide.
The slumb'ring Breeze forgets to breathe,
The Lake is smooth and clear beneath,
Where once again the spangled Show
Descends to meet our Eyes below.

The Grounds which on the right aspire,
In dimness from the View retire:
The Left presents a Place of Graves,
Whose Wall the silent Water laves.
That Steeple guides thy doubtful sight
Among the livid gleams of Night.
There pass with melancholy State,
By all the solemn Heaps of Fate,
And think, as softly-sad you tread
Above the venerable Dead,
Time was, like thee they Life possest,
And Time shall be, that thou shalt Rest.

    Those Graves, with bending Osier bound,
That nameless heave the crumbled Ground,
Quick to the glancing Thought disclose
Where *Toil* and *Poverty* repose.

    The flat smooth Stones that bear a Name,
The Chissels slender help to Fame,
(Which e'er our Sett of Friends decay
Their frequent Steps may wear away)
A *middle Race* of Mortals own,
Men, half ambitious, all unknown.

    The Marble Tombs that rise on high,
Whose Dead in vaulted Arches lye,
Whose Pillars swell with sculptur'd Stones,
Arms, Angels, Epitaphs and Bones,
These (all the poor Remains of State)
Adorn the *Rich*, or praise the *Great*;
Who while on Earth in Fame they live,
Are sensless of the Fame they give.

    Ha! while I gaze, pale *Cynthia* fades,
The bursting Earth unveils the Shades!

All slow, and wan, and wrap'd with Shrouds,
They rise in visionary Crouds,
And all with sober Accent cry,
Think, Mortal, what it is to dye.

Now from yon black and fun'ral Yew,
That bathes the Charnel House with Dew,
Methinks I hear a *Voice* begin;
(Ye Ravens, cease your croaking Din,
Ye tolling Clocks, no Time resound
O'er the long Lake and midnight Ground)
It sends a Peal of hollow Groans,
Thus speaking from among the Bones:

When Men my Scythe and Darts supply,
How great a *King* of *Fears* am I!
They view me like the last of Things:
They make, and then they dread, my Stings.
Fools! if you less provok'd your Fears,
No more my Spectre-Form appears.
Death's but a Path that must be trod,
If Man wou'd ever pass to God:
A Port of Calms, a State of Ease
From the rough Rage of swelling Seas.

Why then thy flowing sable Stoles,
Deep pendent Cypress, mourning Poles,
Loose Scarfs to fall athwart thy Weeds,
Long Palls, drawn Herses, cover'd Steeds,
And Plumes of black, that as they tread,
Nod o'er the 'Scutcheons of the Dead?

Nor can the parted Body know,
Nor wants the Soul, these Forms of Woe:
As Men who long in Prison dwell,
With Lamps that glimmer round the Cell,

THOMAS PARNELL

When e'er their suffering Years are run,
Spring forth to greet the glitt'ring Sun:
Such Joy, tho' far transcending Sense,
Have pious Souls at parting hence.
On Earth, and in the Body plac't,
A few, and evil Years, they wast:
But when their Chains are cast aside,
See the glad Scene unfolding wide,
Clap the glad Wing and tow'r away,
And mingle with the Blaze of Day.

Poems on Several Occasions, 1722

JOHN GAY

1685–1732

99

Blouzelinda's Funeral

TO show their love, the neighbours far and near,
Follow'd with wistful look the damsel's bier.
Sprigg'd rosemary the lads and lasses bore,
While dismally the Parson walk'd before.
Upon her grave the rosemary they threw,
The daisie, butter-flow'r and endive blue.

After the good man warn'd us from his text,
That none cou'd tell whose turn would be the next;
He said, that heav'n would take her soul, no doubt,
And spoke the hour-glass in her praise—quite out.

To her sweet mem'ry flow'ry garlands strung,
O'er her now empty seat aloft were hung.
With wicker rods we fenc'd her tomb around,
To ward from man and beast the hallow'd ground,
Lest her new grave the Parson's cattle raze,
For both his horse and cow the church-yard graze.

160

Now we trudg'd homeward to her mother's farm,
To drink new cyder mull'd, with ginger warm.
For gaffer *Tread-well* told us by the by,
Excessive sorrow is exceeding dry.

While bulls bear horns upon their curled brow,
Or lasses with soft stroakings milk the cow;
While padling ducks the standing lake desire,
Or batt'ning hogs roll in the sinking mire;
While moles the crumbled earth in hillocks raise,
So long shall swains tell *Blouzelinda*'s praise.

Thus wail'd the louts in melancholy strain,
'Till bonny *Susan* sped a-cross the plain;
They seiz'd the lass in apron clean array'd,
And to the ale-house forc'd the willing maid;
In ale and kisses they forget their cares,
And *Susan Blouzelinda*'s loss repairs.

The Shepherd's Week, Friday, 1714

100 *The Great Frost*

O ROVING Muse, recal that wond'rous year,
 When winter reign'd in bleak *Britannia*'s air;
When hoary *Thames*, with frosted oziers crown'd,
Was three long moons in icy fetters bound.
The waterman, forlorn along the shore,
Pensive reclines upon his useless oar,
Sees harness'd steeds desert the stony town;
And wander roads unstable, not their own:
Wheels o'er the harden'd waters smoothly glide,
And rase with whiten'd tracks the slipp'ry tide.
Here the fat cook piles high the blazing fire,
And scarce the spit can turn the steer entire.

Booths sudden hide the *Thames,* long streets appear,
And num'rous games proclaim the crouded fair.
So when a gen'ral bids the martial train
Spread their encampment o'er the spacious plain;
Thick-rising tents a canvas city build,
And the loud dice resound thro' all the field.

Trivia, ii, 1716

101 *Sweet William's Farewell to*
    Black-Ey'd Susan

ALL in the *Downs* the fleet was moor'd,
 The streamers waving in the wind,
When black-ey'd *Susan* came aboard.
 Oh! where shall I my true love find!
Tell me, ye jovial sailors, tell me true,
If my sweet *William* sails among the crew.

William, who high upon the yard,
 Rock'd with the billow to and fro,
Soon as her well-known voice he heard,
 He sigh'd, and cast his eyes below:
The cord slides swiftly through his glowing hands
And, (quick as lightning,) on the deck he stands.

So the sweet lark, high-pois'd in air,
 Shuts close his pinions to his breast,
(If, chance, his mate's shrill call he hear)
 And drops at once into her nest.
The noblest Captain in the *British* fleet,
Might envy *William's* lip those kisses sweet.

JOHN GAY

O *Susan, Susan*, lovely dear,
    My vows shall ever true remain:
Let me kiss off that falling tear,
    We only part to meet again.
Change, as ye list, ye winds; my heart shall be
The faithful compass that still points to thee.

Believe not what the landmen say,
    Who tempt with doubts thy constant mind:
They'll tell thee, sailors, when away,
    In ev'ry port a mistress find.
Yes, yes, believe them when they tell thee so,
For thou art present wheresoe'er I go.

If to far *India*'s coast we sail,
    Thy eyes are seen in di'monds bright,
Thy breath is *Africk*'s spicy gale,
    Thy skin is ivory, so white.
Thus ev'ry beauteous object that I view,
Wakes in my soul some charm of lovely *Sue*.

Though battel call me from thy arms,
    Let not my pretty *Susan* mourn;
Though cannons roar, yet safe from harms,
    William shall to his Dear return.
Love turns aside the balls that round me fly,
Lest precious tears should drop from *Susan*'s eye.

The boatswain gave the dreadful word,
    The sails their swelling bosom spread,
No longer must she stay aboard:
    They kiss'd, she sigh'd, he hung his head.
Her less'ning boat, unwilling rows to land:
Adieu, she cries! and wav'd her lilly hand.

Sweet William's Farewell, 1720

102 *Mr. Pope's Welcome from Greece*

Upon his having finished his translation of Homer's Iliad

LONG hast thou, friend! been absent from thy soil,
   Like patient *Ithacus* at siege of *Troy*;
I have been witness of thy six years toil,
   Thy daily labours, and thy night's annoy,
Lost to thy native land, with great turmoil,
   On the wide sea, oft threat'ning to destroy:
Methinks with thee I've trod *Sigæan* ground,
And heard the shores of *Hellespont* resound.

Did I not see thee when thou first sett'st sail
   To seek adventures fair in *Homer*'s land?
Did I not see thy sinking spirits fail,
   And wish thy bark had never left the strand?
Ev'n in mid ocean often didst thou quail,
   And oft lift up thy holy eye and hand,
Praying the Virgin dear, and saintly choir,
Back to the port to bring thy bark entire.

Chear up, my friend, thy dangers now are o'er;
   Methinks—nay, sure the rising coasts appear;
Hark how the guns salute from either shore,
   As thy trim vessel cuts the *Thames* so fair:
Shouts answ'ring shouts, from *Kent* and *Essex* roar,
   And bells break loud thro' every gust of air:
Bonfires do blaze, and bones and cleavers ring,
As at the coming of some mighty king.

Now pass we *Gravesend* with a friendly wind,
   And *Tilbury*'s white fort, and long *Blackwall*;
Greenwich, where dwells the friend of human kind,
   More visited than or her park or hall,

164

JOHN GAY

Withers the good, and (with him ever join'd)
  Facetious *Disney*, greet thee first of all:
I see his chimney smoke, and hear him say,
Duke! that's the room for *Pope*, and that for *Gay*.

Come in, my friends, here shall ye dine and lie,
  And here shall breakfast, and here dine again;
And sup, and breakfast on, (if ye comply)
  For I have still some dozens of champaign:
His voice still lessens as the ship sails by;
  He waves his hand to bring us back in vain;
For now I see, I see proud *London*'s spires;
Greenwich is lost, and *Deptford* dock retires.

Oh, what a concourse swarms on yonder key!
  The sky re-echoes with new shouts of joy:
By all this show, I ween, 'tis Lord May'r's day
  I hear the voice of trumpet and hautboy.—
No, now I see them near—oh, these are they
  Who come in crowds to welcome thee from *Troy*.
Hail to the bard whom long as lost we mourn'd,
From siege, from battle, and from storm return'd!

. . . .

See generous *Burlington*, with goodly *Bruce*,
  (But *Bruce* comes wafted in a soft sedan)
Dan *Prior* next, belov'd by every muse,
  And friendly *Congreve*, unreproachful man!
(*Oxford* by *Cunningham* hath sent excuse)
  See hearty *Watkins* comes with cup and cann;
And *Lewis*, who has never friend forsaken;
And *Laughton* whisp'ring asks—Is *Troy* town taken?

Earl *Warwick* comes, of free and honest mind;
  Bold, gen'rous *Craggs*, whose heart was ne'er disguis'd:
Ah why, sweet *St. John*, cannot I thee find?
  St. John for ev'ry social virtue priz'd.—
Alas! to foreign climates he 's confin'd,
  Or else to see thee here I well surmiz'd:
Thou too, my *Swift*, dost breathe *Bœotian* air;
When wilt thou bring back wit and humour here?

Harcourt I see for eloquence renown'd,
  The mouth of justice, oracle of law!
Another *Simon* is beside him found,
  Another *Simon*, like as straw to straw.
How *Lansdown* smiles, with lasting laurel crown'd!
  What mitred prelate there commands our awe?
See *Rochester* approving nods his head,
And ranks one modern with the mighty dead.

Carlton and *Chandois* thy arrival grace;
  Hanmer, whose eloquence th' unbiass'd sways;
Harley, whose goodness opens in his face,
  And shews his heart the seat where virtue stays.
Ned Blount advances next, with busy pace,
  In haste, but sauntring, hearty in his ways:
I see the friendly *Carylls* come by dozens,
Their wives, their uncles, daughters, sons, and cousins.

Arbuthnot there I see, in physick's art,
  As *Galen* learn'd, or famed *Hippocrate*;
Whose company drives sorrow from the heart,
  As all disease his medicines dissipate:

166

Kneller amid the triumph bears his part,
   Who could (were mankind lost) a new create:
What can th' extent of his vast soul confine?
A painter, critick, engineer, divine!

Thee *Jervas* hails, robust and debonair,
   Now have we conquer'd *Homer*, friends, he cries:
Dartneuf, grave joker, joyous *Ford* is there,
   And wond'ring *Maine*, so fat with laughing eyes:
(*Gay*, *Maine*, and *Cheney*, boon companions dear,
   Gay fat, *Maine* fatter, *Cheney* huge of size)
Yea *Dennis*, *Gildon*, (hearing thou hast riches)
And honest, hatless *Cromwell*, with red breeches.

O *Wanley*, whence com'st thou with shorten'd hair,
   And visage from thy shelves with dust besprent?
' Forsooth (quoth he) from placing *Homer* there,
   ' For ancients to compyle is myne entente:
' Of ancients only hath Lord *Harley* care;
   ' But hither me hath my meeke lady sent:—
' In manuscript of Greeke rede we thilke same,
' But book yprint best plesyth myn gude dame.'

Yonder I see, among th' expecting croud,
   Evans with laugh jocose, and tragick *Young*;
High-buskin'd *Booth*, grave *Mawbert*, wand'ring *Frowd*,
   And *Titcomb*'s belly waddles slow along.
See *Digby* faints at *Southern* talking loud,
   Yea *Steele* and *Tickell* mingle in the throng;
Tickell whose skiff (in partnership they say)
Set forth for *Greece*, but founder'd in the way.

  .   .   .   .

How lov'd! how honour'd thou! yet be not vain;
　　And sure thou art not, for I hear thee say,
All this, my friends, I owe to *Homer*'s strain,
　　On whose strong pinions I exalt my lay.
What from contending cities did he gain;
　　And what rewards his grateful country pay?
None, none were paid—why then all this for me?
These honours, *Homer*, had been just to thee.

Written 1720; published in *Additions
to the Works of Pope*, 1776

103　　　　　　　　*To a Lady*

On her Passion for Old China

WHAT ecstasies her bosom fire!
　　How her eyes languish with desire!
How blest, how happy should I be,
Were that fond glance bestow'd on me!
New doubts and fears within me war:
What rival's near? a *China* Jar.

　　China's the passion of her soul;
A cup, a plate, a dish, a bowl
Can kindle wishes in her breast,
Inflame with joy, or break her rest.

　　Some gems collect; some medals prize,
And view the rust with lovers eyes;
Some court the stars at midnight hours;
Some doat on Nature's charms in flowers!
But ev'ry beauty I can trace
In *Laura*'s mind, in *Laura*'s face;
My stars are in this brighter sphere,
My lilly and my rose is here.

Philosophers more grave than wise
Hunt science down in Butterflies;
Or fondly poring on a Spider,
Stretch human contemplation wider;
Fossiles give joy to *Galen*'s soul,
He digs for knowledge, like a Mole;
In shells so learn'd, that all agree
No fish that swims knows more than he!
In such pursuits if wisdom lies,
Who, *Laura*, shall thy taste despise?

When I some antique Jar behold,
Or white, or blue, or speck'd with gold,
Vessels so pure, and so refin'd
Appear the types of woman-kind:
Are they not valu'd for their beauty,
Too fair, too fine for houshold duty?
With flowers and gold and azure dy'd,
Of ev'ry house the grace and pride?
How white, how polish'd is their skin,
And valu'd most when only seen!
She who before was highest priz'd
Is for a crack or flaw despis'd;
I grant they're frail, yet they're so rare,
The treasure cannot cost too dear!
But Man is made of courser stuff,
And serves convenience well enough;
He's a strong earthen vessel made,
For drudging, labour, toil and trade;
And when wives lose their other self,
With ease they bear the loss of *Delf*.

Husbands more covetous than sage
Condemn this *China*-buying rage;

They count that woman's prudence little,
Who sets her heart on things so brittle.
But are those wise-men's inclinations
Fixt on more strong, more sure foundations?
If all that's frail we must despise,
No human view or scheme is wise.
Are not Ambition's hopes as weak?
They swell like bubbles, shine and break.
A Courtier's promise is so slight,
'Tis made at noon, and broke at night.
What pleasure's sure?   The Miss you keep
Breaks both your fortune and your sleep.
The man who loves a country life,
Breaks all the comforts of his wife;
And if he quit his farm and plough,
His wife in town may break her vow.
Love, *Laura*, love, while youth is warm,
For each new winter breaks a charm;
And woman's not like *China* sold,
But cheaper grows in growing old;
Then quickly chuse the prudent part,
Or else you break a faithful heart.

To a Lady, &c., **1725**

104   *The Fox at the Point of Death*

A FOX, in life's extream decay,
  Weak, sick and faint, expiring lay;
All appetite had left his maw,
And age disarm'd his mumbling jaw.
His num'rous race around him stand
To learn their dying sire's command;

He raised his head with whining moan,
And thus was heard the feeble tone.

Ah sons, from evil ways depart,
My crimes lye heavy on my heart.
See, see, the murder'd geese appear!
Why are those bleeding turkeys there?
Why all around this cackling train,
Who haunt my ears for chicken slain?

The hungry foxes round them star'd,
And for the promis'd feast prepar'd.

Where, Sir, is all this dainty cheer?
Nor turkey, goose, nor hen is here:
These are the phantoms of your brain,
And your sons lick their lips in vain.

O gluttons, says the drooping sire;
Restrain inordinate desire;
Your liqu'rish taste you shall deplore,
When peace of conscience is no more.
Does not the hound betray our pace,
And gins and guns destroy our race?
Thieves dread the searching eye of power,
And never feel the quiet hour.
Old-age, (which few of us shall know)
Now puts a period to my woe.
Would you true happiness attain,
Let honesty your passions rein;
So live in credit and esteem,
And, the good-name you lost, redeem.

The counsel's good, a fox replies,
Could we perform what you advise.
Think, what our ancestors have done;
A line of thieves from son to son:

To us descends the long disgrace,
And infamy hath mark'd our race.
Though we, like harmless sheep, should feed,
Honest in thought, in word, and deed
Whatever hen-roost is decreas'd,
We shall be thought to share the feast.
The change shall never be believ'd,
A lost good-name is ne'er retriev'd.

   Nay then, replys the feeble Fox,
(But, hark! I hear a hen that clocks)
Go, but be mod'rate in your food;
A chicken too might do me good.

Fables, 1727

105   *Song*

Macheath. WERE I laid on *Greenland*'s Coast,
            And in my Arms embrac'd my Lass;
            Warm amidst eternal Frost,
            Too soon the Half Year's Night would pass.
Polly. Were I sold on *Indian* Soil,
            Soon as the burning Day was clos'd,
            I could mock the sultry Toil
            When on my Charmer's Breast repos'd.
Macheath. And I would love you all the Day,
Polly. Every Night would kiss and play,
Macheath. If with me you'd fondly stray
Polly. Over the Hills and far away.

The Beggar's Opera, Act i, 1728

JOHN GAY

106

Song

YOUTH'S the Season made for Joys,
   Love is then our Duty,
She alone who that employs,
   Well deserves her Beauty.
     Let's be gay,
     While we may,
Beauty's a Flower, despis'd in Decay.
Chorus. Youth's the Season, *&c.*

   Let us drink and sport to-day,
     Ours is not to-morrow.
   Love with Youth flies swift away,
     Age is nought but Sorrow.
     Dance and sing,
     Time's on the Wing,
Life never knows the Return of Spring.
Chorus. Let us drink, *&c.*

             The Beggar's Opera, Act ii, 1728

107

Song

LOVE in her Eyes sits playing,
   And sheds delicious Death;
Love in her Lips is straying,
   And warbling in her Breath;
Love on her Breast sits panting,
   And swells with soft Desire;
Nor Grace, nor Charm, is wanting
   To set the Heart on Fire.

             Acis and Galatea, Act i, 1732

108 *Song*

O RUDDIER than the Cherry,
   O sweeter than the Berry,
O Nymph more bright
Than Moonshine Night,
Like Kidlings blith and merry.
Ripe as the melting Cluster,
No Lilly has such Lustre,
   Yet hard to tame,
   As raging Flame,
And fierce as Storms that bluster.

Acis and Galatea, Act ii, 1732

109 *Song*

T HINK of Dress in ev'ry Light
   'Tis Woman's chiefest Duty;
Neglecting that, our selves we slight
   And undervalue Beauty.
That allures the Lover's Eye,
   And graces ev'ry Action;
Besides, when not a Creature's by,
   'Tis inward Satisfaction.

Achilles, Act iii, 1733

THOMAS TICKELL

110   *To the Earl of Warwick*

On the Death of Mr. Addison

I F, dumb too long, the drooping Muse hath stay'd,
And left her debt to *Addison* unpaid,
Blame not her silence, *Warwick*, but bemoan,
And judge, oh judge, my bosom by your own.
What mourner ever felt poetic fires!
Slow comes the verse, that real woe inspires:
Grief unaffected suits but ill with art,
Or flowing numbers with a bleeding heart.

Can I forget the dismal night, that gave
My soul's best part for-ever to the grave!
How silent did his old companions tread,
By mid-night lamps, the mansions of the dead,
Through breathing statues, then unheeded things,
Through rowes of warriors, and through walks of kings!
What awe did the slow solemn knell inspire;
The pealing organ, and the pausing choir;
The duties by the lawn-robed prelate pay'd;
And the last words, that dust to dust convey'd!
While speechless o'er thy closing grave we bend,
Accept these tears, thou dear departed friend,
Oh gone for-ever, take this long adieu;
And sleep in peace, next thy lov'd *Montagu*!

To strew fresh laurels let the task be mine,
A frequent pilgrim, at thy sacred shrine;
Mine with true sighs thy absence to bemoan,
And grave with faithful epitaphs thy stone.

If e'er from me thy lov'd memorial part,
May shame afflict this alienated heart;
Of thee forgetful if I form a song,
My lyre be broken, and untun'd my tongue,
My grief be doubled, from thy image free,
And mirth a torment, unchastised by thee.

Oft let me range the gloomy Iles alone
(Sad luxury! to vulgar minds unknown)
Along the walls where speaking marbles show
What worthies form the hallow'd mold below:
Proud names, who once the reins of empire held;
In arms who triumph'd; or in arts excell'd;
Chiefs, grac'd with scars, and prodigal of blood;
Stern patriots, who for sacred freedom stood;
Just men, by whom impartial laws were given;
And saints, who taught, and led, the way to heaven.
Ne'er to these chambers, where the mighty rest,
Since their foundation, came a nobler guest,
Nor e'er was to the bowers of bliss convey'd
A fairer spirit, or more welcome shade.

In what new region, to the just assign'd,
What new employments please th' unbody'd mind?
A winged *Virtue* thro' th' ethereal sky,
From world to world unweary'd does he fly?
Or curious trace the long laborious maze
Of heaven's decrees where wondering angels gaze?
Does he delight to hear bold Seraphs tell
How *Michael* battel'd, and the Dragon fell?
Or, mixt with milder Cherubim, to glow
In hymns of love, not ill essay'd below?
Or do'st thou warn poor mortals left behind,
A task well suited to thy gentle mind?

Oh, if sometimes thy spotless form descend,
To me thy aid, thou guardian Genius, lend!
When rage misguides me, or when fear alarms,
When pain distresses, or when pleasure charms,
In silent whisperings purer thoughts impart,
And turn from Ill a frail and feeble heart;
Lead through the paths thy virtue trode before,
'Till bliss shall join, nor death can part us more.

That awful form (which, so ye heavens decree,
Must still be lov'd and still deplor'd by me)
In nightly visions seldom fails to rise,
Or, rous'd by fancy, meets my waking eyes.
If business calls, or crowded courts invite,
Th' unblemish'd statesman seems to strike my sight;
If in the stage I seek to soothe my care,
I meet his soul, which breathes in *Cato* there;
If pensive to the rural shades I rove,
His shape o'ertakes me in the lonely grove:
'Twas there of Just and Good he reason'd strong,
Clear'd some great truth, or rais'd some serious song;
There patient show'd us the wise course to steer,
A candid censor, and a friend severe;
There taught us how to live; and (oh! too high
The price for knowledge) taught us how to die.

Thou Hill, whose brow the antique structures grace,
Rear'd by bold chiefs of *Warwick*'s noble race,
Why, once so lov'd, when-e'er thy bower appears,
O'er my dim eye-balls glance the sudden tears!
How sweet were once thy prospects fresh and fair,
Thy sloping walks, and unpolluted air!
How sweet the gloomes beneath thy aged trees,
Thy noon-tide shadow, and thy evening breeze!

His image thy forsaken bowers restore
Thy walks and airy prospects charm no more,
No more the summer in thy gloomes allay'd,
Thy ev'ning breezes, and thy noon-day shade.
 From other ills, however fortune frown'd,
Some refuge in the muse's art I found:
Reluctant now I touch the trembling string,
Bereft of him, who taught me how to sing,
And these sad accents, murmur'd o'er his urn,
Betray that absence, they attempt to mourn.
Oh! must I then (now fresh my bosom bleeds,
And *Craggs* in death to *Addison* succeeds)
The verse, begun to one lost friend, prolong,
And weep a second in th' unfinish'd song!
 These works divine, which on his death-bed laid
To thee, O *Craggs*, th' expiring Sage convey'd,
Great, but ill-omen'd monument of fame,
Nor he surviv'd to give, nor thou to claim.
Swift after him thy social spirit flies,
And close to his, how soon! thy coffin lies.
Blest pair! whose union future bards shall tell
In future tongues: each other's boast! farewel.
Farewel! whom join'd in fame, in friendship try'd,
No chance could sever, nor the grave divide.

Works of Addison, i, 1721

111   *An Ode*

Inscribed to the Earl of Sunderland at Windsor

THOU Dome, where *Edward* first enroll'd
    His Red-cross Knights and Barons bold,
Whose vacant seats, by Virtue bought,
Ambitious Emperours have sought;

THOMAS TICKELL

Where *Britain*'s Foremost names are found,
In Peace belov'd, in War renown'd,
Who made the Hostile nations moan,
Or brought a Blessing on their own:

Once more a Son of *Spencer* waits,
A name Familiar to thy gates,
Sprung from the Chief whose Prowess gain'd
The Garter while thy Founder reign'd.
He offer'd here his dinted Shield,
The Dread of *Gauls* in *Cressi*'s field,
Which in thy high-arch'd Temple rais'd
For Four long Centuries hath blaz'd.

These Seats our Sires, a hardy Kind,
To the fierce sons of War confin'd,
The Flow'r of Chivalry, who drew
With sinew'd arm the stubborn Yew;
Or with heav'd Poll-Axe clear'd the field;
Or who, in Jousts and Tourneys skill'd,
Before their Ladies' eyes renown'd
Threw Horse and Horseman to the Ground.

In After-times, as Courts refin'd,
Our Patriots in the List were join'd.
Not only *Warwick* stain'd with blood,
Or *Marlbrough* near the *Danube*'s flood,
Have in their crimson Crosses glow'd;
But, on just Lawgivers bestow'd,
These Emblems *Cecil* did invest,
And gleam'd on wise *Godolphin*'s breast.

So *Greece*, e'er Arts began to rise,
Fix'd huge *Orion* in the Skies,

THOMAS TICKELL

And stern *Alcides*, fam'd in Wars,
Bespangled with a thousand Stars;
'Till letter'd *Athens* round the Pole
Made gentler Constellations rowle,
In the blue Heavens the *Lyre* she strung,
And near the *Maid* the *Balance* hung.

Then, *Spencer*, mount amid the Band,
Where Knights and Kings promiscuous stand.
What though the Hero's flame represt
Burns Calmly in thy generous breast!
Yet who more Dauntless to oppose
In doubtful days our Home-bred foes!
Who rais'd his Country's Wealth so high,
Or view'd with less desiring eye !

The Sage who large of soul surveys
The Globe, and all its Empires weighs,
Watchful the various climes to guide
Which Seas, and Tongues, and Faiths divide,
A nobler Name in *Windsor*'s shrine
Shall leave, if right the Muse divine,
Than sprung of old, abhorr'd and vain,
From ravag'd Realms and Myriads slain.

Why praise we, Prodigal of fame,
The Rage that sets the World on flame?
My guiltless Muse his brow shall bind
Whose God-like bounty Spares mankind.
For those, whom Bloody garlands crown,
The Brass may breathe, the Marble frown;
To Him, through every rescu'd land,
Ten thousand Living trophies stand.

Ode to the Earl of Sunderland, 1720

112 *Fairies*

THAT Hollow space, where now in living rowes
   Line above line the Yew's sad verdure grows,
Was, e'er the planter's hand it's beauty gave,
A common Pit, a rude unfashion'd Cave.
The landskip now so sweet we well may praise:
But far far sweeter in its ancient days,
Far sweeter was it, when it's peopled ground
With Fairy domes and dazling tow'rs was crown'd.
Where in the midst those verdant Pillars spring,
Rose the proud Palace of the Elfin King;
For ev'ry hedge of vegetable green
In happier years a crowded street was seen;
Nor all those leaves, that now the prospect grace,
Could match the numbers of its Pygmy race.
   When *Albion* rul'd the land, whose lineage came
From *Neptune* mingling with a mortal dame,
Their midnight pranks the sprightly Fairies play'd
On ev'ry hill, and danc'd in ev'ry shade.
But, foes to sun-shine, most they took delight
In dells and dales conceal'd from human sight:
There hew'd their houses in the arching rock;
Or scoop'd the bosom of the blasted oak;
Or heard, o'ershadow'd by some shelving hill,
The distant murmurs of the falling rill.
They, rich in pilfer'd spoils, indulg'd their mirth,
And pity'd the huge wretched sons of Earth.
Even now, 'tis said, the Hinds o'erhear their strain,
And strive to view their airy forms in vain:

They to their cells at Man's approach repair,
Like the shy Leveret, or the mother Hare,
The whilst poor mortals startle at the sound
Of unseen footsteps on the haunted ground.

Kensington Garden, 1722

113   *Colin and Lucy*

OF *Leinster*, fam'd for maidens fair,
    Bright *Lucy* was the grace;
Nor e'er did *Liffy*'s limpid stream
    Reflect so sweet a face:
Till luckless love, and pining care,
    Impair'd her rosy hue,
Her coral lips, and damask cheeks,
    And eyes of glossy blue.

Oh! have you seen a lilly pale,
    When beating rains descend?
So droop'd the slow-consuming maid,
    Her life now near its end.
By *Lucy* warn'd, of flatt'ring swains
    Take heed, ye easy fair:
Of vengeance due to broken vows,
    Ye perjur'd swains, beware.

Three times, all in the dead of night,
    A bell was heard to ring;
And shrieking at her window thrice,
    The raven flap'd his wing.
Too well the love-lorn maiden knew
    The solemn boding sound;

And thus, in dying words, bespoke
   The virgins weeping round:

‘ I hear a voice, you cannot hear,
   ‘ Which says, I must not stay;
‘ I see a hand, you cannot see,
   ‘ Which beckons me away.
‘ By a false heart, and broken vows,
   ‘ In early youth I die:
‘ Was I to blame, because his bride
   ‘ Was thrice as rich as I?

‘ Ah, *Colin*! give not her thy vows,
   ‘ Vows due to me alone;
‘ Nor thou, fond maid, receive his kiss,
   ‘ Nor think him all thy own.
‘ To-morrow, in the church to wed,
   ‘ Impatient, both prepare;
‘ But know, fond maid, and know, false man,
   ‘ That *Lucy* will be there!

‘ Then bear my corse, my comrades, bear,
   ‘ This bridegroom blythe to meet,
‘ He in his wedding-trim so gay,
   ‘ I in my winding-sheet.’
She spoke; she dy’d; her corse was born,
   The bridegroom blythe to meet,
He in his wedding-trim so gay,
   She in her winding-sheet.

Then what were perjur’d *Colin*’s thoughts?
   How were these nuptials kept?
The bridesmen flock’d round *Lucy* dead,
   And all the village wept.

Confusion, shame, remorse, despair,
 At once his bosom swell:
The damps of death bedew'd his brow,
 He shook, he groan'd, he fell.

From the vain bride, (ah bride no more!)
 The varying crimson fled,
When, stretch'd before her rival's corse,
 She saw her husband dead.
Then to his *Lucy*'s new-made grave
 Convey'd by trembling swains,
One mould with her, beneath one sod,
 For ever he remains.

Oft at this grave, the constant hind,
 And plighted maid are seen;
With garlands gay, and true-love knots,
 They deck the sacred green;
But, swain forsworn, whoe'er thou art,
 This hallow'd spot forbear;
Remember *Colin*'s dreadful fate,
 And fear to meet him there.

Broadside (Dublin), 1725

RICHARD BENTLEY

1662–1742

*114 A Reply to an Imitation of the Second
 Ode in the Third Book of Horace*

WHO strives to mount *Parnassus* Hill,
 And thence Poetick Laurels bring,
Must first acquire due Force and Skill,
 Must fly with Swan's, or Eagle's, Wing.

RICHARD BENTLEY

Who Nature's Treasures wou'd explore,
  Her Mysteries and Arcana know,
Must high, as lofty *Newton*, soar,
  Must stoop, as searching *Woodward*, low.

Who studies ancient Laws and Rites,
  Tongues, Arts and Arms, all History,
Must drudge like *Selden*, Days and Nights,
  And in the endless Labour dye.

Who travels in Religious Jars,
  (Truth mixt with Errors, Shade with Rays,)
Like *Whiston*, wanting *Pyx and Stars,
  In Ocean wide or sinks, or strays.

But grant, our Heroe's Hopes long Toil,
  And comprehensive Genius, crown;
All Sciences, all Arts, his Spoil,
  Yet what Reward, or what Renown?

Envy innate in vulgar Souls,
  Envy steps in, and stops his Rise;
Envy with poison'd Tarnish fouls
  His Lustre, and his Worth decrys.

Inglorious, or by Wants inthrall'd,
  To Colledge, and old Books, confin'd,
A Pedant from his Learning call'd,
  Dunces advanc'd, he's left behind;
Yet left *Content*, a Genuine *Stoick* He,
Great without *Patron*, *rich* without *South-Sea*!

                                    The Grove, 1721

* The Compass.

ELIJAH FENTON

115

To a Lady

Sitting before her Glass

SO smooth and clear the Fountain was
In which his Face *Narcissus* spy'd,
When gazing in that liquid Glass,
    He for himself despair'd and dy'd:
Nor, *Chloris*, can you safer see
Your own Perfections here than he.

The Lark before the Mirror plays,
    Which some deceitful Swain has set;
Pleas'd with her self she fondly stays
    To die deluded in the Net:
Love may such Frauds for you prepare,
Your self the Captive, and the Snare.

But, *Chloris*, whilst you there review
    Those Graces op'ning in their Bloom,
Think how Disease and Age pursue,
    Your riper Glories to consume:
Then sighing you will wish your Glass
Cou'd shew to *Chloris* what she *was*.

Let Pride no more give Nature Law,
    But free the Youth your Pow'r enslaves:
Her Form, like yours, bright *Cynthia* saw
    Reflected on the Crystal Waves,
Yet priz'd not all her Charms above
The Pleasure of *Endymion*'s Love.

ELIJAH FENTON

No longer let your Glass supply
   Too just an Emblem of your Breast;
Where oft' to my deluded Eye
   Love's Image has appear'd imprest;
But play'd so lightly on your Mind,
It left no lasting Print behind.

Miscellaneous Poems and Translations, 1712

WILLIAM BROOME

1689–1745

116
The Rose-Bud
To the Lady Jane Wharton

QUEEN of Fragrance, lovely Rose,
   The Beauties of thy Leaves disclose!
The Winter's past, the Tempests fly,
Soft Gales breathe gently thro' the Sky;
The Lark sweet warbling on the Wing
Salutes the gay Return of Spring:
The silver Dews, the vernal Show'rs,
Call forth a bloomy Waste of Flow'rs;
The joyous Fields, the shady Woods,
Are cloath'd with Green, or swell with Buds;
Then haste thy Beauties to disclose,
Queen of Fragrance, lovely Rose!

   Thou, beauteous Flow'r, a welcome Guest,
Shalt flourish on the Fair-one's Breast,
Shalt grace her Hand, or deck her Hair,
The Flow'r most sweet, the Nymph most fair;
Breathe soft, ye Winds! be calm, ye Skies!
Arise ye flow'ry Race, arise!
And haste thy Beauties to disclose,
Queen of Fragrance, lovely Rose!

But thou, fair Nymph, thy self survey
In this sweet Offspring of a Day;
That Miracle of Face must fail,
Thy Charms are sweet, but Charms are frail:
Swift as the short-liv'd Flow'r they fly,
At Morn they bloom, at Evening die:
Tho' Sickness yet a while forbears,
Yet Time destroys, what Sickness spares;
Now *Helen* lives alone in Fame,
And *Cleopatra*'s but a Name;
Time must indent that heav'nly Brow,
And thou must be, what they are now.
    This Moral to the Fair disclose,
Queen of Fragrance, lovely Rose.

Poems on Several Occasions, 1727

HENRY CAREY

16..–1743

117   *The Ballad of Sally in our Alley*

O F all the Girls that are so smart
        There's none like pretty *Sally*,
She is the Darling of my Heart,
    And she lives in our Alley.
There is no Lady in the Land,
    Is half so sweet as *Sally*,
She is the Darling of my Heart,
    And she lives in our Alley.

Her Father he makes Cabbage-nets,
    And through the Streets does cry 'em;
Her Mother she sells Laces long,
    To such as please to buy 'em:

But sure such Folks could ne'er beget
    So sweet a Girl as *Sally*!
She is the Darling of my Heart,
    And she lives in our Alley.

When she is by I leave my Work,
    (I love her so sincerely)
My Master comes like any Turk,
    And bangs me most severely;
But, let him bang his Belly-full,
    I'll bear it all for *Sally*;
She is the Darling of my Heart,
    And she lives in our Alley.

Of all the Days that's in the Week,
    I dearly love but one Day,
And that's the Day that comes betwixt
    A Saturday and Monday;
For then I'm dress'd, all in my best,
    To walk abroad with *Sally*;
She is the Darling of my Heart,
    And she lives in our Alley.

My Master carries me to Church,
    And often am I blamed,
Because I leave him in the lurch,
    As soon as Text is named:
I leave the Church in Sermon time,
    And slink away to *Sally*;
She is the Darling of my Heart,
    And she lives in our Alley.

When Christmas comes about again,
  O then I shall have Money;
I'll hoard it up, and box and all
  I'll give it to my Honey:
And, would it were ten thousand Pounds,
  I'd give it all to *Sally*;
She is the Darling of my Heart,
  And she lives in our Alley.

My Master and the Neighbours all
  Make game of me and *Sally*;
And (but for her) I'd better be
  A Slave and row a Galley:
But when my seven long Years are out,
  O then I'll marry *Sally*!
O then we'll wed and then we'll bed,
  But not in our Alley.

Poems on Several Occasions, 1729

118   ANONYMOUS

IN good King *Charles*'s golden days,
  When Loyalty no harm meant;
A Furious High-Church Man I was,
  And so I gain'd Preferment.
Unto my Flock I daily Preach'd,
  Kings are by God appointed,
And Damn'd are those who dare resist,
  Or touch the Lord's Anointed.
    And this is Law, I will maintain
      Unto my Dying Day, Sir,
    That whatsoever King shall Reign,
      I will be Vicar of *Bray*, Sir!

ANONYMOUS

When Royal *James* possest the Crown,
  And Popery grew in fashion;
The Penal Law I houted down,
  And read the Declaration:
The Church of *Rome*, I found would fit,
  Full well my Constitution,
And I had been a Jesuit,
  But for the Revolution.
    And this is Law, &c.

When *William* our Deliverer came,
  To heal the Nation's Grievance,
I turned the Cat in Pan again,
  And swore to him Allegiance:
Old Principles I did revoke,
  Set Conscience at a distance,
Passive Obedience is a Joke,
  A Jest is Non-resistance.
    And this is Law, &c.

When glorious *Ann* became our Queen,
  The Church of *England*'s Glory,
Another face of things was seen,
  And I became a Tory:
Occasional Conformists base,
  I Damn'd, and Moderation,
And thought the Church in danger was,
  From such Prevarication.
    And this is Law, &c.

When *George* in Pudding time came o'er,
  And Moderate Men looked big, Sir,

ANONYMOUS

My Principles I chang'd once more,
   And so became a Whig, Sir:
And thus Preferment I procur'd,
   From our Faith's Great Defender,
And almost every day abjur'd
    The Pope, and the Pretender.
      And this is Law, &c.

The Illustrious House of *Hannover*,
   And Protestant Succession,
To these I lustily will swear,
   Whilst they can keep possession:
For in my Faith, and Loyalty,
   I never once will faulter,
But *George*, my Lawful King shall be,
   Except the Times shou'd alter.
      And this is Law, &c.

The British Musical Miscellany, i, 1734

ALLAN RAMSAY

1686–1758

119   *The Poet's Wish : An Ode*

FRAE great *Apollo*, poet say,
   What is thy wish, what wadst thou hae,
   When thou bows at his shrine?
Not *Karss* o' *Gowrie*'s fertile field,
Nor a' the flocks the *Grampians* yield,
   That are baith sleek and fine:
Not costly things brought frae afar,
   As ivory, pearl and gems;

Nor those fair straths that water'd are
　　　With *Tay* and *Tweed*'s smooth streams,
　　　　　Which gently and daintily
　　　　　Eat down the flowry braes,
　　　　　As greatly and quietly
　　　　　They wimple to the seas.

Whaever by his kanny fate
Is master of a good estate,
　　　That can ilk thing afford,
Let him enjoy't withoutten care,
And with the wale of curious fare
　　　Cover his ample board.
Much dawted by the gods is he,
　　　Wha to the *Indian* plain
Successfu' ploughs the wally sea,
　　　And safe returns again,
　　　　　With riches that hitches
　　　　　Him high aboon the rest
　　　　　Of sma' fowk, and a' fowk
　　　　　That are wi' poortith prest.

For me I can be well content
To eat my bannock on the bent,
　　　And kitchen't wi' fresh air;
Of lang-kail I can make a feast,
And cantily had up my crest,
　　　And laugh at dishes rare.
Nought frae *Apollo* I demand,
　　　But throw a lengthen'd life

the wale] the choicest　　　dawted] favoured　　　wally] wavy
poortith] poverty　　　had up] hold up

My outer fabrick firm may stand,
    And saul clear without strife.
             May he then but gie then
             Those blessings for my skair,
             I'll fairly and squairly
             Quite a' and seek nae mair.

Poems, 1721

120   *Sang*

MY *Peggy* is a young thing,
    Just enter'd in her teens,
Fair as the day, and sweet as *May*,
Fair as the day, and always gay.
    My *Peggy* is a young thing,
      And I'm not very auld,
    Yet well I like to meet her at
      The wawking of the fauld.

My *Peggy* speaks sae sweetly,
    When'er we meet alane,
I wish nae mair to lay my care,
I wish nae mair of a' that's rare.
    My *Peggy* speaks sae sweetly,
      To a' the lave I'm cauld;
    But she gars a' my spirits glow
      At wawking of the fauld.

My *Peggy* smiles sae kindly,
    Whene'er I whisper love,
That I look down on a' the town,
That I look down upon a crown.

skair] share   the lave] the rest

My *Peggy* smiles sae kindly,
　　It makes me blythe and bauld,
And naithing gi'es me sic delight,
　　As wawking of the fauld.

My *Peggy* sings sae saftly,
　　When on my pipe I play;
By a' the rest it is confest,
By a' the rest, that she sings best.
My *Peggy* sings sae saftly,
　　And in her sangs are tald,
With innocence, the wale of sense,
　　At wawking of the fauld.

The Gentle Shepherd, Act i, 1725

121　　　　　*A Dainty Sang*

*J*OCKY said to *Jenny*, *Jenny* wilt thou do't,
　Ne'er a fit, quoth *Jenny*, for my tocher-good;
For my tocher-good, I winna marry thee,
E'en's ye like, quoth *Jocky*, ye may let it be.

I hae gowd and gear, I hae land enough,
I hae seen good owsen ganging in a pleugh;
Ganging in a pleugh, and linkan o'er the lee,
And gin ye winna tak me, I can let ye be.

I hae a good ha' house, a barn and a byre,
A peatstack 'fore the door, we'll make a rantin fire;
I'll make a rantin fire, and merry sall we be,
And gin ye winna tak me, I can let ye be.

tocher] dowry　　　owsen] oxen　　　linkan] moving

195

ALLAN RAMSAY

Jenny said to *Jocky*, gin ye winna tell,
Ye shall be the lad, I'll be the lass my sell;
Ye're a bony lad, and I'm a lassie free;
Ye're welcomer to tak me, than to let me be.

The Gentle Shepherd, Act iv, 1725

WILLIAM HAMILTON, OF BANGOUR

1704–1754

122   *The Braes of Yarrow*

In imitation of the ancient Scottish manner

A. BUSK ye, busk ye, my bony bony bride,
  Busk ye, busk ye, my winsome marrow,
Busk ye, busk ye, my bony bony bride,
  And think nae mair on the Braes of Yarrow.

B. Where gat ye that bony bony bride?
  Where gat ye that winsome marrow?
A. I gat her where I dare na weil be seen,
  Puing the birks on the Braes of Yarrow.

Weep not, weep not, my bony bony bride,
  Weep not, weep not, my winsome marrow,
Nor let thy heart lament to leave
  Puing the birks on the Braes of Yarrow.

B. Why does she weep, thy bony bony bride?
  Why does she weep, thy winsome marrow?
And why dare ye nae mair weil be seen
  Puing the birks on the Braes of Yarrow?

busk] dress, deck   marrow] mate

196

A. Lang maun she weep, lang maun she, maun she weep,
 Lang maun she weep with dule and sorrow,
And lang maun I nae mair weil be seen
 Puing the birks on the Braes of Yarrow.

For she has tint her luver luver dear,
 Her luver dear, the cause of sorrow,
And I hae slain the comliest swain
 That e'er pu'd birks on the Braes of Yarrow.

Why runs thy stream, O Yarrow, Yarrow red?
 Why on thy braes heard the voice of sorrow?
And why yon melancholeous weids
 Hung on the bony birks of Yarrow!

What yonder floats on the rueful rueful flude?
 What's yonder floats? O dule and sorrow!
'Tis he the comely swain I slew
 Upon the duleful Braes of Yarrow.

Wash, O wash his wounds his wounds in tears,
 His wounds in tears, with dule and sorrow,
And wrap his limbs in mourning weids,
 And lay him on the Braes of Yarrow.

Then build, then build, ye sisters sisters sad,
 Ye sisters sad, his tomb with sorrow,
And weep around in waeful wise,
 His helpless fate on the Braes of Yarrow.

Curse ye, curse ye, his useless useless shield,
 My arm that wrought the deed of sorrow,
The fatal spear that pierc'd his breast,
 His comely breast on the Braes of Yarrow.

     tint] lost

WILLIAM HAMILTON, OF BANGOUR

Did I not warn thee not to, not to lue,
  And warn from fight, but to my sorrow,
O'er rashly bald a stronger arm
  Thou met'st, and fell on the Braes of Yarrow.

Sweet smells the birk, green grows, green grows the grass,
  Yellow on Yarrow's bank the gowan,
Fair hangs the apple frae the rock,
  Sweet the wave of Yarrow flowan.

Flows Yarrow sweet? as sweet, as sweet flows Tweed,
  As green its grass, its gowan yellow,
As sweet smells on its braes the birk,
  The apple frae the rock as mellow.

Fair was thy luve, fair fair indeed thy luve,
  In floury bands thou him did'st fetter,
Tho' he was fair and weil beluv'd again,
  Than me, he never lued thee better.

Busk ye, then busk, my bony bony bride,
  Busk ye, busk ye, my winsome marrow,
Busk ye, and lue me on the banks of Tweed,
  And think nae mair on the Braes of Yarrow.

C. How can I busk a bony bony bride,
  How can I busk a winsome marrow,
How lue him on the banks of Tweed,
  That slew my luve on the Braes of Yarrow?

O Yarrow fields, may never never rain,
  No dew thy tender blossoms cover,
For there was basely slain my luve,
  My luve, as he had not been a lover.

WILLIAM HAMILTON, OF BANGOUR

The boy put on his robes, his robes of green,
  His purple vest, 'twas my awn seuing,
Ah! wretched me! I little little ken'd
  He was in these to meet his ruin.

The boy took out his milk-white milk-white steed,
  Unheedful of my dule and sorrow,
But e'er the toofall of the night
  He lay a corps on the Braes of Yarrow.

Much I rejoic'd that waeful waeful day;
  I sang, my voice the woods returning,
But lang e'er night the spear was flown
  That slew my luve, and left me mourning.

What can my barbarous barbarous father do,
  But with his cruel rage pursue me?
My luver's blood is on thy spear,
  How can'st thou, barbarous man, then woo me?

My happy sisters may be may be proud,
  With cruel, and ungentle scoffin,
May bid me seek on Yarrow Braes
  My luver nailed in his coffin.

My brother Douglas may upbraid,
  And strive with threatning words to muve me,
My luver's blood is on thy spear,
  How can'st thou ever bid me luve thee?

Yes yes, prepare the bed, the bed of luve,
  With bridal sheets my body cover,
Unbar ye bridal maids the door,
  Let in the expected husband lover.
           toofall] oncoming

But who the expected husband husband is?
　His hands, methinks, are bath'd in slaughter,
Ah me! what ghastly spectre's yon,
　Comes, in his pale shroud, bleeding after.

Pale as he is, here lay him lay him down,
　O lay his cold head on my pillow;
Take aff take aff these bridal weids,
　And crown my careful head with willow.

Pale tho' thou art, yet best yet best beluv'd,
　O could my warmth to life restore thee,
Yet lye all night between my briests,
　No youth lay ever there before thee.

Pale pale indeed, O lovely lovely youth,
　Forgive, forgive so foul a slaughter,
And lye all night between my briests,
　No youth shall ever lye there after.

A. Return return, O mournful mournful bride,
　Return and dry thy useless sorrow,
Thy luver heeds nought of thy sighs,
　He lyes a corps on the Braes of Yarrow.

The Tea Table Miscellany, 1724 ; *Poems on*
Several Occasions, 1749

ANONYMOUS

123　*Translation from the Ancient British*

AWAY; let nought to Love displeasing,
　My *Winifreda*, move your Care;
Let nought delay the Heav'nly Blessing,
　Nor squeamish Pride, nor gloomy Fear.

ANONYMOUS

What tho' no Grants of Royal Donors
  With pompous Titles grace our Blood?
We'll shine in more substantial Honours,
  And, to be Noble, we'll be Good.

Our Name, while Virtue thus we tender,
  Will sweetly sound where-e'er 'tis spoke:
And all the Great ones, they shall wonder,
  How they respect such little Folk.

What tho', from Fortune's lavish Bounty,
  No mighty Treasures we possess?
We'll find, within our Pittance, Plenty,
  And be content without Excess.

Still shall each kind returning Season
  Sufficient for our Wishes give:
For we will live a Life of Reason,
  And that's the only Life to live.

Through Youth and Age, in Love excelling,
  We'll Hand in Hand together tread;
Sweet-smiling Peace shall crown our Dwelling,
  And Babes, sweet-smiling Babes, our Bed.

How should I love the pretty Creatures,
  While round my Knees they fondly clung,
To see them look their Mother's Features,
  To hear them lisp their Mother's Tongue!

And, when with Envy Time transported
  Shall think to rob us of our Joys;
You'll, in your Girls, again be courted,
  And I'll go wooing in my Boys.

D. Lewis's Miscellaneous Poems, 1726

124

The Retirement

'TIS weak and worldly to conclude
Retirement all a Solitude;
The Wise and Good will always own,
That Man is never less alone,
Than when alone; 'tis so with Me,
When in my own large Company.

Withdrawn and pensive while I move,
Beneath the Shade of yonder Grove;
Monarchs, that triple Circles wear,
Feel not the Weight of half my Care:
In Sighs and Pray'rs my Soul I bend,
But rise to Transports in the End.

When from the World retir'd apart,
To dress the Temple of my Heart;
To make it beautiful and fair,
Fit for the God residing there:
'Tis then, and only then I live,
Enjoying all this Globe can give.

Think'st thou to treat Almighty Pow'r
Is but the Bus'ness of an Hour?
Or who, that gets so dear a Guest,
But once enshrin'd within his Breast,
Would, for this World's Impertinence,
Neglect him there, or drive him thence?

My *Eden* then be my Abode,
And the great Visitant, my God!
He only my Companion be,
From whom I hope Eternity!

They who below their Heav'n fore-date,
Ne'er dread th' up-lifted Hand of Fate,
Tasting the Glories that shall crown
An endless Life when this is done.

> D. Lewis's *Miscellaneous Poems*, 1730

DAVID LEWIS

1683?–1760

125

When none shall rail

WHILE Malice, *Pope*, denies thy Page
　　It's own celestial Fire;
While Critics, and while Bards in Rage
　　Admiring, won't admire;

While wayward Pens thy Worth assail,
　　And envious Tongues decry,
These Times tho' many a Friend bewail,
　　These Times bewail not I.

But when the World's loud praise is thine,
　　And Spleen no more shall blame,
When with thy *Homer* Thou shalt shine
　　In one establish'd Fame,

When none shall rail, and ev'ry Lay
　　Devote a Wreath to Thee;
That Day (for come it will) that Day
　　Shall I lament to see.

> *Pieces publish'd on occasion of the*
> *Dunciad*, 1732

126   *On the setting up Mr. Butler's Monument
in Westminster-Abbey*

WHILE *Butler*, needy Wretch! was yet alive,
No gen'rous Patron would a Dinner give:
See him, when starv'd to Death and turn'd to Dust,
Presented with a Monumental Bust!
The Poet's Fate is here in Emblem shown;
He ask'd for Bread, and he receiv'd a Stone.

D. Lewis's Miscellaneous Poems, 1726

127   *From a Hint in the Minor Poets*

NO; not for Those of Women born,
Not so unlike the Die is cast;
For, after all our Vaunt and Scorn,
How very small the Odds at last!

Him, rais'd to Fortune's utmost Top,
With Him beneath her Feet compare;
And One has Nothing more to hope,
And One has Nothing more to fear.

D. Lewis's Miscellaneous Poems, 1730

128   *Epigram on Miltonicks*

After the Manner of the Moderns

WHAT makes You write at this odd Rate?
Why, Sirs, it is to imitate.
What makes You rant and ramble so?
Why, 'tis to do as others do.
But there's no Meaning to be seen:
Why, that's the very Thing I mean.

Pieces publish'd on occasion of the Dunciad, 1732;
Poems on Several Occasions, 1736

ABEL EVANS

1679–1737

129   *On Blenheim House*

SEE, Sir, here 's the grand approach,
   This way is for his Grace's coach;
There lies the bridge, and here 's the clock:
Observe the lion and the cock,
The spacious court, the colonade,
And mark how wide the hall is made!
The chimneys are so well design'd,
They never smoke in any wind.
This gallery 's contriv'd for walking,
The windows to retire and talk in;
The council-chamber for debate,
And all the rest are rooms of state.

   Thanks, Sir, cry'd I, 'tis very fine,
But where d' ye sleep, or where d' ye dine?
I find, by all you have been telling,
That 'tis a house, but not a dwelling.

Original Poems and Translations (Curll), 1714

130   *On Sir John Vanbrugh*

An Epigrammatical Epitaph

UNDER this stone, Reader, survey
   Dead Sir John Vanbrugh's house of clay.
Lie heavy on him, Earth! for he
Laid many heavy loads on thee!

Hackett's *Epitaphs*, i, 1754; Nichols's
Select Collection, iii, 1780

131   *Time's Changes*

LIKE *South-Sea Stock*, Expressions rise and fall:
   King *Edward*'s Words are now no Words at all.
Did ought your Predecessors Genius cramp?
Sure ev'ry Reign may have its proper Stamp.
All Sublunary things of Death partake;
What Alteration does a Cent'ry make?
Kings and Comedians all are mortal found,
Cæsar and *Pinkethman* are under Ground.
What's not destroy'd by Time's devouring Hand?
Where's *Troy*, and where's the *May-Pole* in the *Strand?*
Pease, Cabbages, and Turnips once grew, where
Now stands new *Bond-street*, and a newer Square;
Such Piles of Buildings now rise up and down;
London itself seems going out of *Town*.
Our Fathers cross'd from *Fulham* in a Wherry,
Their Sons enjoy a Bridge at *Putney-Ferry*.
Think we that modern Words eternal are?
Toupet, and *Tompion*, *Cosins*, and *Colmar*
Hereafter will be call'd by some plain Man
A *Wig*, a *Watch*, a *Pair of Stays*, a *Fan*.
To Things themselves if Time such change affords,
Can there be any trusting to our Words?

   .   .   .   .

   When *James* the *first*, at great *Britannia*'s helm,
Rul'd this word-clipping and word-coining Realm,
No words to Royal favour made pretence,
But what agreed in sound and clash'd in sense.

   Pinkethman] Comic actor at Drury Lane Theatre.

JAMES BRAMSTON

Thrice happy he! how great that Speaker's praise,
Whose ev'ry Period look'd an hundred ways.
What then? we now with just abhorrence shun
The trifling Quibble, and the School-boy's Pun;
Tho' no great Connoisseur, I make a shift
Just to find out a *Durfey* from a *Swift*;
I can discern with half an eye, I hope,
Mist from *Jo Addison*, from *Eusden Pope*:
I know a Farce from one of *Congreve*'s Plays,
And *Cibber*'s Opera from *Johnny Gay*'s.

The Art of Politicks, 1729

JAMES MILLER

1706–1744

132   *Italian Opera*

IN Days of Old, when *Englishmen* were—*Men*,
  Their Musick, like themselves, was grave and plain;
The manly Trumpet, and the simple Reed,
Alike with *Citizen* and *Swain* agreed;
Whose Songs, in lofty Sense, but humble Verse,
Their Loves and Wars alternately rehearse;
Sung by themselves, their homely Cheer to crown,
In Tunes from Sire to Son deliver'd down.

But now, since *Britains* are become polite,
Since Few can *read*, and Fewer still can *write*;
Since Trav'ling has so much improv'd our *Beaux*,
That each brings home a foreign *Tongue*, or—*Nose*;
And Ladies paint with that amazing Grace,
That their best *Vizard* is their natural *Face*;
Since *South-Sea Schemes* have so inrich'd the Land,
That *Footmen* 'gainst their *Lords* for *Boroughs* stand;

Since *Masquerades* and *Op'ras* made their Entry,
And *Heydegger* reign'd *Guardian* of our Gentry;
A hundred various Instruments combine,
And foreign *Songsters* in the Concert join:
The *Gallick Horn,* whose winding Tube in vain
Pretends to emulate the *Trumpet's* Strain;
The *shrill-ton'd Fiddle,* and the *warbling Flute,*
The *grave Bassoon, deep Base,* and *tinkling Lute,*
The *jingling Spinnet,* and the *full-mouth'd Drum,*
A *Roman Capon,* and *Venetian Strum,*
All league, melodious Nonsense to dispense,
And give us *Sound,* and *Show,* instead of *Sense;*
In unknown Tongues mysterious Dullness chant,
Make Love in *Tune,* or *thro' the Gamut rant.*

*Harlequin-Horace ; or, The Art of
Modern Poetry,* 1731

133 *The Life of a Beau*

HOW brim-full of *nothing's* the Life of a *Beau!*
They've *nothing* to think of, they've *nothing* to do;
Nor they've *nothing* to talk of, for—*nothing* they know:
    Such, such is the Life of a *Beau.*

For *nothing* they rise, but to draw the fresh Air;
Spend the Morning in *nothing* but curling their Hair;
And do *nothing* all Day but Sing, Santer and Stare:
    Such, such is the Life of a *Beau.*

For *nothing* at Night to the Playhouse they croud,
For to mind *nothing* done there they always are proud,
But to bow, and to grin, and talk—*nothing* aloud:
    Such, such is the Life of a *Beau.*

Heydegger] Operatic manager at the Haymarket.
208

For *nothing* they run to th' Assembly and Ball;
And for *nothing* at Cards a fair Partner call,
For they still must be *beasted* who've—*Nothing* at all:
    Such, such is the Life of a *Beau*.

For *nothing* on *Sundays* at Church they appear,
For they've *nothing* to hope, nor they've *nothing* to fear;
They can be *nothing* no where, who—*nothing* are here:
    Such, such is the Life of a *Beau*.

The Coffee House, 1737

RICHARD SAVAGE

1698–1743

134   *The Bastard's Lot*

IN Gayer Hours, when high my Fancy run,
  The Muse, Exulting, thus her Lay begun.
  Blest be the *Bastard*'s Birth! thro' wond'rous ways
He shines excentric like a Comet's Blaze!
No sickly Fruit of faint Compliance He!
He! stampt in Nature's Mint of Extacy!
He lives to build, not boast a generous Race:
No Tenth Transmitter of a foolish Face.
His daring Hope, no Sire's Example Bounds;
His First-born Lights no Prejudice Confounds.
He, kindling from within, requires no Flame;
He glories in a *Bastard*'s glowing Name.
  Born to himself, by no Possession led,
In Freedom foster'd, and by Fortune fed;
Nor Guides, nor Rules, his Sov'reign Choice controul,
His Body Independent, as his Soul.
Loos'd to the World's wide Range,—enjoyn'd no Aim
Prescrib'd no Duty, and assign'd no Name:

       beasted] beaten *or* penalized.

Nature's unbounded Son, he stands alone,
His Heart unbyass'd, and his Mind his own.

O *Mother*, yet *no* Mother!—'tis to you
My Thanks for such distinguish'd Claims are due.
You, unenslav'd to Nature's narrow Laws,
Warm Championess for *Freedom*'s Sacred Cause,
From all the dry Devoirs of Blood and Line,
From Ties Maternal, Moral and Divine,
Discharg'd my grasping Soul; push'd me from Shore,
And launch'd me into Life without an Oar.

What had I lost, if Conjugally kind,
By Nature hating, yet by Vows confin'd,
Untaught the Matrimonial Bounds to slight,
And coldly Conscious of a Husband's Right,
You had *faint-drawn* me with a Form alone,
A Lawful Lump of Life by Force your own!
Then, while your backward Will retrench'd Desire,
And unconcurring Spirits lent no Fire,
I had been born your dull, domestic *Heir*;
Load of your Life, and Motive of your Care;
Perhaps been poorly Rich, and meanly Great;
The Slave of Pomp, a Cypher in the State;
Lordly neglectful of a Worth unknown,
And slumb'ring in a *Seat*, by Chance my own.

Far nobler Blessings wait the *Bastard*'s Lot;
Conceiv'd in Rapture, and with Fire begot!
Strong as Necessity, he starts away,
Climbs against Wrongs, and brightens into Day.

Thus Unprophetic, lately misinspir'd,
I sang: Gay flatt'ring Hope my Fancy fir'd;
Inly secure, thro' conscious Scorn of Ill,
Nor taught by Wisdom, how to bailance Will,

Rashly deceiv'd, I saw no Pits to shun;
But thought to *purpose*, and to *act* were *One*;
Heedless what pointed Cares pervert his Way,
Whom Caution arms not, and whom Woes betray;
But now expos'd and shrinking from Distress,
I flie to Shelter, while the Tempests press;
My Muse to Grief resigns the varying Tone,
The Raptures languish, and the Numbers groan.

The Bastard, 1728

135   *To a Young Lady*

POLLY, from me, tho' now a love-sick youth,
  Nay, tho' a poet, hear the voice of truth!
Polly, you're not a beauty, yet you're pretty;
So grave, yet gay; so silly, yet so witty;
A heart of softness, yet a tongue of satire;
You've cruelty, yet, ev'n in that, good-nature:
Now you are free, and now reserv'd a while;
Now a forc'd frown betrays a willing smile.
Reproach'd for absence, yet your sight deny'd;
My tongue you silence, yet my silence chide.
How wou'd you praise me, shou'd your sex defame!
Yet, shou'd they praise, grow jealous, and exclaim.
If I despair, with some kind look you bless;
But if I hope, at once all hope suppress.
You scorn; yet shou'd my passion change or fail,
Too late you'd whimper out a softer tale.
You love; yet from your lover's wish retire;
Doubt, yet discern; deny, and yet desire,
Such, *Polly*, are your sex—part truth, part fiction,
Some thought, much whim, and all a contradiction.

The Gentleman's Magazine, August 1733 and March 1734

1689–1762

136 *The Lover: A Ballad*

AT length, by so much importunity press'd,
Take, C——, at once, the inside of my breast;
This stupid indiff'rence so often you blame,
Is not owing to nature, to fear, or to shame:
I am not as cold as a virgin in lead,
Nor is Sunday's sermon so strong in my head:
I know but too well how Time flies along,
That we live but few years, and yet fewer are young.

But I hate to be cheated, and never will buy
Long years of repentance for moments of joy.
Oh! was there a man (but where shall I find
Good sense and good nature so equally join'd?)
Would value his pleasure, contribute to mine;
Not meanly would boast, nor would lewdly design;
Not over severe, yet not stupidly vain,
For I would have the power, tho' not give the pain.

No pedant, yet learned; no rake-helly gay,
Or laughing, because he has nothing to say;
To all my whole sex obliging and free,
Yet never be fond of any but me;
In public preserve the decorum that's just,
And shew in his eyes he is true to his trust;
Then rarely approach, and respectfully bow,
But not fulsomely pert, nor yet foppishly low.

But when the long hours of public are past,
And we meet with champagne and a chicken at last,
May ev'ry fond pleasure that moment endear;
Be banish'd afar both discretion and fear!

212

Forgetting or scorning the airs of the crowd,
He may cease to be formal, and I to be proud,
'Till lost in the joy, we confess that we live,
And he may be rude, and yet I may forgive.

And that my delight may be solidly fix'd,
Let the friend and the lover be handsomely mix'd;
In whose tender bosom my soul may confide,
Whose kindness can sooth me, whose counsel can guide.
From such a dear lover as here I describe,
No danger should fright me, no millions should bribe;
But till this astonishing creature I know,
As I long have liv'd chaste, I will keep myself so.

I never will share with the wanton coquet,
Or be caught by a vain affectation of wit.
The toasters and songsters may try all their art,
But never shall enter the pass of my heart.
I loath the lewd rake, the dress'd fopling despise:
Before such pursuers the nice virgin flies:
And as OVID has sweetly in parable told,
We harden like trees, and like rivers grow cold.

Six Town Eclogues, 1747

137 *In Answer to a Lady who advised Retirement*

YOU little know the heart that you advise;
I view this various scene with equal eyes:
In crowded courts I find myself alone,
And pay my worship to a nobler throne.
Long since the value of this world I know,
Pity the madness, and despise the show.

Well as I can my tedious part I bear,
And wait for my dismission without fear.
Seldom I mark mankind's detested ways,
Not hearing censure, nor affecting praise;
And, unconcern'd, my future state I trust
To that sole Being, merciful and just.

The London Magazine, May 1750

EDWARD YOUNG

1683·-1765

138 *Characters of Women*
The Languid Lady

THE *languid* lady next appears in state,
 Who was not born to carry her own weight;
She lolls, reels, staggers, 'till some foreign aid
To her own stature lifts the feeble maid.
Then, if ordain'd to so *severe* a doom,
She, by just stages, *journeys* round the room:
But knowing her own weakness, she despairs
To scale the *Alps*—that is, ascend the *stairs*.
My fan! let others say who laugh at toil;
Fan! hood! glove! scarf! is her *laconick* style.
And that is spoke with such a dying fall,
That *Betty* rather *sees*, than *hears* the call:
The motion of her lips, and meaning eye
Piece out the Idea her faint words deny.
O listen with attention most profound!
Her voice is but the shadow of a sound.
And help! O help! her spirits are so dead,
One hand scarce lifts the other to her head
If, there, a stubborn pin it triumphs o'er,
She pants! she sinks away! and is no more.

Let the robust, and the gygantick *carve*,
Life is not worth so much, she'd rather *starve*;
But *chew* she must herself, ah cruel fate!
That *Rosalinda* can't by *proxy* eat.

The Manly Lady

Thalestris triumphs in a manly mein,
Loud in her accent, and her phrase obscene.
In fair and open dealing where's the shame?
What nature dares to *give*, she dares to *name*.
This *honest fellow* is sincere, and plain,
And justly gives the jealous husband pain.
(Vain is the task to Petticoats assign'd,
If wanton language shews a *naked* mind.)
And now and then, to grace her eloquence,
An oath supplies the vacancys of sense.
Hark! the shrill notes transpierce the yielding air,
And teach the neighb'ring ecchos how to swear
By *Jove*, is faint, and for the simple swain;
She, on the christian System, is prophane.
But tho' the volly rattles in your ear,
Believe her *dress*, she's not a granadeer.
If thunder's awful, how much more our dread,
When *Jove* deputes a Lady in his stead
A *Lady!* pardon my mistaken pen,
A shameless woman is the worst of *Men*.

The Modern Maid

Few to good-breeding make a just pretence,
Good-breeding is the blossom of good sense;
The last result of an accomplisht mind,
With outward grace, the *body's virtue*, join'd.

A violated decency, now, reigns;
And Nymphs for *failings* take peculiar pains.
With *Indian* painters modern *toasts* agree,
The point they aim at is *deformity*:
They *throw* their persons with a hoydon-air
Across the room, and *toss* into the chair.
So far their commerce with mankind is gone,
They, for our manners, have exchang'd their own.
The modest look, the castigated grace,
The gentle movement, and slow-measur'd pace,
For which her lovers *dy'd*, her parents *pay'd*,
Are indecorums with the *modern* maid.
Stiff forms are bad, but let not worse intrude,
Nor conquer *art*, and *nature*, to be rude.

Love of Fame, Satire V, 1725

139

Night

TIR'D nature's sweet Restorer, balmy *Sleep!*
He, like the World, his ready visit pays,
Where Fortune smiles; the wretched he forsakes:
Swift on his downy pinion flies from Woe,
And lights on Lids unsully'd with a Tear.

From short, (as usual) and disturb'd Repose,
I wake: How happy they who wake no more!
Yet that were vain, if Dreams infest the Grave.
I wake, emerging from a sea of Dreams
Tumultuous; where my wreck'd, desponding Thought
From wave to wave of *fancy'd* Misery,
At random drove, her helm of Reason lost;
Tho' now restor'd, 'tis only Change of pain,
A bitter change; severer for severe:
The *Day* too short for my Distress! and *Night*

Even in the *Zenith* of her dark Domain,
Is Sun-shine, to the colour of my Fate.

 Night, sable Goddess! from her *Ebon* throne,
In rayless Majesty, now stretches forth
Her leaden Scepter o'er a slumbering world:
Silence, how dead? and Darkness how profound?
Nor Eye, nor list'ning Ear an Object finds;
Creation sleeps. 'Tis, as the general Pulse
Of life stood still, and Nature made a Pause;
An aweful pause! prophetic of her End.

   .   .   .   .

 The Bell strikes *One* : We take no note of Time,
But from its Loss. To give it then a Tongue,
Is wise in man. As if an Angel spoke,
I feel the solemn Sound. If heard aright,
It is the *Knell* of my departed Hours;
Where are they? with the years beyond the Flood:
It is the *Signal* that demands Dispatch;
How Much is to be done? my Hopes and Fears
Start up alarm'd, and o'er life's narrow Verge
Look down—on what? a fathomless Abyss;
A dread Eternity! how surely *mine !*
And can Eternity belong to me,
Poor Pensioner on the bounties of an Hour?

          Night Thoughts, i, 1742

140   *Procrastination*

BE wise to day, 'tis madness to defer;
 Next day the fatal Precedent will plead;
Thus on, till Wisdom is push'd out of life:
Procrastination is the Thief of Time,

Year after year it steals, till all are fled,
And to the mercies of a Moment leaves
The vast Concerns of an Eternal scene.
If not so frequent, would not This be strange?
That 'tis so frequent, *This* is stranger still.

Of Man's miraculous Mistakes, This bears
The Palm, ' That all Men are about to live.'
For ever on the Brink of being born:
All pay themselves the compliment to think
They, one day, shall not drivel; and their Pride
On this Reversion takes up ready Praise;
At least, their own; their future selves applauds;
How excellent that Life they *ne'er* will lead?
Time lodg'd in their *own* hands is *Folly*'s Vails;
That lodg'd in *Fate*'s, to *Wisdom* they consign;
The thing they can't but *purpose*, they *postpone*;
'Tis not in *Folly*, not to scorn a Fool;
And scarce in human *Wisdom* to do more:
All *Promise* is poor dilatory man,
And that thro' every Stage: When young, indeed,
In full content, we sometimes nobly rest,
Unanxious for ourselves; and only wish,
As duteous sons, our Fathers were more Wise:
At *thirty* man *suspects* himself a Fool;
Knows it at *forty*, and reforms his Plan;
At *fifty* chides his infamous Delay,
Pushes his prudent Purpose to *Resolve*;
In all the magnanimity of Thought
Resolves; and re-resolves: then dies the same.

Night Thoughts, i, 1742

EDWARD YOUNG

141   *Happiness an Art*

NO Man e'er found a *happy Life* by Chance,
 Or yawn'd it into Being, with a Wish;
Or, with the Snout of grov'ling *Appetite*,
E'er smelt it out, and grubb'd it from the Dirt;
An *Art* it is, and must be learnt; and learnt
With unremitting Effort, or be lost;
And leave us perfect Blockheads, in our Bliss:
The Clouds may drop down Titles, and Estates;
Wealth may seek Us; but *Wisdom* must be Sought;
Sought before All; but (how unlike All else
We seek on Earth?) 'tis never sought in vain.

Night Thoughts, viii, 1745

GEORGE BERKELEY, BISHOP OF CLOYNE

1685–1753

142   *Verses on the Prospect of planting Arts*
and Learning in America

THE Muse, disgusted at an age and clime
 Barren of every glorious theme,
In distant lands now waits a better time,
 Producing subjects worthy fame:

In happy climes, where from the genial sun
 And virgin earth such scenes ensue,
The force of art by nature seems outdone,
 And fancied beauties by the true:

In happy climes the seat of innocence,
 Where nature guides and virtue rules,
Where men shall not impose for truth and sense,
 The pedantry of courts and schools:

219

There shall be sung another golden age,
　　The rise of empire and of arts,
The good and great inspiring epic rage,
　　The wisest heads and noblest hearts.

Not such as Europe breeds in her decay;
　　Such as she bred when fresh and young,
When heav'nly flame did animate her clay,
　　By future poets shall be sung.

Westward the course of empire takes its way;
　　The four first acts already past,
A fifth shall close the drama with the day;
　　Time's noblest offspring is the last.

Dodsley's Collection, vi, 1758

JOHN BYROM

1692–1763

143　　　　*A Pastoral*

MY Time, O ye Muses, was happily spent,
　　When *Phebe* went with me wherever I went;
Ten thousand sweet Pleasures I felt in my Breast:
Sure never fond Shepherd like *Colin* was blest!
But now she is gone, and has left me behind,
What a marvellous Change on a sudden I find!
When Things were as fine as could possibly be,
I thought 'twas the Spring; but alas! it was she.

　　With such a Companion to tend a few Sheep,
To rise up and play, or to lie down and sleep,
I was so good-humour'd, so chearful and gay,
My Heart was as light as a Feather all Day.

220

But now I so cross and so peevish am grown,
So strangely uneasy as never was known.
My Fair one is gone, and my Joys are all drown'd,
And my Heart—I am sure it weighs more than a Pound.

The Fountain that wont to run sweetly along,
And dance to soft Murmurs the Pebbles among,
Thou know'st, little *Cupid*, if *Phebe* was there,
'Twas Pleasure to look at, 'twas Musick to hear:
But now she is absent, I walk by its Side,
And still as it murmurs do nothing but chide,
Must you be so chearful, while I go in Pain?
Peace there with your Bubbling, and hear me complain.

When my Lambkins around me would oftentime play,
And when *Phebe* and I were as joyful as they,
How pleasant their Sporting, how happy the Time,
When Spring, Love, and Beauty, were all in their Prime!
But now in their Frolicks when by me they pass,
I fling at their Fleeces an handful of Grass;
Be still then, I cry, for it makes me quite mad
To see you so merry, while I am so sad.

My dog I was ever well pleased to see
Come wagging his Tail to my fair one and me;
And *Phebe* was pleas'd too, and to my Dog said,
Come hither, poor Fellow; and patted his Head.
But now, when he's fawning, I with a sour Look
Cry, Sirrah; and give him a Blow with my Crook:
And I'll give him another; for why should not *Tray*
Be as dull as his Master, when *Phebe*'s away?

JOHN BYROM

When walking with *Phebe*, what Sights have I seen?
How fair was the Flower, how fresh was the Green?
What a lovely appearance the Trees and the Shade,
The Corn-fields and Hedges, and ev'ry thing made?
But now she has left me, tho' all are still there,
They none of 'em now so delightful appear:
'Twas nought but the Magick, I find, of her Eyes,
Made so many beautiful Prospects arise.

Sweet Musick went with us both all the Wood thro',
The Lark, Linnet, Throstle, and Nightingale too;
Winds over us whisper'd, Flocks by us did bleat,
And chirp went the Grasshopper under our Feet.
But now she is absent, tho' still they sing on,
The Woods are but lonely, the Melody's gone:
Her Voice in the Consort, as now I have found
Gave ev'ry thing else its agreeable Sound.

Rose, what is become of thy delicate Hue?
And where is the Violet's beautiful Blue?
Does ought of its Sweetness the Blossom beguile,
That Meadow, those Daisies, why do they not smile?
Ah! Rivals, I see what it was that you drest,
And made your selves fine for; a Place in her Breast:
You put on your Colours to pleasure her Eye,
To be pluckt by her Hand, on her Bosom to die.

How slowly Time creeps till my *Phebe* return!
While amidst the soft Zephyrs, cool Breezes, I burn;
Methinks if I knew whereabouts he would tread,
I could breathe on his Wings, and 'twould melt down the
     Lead.

222

Fly swifter, ye Minutes, bring hither my Dear,
And rest so much longer for't when she is here.
Ah *Colin !* old Time is full of Delay,
Nor will budge one Foot faster for all thou canst say.

Will no pitying Power that hears me complain,
Or cure my Disquiet, or soften my Pain?
To be cur'd, thou must, *Colin*, thy Passion remove;
But what Swain is so silly to live without Love?
No, Deity, bid the dear Nymph to return,
For ne'er was poor Shepherd so sadly forlorn.
Ah! What shall I do? I shall die with Despair;
Take Heed, all ye Swains, how you love one so fair.

The Spectator, October 6, **1714**

144 *Epigram on Handel and Bononcini*

SOME say, compar'd to *Bononcini*
That Mynheer *Handel*'s but a Ninny;
Others aver, that he to *Handel*
Is scarcely fit to hold a *Candle*.
Strange all this Difference should be
'Twixt Tweedle-*dum* and Tweedle-*dee* !

Written 1725 ; Swift's *Miscellanies,* 1728

145 *Extempore Verses*

Intended to allay the Violence of Party-Spirit

GOD bless the King, I mean the Faith's Defender;
God bless—no Harm in blessing—the Pretender:
But who Pretender is, or who is King,
God bless us all—that's quite another Thing.

Miscellaneous Poems, 1773

*146   Extempore Verses Upon a Trial of Skill
between the Two Great Masters of the Noble
Science of Defence, Messrs. Figg and Sutton*

LONG was the great *Figg* by the prize fighting Swains
    Sole Monarch acknowledg'd of *Marybone* Plains;
To the Towns, far and near, did his Valour extend,
And swam down the River from *Thame* to *Gravesend*;
Where liv'd Mr. *Sutton*, Pipe-maker by Trade,
Who, hearing that *Figg* was thought such a stout Blade,
Resolv'd to put in for a Share of his Fame,
And so sent to challenge the Champion of *Thame*.

With alternate Advantage two Tryals had past,
When they fought out the Rubbers on *Wednesday* last.
To see such a Contest the House was so full,
There hardly was room left to thrust in your Skull.
With a Prelude of Cudgels we first were saluted,
And two or three Shoulders most handsomely fluted;
'Till, wearied at last with inferior Disasters,
All the Company cry'd, *Come, the Masters, the Masters.*

Whereupon the bold *Sutton* first mounted the Stage,
Made his Honours, as usual, and yearn'd to engage;
Then *Figg*, with a Visage so fierce and sedate,
Came and enter'd the List with his fresh-shaven Pate;
Their Arms were encircled by Armigers two,
With a red Ribbon *Sutton*'s and *Figg*'s with a blue.
Thus adorn'd, the two Heroes, 'twixt Shoulder and Elbow,
Shook Hands, and went to't, and the Word it was *Bilbo*.

JOHN BYROM

Sure such a Concern in the Eyes of Spectators
Was never yet seen in our Amphitheatres:
Our Commons, and Peers, from their several Places,
To half an Inch Distance all pointed their Faces;
While the Rays of old *Phœbus*, that shot thro' the Sky-light,
Seem'd to make on the Stage a new kind of Twilight;
And the Gods, without doubt, if one could but have seen 'em,
Were peeping there thro' to do Justice between 'em.

Figg struck the first Stroke, and with such a vast Fury,
That he broke his huge Weapon in Twain, I assure you;
And, if his brave Rival this Blow had not warded,
His Head from his Shoulders had quite been discarded.
Figg arm'd him again, and they took t'other Tilt,
And then *Sutton*'s Blade run away from its Hilt.
The Weapons were frighted, but as for the Men,
In Truth they ne'er minded, but at it again.

Such a Force in their Blows, you'd have thought it a
    Wonder
Every Stroke they receiv'd did not cleave them asunder;
Yet so great was their Courage, so equal their Skill,
That they both seem'd as safe as a Thief in a Mill:
While in doubtful Attention Dame *Victory* stood,
And which Side to take could not tell for her Blood,
But remain'd, like the Ass 'twixt two Bottles of Hay,
Without ever moving an Inch either way.

Till *Jove*, to the Gods, signified his Intention,
In a Speech that he made them, too tedious to mention;
But the Upshot on't was, that, at that very Bout,
From a Wound in *Figg*'s Side the hot Blood spouted out.

Her Ladyship then seem'd to think the Case plain;
But *Figg* stepping forth with a sullen disdain,
Shew'd the Gash, and appeal'd to the Company round,
If his own broken Sword had not given him the Wound?

That Bruises and Wounds a Man's Spirit should touch,
With Danger so little, with Honour so much!—
Well, they both took a Dram, and return'd to the Battle,
And with a fresh Fury they made the Swords rattle;
While *Sutton*'s Right Arm was observed to bleed,
By a Touch from his Rival; so *Jove* had decreed;
Just enough for to shew that his Blood was not Icor,
But made up, like *Figg*'s, of the common red Liquor.

Again they both rush'd with so equal a Fire on,
That the Company cry'd,—*Hold, enough of cold Iron.*
To the Quarter Staff, now Lads.—So first having dram'd it,
They took to their Wood, and i'faith never sham'd it:
The first Bout they had was so fair, and so handsome,
That to make a fair Bargain, 'twas worth a King's Ransom;
And *Sutton* such Bangs to his Neighbour imparted,
Wou'd have made any Fibres but *Figg*'s to have smarted.

Then after that Bout they went on to another,
But the Matter must end on some Fashion or other;
So *Jove* told the Gods he had made a Decree,
That *Figg* should hit *Sutton* a stroke on the Knee.
Tho' *Sutton* disabled, as soon as he hit him,
Wou'd still have fought on, but *Jove* wou'd not permit him;
'Twas his Fate, not his Fault, that constrain'd him to yield,
And thus the great *Figg* became Lord of the Field.

Now, after such Men, who can bear to be told
Of your *Roman* and *Greek* puny Heroes of old?

To compare such poor Dogs as *Alcides* and *Theseus*
To *Sutton* and *Figg* would be very facetious.
Were *Hector* himself, with *Apollo* to back him,
To encounter with *Sutton*,—zooks, how he would thwack
    him!
Or *Achilles*, tho' old Mother *Thetis* had dipt him,
With *Figg*—odds my Life, how he would have unript him!

  To *Cæsar*, and *Pompey*, for want of Things juster,
We compare these brave Boys, but 'twill never pass Muster:
Did those mighty Fellows e'er fight Hand to Fist once?
No, I thank you; they kept at a suitable Distance.
What is *Pompey* the Great, with his Armour begirt,
To the much greater *Sutton*, who fought in his Shirt?
Or is *Figg* to be pair'd with a Cap-a-pee Roman,
Who scorn'd any Fence but a jolly Abdomen?

                    Written 1725 ; *Miscellaneous Poems*, 1773

147   *Careless Content*

I AM Content, I do not care,
  Wag as it will the World for me;
When Fuss and Fret was all my Fare,
    It got no ground, as I could see:
So when away my Caring went,
I counted Cost, and was Content.

With more of Thanks, and less of Thought,
  I strive to make my Matters meet;
To seek what ancient Sages sought,
    Physic and Food, in sour and sweet:
To take what passes in good Part,
And keep the Hiccups from the Heart.

JOHN BYROM

With good and gentle-humour'd Hearts
    I choose to chat where e'er I come,
Whate'er the Subject be that starts;
    But if I get among the Glum,
I hold my Tongue to tell the Troth,
And keep my Breath to cool my Broth.

For Chance or Change, of Peace or Pain,
    For Fortune's Favour, or her Frown,
For Lack or Glut, for Loss or Gain,
    I never dodge, nor up nor down:
But swing what Way the Ship shall swim,
Or tack about, with equal Trim.

I suit not where I shall not speed,
    Nor trace the Turn of ev'ry Tide;
If simple Sense will not succeed,
    I make no Bustling, but abide:
For shining Wealth, or scaring Woe,
I force no Friend, I fear no Foe.

Of *Ups* and *Downs*, of *Ins* and *Outs*,
    Of *they're i' th' wrong*, and *we're i' th' right*,
I shun the Rancours, and the Routs,
    And wishing well to every Wight,
Whatever Turn the Matter takes,
I deem it all but Ducks and Drakes.

With whom I feast I do not fawn,
    Nor if the Folks should flout me, faint
If wonted Welcome be withdrawn,
    I cook no Kind of a Complaint,
With none dispos'd to disagree,
But like them best, who best like me.

JOHN BYROM

Not that I rate myself the Rule
   How all my Betters should behave;
But Fame shall find me no Man's Fool,
   Nor to a Set of Men a Slave:
I love a Friendship free and frank,
And hate to hang upon a Hank.

Fond of a true and trusty Tie,
   I never loose where'er I link;
Tho' if a Bus'ness budges by,
   I talk thereon just as I think:
My Word, my Work, my Heart, my Hand,
Still on a Side together stand.

If Names or Notions make a noise,
   Whatever Hap the Question hath,
The Point impartially I poise,
   And read, or write, but without Wrath;
For should I burn or break my Brains,
Pray, who will pay me for my Pains?

I love my Neighbour as myself,
   Myself like him too, by his Leave;
Nor to his Pleasure, Pow'r, or Pelf,
   Came I to crouch, as I conceive:
Dame Nature doubtless has design'd
A Man the Monarch of his Mind.

Now taste and try this Temper, Sirs,
   Mood it, and brood it in your Breast;
Or if ye ween, for worldly Stirs,
   That Man does right to mar his Rest,
Let me be deft, and debonair:
I am Content, I do not care.

Miscellaneous Poems, 1773

JOHN BYROM

148 Contentment, or The Happy Workman's Song

I AM a poor Workman as rich as a *Jew*,
  A strange sort of Tale, but however 'tis true;
Come listen a while, and I'll prove it to you
  So as No-body can deny, &c.

I am a poor Workman, you'll easily grant,
And I'm rich as a *Jew*, for there's nothing I want,
I have Meat, Drink, and Cloaths, and am hearty and cant,
  Which No-body can deny, &c.

I live in a Cottage, and yonder it stands,
And while I can work with these two honest Hands,
I'm as happy as they that have Houses and Lands,
  Which No-body can deny, &c.

I keep to my Workmanship all the Day long,
I sing and I whistle, and this is my Song,
Thank God, that has made me so lusty and strong,
  Which No-body can deny, &c.

I never am greedy of delicate Fare,
If he give me enough, tho' 'tis never so bare,
The more is his Love, and the less is my Care,
  Which No-body can deny, &c.

My Cloaths on a working day looken but lean,
But when I can dress me——on Sundays, I mean,
Tho' cheap, they are warm, and tho' coarse, they are clean.
  Which No-body can deny, &c.

•   •   •   •   •   •   •   •

cant] hale, lively

With Quarrels o' th' Country, and Matters of State,
With *Tories* and *Whigs*, I ne'er puzzle my Pate;
There's some that I love, and there's none that I hate,
Which No-body can deny, &c.

What tho' my Condition be ever so coarse,
I strive to embrace it for better and worse,
And my Heart, I thank God, is as light as my Purse,
Which No-body can deny, &c.

In short, my Condition, whatever it be,
'Tis God that appoints it, as far as I see,
And I'm sure I can never do better than he,
Which No-body can deny, &c.
Miscellaneous Works, 1773

149   *Hymn for Christmas Day*

CHRISTIANS awake, salute the happy Morn,
Whereon the SAVIOUR of the World was born;
Rise, to adore the Mystery of Love,
Which Hosts of Angels chanted from above:
With them the joyful Tidings first begun
Of GOD incarnate, and the Virgin's Son:
Then to the watchful Shepherds it was told,
Who heard th' Angelic Herald's Voice——*Behold !*
I bring good Tidings of a SAVIOUR'S *Birth*
To you, and all the Nations upon Earth ;
This Day hath GOD *fulfill'd his promis'd Word ;*
This Day is born a SAVIOUR, CHRIST, *the* LORD :
In David's *City, Shepherds, ye shall find*
The long foretold Redeemer of Mankind ;
Wrapt up in swaddling Cloaths, the Babe divine
Lies in a Manger ; this shall be your Sign.
He spake, and straightway the Celestial Choir,

JOHN BYROM

In Hymns of Joy, unknown before, conspire:
The Praises of redeeming Love they sung,
And Heav'ns whole Orb with Hallelujahs rung:
GOD's highest Glory was their Anthem still;
Peace upon Earth, and mutual Good-will.
To *Bethlehem* straight th' enlightened Shepherds ran,
To see the Wonder GOD had wrought for Man;
And found, with *Joseph* and the blessed Maid,
Her Son, the SAVIOUR, in a Manger laid.
Amaz'd, the wond'rous Story they proclaim;
The first Apostles of his Infant Fame:
While *Mary* keeps, and ponders in her Heart,
The heav'nly Vision, which the Swains impart;
They to their Flocks, still praising GOD, return,
And their glad Hearts within their Bosoms burn.

Let us, like these good Shepherds then, employ
Our grateful Voices to proclaim the Joy:
Like *Mary*, let us ponder in our Mind
GOD's wond'rous Love in saving lost Mankind;
Artless, and watchful, as these favour'd Swains,
While Virgin Meekness in the Heart remains:
Trace we the Babe, who has retriev'd our Loss,
From his poor Manger to his bitter Cross;
Treading his Steps, assisted by his Grace,
'Till Man's first heav'nly State again takes Place:
Then may we hope, th' Angelic Thrones among,
To sing, redeem'd, a glad triumphal Song:
He that was born, upon this joyful Day,
Around us all, his Glory shall display;
Sav'd by his Love, incessant we shall sing
Of Angels, and of Angel-Men, the King.

Written about 1750; *Miscellaneous Poems*, 1773

150 *The Desponding Soul's Wish*

MY Spirit longeth for thee,
  Within my troubled Breast;
Altho' I be unworthy
  Of so divine a Guest.

Of so divine a Guest,
  Unworthy tho' I be;
Yet has my Heart no Rest,
  Unless it come from Thee.

Unless it come from Thee,
  In vain I look around;
In all that I can see,
  No Rest is to be found.

No Rest is to be found,
  But in thy blessed Love;
O! let my Wish be crown'd,
  And send it from above!

Miscellaneous Poems, 1773

COLLEY CIBBER

1671–1757

151 *The Blind Boy*

O SAY! what is that Thing call'd Light,
  Which I can ne'er enjoy;
What is the Blessing of the Sight,
  O tell your poor Blind Boy!

You talk of wond'rous Things you see,
  You say the Sun shines bright;
I feel him warm, but how can he
  Then make it Day or Night?

COLLEY CIBBER

My Day or Night myself I make,
    Whene'er I wake or play,
And cou'd I ever keep awake,
    It wou'd be always Day.

With heavy Sighs, I often hear,
    You mourn my hopeless Woe;
But sure, with Patience I may bear
    A Loss I ne'er can know.

Then let not what I cannot have
    My Chear of Mind destroy;
Whilst thus I sing, I am a King,
    Altho' a poor Blind Boy.
            The British Musical Miscellany, i, 1734

BARTON BOOTH

1681–1733

152   *Song*

SWEET are the Charms of her I love,
    More fragrant than the Damask Rose;
Soft as the Down on Turtle-Dove;
    Gentle as Air when *Zephir* blows;
Refreshing as descending Rains,
To Sun-burnt Climes and thirsty Plains.

True as the Needle to the Pole,
    Or as the Dial to the Sun;
Constant as gliding Waters roll,
    Whose swelling Tides obey the Moon:
From ev'ry other Charmer free,
My Life and Love shall follow thee.

BARTON BOOTH

The Lamb the flow'ry Thyme devours,
  The Dam the tender Kid pursues;
Sweet *Philomel*, in shady Bowers
  Of verdant Spring, his Note renews:
All follow what they most admire,
As I pursue my Soul's Desire.

Nature must change her beauteous Face,
  And vary as the Seasons rise;
As Winter to the Spring gives place,
  Summer th' Approach of Autumn flies:
No Change in Love the Seasons bring,
Love only knows perpetual Spring.

Devouring Time, with stealing Pace,
  Makes lofty Oaks and Cedars bow;
And marble Tow'rs, and Walls of Brass,
  In his rude March he levels low:
But Time, destroying far and wide,
Love from the Soul can ne'er divide.

Death only, with his cruel Dart,
  The gentle Godhead can remove;
And drive him from the bleeding Heart,
  To mingle with the Bless'd above:
Where, known to all his kindred Train,
He finds a lasting Rest from Pain.

Love, and his Sister fair, the Soul,
  Twin-born, from Heav'n together came;
Love will the Universe controul,
  When dying Seasons lose their Name:
Divine Abodes shall own his Pow'r,
When Time and Death shall be no more.

The Hive, i, 1726

WILLIAM OLDYS

1696–1761

153　　　*The Fly*

An Anacreontick

BUSY, curious, thirsty Fly,
　Gently drink, and drink as I;
Freely welcome to my Cup,
Could'st thou sip, and sip it up;
Make the most of Life you may,
Life is short and wears away.

Just alike, both mine and thine,
Hasten quick to their Decline;
Thine's a Summer, mine's no more,
Though repeated to threescore;
Threescore Summers when they're gone,
Will appear as short as one.

The Scarborough Miscellany, 1732

JAMES THOMSON

1700–1748

154　　*Approach of Winter*

SEE, WINTER comes, to rule the vary'd Year,
　Sullen, and sad, with all his rising Train;
Vapours, and *Clouds*, and *Storms*. Be these my Theme,
These, that exalt the Soul to solemn Thought,
And heavenly Musing. Welcome, kindred Glooms!
Cogenial Horrors, hail! with frequent Foot,
Pleas'd have I, in my chearful Morn of Life,
When nurs'd by careless Solitude I liv'd.

236

And sung of Nature with unceasing Joy,
Pleas'd have I wander'd thro' your rough Domain;
Trod the pure Virgin-Snows, myself as pure;
Heard the Winds roar, and the big Torrent burst;
Or seen the deep fermenting Tempest brew'd,
In the grim Evening-Sky. Thus pass'd the Time,
Till thro' the lucid Chambers of the South
Look'd out the joyous Spring, look'd out, and smil'd.

Winter, 1726

155 *A Winter Scene*

THRO' the hush'd Air the whitening Shower descends,
At first thin-wavering; till at last the Flakes
Fall broad, and wide, and fast, dimming the Day,
With a continual Flow. The cherish'd Fields
Put on their Winter-Robe, of purest White.
'Tis Brightness all; save where the new Snow melts,
Along the mazy Current. Low, the Woods
Bow their hoar Head; and, ere the languid Sun
Faint from the West emits his Evening-Ray,
Earth's universal Face, deep-hid, and chill,
Is one wild dazzling Waste, that buries deep
The Works of Man. Drooping, the Labourer-Ox
Stands cover'd o'er with Snow, and then demands
The Fruit of all his Toil. The Fowls of Heaven,
Tam'd by the cruel Season, croud around
The winnowing Store, and claim the little Boon
Which Providence assigns them. One alone,
The Red-Breast, sacred to the houshold Gods,
Wisely regardful of th' embroiling Sky,
In joyless Fields, and thorny Thickets, leaves

His shivering Mates, and pays to trusted Man
His annual Visit. Half-afraid, he first
Against the Window beats; then, brisk, alights
On the warm Hearth; then, hopping o'er the Floor,
Eyes all the smiling Family askance,
And pecks, and starts, and wonders where he is:
Till more familiar grown, the Table-Crumbs
Attract his slender Feet. The foodless Wilds
Pour forth their brown Inhabitants. The Hare,
Tho' timorous of Heart, and hard beset
By Death in various Forms, dark Snares, and Dogs,
And more unpitying Men, the Garden seeks,
Urg'd on by fearless Want. The bleating Kind
Eye the bleak Heaven, and next the glistening Earth,
With Looks of dumb Despair; then, sad-dispers'd,
Dig for the wither'd Herb thro' Heaps of Snow.

Winter, 1726

156 *Frost at Night*

WITH the fierce Rage of Winter deep suffus'd,
   An icy Gale, oft shifting, o'er the Pool
Breathes a blue Film, and in its mid Career
Arrests the bickering Stream. The loosen'd Ice,
Let down the Flood, and half dissolv'd by Day,
Rustles no more; but to the sedgy Bank
Fast grows, or gathers round the pointed Stone,
A crystal Pavement, by the Breath of Heaven
Cemented firm; till, seiz'd from Shore to Shore,
The whole imprison'd River growls below.
Loud rings the frozen Earth, and hard reflects
A double Noise; while, at his evening Watch,
The village Dog deters the nightly Thief;

The Heifer lows; the distant Water-fall
Swells in the Breeze; and, with the hasty Tread
Of Traveller, the hollow-sounding Plain
Shakes from afar. The full ethereal Round,
Infinite Worlds disclosing to the View,
Shines out intensely keen; and, all one Cope
Of starry Glitter, glows from Pole to Pole.
From Pole to Pole the rigid Influence falls,
Thro' the still Night, incessant, heavy, strong,
And seizes Nature fast. It freezes on;
Till Morn, late-rising o'er the drooping World,
Lifts her pale Eye unjoyous. Then appears
The various Labour of the silent Night:
Prone from the dripping Eave, and dumb Cascade,
Whose idle Torrents only seem to roar,
The pendant Icicle; the Frost-Work fair,
Where transient Hues, and fancy'd Figures rise;
Wide-spouted o'er the Hill, the frozen Brook,
A livid Tract, cold-gleaming on the Morn;
The Forest bent beneath the plumy Wave;
And by the Frost refin'd the whiter Snow,
Incrusted hard, and sounding to the Tread
Of early Shepherd, as he pensive seeks
His pining Flock, or from the Mountain-top,
Pleas'd with the slippery Surface, swift descends.

Winter, 1726

157 *Spring Flowers*

ALONG the blushing Borders, bright with Dew,
And in yon mingled Wilderness of Flowers,
Fair-handed Spring unbosoms every Grace:
Throws out the Snow-drop, and the Crocus first;

The Daisy, Primrose, Violet darkly blue,
And Polyanthus of unnumber'd Dyes;
The yellow Wall-Flower, stain'd with iron Brown;
And lavish Stock that scents the Garden round:
From the soft Wing of vernal Breezes shed,
Anemonies; Auriculas, enrich'd
With shining Meal o'er all their velvet Leaves;
And full Renunculas, of glowing Red.
Then comes the Tulip-Race, where Beauty plays
Her idle Freaks: from Family diffus'd
To Family, as flies the Father-Dust,
The varied Colours run; and while they *break*
On the charm'd Eye, th' exulting Florist marks,
With secret Pride, the Wonders of his Hand.
No gradual Bloom is wanting; from the Bud,
First-born of Spring, to Summer's musky Tribes:
Nor Hyacinths, deep-purpled; nor Jonquils,
Of potent Fragrance; nor Narcissus fair,
As o'er the fabled Fountain hanging still;
Nor broad Carnations; nor gay-spotted Pinks;
Nor, shower'd from every Bush, the Damask-rose:
Infinite Numbers, Delicacies, Smells,
With Hues on Hues Expression cannot paint,
The Breath of Nature, and her endless Bloom.

Spring, 1728

158 *Birds in Spring*

THE Black-bird whistles from the thorny Brake;
The mellow Bullfinch answers from the Grove:
Nor are the Linnets, o'er the flowering Furze
Pour'd out profusely, silent. Join'd to These

JAMES THOMSON

Innumerous Songsters, in the freshening Shade
Of new-sprung Leaves, their Modulations mix
Mellifluous. The Jay, the Rook, the Daw,
And each harsh Pipe discordant heard alone,
Aid the full Concert: while the Stock-dove breathes
A melancholy Murmur thro' the whole.

Spring, 1728

159   *Summer Morning*

THE meek-ey'd Morn appears, Mother of Dews,
    At first faint-gleaming in the dappled East:
Till far o'er Ether spreads the widening Glow;
And, from before the Lustre of her Face,
White break the Clouds away. With quicken'd Step,
Brown Night retires. Young Day pours in apace,
And opens all the lawny Prospect wide.
The dripping Rock, the Mountain's misty Top,
Swell on the Sight, and brighten with the Dawn.
Blue, thro' the Dusk, the smoking Currents shine;
And from the bladed Field the fearful Hare
Limps, aukward: while along the Forest-glade
The wild Deer trip, and often turning gaze
At early Passenger. Musick awakes,
The native Voice of undissembled Joy;
And thick around the woodland Hymns arise.
Rous'd by the Cock, the soon-clad Shepherd leaves
His mossy Cottage, where with *Peace* he dwells;
And from the crouded Fold, in Order, drives
His Flock, to taste the Verdure of the Morn.

Summer, 1727

Happy Britannia

HEAVENS! what a goodly Prospect spreads around,
Of Hills, and Dales, and Woods, and Lawns, and
Spires,
And glittering Towns, and gilded Streams, till all
The stretching Landskip into Smoke decays!
Happy BRITANNIA! where the QUEEN OF ARTS,
Inspiring Vigor, LIBERTY abroad
Walks, unconfin'd, even to thy farthest Cotts,
And scatters Plenty with unsparing Hand.

Rich is thy Soil, and merciful thy Clime;
Thy Streams unfailing in the Summer's Drought;
Unmatch'd thy Guardian-Oaks; thy Valleys float
With golden Waves; and on thy Mountains Flocks
Bleat numberless; while, roving round their Sides,
Bellow the blackening Herds in lusty Droves.
Beneath, thy Meadows glow, and rise unquell'd
Against the Mower's Scythe. On every hand,
Thy Villas shine. Thy Country teems with Wealth;
And Property assures it to the Swain,
Pleas'd, and unweary'd, in his guarded Toil.

Full are thy Cities with the Sons of Art;
And Trade and Joy, in every busy Street,
Mingling are heard: even Drudgery himself,
As at the Car he sweats, or dusty hews
The Palace-Stone, looks gay. Thy crouded Ports,
Where rising Masts an endless Prospect yield,
With Labour burn, and echo to the Shouts
Of hurry'd Sailor, as he hearty waves
His last Adieu, and loosening every Sheet,
Resigns the spreading Vessel to the Wind.

Bold, firm, and graceful, are thy generous Youth,
By Hardship sinew'd, and by Danger fir'd,
Scattering the Nations where they go; and first
Or in the listed Plain, or wintry Seas.
Mild are thy Glories too, as o'er the Plans
Of thriving Peace thy thoughtful Sires preside;
In Genius, and substantial Learning, high;
For every Virtue, every Worth, renown'd;
Sincere, plain-hearted, hospitable, kind;
Yet like the mustering Thunder when provok'd,
The Dread of Tyrants, and the sole Resource
Of those that under grim Oppression groan.

Summer, 1727

161 *Summer Evening and Night*

CONFESS'D from yonder slow-extinguish'd Clouds,
All Ether softening, sober *Evening* takes
Her wonted Station in the middle Air;
A thousand *Shadows* at her Beck. First *This*
She sends on Earth; then *That* of deeper Dye
Steals soft behind; and then a *Deeper* still,
In Circle following Circle, gathers round,
To close the Face of Things. A fresher Gale
Begins to wave the Wood, and stir the Stream,
Sweeping with shadowy Gust the Fields of Corn;
While the Quail clamours for his running Mate.
Wide o'er the thistly Lawn, as swells the Breeze,
A whitening Shower of vegetable Down
Amusive floats. The kind impartial Care
Of Nature nought disdains: thoughtful to feed
Her lowest Sons, and clothe the coming Year,

From Field to Field the feather'd Seeds she wings.

His folded Flock secure, the Shepherd home
Hies, merry-hearted; and by turns relieves
The ruddy Milk-Maid of her brimming Pail;
The Beauty whom perhaps his witless Heart,
Unknowing what the Joy-mixt Anguish means,
Sincerely loves, by that best Language shown
Of cordial Glances, and obliging Deeds.
Onward they pass, o'er many a panting Height,
And Valley sunk, and unfrequented; where
At Fall of Eve the Fairy People throng,
In various Game, and Revelry to pass
The Summer-Night, as Village-Stories tell.
But far about they wander from the Grave
Of him, whom his ungentle Fortune urg'd
Against his own sad Breast to lift the hand
Of impious Violence. The lonely Tower
Is also shunn'd; whose mournful Chambers hold,
So night-struck Fancy dreams, the yelling Ghost.

Among the crooked Lanes, on every Hedge,
The Glow-Worm lights his Gem; and, thro' the Dark,
A moving Radiance twinkles. *Evening* yields
The World to *Night*; not in her Winter-Robe
Of massy Stygian Woof, but loose array'd
In Mantle dun. A faint erroneous Ray,
Glanc'd from th' imperfect Surfaces of Things,
Flings half an Image on the straining Eye;
While wavering Woods, and Villages, and Streams,
And Rocks, and Mountain-tops, that long retain'd
Th' ascending Gleam, are all one swimming Scene,
Uncertain if beheld. Sudden to Heaven
Thence weary Vision turns; where, leading soft

The silent Hours of Love, with purest Ray
Sweet *Venus* shines; and from her genial Rise,
When Day-Light sickens till it springs afresh,
Unrival'd reigns, the fairest Lamp of Night.

Summer, 1727

162   *Lavinia*

THE lovely young LAVINIA once had Friends;
        And Fortune smil'd, deceitful, on her Birth.
For in her helpless Years depriv'd of all,
Of every Stay, save Innocence and HEAVEN,
She with her widow'd Mother, feeble, old,
And poor, liv'd in a Cottage, far retir'd
Among the Windings of a Woody Vale;
By Solitude and deep surrounding Shades,
But more by bashful Modesty, conceal'd.
Together thus they shunn'd the cruel Scorn
Which Virtue, sunk to Poverty, would meet
From giddy Fashion and low-minded Pride:
Almost on Nature's common Bounty fed,
Like the gay Birds that sung them to Repose,
Content, and careless of to-morrow's Fare.
Her Form was fresher than the Morning-Rose,
When the Dew wets its Leaves; unstain'd, and pure,
As is the Lilly, or the Mountain Snow.
The modest Virtues mingled in her Eyes,
Still on the Ground dejected, darting all
Their humid Beams into the blooming Flowers:
Or when the mournful Tale her Mother told,
Of what her faithless Fortune promis'd once,
Thrill'd in her Thought, they, like the dewy Star
Of Evening, shone in Tears. A native Grace

Sat fair-proportion'd on her polish'd Limbs,
Veil'd in a simple Robe, their best Attire,
Beyond the Pomp of Dress; for Loveliness
Needs not the foreign Aid of Ornament,
But is when unadorn'd adorn'd the most.
Thoughtless of Beauty, she was Beauty's Self,
Recluse amid the close-embowering Woods.

Autumn, 1730

163　　*Moonlight in Autumn*

THE Western Sun withdraws the shorten'd Day;
　And humid Evening, gliding o'er the Sky,
In her chill Progress, to the Ground condens'd
The Vapours throws. Where creeping Waters ooze,
Where Marshes stagnate, and where Rivers wind,
Cluster the rolling Fogs, and swim along
The dusky-mantled Lawn. Mean-while the Moon
Full-orb'd, and breaking thro' the scatter'd Clouds,
Shews her broad Visage in the crimson'd East.
Turn'd to the Sun direct, her spotted Disk,
(Where Mountains rise, umbrageous Dales descend,
And Oceans roll, as optic Tube descries,)
A smaller Earth, gives all its Blaze again,
Void of its Flame, and sheds a softer Day.
Now thro' the passing Cloud she seems to stoop,
Now up the pure Cerulean rides sublime.
Wide the pale Deluge floats, and streaming mild
O'er the sky'd Mountain to the shadowy Vale,
While Rocks and Floods reflect the quivering Gleam,
The whole Air whitens with a boundless Tide
Of silver Radiance, trembling round the World.

The lengthen'd Night elaps'd, the Morning shines
Serene, in all her dewy Beauty bright,
Unfolding fair the last Autumnal Day.
And now the mounting Sun dispels the Fog;
The rigid Hoar-Frost melts before his Beam;
And hung on every Spray, on every Blade
Of Grass, the myriad Dew-Drops twinkle round.

Autumn, 1730

164   *Love of Nature*

THE FALL of Kings,
The Rage of Nations, and the Crush of States,
Move not the Man, who, from the World escap'd,
In still Retreats, and flowery Solitudes,
To Nature's Voice attends, from Month to Month,
And Day to Day, thro' the revolving Year;
Admiring, sees Her in her every Shape;
Feels all her sweet Emotions at his Heart;
Takes what she liberal gives, nor thinks of more.
He, when young Spring protrudes the bursting Gems,
Marks the first Bud, and sucks the healthful Gale
Into his freshen'd Soul; her genial Hours
He full enjoys; and not a Beauty blows,
And not an opening Blossom breathes in vain.
In Summer he, beneath the living Shade,
Such as o'er frigid *Tempe* wont to wave,
Or *Hemus* cool, reads what the Muse, of These
Perhaps, has in immortal Numbers sung;
Or what she dictates writes; and, oft an Eye
Shot round, rejoices in the vigorous Year.
When Autumn's yellow Luster gilds the World,

And tempts the sickled Swain into the Field,
Seiz'd by the general Joy, his Heart distends
With gentle Throws; and, thro' the tepid Gleams
Deep-musing, then he *best* exerts his Song.
Even Winter wild to him is full of Bliss.
The mighty Tempest, and the hoary Waste,
Abrupt, and deep, stretch'd o'er the bury'd Earth,
Awake to solemn Thought. At Night the Skies,
Disclos'd, and kindled, by refining Frost,
Pour every Luster on th' exalted Eye.
A Friend, a Book, the stealing Hours secure,
And mark them down for Wisdom. With swift Wing,
O'er Land and Sea Imagination roams;
Or Truth, divinely breaking on his Mind,
Elates his Being, and unfolds his Powers;
Or in his Breast heroic Virtue burns.
The Touch of Kindred too and Love he feels;
The modest Eye, whose Beams on His alone
Extatic shine; the little strong Embrace
Of prattling Children, twin'd around his Neck,
And emulous to please him, calling forth
The fond parental Soul. Nor Purpose gay,
Amusement, Dance, or Song, he sternly scorns;
For Happiness and true Philosophy
Are of the social, still, and smiling Kind.
This is the Life which those who fret in Guilt,
And guilty Cities, never knew; the Life,
Led by primeval Ages, uncorrupt,
When Angels dwelt, and GOD himself, with Man!

Autumn, 1730

165   *Hymn on Solitude*

HAIL, mildly pleasing solitude,
   Companion of the wise, and good;
But, from whose holy, piercing eye,
The herd of fools, and villains fly.
Oh! how I love with thee to walk,
And listen to thy whisper'd talk,
Which innocence, and truth imparts,
And melts the most obdurate hearts.

A thousand shapes you wear with ease,
And still in every shape you please.
Now wrapt in some mysterious dream,
A lone philosopher you seem;
Now quick from hill to vale you fly,
And now you sweep the vaulted sky;
A shepherd next, you haunt the plain,
And warble forth your oaten strain;
A lover now, with all the grace
Of that sweet passion in your face:
Then, calm'd to friendship, you assume
The gentle-looking HARFORD's bloom,
As, with her MUSIDORA, she,
(Her MUSIDORA fond of thee)
Amid the long withdrawing vale,
Awakes the rival'd nightingale.

Thine is the balmy breath of morn,
Just as the dew-bent rose is born;
And while Meridian fervours beat,
Thine is the woodland dumb retreat;
But chief, when evening scenes decay,
And the faint landskip swims away,

Thine is the doubtful soft decline,
And that best hour of musing thine.

    Descending angels bless thy train,
The Virtues of the sage, and swain;
Plain Innocence in white array'd,
Before thee lifts her fearless head;
Religion's beams around thee shine,
And chear thy glooms with light divine;
About thee sports sweet Liberty;
And rapt *Urania* sings to thee.

    Oh, let me pierce thy secret cell,
And in thy deep recesses dwell!
Perhaps from *Norwood*'s oak-clad hill,
When meditation has her fill,
I just may cast my careless eyes
Where *London*'s spiry turrets rise,
Think of its crimes, its cares, its pain,
Then shield me in the woods again.

                Ralph's *Miscellaneous Poems,* 1729

166   *Britannia's Empire*

AND what, my thoughtless Sons, should fire you more,
   Than when your well-earn'd Empire of the Deep
The least beginning Injury receives?
What better Cause can call your Lightning forth?
Your Thunder wake? Your dearest Life demand?
What better Cause, than when your Country sees
The sly Destruction at her Vitals aim'd?
For oh it much imports you, 'tis your All,
To keep your Trade intire, intire the Force
And Honour of your Fleets; o'er that to watch,

Even with a Hand severe, and jealous Eye.
In Intercourse be gentle, generous, just,
By Wisdom polish'd, and of Manners fair;
But on the Sea be terrible, untam'd,
Unconquerable still: let none escape,
Who shall but aim to touch your Glory there.
Is there the Man, into the Lion's Den
Who dares intrude, to snatch his Young away?
And is a *Briton* seiz'd? and seiz'd beneath
The slumbring Terrors of a *British* Fleet?
Then ardent rise! Oh great in Vengeance rise!
O'erturn the Proud, teach Rapine to restore:
And as you ride sublimely round the World,
Make every Vessel stoop, make every State
At once their Welfare and their Duty know.
This is your Glory; this your Wisdom; this
The native Power for which you were design'd
By Fate, when Fate design'd the firmest State,
That e'er was seated on the subject Sea;
A State, alone, where *Liberty* should live,
In these late Times, this Evening of Mankind,
When *Athens*, *Rome*, and *Carthage* are no more,
The World almost in slavish Sloth dissolv'd.
For this, these Rocks around your Coast were thrown;
For this, your Oaks, peculiar harden'd, shoot
Strong into sturdy Growth; for this, your Hearts
Swell with a sullen Courage, growing still
As Danger grows; and Strength, and Toil for this
Are liberal pour'd o'er all the fervent Land.
Then cherish this, this unexpensive Power,
Undangerous to the Public, ever prompt,
By lavish Nature thrust into your Hand:

And, unencumber'd with the Bulk immense
Of Conquest, whence huge Empires rose, and fell,
Self-crush'd, extend your Reign from Shore to Shore,
Where'er the Wind your high Behests can blow,
And fix it deep on this eternal Base.

Britannia, **1729**

167 *British Commerce*

FOR BRITONS, chief,
It was reserv'd, with star-directed Prow,
To dare the middle Deep, and drive assur'd
To distant Nations thro' the pathless Main.
Chief, for their fearless Hearts the Glory waits,
Long Months from Land, while the black stormy Night
Around them rages, on the groaning Mast
With unshook Knee to know their giddy Way;
To sing, unquell'd, amid the lashing Wave;
To laugh at Danger. Theirs the Triumph be,
By deep *Invention*'s keen pervading Eye,
The Heart of *Courage,* and the Hand of *Toil,*
Each conquer'd Ocean staining with their Blood,
Instead of Treasure robb'd by ruffian War,
Round social Earth to circle fair Exchange,
And bind the Nations in a golden Chain.

Liberty, **iv,** 1736

168 *Rule Britannia*

WHEN *Britain* first, at heaven's command,
 Arose from out the azure main;
This was the charter of the land,
 And guardian Angels sung *this* strain:
 ' Rule, *Britannia,* rule the waves;
 ' *Britons* never will be slaves.'

JAMES THOMSON

The nations, not so blest as thee,
    Must, in their turns, to tyrants fall:
While thou shalt flourish great and free,
    The dread and envy of them all.
        ' Rule, &c.

Still more majestic shalt thou rise,
    More dreadful, from each foreign stroke:
As the loud blast that tears the skies,
    Serves but to root thy native oak.
        ' Rule, &c.

Thee haughty tyrants ne'er shall tame:
    All their attempts to bend thee down,
Will but arrouse thy generous flame;
    But work their woe, and thy renown.
        ' Rule, &c.

To thee belongs the rural reign;
    Thy cities shall with commerce shine:
All thine shall be the subject main,
    And every shore it circles thine.
        ' Rule, &c.

The Muses, still with freedom found,
    Shall to thy happy coast repair:
Blest isle! with matchless beauty crown'd,
    And manly hearts to guard the fair.
        ' Rule, *Britannia*, rule the waves:
        ' *Britons* never will be slaves.'
                        Alfred : A Masque, Act ii, 1740

JAMES THOMSON

169   *Verses occasioned by the Death*
          of Dr. Aikman

A particular Friend of the Author's

AS those we love decay, we die in part,
    String after string is sever'd from the heart;
Till loosen'd life, at last, but breathing clay,
Without one pang is glad to fall away.
Unhappy he, who latest feels the blow,
Whose eyes have wept o'er every friend laid low,
Drag'd ling'ring on from partial death to death,
Till, dying, all he can resign is breath.

Poems on Several Occasions, 1750

170   *Ode*

TELL me, thou soul of her I love,
    Ah! tell me, whither art thou fled;
To what delightful world above,
    Appointed for the happy dead?

Or dost thou, free, at pleasure, roam,
    And sometimes share thy lover's woe;
Where, void of thee, his chearless home
    Can now, alas! no comfort know?

Oh! if thou hover'st round my walk,
    While, under ev'ry well-known tree,
I to thy fancy'd shadow talk,
    And every tear is full of thee,

Should then the weary eye of grief,
   Beside some sympathetic stream,
In slumber find a short relief,
   Oh visit thou my soothing dream!

Poems on Several Occasions, 1750

171   *To the Reverend Mr. Murdoch*

Rector of Straddishall in Suffolk

THUS safely low, my friend, thou can'st not fall:
   Here reigns a deep tranquillity o'er all:
No noise, no care, no vanity, no strife;
Men, woods and fields, all breathe untroubled life
Then keep each passion down, however dear;
Trust me, the tender are the most severe.
Guard, while 'tis thine, thy philosophic ease,
And ask no joy but that of virtuous peace;
That bids defiance to the storms of fate:
High bliss is only for a higher state.

Poems on Several Occasions, 1750

172   *The Land of Indolence*

IN lowly Dale, fast by a River's Side,
   With woody Hill o'er Hill encompass'd round,
A most enchanting Wizard did abide,
Than whom a Fiend more fell is no where found.
It was, I ween, a lovely Spot of Ground;
And there a Season atween June and May,
Half prankt with Spring, with Summer half imbrown'd,
A listless Climate made, where, Sooth to say,
No living Wight could work, ne cared even for Play.

Was nought around but Images of Rest:
Sleep-soothing Groves, and quiet Lawns between;
And flowery Beds that slumbrous Influence kest,
From Poppies breath'd; and Beds of pleasant Green,
Where never yet was creeping Creature seen.
Mean time unnumber'd glittering Streamlets play'd,
And hurled every-where their Waters sheen;
That, as they bicker'd through the sunny Glade,
Though restless still themselves, a lulling Murmur made.

Join'd to the Prattle of the purling Rills,
Were heard the lowing Herds along the Vale,
And Flocks loud-bleating from the distant Hills,
And vacant Shepherds piping in the Dale;
And now and then sweet Philomel would wail,
Or Stock-Doves plain amid the Forest deep,
That drowsy rustled to the sighing Gale;
And still a Coil the Grashopper did keep:
Yet all these Sounds yblent inclined all to Sleep.

Full in the Passage of the Vale, above,
A sable, silent, solemn Forest stood;
Where nought but shadowy Forms were seen to move,
As *Idless* fancy'd in her dreaming Mood.
And up the Hills, on either Side, a Wood
Of blackening Pines, ay waving to and fro,
Sent forth a sleepy Horror through the Blood;
And where this Valley winded out, below,
The murmuring Main was heard, and scarcely heard, to flow.

A pleasing Land of Drowsy-hed it was:
Of Dreams that wave before the half-shut Eye;
And of gay Castles in the Clouds that pass,
For ever flushing round a Summer-Sky:

There eke the soft Delights, that witchingly
Instil a wanton Sweetness through the Breast,
And the calm Pleasures always hover'd nigh;
But whate'er smack'd of Noyance, or Unrest,
Was far far off expell'd from this delicious Nest.

The Castle of Indolence, i, 1748

173 *A Witching Song*

WHAT, what, is Virtue, but Repose of Mind?
  A pure ethereal Calm! that knows no Storm;
Above the Reach of wild Ambition's Wind,
Above those Passions that this World deform,
And torture Man, a proud malignant Worm!
But here, instead, soft Gales of Passion play,
And gently stir the Heart, thereby to form
A quicker Sense of Joy; as Breezes stray
Across th' enliven'd Skies, and make them still more gay.

The Best of Men have ever lov'd Repose:
They hate to mingle in the filthy Fray;
Where the Soul sowrs, and gradual Rancour grows,
Imbitter'd more from peevish Day to Day.
Even Those whom Fame has lent her fairest Ray,
The most renown'd of worthy Wights of Yore,
From a base World at last have stolen away:
So SCIPIO, to the soft *Cumæan* Shore
Retiring, tasted Joy he never knew before.

But if a little Exercise you chuse,
Some Zest for Ease, 'tis not forbidden here.
Amid the Groves you may indulge the Muse,
Or tend the Blooms, and deck the vernal Year;

Or softly stealing, with your watry Gear,
Along the Brooks, the crimson-spotted Fry
You may delude: The whilst, amus'd, you hear
Now the hoarse Stream, and now the Zephir's Sigh,
Attuned to the Birds, and woodland Melody.

O grievous Folly! to heap up Estate,
Losing the Days you see beneath the Sun;
When, sudden, comes blind unrelenting Fate,
And gives th' untasted Portion you have won,
With ruthless Toil, and many a Wretch undone,
To Those who mock you gone to *Pluto*'s Reign,
There with sad Ghosts to pine, and Shadows dun:
But sure it is of Vanities most vain,
To toil for what you here untoiling may obtain.

The Castle of Indolence, i, 1748

174   *A Wondrous Show*

THIS Rite perform'd, All inly pleas'd and still,
    Withouten Tromp, was Proclamation made.
' Ye Sons of INDOLENCE, do what you will;
' And wander where you list, through Hall or Glade:
' Be no Man's Pleasure for another's staid;
' Let Each as likes him best his Hours employ,
' And curs'd be he who minds his Neighbour's Trade!
' Here dwells kind Ease and unreproving Joy:
' He little merits Bliss who Others can annoy.'

Strait of these endless Numbers, swarming round,
As thick as idle Motes in sunny Ray,
Not one eftsoons in View was to be found,
But every Man stroll'd off his own glad Way.

258

Wide o'er this ample Court's blank Area,
With all the Lodges that thereto pertain'd,
No living Creature could be seen to stray;
While Solitude, and perfect Silence reign'd:
So that to think you dreamt you almost was constrain'd.

As when a Shepherd of the *Hebrid-Isles*,
Plac'd far amid the melancholy Main,
(Whether it be lone Fancy him beguiles;
Or that aerial Beings sometimes deign
To stand, embodied, to our Senses plain)
Sees on the naked Hill, or Valley low,
The whilst in Ocean *Phœbus* dips his Wain,
A vast Assembly moving to and fro:
Then all at once in Air dissolves the wondrous Show.

The Castle of Indolence, i, 1748

175 *Sons of Indolence*

OF all the gentle Tenants of the Place,
There was a Man of special grave Remark:
A certain tender Gloom o'erspread his Face,
Pensive not sad, in Thought involv'd not dark,
As soot this Man could sing as Morning-Lark,
And teach the noblest Morals of the Heart:
But These his Talents were ybury'd stark;
Of the fine Stores he Nothing would impart,
Which or boon Nature gave, or Nature-painting Art.

To Noontide Shades incontinent he ran,
Where purls the Brook with Sleep-inviting Sound;
Or where Dan *Sol* to slope his Wheels began,
Amid the Broom he bask'd him on the Ground,

Where the wild Thyme and Camomil are found:
There would he linger, till the latest Ray
Of Light sat trembling on the Welkin's Bound:
Then homeward through the twilight Shadows stray,
Sauntring and slow. So had he passed many a Day.

Yet not in thoughtless Slumber were they past:
For oft the heavenly Fire, that lay conceal'd
Beneath the sleeping Embers, mounted fast,
And all its native Light anew reveal'd;
Oft as he travers'd the Cerulean Field,
And mark'd the Clouds that drove before the Wind,
Ten thousand glorious Systems would he build,
Ten thousand great Ideas fill'd his Mind;
But with the Clouds they fled, and left no Tract behind.

With him was sometimes join'd, in silent Walk,
(Profoundly silent, for they never spoke)
One shyer still, who quite detested Talk:
Oft, stung by Spleen, at once away he broke,
To Groves of Pine, and broad o'ershadowing Oak;
There, inly thrill'd, he wander'd all alone,
And on himself his pensive Fury wroke,
Ne ever utter'd Word, save when first shone
The glittering Star of Eve—' Thank Heaven! the Day is
    done.'

One Day there chaunc'd into these Halls to rove
A joyous Youth, who took you at first Sight;
Him the wild Wave of Pleasure hither drove,
Before the sprightly Tempest tossing light:
Certes, he was a most engaging Wight,

Of social Glee, and Wit humane though keen,
Turning the Night to Day and Day to Night;
For him the merry Bells had rung, I ween,
If in this Nook of Quiet Bells had ever been.

But not even Pleasure to Excess is good,
What most elates then sinks the Soul as low;
When Spring-Tide Joy pours in with copious Flood,
And higher still th' exulting Billows flow,
The farther back again they flagging go,
And leave us groveling on the dreary Shore:
Taught by this Son of Joy, we found it so;
Who, whilst he staid, kept in a gay Uproar
Our madden'd Castle all, th' Abode of Sleep no more.

As when in Prime of June a burnish'd Fly,
Sprung from the Meads, o'er which he sweeps along,
Chear'd by the breathing Bloom and vital Sky,
Tunes up amid these airy Halls his Song,
Soothing at first the gay reposing Throng:
And oft he sips their Bowl; or nearly drown'd,
He, thence recovering, drives their Beds among,
And scares their tender Sleep, with Trump profound;
Then out again he flies, to wing his mazy Round.

Full oft by Holy Feet our Ground was trod,
Of Clerks good Plenty here you mote espy.
A little, round, fat, oily Man of God,
Was one I chiefly mark'd among the Fry:
He had a roguish Twinkle in his Eye,
And shone all glittering with ungodly Dew,
If a tight Damsel chaunc'd to trippen by;
Which when observ'd, he shrunk into his Mew,
And strait would recollect his Piety anew.

Nor be forgot a Tribe, who minded Nought
(Old Inmates of the Place) but State-Affairs:
They look'd, perdie, as if they deeply thought;
And on their Brow sat every Nation's Cares.
The World by them is parcel'd out in Shares,
When in the *Hall of Smoak* they Congress hold,
And the sage Berry sun-burnt *Mocha* bears
Has clear'd their inward Eye: then, smoak-enroll'd,
Their Oracles break forth mysterious as of old.

Here languid Beauty kept her pale-fac'd Court:
Bevies of dainty Dames, of high Degree,
From every Quarter hither made Resort;
Where, from gross mortal Care and Business free,
They lay, pour'd out in Ease and Luxury.
Or should they a vain Shew of Work assume,
Alas! and well-a-day! what can it be?
To knot, to twist, to range the vernal Bloom;
But far is cast the Distaff, Spinning-Wheel, and Loom.

Their only Labour was to kill the Time;
And Labour dire it is, and weary Woe.
They sit, they loll, turn o'er some idle Rhyme;
Then, rising sudden, to the Glass they go,
Or saunter forth, with tottering Step and slow:
This soon too rude an Exercise they find;
Strait on the Couch their Limbs again they throw,
Where Hours on Hours they sighing lie reclin'd,
And court the vapoury God soft-breathing in the Wind.

The Castle of Indolence, i, 1748

176   *Indifference to Fortune*

I CARE not, Fortune, what you me deny:
   You cannot rob me of free Nature's Grace;
You cannot shut the Windows of the Sky,
   Through which *Aurora* shews her brightening Face;
You cannot bar my constant Feet to trace
   The Woods and Lawns, by living Stream, at Eve:
Let Health my Nerves and finer Fibres brace,
   And I their Toys to the *great Children* leave;
Of Fancy, Reason, Virtue, nought can me bereave.

The Castle of Indolence, ii, **1748**

177   *The Praise of Industry*

IT was not by vile Loitering in Ease,
   That GREECE obtain'd the brighter Palm of Art,
That soft yet ardent ATHENS learn'd to please,
   To keen the Wit, and to sublime the Heart,
In all supreme! compleat in every Part!
   It was not thence majestic ROME arose,
And o'er the Nations shook her conquering Dart:
   For Sluggard's Brow the Laurel never grows;
Renown is not the Child of indolent Repose.

Had unambitious Mortals minded Nought
   But in loose Joy their Time to wear away;
Had they alone the Lap of Dalliance sought,
   Pleas'd on her Pillow their dull Heads to lay:
Rude Nature's State had been our State To-day;
   No Cities e'er their towery Fronts had rais'd,
No Arts had made us opulent and gay;
   With Brother-Brutes the Human Race had graz'd;
None e'er had soar'd to Fame, None honour'd been, None
      prais'd.

JAMES THOMSON

Great HOMER's Song had never fir'd the Breast,
To Thirst of Glory, and heroic Deeds;
Sweet MARO's Muse, sunk in inglorious Rest,
Had silent slept amid the *Mincian* Reeds:
The Wits of modern Time had told their Beads,
And monkish Legends been their only Strains;
Our MILTON's *Eden* had lain wrapt in Weeds,
Our SHAKESPEAR stroll'd and laugh'd with *Warwick*
        Swains,
Ne had my Master SPENSER charm'd his *Mulla*'s Plains.

Dumb too had been the sage Historic Muse,
And perish'd all the Sons of antient Fame;
Those starry Lights of Virtue, that diffuse
Through the dark Depth of Time their vivid Flame,
Had All been lost with Such as have no Name.
Who then had scorn'd his Ease for others' Good?
Who then had toil'd rapacious Men to tame?
Who in the Public Breach devoted stood,
And for his Country's Cause been prodigal of Blood?

But should to Fame your Hearts impervious be,
If right I read, you Pleasure All require:
Then hear how best may be obtain'd this Fee,
How best enjoy'd this Nature's wide Desire.
Toil, and be glad! Let Industry inspire
Into your quicken'd Limbs her buoyant Breath!
Who does not act is dead; absorpt intire
In miry Sloth, no Pride no Joy he hath:
O Leaden-hearted Men, to be in Love with Death!

Better the toiling Swain, oh happier far!
Perhaps the happiest of the Sons of Men!

Who vigorous plies the Plough, the Team, or Car;
Who houghs the Field, or ditches in the Glen,
Delves in his Garden, or secures his Pen:
The Tooth of Avarice poisons not his Peace;
He tosses not in Sloth's abhorred Den;
From Vanity he has a full Release;
And, rich in Nature's Wealth, he thinks not of Increase.

Good Lord! how keen are his Sensations all!
His Bread is sweeter than the Glutton's Cates;
The Wines of *France* upon the Palate pall,
Compar'd with What his simple Soul elates,
The native Cup whose Flavour Thirst creates;
At one deep Draught of Sleep he takes the Night;
And for that Heart-felt Joy which Nothing mates,
Of the pure nuptial Bed the chaste Delight,
The Losel is to him a miserable Wight.

But what avail the largest Gifts of HEAVEN,
When sickening Health and Spirits go amiss?
How tasteless then Whatever can be given?
Health is the vital Principle of Bliss,
And Exercise of Health. In Proof of This,
Behold the Wretch, who slugs his Life away,
Soon swallow'd in Disease's sad Abyss;
While he whom Toil has brac'd, or manly Play,
Has light as Air each Limb, each Thought as clear as Day.
The Castle of Indolence, ii, 1748

178 *William and Margaret*

'TWAS at the silent, solemn hour,
  When night and morning meet;
In glided MARGARET's grimly ghost,
  And stood at WILLIAM's feet.

Her face was like an *April* morn,
  Clad in a wintry cloud:
And clay-cold was her lilly hand,
  That held her sable shroud.

So shall the fairest face appear,
  When youth and years are flown:
Such is the robe that kings must wear,
  When death has reft their crown.

Her bloom was like the springing flower,
  That sips the silver dew;
The rose was budded in her cheek,
  Just opening to the view.

But *Love* had, like the canker-worm,
  Consum'd her early prime:
The rose grew pale, and left her cheek;
  She dy'd before her time.

Awake! *she* cry'd, thy *True Love* calls,
  Come from her midnight grave;
Now let thy *Pity* hear the maid,
  Thy *Love* refus'd to save.

DAVID MALLET

This is the dumb and dreary hour,
    When injur'd ghosts complain;
When yauning graves give up their dead
    To haunt the faithless swain.

Bethink thee, WILLIAM, of thy fault,
    Thy pledge, and broken oath:
And give me back my maiden vow,
    And give me back my troth.

Why did you promise love to me,
    And not that promise keep?
Why did you swear my eyes were bright,
    Yet leave those eyes to weep?

How could you say my face was fair,
    And yet that face forsake?
How could you win my virgin heart,
    Yet leave that heart to break?

Why did you say, my lip was sweet,
    And made the scarlet pale?
And why did I, young, witless maid!
    Believe the flattering tale?

That face, alas! no more is fair;
    Those lips no longer red:
Dark are my eyes, now clos'd in death,
    And every charm is fled.

The hungry *worm* my *sister* is;
    This *winding-sheet* I wear:
And cold and weary lasts our *night*,
    Till that *last morn* appear.

But hark!—the *cock* has warn'd me hence;
  A long and late adieu!
Come, see, false *man*, how low *she* lies,
  Who dy'd for love of you.

The lark sung loud; the morning smil'd,
  And rais'd her glistering head:
Pale WILLIAM quak'd in every limb,
  And raving left his bed.

He hy'd him to the fatal place
  Where MARGARET's body lay:
And stretch'd him on the grass-green turf,
  That wrap'd her breathless clay.

And thrice he call'd on MARGARET's name,
  And thrice he wept full sore:
Then laid his cheek to her cold grave,
  And word spake never more.

The Plain Dealer, July 24, 1724

179   *The Birks of Endermay*

THE smiling Morn, the breathing Spring,
  Invite the tuneful Birds to sing:
And while they warble from each Spray,
Love melts the universal Lay.
Let us, *Amanda*, timely wise,
Like them improve the Hour that flies;
And in soft Raptures waste the Day,
Among the Birks of *Endermay*.

For soon the Winter of the Year,
And Age, Life's Winter, will appear:
At this, thy living Bloom will fade;
As that will strip the verdant Shade.

DAVID MALLET

Our Taste of Pleasure then is o'er;
The feather'd Songsters love no more:
And when they droop, and we decay,
Adieu the Birks of *Endermay*.

Orpheus Caledonius, ii, **1733**

JOHN DYER

1700–1758

180

Grongar Hill

SILENT *Nymph*, with curious Eye!
Who, the purple Ev'ning, lye
On the Mountain's lonely Van,
Beyond the Noise of busy Man,
Painting fair the form of Things,
While the yellow Linnet sings;
Or the tuneful Nightingale
Charms the Forest with her Tale;
Come with all thy various Hues,
Come, and aid thy Sister Muse;
Now while *Phœbus* riding high
Gives Lustre to the Land and Sky!
Grongar Hill invites my Song,
Draw the Landskip bright and strong;
Grongar, in whose Mossie Cells
Sweetly-musing Quiet dwells:
Grongar, in whose silent Shade,
For the modest Muses made,
So oft I have, the Even still,
At the Fountain of a Rill,
Sate upon a flow'ry Bed,
With my Hand beneath my Head;

And stray'd my Eyes o'er *Towy*'s Flood,
Over Mead, and over Wood,
From House to House, from Hill to Hill,
'Till Contemplation had her fill.

   About his chequer'd Sides I wind,
And leave his Brooks and Meads behind,
And Groves, and Grottoes where I lay,
And Vistoes shooting Beams of Day:
Wider and wider spreads the Vale;
As Circles on a smooth Canal:
The Mountains round, unhappy Fate,
Sooner or later, of all Height!
Withdraw their Summits from the Skies,
And lessen as the others rise:
Still the Prospect wider spreads,
Adds a thousand Woods and Meads,
Still it widens, widens still,
And sinks the newly-risen Hill.

   Now, I gain the Mountain's Brow,
What a Landskip lies below!
No Clouds, no Vapours intervene,
But the gay, the open Scene
Does the Face of Nature show,
In all the Hues of Heaven's Bow!
And, swelling to embrace the Light,
Spreads around beyond the Sight.

   Old Castles on the Cliffs arise,
Proudly tow'ring in the Skies!
Rushing from the Woods, the Spires
Seem from hence ascending Fires!
Half his Beams *Apollo* sheds,
On the yellow Mountain-Heads!

Gilds the Fleeces of the Flocks;
And glitters on the broken Rocks!
  Below me Trees unnumber'd rise,
Beautiful in various Dies:
The gloomy Pine, the Poplar blue,
The yellow Beech, the sable Yew,
The slender Firr, that taper grows,
The sturdy Oak with broad-spread Boughs.
And beyond the purple Grove,
Haunt of *Phillis*, Queen of Love!
Gawdy as the op'ning Dawn,
Lies a long and level Lawn,
On which a dark Hill, steep and high,
Holds and charms the wand'ring Eye!
Deep are his Feet in *Towy*'s Flood,
His Sides are cloath'd with waving Wood,
And antient Towers crown his Brow,
That cast an awful Look below;
Whose ragged Walls the Ivy creeps,
And with her Arms from falling keeps.
So both a Safety from the Wind
On mutual Dependance find.
  'Tis now the Raven's bleak Abode;
'Tis now th' Apartment of the Toad;
And there the Fox securely feeds;
And there the pois'nous Adder breeds,
Conceal'd in Ruins, Moss and Weeds:
While, ever and anon, there falls,
Huge heaps of hoary moulder'd Walls.
Yet Time has seen, that lifts the low,
And level lays the lofty Brow,
Has seen this broken Pile compleat,

Big with the Vanity of State;
But transient is the Smile of Fate!
A little Rule, a little Sway,
A Sun-beam in a Winter's Day
Is all the Proud and Mighty have,
Between the Cradle and the Grave.

And see the Rivers how they run,
Thro' Woods and Meads, in Shade and Sun,
Sometimes swift, and sometimes slow,
Wave succeeding Wave they go
A various Journey to the Deep,
Like human Life to endless Sleep!
Thus is Nature's Vesture wrought,
To instruct our wand'ring Thought;
Thus she dresses green and gay,
To disperse our Cares away.

Ever charming, ever new,
When will the Landskip tire the View!
The Fountain's Fall, the River's Flow,
The woody Vallies, warm and low;
The windy Summit, wild and high,
Roughly rushing on the Sky!
The pleasent Seat, the ruin'd Tow'r,
The naked Rock, the shady Bow'r;
The Town and Village, Dome and Farm,
Each give each a double Charm,
As Pearls upon an *Æthiop*'s Arm.

See on the Mountain's southern side,
Where the Prospect opens wide,
Where the Ev'ning gilds the Tide;
How close and small the Hedges lie!
What streaks of Meadows cross the Eye!

JOHN DYER

A Step methinks may pass the Stream,
So little distant Dangers seem;
So we mistake the Future's face,
Ey'd thro' Hope's deluding Glass;
As yon Summits soft and fair,
Clad in Colours of the Air,
Which, to those who journey near,
Barren, and brown, and rough appear.
Still we tread tir'd the same coarse Way
The Present's still a cloudy Day.

O may I with my self agree,
And never covet what I see:
Content me with an humble Shade,
My Passions tam'd, my Wishes laid;
For while our Wishes wildly roll,
We banish Quiet from the Soul:
'Tis thus the Busy beat the Air;
And Misers gather Wealth and Care.

Now, ev'n now, my Joy runs high,
As on the Mountain-turf I lie;
While the wanton *Zephir* sings,
And in the Vale perfumes his Wings;
While the Waters murmur deep;
While the Shepherd charms his Sheep;
While the Birds unbounded fly,
And with Musick fill the Sky.
Now, ev'n now, my Joy runs high.

Be full, ye Courts, be great who will;
Search for Peace, with all your Skill:
Open wide the lofty Door,
Seek her on the marble Floor,
In vain ye search, she is not there;

In vain ye search the Domes of Care!
Grass and Flowers Quiet treads,
On the Meads, and Mountain-heads,
Along with Pleasure, close ally'd,
Ever by each other's Side:
And often, by the murm'ring Rill,
Hears the Thrush, while all is still,
Within the Groves of *Grongar Hill.*

D. Lewis's *Miscellaneous Poems,* 1726

181 *The Enquiry*

YE poor little Sheep, ah well may ye stray,
  While sad is your Shepherd, and *Clio* away!
Tell where have you been, have you met with my Love,
On the Mountain, or Valley, or Meadow, or Grove?
Alas-aday, No—Ye are starv'd and half dead,
Ye saw not my Love, or ye all had been fed.

Oh, Sun, did you see her?—Ay surely you did:
Mong what Willows, or Woodbines, or Reeds, is she hid?
Ye tall, whistling Pines, that on yonder Hill grow,
And o'erlook the beautiful Valley below,
Did you see her a roving in Wood or in Brake?
Or bathing her fair Limbs in some silent Lake?

Ye Mountains, that look on the vigorous East,
And the North, and the South, and the wearisom West,
Pray tell where she hides her, you surely do know,
And let not her Lover pine after her so.

Oh, had I the Wings of an Eagle, I'd fly,
Along with bright *Phœbus* all over the Sky.
Like an Eagle, look down, with my Wings wide display'd,
And dart in my Eyes at each whisp'ring Shade:

I'd search ev'ry Tuft in my diligent Tour,
I'd unravel the Woodbines, and look in each Bow'r,
Till I found out my *Clio*, and ended my Pain,
And made my self quiet, and happy again.

Savage's *Miscellaneous Poems*, 1726

182   *The Ruins of Rome*

FALL'N, fall'n, a silent Heap; her Heroes all
 Sunk in their Urns; behold the Pride of Pomp,
The Throne of Nations fall'n; obscur'd in dust;
Ev'n yet Majestical: The solemn Scene
Elates the soul, while now the rising Sun
Flames on the Ruins, in the purer air
Tow'ring aloft, upon the glitt'ring plain,
Like broken Rocks, a vast circumference;
Rent Palaces, crush'd Columns, rifted Moles,
Fanes roll'd on Fanes, and Tombs on buried Tombs.

.   .   .   .

                 The Pilgrim oft
At dead of Night, mid his Oraison hears
Aghast the Voice of Time, disparting Tow'rs,
Tumbling all precipitate down dash'd,
Rattling around, loud thundring to the Moon:
While Murmurs sooth each awful Interval
Of ever-falling Waters; shrouded *Nile*,[1]
Eridanus, and *Tiber* with his Twins,
And palmy *Euphrates*; they with dropping locks
Hang o'er their Urns, and mournfully among
The plaintive-ecchoing Ruins pour their streams.

.   .   .   .

[1] Fountains at *Rome* adorned with the Statues of those Rivers.

JOHN DYER

There is a Mood,
(I sing not to the vacant and the young)
There is a kindly Mood of Melancholy,
That wings the Soul and points her to the Skies;
When Tribulation cloaths the child of Man,
When Age descends with sorrow to the grave,
'Tis sweetly-soothing Sympathy to Pain,
A gently-wak'ning Call to Health and Ease,
How musical! When all-devouring Time,
Here sitting on his Throne of Ruins hoar,
With Winds and Tempests sweeps his various Lyre,
How sweet thy Diapason, Melancholy!

The Ruins of Rome, 1740

183   *English Weather*

HOW erring oft the judgment in its hate,
Or fond desire! Those slow-descending show'rs,
Those hov'ring fogs, that bathe our growing vales
In deep November (loath'd by trifling Gaul,
Effeminate), are gifts the Pleiads shed,
Britannia's handmaids. As the bev'rage falls,
Her hills rejoice, her vallies laugh and sing.

HAIL noble Albion! where no golden mines,
No soft perfumes, nor oils, nor myrtle bow'rs,
The vig'rous frame and lofty heart of man
Enervate: round whose stern cerulean brows
White-winged snow, and cloud, and pearly rain,
Frequent attend, with solemn majesty:
Rich queen of mists and vapours!

The Fleece, i, 1757

184 *The Wool Trade*

THUS all is here in motion, all is life:
   The creaking wain brings copious store of corn:
The grazier's sleeky kine obstruct the roads;
The neat-dress'd housewives, for the festal board
Crown'd with full baskets, in the field-way paths
Come tripping on; th' echoing hills repeat
The stroke of ax and hammer; scaffolds rise,
And growing edifices; heaps of stone,
Beneath the chissel, beauteous shapes assume
Of frize and column. Some, with even line,
New streets are marking in the neighb'ring fields,
And sacred domes of worship. Industry,
Which dignifies the artist, lifts the swain,
And the straw cottage to a palace turns,
Over the work presides. Such was the scene
Of hurrying Carthage, when the Trojan chief
First view'd her growing turrets. So appear
Th' increasing walls of busy Manchester,
Sheffield, and Birmingham, whose redd'ning fields
Rise and enlarge their suburbs. Lo, in throngs,
For ev'ry realm, the careful factors meet,
Whisp'ring each other. In long ranks the bales,
Like war's bright files, beyond the sight extend.
              .   .   .   .   Pursue,
Ye sons of Albion, with unyielding heart,
Your hardy labors: let the sounding loom
Mix with the melody of ev'ry vale.

                              The Fleece, iii, 1757

277

185 *A Nation's Wealth*

BUT chief by numbers of industrious hands
A nation's wealth is counted: numbers raise
Warm emulation: where that virtue dwells,
There will be traffick's seat; there will she build
Her rich emporium. Hence, ye happy swains,
With hospitality inflame your breast,
And emulation: the whole world receive,
And with their arts, their virtues, deck your isle.
Each clime, each sea, the spacious orb of each,
Shall join their various stores, and amply feed
The mighty brotherhood; while ye proceed,
Active and enterprising, or to teach
The stream a naval course, or till the wild,
Or drain the fen, or stretch the long canal,
Or plough the fertile billows of the deep.
Why to the narrow circle of our coast
Should we submit our limits, while each wind
Assists the stream and sail, and the wide main
Wooes us in ev'ry port?

The Fleece, iii, 1757

186 *British Commerce*

REJOICE, ye nations, vindicate the sway
Ordain'd for common happiness. Wide, o'er
The globe terraqueous, let Britannia pour
The fruits of plenty from her copious horn.
What can avail to her, whose fertile earth
By ocean's briny waves are circumscrib'd,
The armed host, and murd'ring sword of war,
And conquest o'er her neighbours? She ne'er breaks

JOHN DYER

Her solemn compacts, in the lust of rule:
Studious of arts and trade, she ne'er disturbs
The holy peace of states. 'Tis her delight
To fold the world with harmony, and spread,
Among the habitations of mankind,
The various wealth of toil, and what her fleece,
To clothe the naked, and her skilful looms,
Peculiar give. Ye too rejoice, ye swains;
Increasing commerce shall reward your cares.
A day will come, if not too deep we drink
The cup, which luxury on careless wealth,
Pernicious gift, bestows; a day will come,
When, through new channels sailing, we shall clothe
The Californian coast, and all the realms
That stretch from Anian's streights to proud Japan;
And the green isles, which on the left arise
Upon the glassy brine, whose various capes
Not yet are figur'd on the sailors chart:
Then ev'ry variation shall be told
Of the magnetic steel; and currents mark'd,
Which drive the heedless vessel from her course.

The Fleece, iv, 1757

WILLIAM SOMERVILE

1675–1742

187 *On presenting to a Lady a White Rose
and a Red on the Tenth of June*

IF this pale Rose offend your Sight,
It in your Bosom wear;
'Twill blush to find itself less white,
And turn *Lancastrian* there.

But, *Celia*, should the Red be chose,
  With gay Vermilion bright;
'Twould sicken at each Blush that glows,
  And in Despair turn White.

Let Politicians idly prate,
  Their *Babels* build in vain;
As uncontrolable as Fate,
  Imperial Love shall reign.

Each haughty Faction shall obey,
  And Whigs, and Tories join,
Submit to your Despotick Sway,
  Confess your Right Divine.

Yet this (my gracious Monarch) own,
  They're Tyrants that oppress;
'Tis Mercy must support your Throne,
  And 'tis like Heav'n to Bless.

Occasional Poems, 1727

188   *Hare-hunting*

HARK! from yon Covert, where those tow'ring Oaks
  Above the humble Copse aspiring rise,
What glorious Triumphs burst in ev'ry Gale
Upon our ravish'd Ears! The Hunters shout,
The clanging Horns swell their sweet-winding Notes,
The Pack wide-op'ning load the trembling Air
With various Melody; from Tree to Tree
The propagated Cry, redoubling bounds,
And winged Zephyrs waft the floating Joy
Thro' all the Regions near: Afflictive Birch
No more the School-boy dreads, his Prison broke,

Scamp'ring he flies, nor heeds his Master's Call;
The weary Traveller forgets his Road,
And climbs th' adjacent Hill; the Ploughman leaves
Th' unfinish'd Furrow; nor his bleating Flocks
Are now the Shepherd's Joy; Men, Boys, and Girls
Desert th' unpeopled Village; and wild Crowds
Spread o'er the Plain, by the sweet Frenzy seiz'd.
Look, how she pants! and o'er yon op'ning Glade
Slips glancing by; while, at the further End,
The puzzling Pack unravel Wile by Wile
Maze within Maze. The Covert's utmost Bound
Slyly she skirts; behind them cautious creeps,
And in that very Track, so lately stain'd
By all the steaming Crowd, seems to pursue
The Foe she flies. Let Cavillers deny
That Brutes have Reason; sure 'tis something more,
'Tis Heav'n directs, and Stratagems inspires,
Beyond the short Extent of human Thought.
But hold——I see her from the Covert break;
Sad on yon little Eminence she sits;
Intent she listens with one Ear erect,
Pond'ring, and doubtful what new Course to take,
And how t' escape the fierce blood-thirsty Crew,
That still urge on, and still in Vollies loud
Insult her Woes, and mock her sore Distress.
As now in louder Peals the loaded Winds
Bring on the gath'ring Storm, her Fears prevail;
And o'er the Plain, and o'er the Mountain's Ridge,
Away she flies; nor Ships with Wind and Tide,
And all their Canvass Wings, skud half so fast.
Once more, ye jovial Train, your Courage try,
And each clean Courser's Speed. We scour along,

In pleasing Hurry and Confusion tost;
Oblivion to be wish'd.   The patient Pack
Hang on the Scent unweary'd, up they climb,
And ardent we pursue; our lab'ring Steeds
We press, we gore; till once the Summit gain'd,
Painfully panting, there we breath awhile;
Then like a foaming Torrent, pouring down
Precipitant, we smoke along the Vale.
Happy the Man, who with unrival'd Speed
Can pass his Fellows, and with Pleasure view
The struggling Pack; how in the rapid Course
Alternate they preside, and justling push
To guide the dubious Scent; how giddy Youth
Oft babbling errs, by wiser Age reprov'd;
How niggard of his Strength, the wise old Hound
Hangs in the Rear, 'till some important Point
Rouse all his Diligence, or 'till the Chace
Sinking he finds; then to the Head he springs
With Thirst of Glory fir'd, and wins the Prize.
Huntsman, take heed; they stop in full career.
Yon crowding Flocks, that at a Distance gaze,
Have haply foil'd the Turf. See! that old Hound,
How busily he works, but dares not trust
His doubtful Sense; draw yet a wider Ring.
Hark! now again the Chorus fills: as Bells
Sally'd a while at once their Peal renew,
And high in Air the tuneful Thunder rolls.
See, how they toss, with animated Rage
Recov'ring all they lost!—That eager Haste
Some doubling Wile foreshews.—Ah! yet once more
They're check'd—hold back with Speed—on either Hand
They flourish round—ev'n yet persist—'Tis right,

Away they spring; the rustling Stubbles bend
Beneath the driving Storm. Now the poor Chace
Begins to flag, to her last Shifts reduc'd.
From Brake to Brake she flies, and visits all
Her well-known Haunts, where once she rang'd secure,
With Love and Plenty blest. See! there she goes,
She reels along, and by her Gate betrays
Her inward Weakness. See, how black she looks!
The Sweat that clogs th' obstructed Pores, scarce leaves
A languid Scent. And now in open View
See, see, she flies! each eager Hound exerts
His utmost Speed, and stretches ev'ry Nerve.
How quick she turns! their gaping Jaws eludes,
And yet a Moment lives; 'till round inclos'd
By all the greedy Pack, with infant Screams
She yields her Breath, and there reluctant dies.

The Chace, ii, 1735

189 *An Address to his Elbow-chair, new cloath'd*

MY dear companion, and my faithful friend!
If Orpheus taught the listening oaks to bend;
If stones and rubbish, at Amphion's call,
Danc'd into form, and built the Theban wall;
Why should'st not *thou* attend my humble lays,
And hear my grateful harp resound thy praise?

True, thou art spruce and fine, a very beau;
But what are trappings, and external show?
To real worth alone I make my court;
Knaves are my scorn, and coxcombs are my sport.

Once I beheld thee far less trim and gay;
Ragged, disjointed, and to worms a prey;

The safe retreat of every lurking mouse;
Derided, shun'd; the lumber of my house!
Thy robe, how chang'd from what it was before!
Thy velvet robe, which pleas'd my sires of yore!
'Tis thus capricious Fortune wheels us round;
Aloft we mount—then tumble to the ground.
Yet grateful *then*, my constancy I prov'd;
I knew thy worth; my friend in rags I lov'd!
I lov'd thee, *more*; nor, like a courtier, spurn'd
My benefactor, when the tide was turn'd.

With conscious shame, yet frankly, I confess,
That in my youthful days—I lov'd thee less.
Where vanity, where pleasure call'd, I stray'd;
And every wayward appetite obey'd.
But sage experience taught me how to prize
Myself; and how, this world: she bade me rise
To nobler flights, regardless of a race
Of factious emmets; pointed where to place
My bliss, and lodg'd me in thy soft embrace.

Here on thy yielding down I sit secure,
And, patiently, what heav'n has sent, endure:
From all the futile cares of business free;
Not *fond* of life, but yet content to *be*:
Here mark the fleeting hours; regret the past;
And seriously prepare, to meet the last.

So safe on shore the pension'd sailor lies,
And all the malice of the storm defies;
With ease of body blest, and peace of mind,
Pities the restless crew he left behind;
Whilst, in his cell, he meditates alone
On his great voyage, to the world unknown.

The Student, January 1750

1696–1737

A Cure for the Spleen

CONTENTMENT, parent of delight,
　So much a stranger to our sight,
Say, goddess, in what happy place
Mortals behold thy blooming face;
Thy gracious auspices impart,
And for thy temple chuse my heart.
They, whom thou deignest to inspire,
Thy science learn, to bound desire;
By happy alchymy of mind
They turn to pleasure all they find;
They both disdain in outward mien
The grave and solemn garb of spleen,
And meretricious arts of dress
To feign a joy, and hide distress;
Unmov'd when the rude tempest blows,
Without an opiate they repose;
And cover'd by your shield defy
The whizzing shafts, that round them fly
Nor, meddling with the Gods' affairs,
Concern themselves with distant cares;
But place their bliss in mental rest,
And feast upon the good possesst.

　Forc'd by soft violence of pray'r,
The blythsome goddess sooths my care;
I feel the deity inspire,
And thus she models my desire.
Two hundred pounds half-yearly paid,
Annuity securely made;

MATTHEW GREEN

A farm some twenty miles from town,
Small, tight, salubrious, and my own;
Two maids, that never saw the town;
A serving-man not quite a clown;
A boy to help to tread the mow,
And drive, while t'other holds the plough
A chief of temper form'd to please,
Fit to converse, and keep the keys,
And better to preserve the peace,
Commission'd by the name of niece;
With understandings of a size
To think their master very wise.
May heav'n (it's all I wish for) send
One genial room to treat a friend,
Where decent cup-board, little plate,
Display benevolence, not state.
And may my humble dwelling stand
Upon some chosen spot of land;
A pond before full to the brim,
Where cows may cool, and geese may swim;
Behind, a green like velvet neat,
Soft to the eye, and to the feet,
Where od'rous plants in evening fair
Breathe all around ambrosial air,
From Eurus, foe to kitchen-ground,
Fenc'd by a slope with bushes crown'd,
Fit dwelling for the feather'd throng,
Who pay their quit-rents with a song;
With op'ning views of hill and dale,
Which sense and fancy too regale. . . .
There see the clover, pea, and bean,
Vie in variety of green,

MATTHEW GREEN

Fresh pastures speckled o'er with sheep,
Brown fields their fallow sabbaths keep;
Plump Ceres golden tresses wear,
And poppy-topknots deck her hair,
And silver streams thro' meadows stray,
And Naiads on the margin play,
And lesser nymphs on side of hills
From play-thing urns pour down the rills.

Thus shelter'd, free from care and strife,
May I enjoy a calm thro' life,
See faction, safe in low degree,
As men at land see storms at sea,
And laugh at miserable elves
Not kind, so much as to themselves,
Curst with such souls of base alloy,
As can possess, but not enjoy,
Debarr'd the pleasure to impart
By av'rice, sphincter of the heart,
Who wealth, hard earn'd by guilty cares,
Bequeath untouch'd to thankless heirs
May I, with look ungloom'd by guile,
And wearing virtue's liv'ry-smile,
Prone the distressed to relieve,
And little trespasses forgive,
With income not in fortune's pow'r,
And skill to make a busy hour,
With trips to town life to amuse,
To purchase books, and hear the news,
To see old friends, brush off the clown,
And quicken taste at coming down,
Unhurt by sickness' blasting rage,
And slowly mellowing in age,

When fate extends its gath'ring gripe,
Fall off like fruit grown fully ripe,
Quit a worn being without pain,
Perhaps to blossom soon again.

The Spleen, 1737

191   *On Even Keel*

THUS, thus I steer my bark, and sail
    On even keel with gentle gale.
At helm I make my reason sit,
My crew of passions all submit.
If dark and blustring prove some nights,
Philosophy puts forth her lights;
Experience holds the cautious glass,
To shun the breakers, as I pass,
And frequent throws the wary lead,
To see what dangers may be hid;
And once in seven years I'm seen
At Bath or Tunbridge to careen.
Tho' pleas'd to see the dolphins play,
I mind my compass and my way,
With store sufficient for relief,
And wisely still prepar'd to reef,
Nor wanting the dispersive bowl
Of cloudy weather in the soul,
I make (may heav'n propitious send
Such wind and weather to the end)
Neither becalm'd, nor over-blown,
Life's voyage to the world unknown.

The Spleen, 1737

1707–1754

192 *Hunting Song*

T HE dusky Night rides down the Sky,
    And ushers in the Morn;
The Hounds all join in glorious Cry,
    The Huntsman winds his Horn:
        And a Hunting we will go.

The Wife around her Husband throws
    Her Arms, and begs his Stay;
My Dear, it rains, and hails, and snows
    You will not hunt to-day.
        But a Hunting we will go.

A brushing Fox in yonder Wood,
    Secure to find we seek;
For why, I carry'd sound and good
    A Cartload there last Week.
        And a Hunting we will go.

Away he goes, he flies the Rout,
    Their Steeds all spur and switch;
Some are thrown in, and some thrown out,
    And some thrown in the Ditch:
        But a Hunting we will go.

At length his Strength to Faintness worn,
    Poor *Renard* ceases Flight;
Then hungry, homeward we return,
    To feast away the Night:
        Then a Drinking we will go.

                    Don Quixote in England, Act ii, 1733

193   *The Roast Beef of Old England*

WHEN mighty rost Beef was the *Englishman's* Food,
   It enobled our Hearts, and enriched our Blood;
Our Soldiers were brave, and our Courtiers were good.
     Oh the Rost Beef of Old *England*,
     And Old *England*'s Rost Beef!

Then, *Britons*, from all nice Dainties refrain,
Which effeminate *Italy*, *France*, and *Spain*;
And mighty Rost Beef shall command on the Main.
     Oh the Rost Beef, &c.

The Grub-Street Opera, 1731; *Don Quixote in England*, 1733

RICHARD LEVERIDGE

1670–1758

194   *A Song in Praise of Old English Roast Beef*

WHEN mighty Roast Beef was the *Englishman's* Food,
   It enobled our Veins and enriched our Blood,
Our Soldiers were brave and our Courtiers were good.
     Oh the Roast Beef of Old England,
     And Old English *Roast Beef*.

But since we have learn'd from all-conquering *France*
To eat their Ragouts as well as to dance,
We are fed up with nothing but vain Complaisance.
     Oh the Roast Beef, &c.

Our Fathers of old were robust, stout, and strong,
And kept open House with good Cheer all Day long,
Which made their plump Tenants rejoice in this song,
     Oh the Roast Beef, &c.

RICHARD LEVERIDGE

But now we are dwindled, to what shall I name?
A sneaking poor Race, half begotten—and tame,
Who sully those Honours that once shone in Fame.
    Oh the Roast Beef, &c.

When good Queen *Elizabeth* was on the Throne,
E'er Coffee, or Tea, and such Slip Slops were known,
The World was in Terror, if e'er she did frown.
    Oh the Roast Beef, &c.

In those Days, if Fleets did presume on the Main,
They seldom or never return'd back again,
As witness the vaunting *Armada* of *Spain*.
    Oh the Roast Beef, &c.

Oh then they had Stomachs to eat and to fight,
And when Wrongs were a-cooking to do themselves right!
But now we're a—I cou'd—but good Night.
    Oh the Roast Beef of Old England,
    And Old English *Roast Beef*.

                    The British Musical Miscellany, iii, 1735

PAUL WHITEHEAD

1710–1774

195   *Hunting Song*

THE sun from the East tips the mountains with gold;
    The meadows all spangled with dew-drops behold!
Hear! the lark's early matin proclaims the new day,
And the Horn's chearful summons rebukes our delay.
    With the sports of the Field there's no pleasure can vye,
    While jocund we follow the Hounds in full cry.

PAUL WHITEHEAD

Let the Drudge of the Town still make Riches his sport
The Slave of the State hunt the smiles of a Court;
No care and ambition our pastime annoy,
But innocence still gives a zest to our joy.
With the sports, &c.

Mankind are all hunters in various degree;
The Priest hunts a Living—the Lawyer a Fee,
The Doctor a Patient—the Courtier a Place,
Though often, like us, he's flung-out in the chace.
With the sports, &c.

The Cit hunts a Plumb—while the Soldier hunts Fame,
The Poet a Dinner—the Patriot a Name;
And the practis'd Coquette, tho' she seems to refuse,
In spite of her airs, still her Lover pursues.
With the sports, &c.

Let the Bold and the Busy hunt Glory and Wealth;
All the blessing we ask is the blessing of Health,
With Hound and with Horn thro' the woodlands to roam,
And, when tired abroad, find Contentment at home.

With the sports of the Field there's no pleasure can vie,
While jocund we follow our Hounds in full cry.
Sung in *Apollo and Daphne*, 1734, or later

PHILIP DORMER STANHOPE
EARL OF CHESTERFIELD

1694–1773

196   *Verses written in a Lady's*
       Sherlock ' Upon Death '

MISTAKEN fair, lay *Sherlock* by,
    His doctrine is deceiving;
For, whilst he teaches us to die,
    He cheats us of our living.

To die's a lesson we shall know
    Too soon, without a master;
Then let us only study now
    How we may live the faster.

To live's to love, to bless, be bless'd
    With mutual inclination;
Share then my ardour in your breast,
    And kindly meet my passion.

But if thus bless'd I may not live,
    And pity you deny,
To me, at least, your *Sherlock* give,
    'Tis I must learn to die.
                The Gentleman's Magazine, May 1733

197   *Advice to a Lady in Autumn*

ASSES milk, half a pint, take at seven, or before;
    Then sleep for an hour or two, and no more.
At nine stretch your arms, and oh! think when alone,
There's no pleasure in bed.—MARY, bring me my gown:

PHILIP DORMER STANHOPE

Slip on that ere you rise; let your caution be such,
Keep all cold from your breast, there's already too much.
Your pinners set right, your twitcher ty'd on,
Your prayers at an end, and your breakfast quite done,
Retire to some author improving and gay,
And with sense like your own, set your mind for the day.
At twelve you may walk, for at this time o'the year,
The sun, like your wit, is as mild as 'tis clear:
But mark in the meadows the ruin of time;
Take the hint, and let life be improv'd in its prime.
Return not in haste, nor of dressing take heed;
For beauty like yours, no assistance can need.
With an appetite, thus, down to dinner you sit,
Where the chief of the feast, is the flow of your wit:
Let this be indulg'd, and let laughter go round;
As it pleases your mind, to your health 'twill redound.
After dinner two glasses at least, I approve;
Name the first to the king, and the last to your love:
Thus cheerful with wisdom, with innocence gay,
And calm with your joys gently glide thro' the day.
The dews of the evening most carefully shun;
Those tears of the sky for the loss of the sun.
Then in chat, or at play, with a dance, or a song,
Let the night, like the day, pass with pleasure along.
All cares, but of love, banish far from your mind;
And those you may end, when you please to be kind.

The Gentleman's Magazine, November 1736

SIR CHARLES HANBURY WILLIAMS
1708–1759

198   *The Old General*

THE gen'ral! one of those brave old commanders,
  Who serv'd through all the glorious wars in Flanders;
Frank and good natur'd, of an honest heart,
Loving to act the steady friendly part:
None led through youth a gayer life than he,
Chearful in converse, smart in repartee.
Sweet was his night, and joyful was his day,
He din'd with Walpole, and with Oldfield lay;
But with old age its vices came along,
And in narration he's extremely long;
Exact in circumstance, and nice in dates,
He each minute particular relates.
If you name one of Malbro's ten campaigns,
He tells you its whole history for your pains:
And Blenheim's field becomes by his reciting,
As long in telling as it was in fighting:
His old desire to please is still express'd;
His hat's well cock'd, his perriwig's well dress'd:
He rolls his stockings still, white gloves he wears,
And in the boxes with the beaux appears:
His eyes through wrinkled corners cast their rays;
Still he looks chearful, still soft things he says:
And still rememb'ring that he once was young
He strains his crippled knees, and struts along.

Isabella, 1740

199   *An Epigram of Martial, imitated*

COME, Chloe, and give me sweet kisses,
    For sweeter sure never girl gave:
But why in the midst of my blisses
    Do you ask me how many I'd have?
I'm not to be stinted in pleasure,
    Then pr'ythee my charmer be kind,
For whilst I love thee above measure,
    To numbers I'll ne'er be confin'd.

Count the bees that on Hybla are playing,
    Count the flow'rs that enamel its fields,
Count the flocks that on Tempe are straying,
    Or the grain that rich Sicily yields;
Go number the stars in the heaven,
    Count how many sands on the shore,
When so many kisses you've given
    I still shall be craving for more.

To a heart full of love let me hold thee,
    To a heart which, dear Chloe, is thine
With my arms I'll for ever enfold thee,
    And twist round thy limbs like a vine.
What joy can be greater than this is?
    My life on thy lips shall be spent;
But the wretch that can number his kisses
    With few will be ever content.

Dodsley's Collection, iv, 1755

200 *An Ode on Miss Harriet Hanbury*
at Six Years old

WHY shou'd I thus employ my time,
　　To paint those cheeks of rosy hue ?
Why should I search my brains for rhyme,
　　To sing those eyes of glossy blue?

The pow'r as yet is all in vain,
　　Thy num'rous charms, and various graces :
They only serve to banish pain,
　　And light up joy in parents' faces.

But soon those eyes their strength shall feel :
　　Those charms their pow'rful sway shall find :
Youth shall in crowds before you kneel,
　　And own your empire o'er mankind.

Then, when on Beauty's throne you sit,
　　And thousands court your wish'd-for arms,
My muse shall stretch her utmost wit,
　　To sing the vict'ries of your charms.

Charms that in time shall ne'er be lost,
　　At least while verse like mine endures :
And future Hanburys shall boast,
　　Of verse like mine, of charms like yours.

A little vain we both may be,
　　Since scarce another house can shew
A poet, that can sing like me,
　　A beauty, that can charm like you.

Dodsley's *Collection*, v, 1758

297

201   *A Pipe of Tobacco*

In imitation of Young

CRITICS avaunt! TOBACCO is my Theme;
    Tremble like Hornets at the blasting Steam.
And you, Court-insects, flutter not too near
Its Light, nor buzz within the scorching Sphere.
Pollio, with Flame like thine, my Verse inspire,
So shall the Muse from Smoke elicit Fire.
Coxcombs prefer the tickling Sting of Snuff;
Yet all their Claim to Wisdom is—a Puff:
Lord *Foplin* smokes not—for his Teeth afraid:
Sir *Tawdry* smokes not—for he wears Brocade.
Ladies, when Pipes are brought, affect to swoon;
They love no *Smoke*, except the *Smoke* of Town:
But Courtiers hate the puffing Tribe,—no matter,
Strange if they love the *Breath* that cannot *flatter !*
Its Foes but shew their Ignorance, can *He*
Who scorns the *Leaf* of Knowledge, love the *Tree?*
The *tainted* Templar (more prodigious yet)
Rails at TOBACCO, tho' it makes him—*spit.*
Citronia vows it has an odious Stink;
She will not smoke (ye Gods!) but she will drink:
And chaste *Prudella* (blame her if you can)
Says, Pipes are us'd by that vile Creature *Man*:
Yet Crowds remain, who still its Worth proclaim,
While some for Pleasure smoke, and some for *Fame*:
Fame, of our Actions universal Spring,
For which we drink, eat, sleep, smoke,—*ev'ry* Thing.

202   *In imitation of Pope*

B LEST Leaf! whose aromatic Gales dispense
  To Templars Modesty, to Parsons Sense:
So raptur'd Priests, at fam'd *Dodona*'s Shrine
Drank Inspiration from the Steam divine.
Poison that cures, a Vapour that affords
Content, more solid than the Smile of Lords:
Rest to the Weary, to the Hungry Food,
The last kind Refuge of the WISE and GOOD:
Inspir'd by Thee, dull Cits adjust the Scale
Of *Europe*'s Peace, when other Statesmen fail.
By Thee protected, and thy Sister, Beer,
Poets rejoice, nor think the Bailiff near.
Nor less, the Critic owns thy genial Aid,
While supperless he plies the piddling Trade.
What tho' to Love and soft Delights a Foe,
By Ladies hated, hated by the Beau,
Yet social Freedom, long to Courts unknown,
Fair Health, fair Truth, and Virtue are thy own.
Come to thy Poet, come with healing Wings,
And let me taste Thee unexcis'd by Kings.

              The London Evening Post, December 2, 1735

203   *The Fire Side: A Pastoral Soliloquy*
      On the Earl of Godolphin's taking the Seals

T HRICE happy, who free from ambition and pride,
  In a rural retreat, has a quiet *fire side*;
I love my *fire side*, there I long to repair,
And to drink a delightful oblivion of care.

Oh! when shall I 'scape to be truly my own,
From the noise, and the smoke, and the bustle of town.
Then I live, then I triumph, whene'er I retire
From the pomp and parade that the Many admire.
Hail ye woods and ye lawns, shady vales, sunny hills,
And the warble of birds, and the murmur of rills,
Ye flow'rs of all hues that embroider the ground,
Flocks feeding, or frisking in gambols around;
Scene of joy to behold! joy, that who would forego,
For the wealth and the pow'r that a court can bestow?
I have said it at home, I have said it abroad,
That the town is Man's world, but that this is of God;
Here my trees cannot flatter, plants nurs'd by my care
Pay with fruit or with fragrance, and incense the air;
Here contemplative solitude raises the mind,
(Least alone, when alone,) to ideas refin'd.
Methinks hid in groves, that no sound can invade,
Save when Philomel strikes up her sweet serenade,
I revolve on the changes and chances of things,
And pity the wretch that depends upon kings.

Now I pass with old authors an indolent hour,
And reclining at ease turn Demosthenes o'er;
Now facetious and vacant, I urge the gay flask
With a set of old friends—who have nothing to ask;
Thus happy, I reck not of FRANCE nor of SPAIN,
Nor the *balance of power* what hand shall sustain.
The *balance of pow'r?* Ah! till that is restor'd,
What solid delight can retirement afford?
Some must be content to be drudges of state,
That the Sage may securely enjoy his retreat.
In weather serene, when the ocean is calm,
It matters not much who presides at the helm;

ISAAC HAWKINS BROWNE

But soon as clouds gather and tempests arise,
Then a pilot there needs, a man *dauntless and wise*.
If such can be found, sure he ought to come forth
And lend to the publick his talents and worth.
Whate'er inclination or ease may suggest,
If the state wants his aid, he has no claim to rest.
But who is the Man, a bad game to redeem?
HE whom TURIN admires, who has PRUSSIA's esteem,
Whom the SPANIARD has felt; and whose iron with dread
Haughty LEWIS saw forging to fall on his head.
HOLLAND loves him, nor less in the NORTH all the pow'rs
Court, honour, revere, and the EMPRESS adores.
Hark! what was that sound? for it seem'd more sublime
Than befits the low genius of pastoral rhyme:
Was it WISDOM I heard? or can fumes of the brain
Cheat my ears with a dream? Ha! repeat me that strain:
Yes, WISDOM, I hear thee; thou deign'st to declare
ME, ME, the sole ATLAS to prop this whole sphere:
Thy voice says, or seems in sweet accents to say,
Haste to save sinking BRITAIN;—resign'd, I obey;
And O! witness ye Powers, that Ambition and Pride
Have no share in this change—*for I love my Fire Side*.
Thus the *Shepherd*; then throwing his crook away steals
Direct to St. JAMES's and takes up the Seals.

Written 1735 ; *The Foundling Hospital
for Wit*, iv, 1747

204 *God save the King*

GOD save Great *George* our King,
Long live our noble King,
God save the King.
Send him Victorious,
Happy and Glorious,
Long to reign over us,
God save the King.

O Lord our God arise,
Scatter his Enemies,
And make them fall:
Confound their Politicks,
Frustrate their Knavish Tricks,
On him our Hopes we fix,
God save us all.

Thy choicest Gifts in Store,
On him be pleas'd to pour,
Long may he reign.
May he defend our Laws,
And ever give us Cause,
To sing with Heart and Voice
God save the King.

Lord grant that Marshal *Wade*
May by thy Mighty Aid
Victory bring.
May he Sedition hush,
And like a Torrent rush,
Rebellious Scots to crush,
God save the King.

Harmonia Anglicana; The Gentleman
Magazine, October 1745

ANONYMOUS

205 *Will he no come back again?*

ROYAL Charlie's now awa,
　　Safely owre the friendly main;
Mony a heart will break in twa,
　　Should he ne'er come back again.
　　　　Will you no come back again?
　　　　Will you no come back again?
　　　　Better lo'ed you'll never be,
　　　　And will you no come back again?

Mony a traitor 'mang the isles
　　Brak the band o' nature's law;
Mony a traitor, wi' his wiles,
　　Sought to wear his life awa.
　　　　Will he no come back again?
　　　　Will he no come back again?
　　　　Better lo'ed he'll never be,
　　　　And will he no come back again?

The hills he trode were a' his ain,
　　And bed beneath the birken tree;
The bush that hid him on the plain,
　　There's none on earth can claim but he
　　　　Will he no come back again, &c.

Whene'er I hear the blackbird sing,
　　Unto the e'ening sinking down,
Or merl that makes the woods to ring,
　　To me they hae nae ither soun',
　　　　Than, Will he no come back again, &c.

Mony a gallant sodger fought,
　　Mony a gallant chief did fa';
Death itself were dearly bought,
　　A' for Scotland's king and law.
　　　　Will he no come back again, &c.

Sweet the lav'rock's note and lang,
　　Lilting wildly up the glen;
And aye the o'erword o' the sang
　　Is ' Will he no come back again? '
　　　　Will he no come back again, &c.

Hogg's Jacobite Relics, ii, 1821

ROBERT BLAIR

1699–1746

206　　*Church and Church-yard at Night*

SEE yonder Hallow'd Fane! the pious Work
　Of Names once fam'd, now dubious or forgot,
And buried 'midst the Wreck of Things which were:
There lie interr'd the more illustrious Dead.
The Wind is up: Hark! how it howls! Methinks
Till now, I never heard a Sound so dreary:
Doors creak, and Windows clap, and Night's foul Bird
Rook'd in the Spire screams loud: The gloomy Isles
Black-plaster'd, and hung round with Shreds of 'Scutcheons
And tatter'd Coats of Arms, send back the Sound
Laden with heavier Airs, from the low Vaults
The Mansions of the Dead. Rous'd from their Slumbers
In grim Array the grizly Spectres rise,
Grin horrible, and obstinately sullen
Pass and repass, hush'd as the Foot of Night.
Again! the Screech-Owl shrieks: Ungracious Sound!
I'll hear no more, it makes one's Blood run chill.

ROBERT BLAIR

Quite round the Pile, a Row of Reverend Elms,
Coæval near with that, all ragged shew,
Long lash'd by the rude Winds: Some rift half down
Their branchless Trunks: Others so thin a Top,
That scarce Two Crows could lodge in the same Tree.
Strange Things, the Neighbours say, have happen'd here:
Wild Shrieks have issu'd from the hollow Tombs,
Dead men have come again, and walk'd about,
And the Great Bell has toll'd, unrung, untouch'd.
(Such Tales their Chear, at Wake or Gossiping,
When it draws near to Witching Time of Night.)
   Oft, in the lone Church-yard at Night I've seen
By Glimpse of Moon-shine, chequering thro' the Trees,
The School-boy with his Satchel in his Hand,
Whistling aloud to bear his Courage up,
And lightly tripping o'er the long flat Stones
(With Nettles skirted, and with Moss o'ergrown,)
That tell in homely Phrase who lie below;
Sudden! he starts, and hears, or thinks he hears
The Sound of something purring at his Heels:
Full fast he flies, and dares not look behind him,
Till out of Breath he overtakes his Fellows;
Who gather round, and wonder at the Tale
Of horrid *Apparition*, tall and ghastly,
That walks at Dead of Night, or takes his Stand
O'er some new-open'd *Grave*; and, strange to tell!
Evanishes at Crowing of the Cock.

The Grave, 1743

207 *Friendship*

OH! when my Friend and I
In some thick Wood have wander'd heedless on,
Hid from the vulgar Eye; and sat us down
Upon the sloping Cowslip-cover'd Bank,
Where the pure limpid Stream has slid along
In grateful Errors thro' the Under-wood
Sweet-murmuring: Methought! the shrill-tongu'd Thrush
Mended his Song of Love; the sooty Black-bird
Mellow'd his Pipe, and soften'd ev'ry Note:
The Eglantine smell'd sweeter, and the Rose
Assum'd a Dye more deep; whilst ev'ry Flower
Vy'd with its Fellow-Plant in Luxury
Of Dress. Oh! then the longest Summer's Day
Seem'd too too much in Haste: Still the full Heart
Had not imparted half: 'Twas Happiness
Too exquisite to last. Of Joys departed
Not to return, how painful the Remembrance!

The Grave, 1743

JOHN ARMSTRONG

1709–1779

208 *The Home of the Naiads*

NOW come, ye Naiads, to the fountains lead;
Now let me wander thro' your gelid reign.
I burn to view th' enthusiastic wilds
By mortal else untrod. I hear the din
Of waters thundering o'er the ruin'd cliffs.
With holy rev'rence I approach the rocks
Whence glide the streams renown'd in ancient song.

Here from the desart down the rumbling steep
First springs the Nile; here bursts the sounding Po
In angry waves; Euphrates hence devolves
A mighty flood to water half the East;
And there, in Gothic solitude reclin'd,
The cheerless Tanais pours his hoary urn.
What solemn twilight! What stupendous shades
Enwrap these infant floods! Thro' every nerve
A sacred horror thrills, a pleasing fear
Glides o'er my frame. The forest deepens round;
And more gigantic still th' impending trees
Stretch their extravagant arms athwart the gloom.
Are these the confines of some fairy world?
A land of Genii? Say, beyond these wilds
What unknown nations? If indeed beyond
Aught habitable lies. And whither leads,
To what strange regions, or of bliss or pain,
That subterraneous way?

The Art of Preserving Health, ii, 1744

209   *Blest Winter Nights*

THRICE happy days! in rural business past.
     Blest winter nights! when, as the genial fire
Chears the wide hall, his cordial family
With soft domestic arts the hours beguile,
And pleasing talk that starts no timerous fame,
With witless wantoness to hunt it down:
Or thro' the fairy-land of tale or song
Delighted wander, in fictitious fates
Engag'd, and all that strikes humanity;
Till lost in fable, they the stealing hour

JOHN ARMSTRONG

Of timely rest forget. Sometimes, at eve,
His neighbours lift the latch, and bless unbid
His festal roof; while, o'er the light repast,
And sprightly cups, they mix in social joy;
And, thro' the maze of conversation, trace
Whate'er amuses or improves the mind.
Sometimes at eve (for I delight to taste
The native zest and flavour of the fruit,
Where sense grows wild, and takes of no manure)
The decent, honest, chearful husbandman
Should drown his labours in my friendly bowl;
And at my table find himself at home.

The Art of Preserving Health, iii, 1744

GEORGE, LORD LYTTELTON

1709–1773

210   *Song*

WHEN Delia on the plain appears,
Aw'd by a thousand tender fears,
I would approach, but dare not move;
Tell me, my heart, if this be love?

Whene'er she speaks, my ravish'd ear
No other voice but her's can hear,
No other wit but her's approve;
Tell me, my heart, if this be love?

If she some other youth commend,
Though I was once his fondest friend,
His instant enemy I prove;
Tell me, my heart, if this be love?

When she is absent, I no more
Delight in all that pleas'd before,
The clearest spring, or shadiest grove;
Tell me, my heart, if this be love?

When fond of pow'r, of beauty vain,
Her nets she spread for ev'ry swain,
I strove to hate, but vainly strove;
Tell me, my heart, if this be love.

Written 1732; *The British Musical Miscellany*, i, 1734

211   *To the Memory of a Lady*

A Monody

IN vain I look around
  O'er the well-known ground,
My LUCY's wonted footsteps to descry;
    Where oft we us'd to walk,
    Where oft in tender talk
We saw the summer sun go down the sky;
    Nor by yon fountain's side,
    Nor where its waters glide
Along the valley, can she now be found:
In all the wide-stretch'd prospect's ample bound
    No more my mournful eye
    Can aught of her espy,
But the sad sacred earth where her dear relics lie.

O shades of Hagley, where is now your boast?
    Your bright inhabitant is lost,
You she preferr'd to all the gay resorts
Where female vanity might wish to shine,
The pomp of cities, and the pride of courts.

Her modest beauties shunn'd the public eye:
  To your sequestred dales
  And flow'r-embroider'd vales
From an admiring world she chose to fly;
With Nature there retir'd, and Nature's GOD,
  The silent paths of wisdom trod,
And banish'd ev'ry passion from her breast,
  But those, the gentlest, and the best,
Whose holy flames with energy divine
The virtuous heart enliven and improve,
The conjugal, and the maternal love.

Sweet babes, who, like the little playful fawns,
Were wont to trip along these verdant lawns
  By your delighted mother's side,
  Who now your infant steps shall guide?
Ah! where is now the hand whose tender care
To ev'ry virtue would have form'd your youth,
And strew'd with flow'rs the thorny ways of truth?
    O loss beyond repair!
    O wretched father! left alone
To weep their dire misfortune, and thy own!
How shall thy weaken'd mind, oppress'd with woe,
  And drooping o'er thy LUCY's grave,
Perform the duties that you doubly owe,
  Now she, alas! is gone,
From folly, and from vice, their helpless age to save?

  .   .   .   .

    O best of wives! O dearer far to me
      Than when thy virgin charms
      Were yielded to my arms,
    How can my soul endure the loss of thee?

How in the world, to me a desart grown,
   Abandon'd, and alone,
Without my sweet companion can I live?
   Without thy lovely smile,
The dear reward of ev'ry virtuous toil,
What pleasures now can pall'd ambition give?
Ev'n the delightful sense of well-earn'd praise,
Unshar'd by thee, no more my lifeless thoughts could raise.

   For my distracted mind
   What succour can I find?
On whom for consolation shall I call?
   Support me, ev'ry friend,
   Your kind assistance lend
To bear the weight of this oppressive woe.
   Alas! each friend of mine,
My dear, departed love, so much was thine,
That none has any comfort to bestow.
   My books, the best relief
   In ev'ry other grief,
Are now with your idea sadden'd all:
Each fav'rite author we together read
My tortur'd mem'ry wounds, and speaks of Lucy dead.

We were the happiest pair of human kind!
The rolling year its varying course perform'd,
   And back return'd again;
Another, and another smiling came,
And saw our happiness unchang'd remain:
   Still in her golden chain
Harmonious Concord did our wishes bind:
   Our studies, pleasures, tastes, the same.

GEORGE, LORD LYTTELTON

O fatal, fatal stroke,
That all this pleasing fabric Love had rais'd
Of rare felicity,
On which ev'n wanton Vice with envy gaz'd,
And every scheme of bliss our hearts had form'd
With soothing hope, for many a future day,
In one sad moment broke!
Yet, O my soul, thy rising murmurs stay,
Nor dare th' all-wise Disposer to arraign,
Or against his supreme decree
With impious grief complain.
That all thy full-blown joys at once should fade,
Was his most righteous will, and be that will obey'd.

Monody, 1747

WILLIAM SHENSTONE

1714-1763

212 *Song*

The Landskip

HOW pleas'd within my native bowers
Erewhile I pass'd the day!
Was ever scene so deck'd with flowers?
Were ever flowers so gay?

How sweetly smil'd the hill, the vale,
And all the landskip round!
The river gliding down the dale!
The hill with beeches crown'd!

But now, when urg'd by tender woes
I speed to meet my dear,
That hill and stream my zeal oppose,
And check my fond career.

No more, since DAPHNE was my theme,
   Their wonted charms I see:
That verdant hill, and silver stream,
   Divide my love and me.

Written 1737–43 ; Dodsley's *Collection*, v, 1758

213   *Pastoral Ballad*

I. *Absence*

YE shepherds so chearful and gay,
   Whose flocks never carelessly roam;
Should CORYDON's happen to stray,
   Oh! call the poor wanderers home.
Allow me to muse and to sigh,
   Nor talk of the change that ye find;
None once was so watchful as I;
   —I have left my dear PHYLLIS behind.

Now I know what it is, to have strove
   With the torture of doubt and desire;
What it is, to admire and to love,
   And to leave her we love and admire.
Ah lead forth my flock in the morn,
   And the damps of each ev'ning repel;
Alas! I am faint and forlorn:
   —I have bade my dear PHYLLIS farewel.

Since PHYLLIS vouchsaf'd me a look,
   I never once dreamt of my vine;
May I lose both my pipe and my crook,
   If I knew of a kid that was mine.

313

I priz'd every hour that went by,
  Beyond all that had pleas'd me before;
But now they are past, and I sigh;
  And I grieve that I priz'd them no more.

But why do I languish in vain?
  Why wander thus pensively here?
Oh! why did I come from the plain,
  Where I fed on the smiles of my dear?
They tell me, my favourite maid,
  The pride of that valley, is flown;
Alas! where with her I have stray'd,
  I could wander with pleasure, alone.

When forc'd the fair nymph to forego,
  What anguish I felt at my heart!
Yet I thought—but it might not be so—
  'Twas with pain that she saw me depart.
She gaz'd, as I slowly withdrew;
  My path I could hardly discern
So sweetly she bade me adieu,
  I thought that she bade me return.

The pilgrim that journeys all day
  To visit some far-distant shrine,
If he bear but a relique away,
  Is happy, nor heard to repine.
Thus widely remov'd from the fair,
  Where my vows, my devotion, I owe,
Soft hope is the relique I bear,
  And my solace wherever I go.

II. *Hope*

MY banks they are furnish'd with bees,
  Whose murmur invites one to sleep;
My grottos are shaded with trees,
  And my hills are white-over with sheep.
I seldom have met with a loss,
  Such health do my fountains bestow;
My fountains all border'd with moss,
  Where the hare-bells and violets grow.

Not a pine in my grove is there seen,
  But with tendrils of woodbine is bound:
Not a beech's more beautiful green,
  But a sweet-briar entwines it around.
Not my fields, in the prime of the year,
  More charms than my cattle unfold;
Not a brook that is limpid and clear,
  But it glitters with fishes of gold.

One would think she might like to retire
  To the bow'r I have labour'd to rear;
Not a shrub that I heard her admire,
  But I hasted and planted it there.
Oh how sudden the jessamine strove
  With the lilac to render it gay!
Already it calls for my love,
  To prune the wild branches away.

From the plains, from the woodlands and groves,
  What strains of wild melody flow!
How the nightingales warble their loves
  From thickets of roses that blow!

And when her bright form shall appear,
   Each bird shall harmoniously join
In a concert so soft and so clear,
   As—she may not be fond to resign.

I have found out a gift for my fair;
   I have found where the wood-pigeons breed:
But let me that plunder forbear,
   She will say 'twas a barbarous deed.
For he ne'er could be true, she aver'd,
   Who could rob a poor bird of its young:
And I lov'd her the more, when I heard
   Such tenderness fall from her tongue.

I have heard her with sweetness unfold
   How that pity was due to—a dove:
That it ever attended the bold,
   And she call'd it the sister of love.
But her words such a pleasure convey,
   So much I her accents adore,
Let her speak, and whatever she say,
   Methinks I should love her the more.

Can a bosom so gentle remain
   Unmov'd, when her CORYDON sighs!
Will a nymph that is fond of the plain,
   These plains and this valley despise?
Dear regions of silence and shade!
   Soft scenes of contentment and ease!
Where I could have pleasingly stray'd,
   If aught, in her absence, could please.

But where does my PHYLLIDA stray?
  And where are her grots and her bow'rs?
Are the groves and the valleys as gay,
  And the shepherds as gentle as ours?
The groves may perhaps be as fair,
  And the face of the valleys as fine;
The swains may in manners compare,
  But their love is not equal to mine.

Written 1743 ; Dodsley's Collection, iv, 1755

214   *Elegy*

He complains how soon the pleasing novelty of life is over

AH me, my friend! it will not, will not last!
  This fairy-scene, that cheats our youthful eyes!
The charm dissolves; th' aerial music's past;
  The banquet ceases, and the vision flies.

Where are the splendid forms, the rich perfumes,
  Where the gay tapers, where the spacious dome?
Vanish'd the costly pearls, the crimson plumes,
  And we, delightless, left to wander home!

Vain now are books, the sage's wisdom vain!
  What has the world to bribe our steps astray?
Ere reason learns by study'd laws to reign,
  The weaken'd passions, self-subdued, obey.

Scarce has the sun sev'n annual courses roll'd,
  Scarce shewn the whole that fortune can supply
Since, not the miser so caress'd his gold,
  As I, for what it gave, was heard to sigh.

317

On the world's stage I wish'd some sprightly part;
    To deck my native fleece with tawdry lace;
'Twas life, 'twas taste, and—oh my foolish heart!
    Substantial joy was fix'd in pow'r and place.

And you, ye works of art! allur'd mine eye,
    The breathing picture, and the living stone:
' Tho' gold, tho' splendour, heav'n and fate deny,
    ' Yet might I call one Titian stroke my own!'

Smit with the charms of fame, whose lovely spoil,
    The wreath, the garland, fire the poet's pride,
I trim'd my lamp, consum'd the midnight oil—
    But soon the paths of health and fame divide!

Oft too I pray'd, 'twas nature form'd the pray'r,
    To grace my native scenes, my rural home;
To see my trees express their planter's care,
    And gay, on Attic models, raise my dome.

But now 'tis o'er, the dear delusion's o'er!
    A stagnant breezeless air becalms my soul:
A fond aspiring candidate no more,
    I scorn the palm, before I reach the goal.

O youth! enchanting state, profusely blest!
    Bliss ev'n obtrusive courts the frolic mind;
Of health neglectful, yet by health carest;
    Careless of favour, yet secure to find.

Then glows the breast, as op'ning roses fair;
    More free, more vivid than the linnet's wing;
Honest as light, transparent ev'n as air,
    Tender as buds, and lavish as the spring.

Not all the force of manhood's active might,
  Not all the craft to subtle age assign'd,
Not science shall extort that dear delight,
  Which gay delusion gave the tender mind.

Adieu soft raptures! transports void of care!
  Parent of raptures, dear deceit, adieu!
And you, her daughters, pining with despair,
  Why, why so soon her fleeting steps pursue!

Tedious again to curse the drizling day!
  Again to trace the wintry tracts of snow!
Or, sooth'd by vernal airs, again survey
  The self-same hawthorns bud, and cowslips blow!

O life! how soon of ev'ry bliss forlorn!
  We start false joys, and urge the devious race:
A tender prey; that chears our youthful morn,
  Then sinks untimely, and defrauds the chace.
        Written about 1748 ; *Works in Verse and Prose*, 1764

215   *Written at an Inn at Henley*

To thee, fair freedom! I retire
  From flattery, cards, and dice, and din:
Nor art thou found in mansions higher
  Than the low cott, or humble inn.

'Tis here with boundless pow'r, I reign;
  And ev'ry health which I begin,
Converts dull port to bright champaigne;
  Such freedom crowns it, at an inn.

I fly from pomp, I fly from plate!
  I fly from falsehood's specious grin!
Freedom I love, and form I hate,
  And chuse my lodgings at an inn.

WILLIAM SHENSTONE

Here, waiter! take my sordid ore,
  Which lacqueys else might hope to win;
It buys, what courts have not in store;
  It buys me freedom, at an inn.

And now once more I shape my way
  Thro' rain or shine, thro' thick or thin,
Secure to meet, at close of day,
  With kind reception, at an inn.

Whoe'er has travell'd life's dull round,
  Where'er his stages may have been,
May sigh to think he still has found
  The warmest welcome, at an inn.

Written 1751 ; Dodsley's *Collection*, v, 1758 *Works*, 1764

SAMUEL JOHNSON
1709-1784

216   *Poverty in London*

BY Numbers here from Shame or Censure free,
  All Crimes are safe, but hated Poverty.
This, only this, the rigid Law persues,
This, only this, provokes the snarling Muse;
The sober Trader at a tatter'd Cloak,
Wakes from his Dream, and labours for a Joke;
With brisker Air the silken Courtiers gaze,
And turn the varied Taunt a thousand Ways.
Of all the Griefs that harrass the Distrest,
Sure the most bitter is a scornful Jest;
Fate never wounds more deep the gen'rous Heart
Than when a Blockhead's Insult points the Dart.

  Has Heaven reserv'd, in Pity to the Poor,
No pathless Waste, or undiscover'd Shore?

No secret Island in the boundless Main?
No peaceful Desart yet unclaim'd by SPAIN?
Quick let us rise, the happy Seats explore,
And bear Oppression's Insolence no more.
This mournful Truth is ev'ry where confest,
SLOW RISES WORTH, BY POVERTY DEPREST:
But here more slow, where all are Slaves to Gold,
Where Looks are Merchandise, and Smiles are sold,
Where won by Bribes, by Flatteries implor'd,
The Groom retails the Favours of his Lord.

London, 1738

217 *An Epitaph upon the celebrated Claudy
Philips, Musician, who died very poor*

*P*HILIPS, whose touch harmonious could remove
The pangs of guilty pow'r and hapless love,
Rest here, distress'd by poverty no more,
Here find that calm, thou gav'st so oft before.
Sleep, undisturb'd, within this peaceful shrine,
Till angels wake thee, with a note like thine.

The Gentleman's Magazine, September 1740

218   *Prologue spoken by Mr. Garrick*
At the Opening of the Theatre in Drury-Lane, 1747

W HEN Learning's Triumph o'er her barb'rous Foes
First rear'd the Stage, immortal SHAKESPEAR rose;
Each Change of many-colour'd Life he drew,
Exhausted Worlds, and then imagin'd new:
Existence saw him spurn her bounded Reign,
And panting Time toil'd after him in vain:

His pow'rful Strokes presiding Truth impress'd,
And unresisted Passion storm'd the Breast.

Then JOHNSON came, instructed from the School,
To please in Method, and invent by Rule;
His studious Patience, and laborious Art,
By regular Approach essay'd the Heart;
Cold Approbation gave the ling'ring Bays,
For those who durst not censure, scarce cou'd praise.
A Mortal born he met the general Doom,
But left, like *Egypt*'s Kings, a lasting Tomb.

The Wits of *Charles* found easier Ways to Fame,
Nor wish'd for JOHNSON's Art, or SHAKESPEAR's Flame;
Themselves they studied, as they felt, they writ,
Intrigue was Plot, Obscenity was Wit.
Vice always found a sympathetick Friend;
They pleas'd their Age, and did not aim to mend.
Yet Bards like these aspir'd to lasting Praise,
And proudly hop'd to pimp in future Days.
Their Cause was gen'ral, their Supports were strong,
Their Slaves were willing, and their Reign was long;
Till Shame regain'd the Post that Sense betray'd,
And Virtue call'd Oblivion to her Aid.

Then crush'd by Rules, and weaken'd as refin'd,
For Years the Pow'r of Tragedy declin'd;
From Bard, to Bard, the frigid Caution crept,
Till Declamation roar'd, while Passion slept.
Yet still did Virtue deign the Stage to tread,
Philosophy remain'd, though Nature fled.
But forc'd at length her antient Reign to quit,
She saw great *Faustus* lay the Ghost of Wit:
Exulting Folly hail'd the joyful Day,
And Pantomime, and Song, confirm'd her Sway.

But who the coming Changes can presage,
And mark the future Periods of the Stage?
Perhaps if Skill could distant Times explore,
New *Behns*, new *Durfeys*, yet remain in Store.
Perhaps, where *Lear* has rav'd, and *Hamlet* dy'd,
On flying Cars new Sorcerers may ride.
Perhaps, for who can guess th' Effects of Chance?
Here *Hunt* may box, or *Mahomet* may dance.

Hard is his Lot, that here by Fortune plac'd,
Must watch the wild Vicissitudes of Taste;
With ev'ry Meteor of Caprice must play,
And chase the new-blown Bubbles of the Day.
Ah! let not Censure term our Fate our Choice,
The Stage but echoes back the publick Voice.
The Drama's Laws the Drama's Patrons give,
For we that live to please, must please to live.

Then prompt no more the Follies you decry,
As Tyrants doom their Tools of Guilt to die;
'Tis yours this Night to bid the Reign commence
Of rescu'd Nature, and reviving Sense;
To chase the Charms of Sound, the Pomp of Show,
For useful Mirth, and salutary Woe;
Bid scenic Virtue form the rising Age,
And Truth diffuse her Radiance from the Stage.

Prologue and Epilogue spoken at . . . Drury-Lane, 1747

Hunt] Edward Hunt, a light-weight pugilist, famous for his
defeat of the Life-guardsman Hawksley, at Broughton's Amphi-
theatre, in June 1746

Mahomet] A rope-dancer who had exhibited at Covent-
Garden Theatre

219　　　*The Scholar's Life*

WHEN first the College Rolls receive his Name,
　　The young Enthusiast quits his Ease for Fame;
Thro' all his Veins the Fever of Renown
Burns from the strong Contagion of the Gown;
O'er *Bodley*'s Dome his future Labours spread,
And *Bacon*'s Mansion trembles o'er his Head;
Are these thy Views? proceed, illustrious Youth,
And Virtue guard thee to the Throne of Truth.
Yet should thy Soul indulge the gen'rous Heat
Till captive Science yields her last Retreat;
Should Reason guide thee with her brightest Ray,
And pour on misty Doubt resistless Day;
Should no false Kindness lure to loose Delight,
Nor Praise relax, nor Difficulty fright;
Should tempting Novelty thy Cell refrain,
And Sloth effuse her opiate Fumes in Vain;
Should Beauty blunt on Fops her fatal Dart,
Nor claim the triumph of a letter'd Heart;
Should no Disease thy torpid Veins invade,
Nor Melancholy's Phantoms haunt thy shade;
Yet hope not Life from Grief or Danger free,
Nor think the Doom of Man revers'd for thee.
Deign on the passing World to turn thine Eyes
And pause awhile from Letters to be wise;
There mark what Ills the Scholar's Life assail,
Toil, Envy, Want, the Patron, and the Jail.
See Nations slowly wise, and meanly just,
To buried Merit raise the tardy Bust.
If Dreams yet flatter, once again attend,
Hear *Lydiat*'s Life, and *Galileo*'s End.

The Vanity of Human Wishes, 1749

Charles XII

ON what Foundation stands the Warrior's Pride?
　　How just his Hopes let *Swedish Charles* decide;
A Frame of Adamant, a Soul of Fire,
No Dangers fright him and no Labours tire;
O'er Love, o'er Fear, extends his wide Domain,
Unconquer'd Lord of Pleasure and of Pain;
No Joys to him pacific Scepters yield,
War sounds the Trump, he rushes to the Field;
Behold surrounding Kings their pow'rs combine,
And One capitulate, and One resign:
Peace courts his Hand, but spreads her Charms in vain;
' Think Nothing gain'd ', he cries, ' till nought remain,
' On *Moscow*'s Walls till *Gothic* standards fly,
' And all be Mine beneath the Polar Sky.'
The March begins in Military State,
And Nations on his Eye suspended wait;
Stern Famine guards the solitary Coast,
And Winter barricades the Realms of Frost;
He comes, nor Want nor Cold his Course delay;—
Hide, blushing Glory, hide *Pultowa*'s day:
The vanquish'd Hero leaves his broken Bands,
And shows his Miseries in distant Lands;
Condemn'd a needy Supplicant to wait,
While Ladies interpose, and Slaves debate.
But did not Chance at length her Error mend?
Did no subverted Empire mark his End?
Did rival Monarchs give the fatal Wound?
Or hostile Millions press him to the Ground?

His Fall was destin'd to a barren Strand,
A petty Fortress, and a dubious Hand;
He left the Name, at which the World grew pale,
To point a Moral, or adorn a Tale.

The Vanity of Human Wishes, 1749

221   *Life's Last Scene*

BUT grant, the Virtues of a temp'rate Prime
   Bless with an Age exempt from Scorn or Crime;
An Age that melts with unperceiv'd Decay,
And glides in modest Innocence away;
Whose peaceful Day Benevolence endears,
Whose Night congratulating Conscience cheers;
The gen'ral Fav'rite as the gen'ral Friend:
Such Age there is, and who shall wish its End?

Yet ev'n on this her Load Misfortune flings,
To press the weary Minutes' flagging Wings;
New Sorrow rises as the Day returns,
A Sister sickens, or a Daughter mourns.
Now Kindred Merit fills the sable Bier,
Now lacerated Friendship claims a Tear.
Year chases Year, Decay pursues Decay,
Still drops some Joy from with'ring Life away;
New Forms arise, and diff'rent views Engage,
Superfluous lags the Vet'ran on the Stage,
Till pitying Nature signs the last Release,
And bids afflicted Worth retire to Peace.

But few there are whom Hours like these await,
Who set unclouded in the Gulphs of Fate.
From *Lydia's* Monarch should the Search descend,
By *Solon* caution'd to regard his End,

In Life's last Scene what Prodigies surprise,
Fears of the Brave, and Follies of the Wise!
From *Marlb'rough*'s Eyes the Streams of Dotage flow,
And *Swift* expires a Driv'ler and a Show.

The Vanity of Human Wishes, 1749

222 *Prayer*

WHERE then shall Hope and Fear their Objects find?
　　Must dull Suspence corrupt the stagnant Mind?
Must helpless Man, in Ignorance sedate,
Roll darkling down the Torrent of his Fate?
Must no Dislike alarm, no Wishes rise,
No Cries attempt the Mercies of the skies?
Enquirer, cease, Petitions yet remain,
Which Heav'n may hear, nor deem Religion vain.
Still raise for Good the supplicating Voice,
But leave to Heav'n the Measure and the Choice:
Safe in his Pow'r, whose Eyes discern afar
The secret Ambush of a specious Pray'r.
Implore his Aid, in his Decisions rest,
Secure, whate'er he gives, he gives the best.
Yet when the Sense of sacred Presence fires,
And strong Devotion to the Skies aspires,
Pour forth thy Fervours for a healthful Mind,
Obedient Passions, and a Will resign'd;
For Love, which scarce collective Man can fill;
For Patience, Sov'reign o'er transmuted ill;
For Faith, that panting for a happier Seat,
Counts Death kind Nature's Signal of Retreat.

327

These Goods for Man the Laws of Heav'n ordain,
These Goods he grants, who grants the Pow'r to gain;
With these celestial Wisdom calms the Mind,
And makes the Happiness she does not find.

The Vanity of Human Wishes, 1749

223   *A Short Song of Congratulation*

LONG-expected one and twenty,
    Ling'ring year, at last is flown;
Pomp and Pleasure, Pride and Plenty,
Great Sir John, are all your own.

Loosen'd from the Minor's tether,
Free to mortgage or to sell,
Wild as wind, and light as feather,
Bid the Slaves of thrift farewel.

Call the Bettys, Kates, and Jennys,
Ev'ry name that laughs at Care,
Lavish of your Grandsire's guineas,
Show the Spirit of an heir.

All that prey on vice and folly
Joy to see their quarry fly,
Here the Gamester light and jolly,
There the Lender grave and sly.

Wealth, Sir John, was made to wander,
Let it wander as it will:
See the Jockey, see the Pander,
Bid them come, and take their fill.

When the bonny Blade carouses,
Pockets full, and Spirits high,
What are acres? What are houses?
Only dirt, or wet or dry.

If the Guardian or the Mother
Tell the woes of wilful waste,
Scorn their counsel and their pother,
You can hang or drown at last.

Written 1780 ; Mrs. Piozzi's British
Synonymy, 1794

224 *On the Death of Mr. Robert Levet*
A Practiser in Physic

CONDEMN'D to Hope's delusive mine,
As on we toil from day to day,
By sudden blasts, or slow decline,
Our social comforts drop away.

Well tried through many a varying year,
See LEVET to the grave descend;
Officious, innocent, sincere,
Of every friendless name the friend.

Yet still he fills affection's eye,
Obscurely wise, and coarsely kind;
Nor, letter'd arrogance, deny
Thy praise to merit unrefin'd.

When fainting nature call'd for aid,
And hovering death prepar'd the blow,
His vigorous remedy display'd
The power of art without the show.

329

In misery's darkest caverns known,
   His useful care was ever nigh,
Where hopeless anguish pour'd his groan,
   And lonely want retir'd to die.

No summons mock'd by chill delay,
   No petty gain disdain'd by pride,
The modest wants of every day
   The toil of every day supplied.

His virtues walk'd their narrow round,
   Nor made a pause, nor left a void;
And sure the Eternal Master found
   The single talent well employ'd.

The busy day, the peaceful night,
   Unfelt, uncounted, glided by;
His frame was firm, his powers were bright,
   Tho' now his *eightieth* year was nigh.

Then with no fiery throbbing pain,
   No cold gradations of decay,
Death broke at once the vital chain,
   And freed his soul the nearest way.

> Written 1782 ; *The Gentleman's Magazine*,
> August 1783

MARK AKENSIDE

1721–1770

225   *Invocation to the Genius of Greece*

GENIUS of ancient Greece! whose faithful steps
   Well-pleas'd I follow thro' the sacred paths
Of nature and of science; nurse divine
Of all heroic deeds and fair desires!
O! let the breath of thy extended praise
Inspire my kindling bosom to the height
Of this untempted theme. Nor be my thoughts

Presumptuous counted, if, amid the calm
That sooths this vernal evening into smiles,
I steal impatient from the sordid haunts
Of strife and low ambition, to attend
Thy sacred presence in the sylvan shade,
By their malignant footsteps ne'er profan'd.
Descend, propitious! to my favour'd eye;
Such in thy mien, thy warm, exalted air,
As when the Persian tyrant, foil'd and stung
With shame and desperation, gnash'd his teeth
To see thee rend the pageants of his throne;
And at the lightning of thy lifted spear
Crouch'd like a slave. Bring all thy martial spoils
Thy palms, thy laurels, thy triumphal songs,
Thy smiling band of arts, thy godlike sires
Of civil wisdom, thy heroic youth
Warm from the schools of glory. Guide my way
Thro' fair Lycéum's walk, the green retreats
Of Academus, and the thymy vale,
Where oft inchanted with Socratic sounds,
Ilissus pure devolv'd his tuneful stream
In gentler murmurs. From the blooming store
Of these auspicious fields, may I unblam'd
Transplant some living blossoms to adorn
My native clime: while far above the flight
Of fancy's plume aspiring, I unlock
The springs of ancient wisdom; while I join
Thy name, thrice honour'd! with th' immortal praise
Of nature; while to my compatriot youth
I point the high example of thy sons,
And tune to Attic themes the British lyre.

The Pleasures of Imagination, Bk. i, 174

331

226 *Nature's Influence on Man*

OH! blest of heav'n, whom not the languid songs
   Of luxury, the Siren! not the bribes
Of sordid wealth, nor all the gaudy spoils
Of pageant honour can seduce to leave
Those ever-blooming sweets, which from the store
Of nature fair imagination culls
To charm th' inliven'd soul! What tho' not all
Of mortal offspring can attain the heights
Of envied life; tho' only few possess
Patrician treasures or imperial state;
Yet nature's care, to all her children just,
With richer treasures and an ampler state
Indows at large whatever happy man
Will deign to use them. His the city's pomp,
The rural honours his. Whate'er adorns
The princely dome, the column and the arch,
The breathing marbles and the sculptur'd gold,
Beyond the proud possessor's narrow claim,
His tuneful breast injoys. For him, the spring
Distills her dews, and from the silken gem
Its lucid leaves unfolds: for him, the hand
Of autumn tinges every fertile branch
With blooming gold and blushes like the morn.
Each passing hour sheds tribute from her wings;
And still new beauties meet his lonely walk;
And loves unfelt attract him. Not a breeze
Flies o'er the meadow, not a cloud imbibes
The setting sun's effulgence, not a strain
From all the tenants of the warbling shade
Ascends, but whence his bosom can partake

Fresh pleasure, unreprov'd. Nor thence partakes
Fresh pleasure only: for th' attentive mind,
By this harmonious action on her pow'rs,
Becomes herself harmonious: wont so long
In outward things to meditate the charm
Of sacred order, soon she seeks at home
To find a kindred order, to exert
Within herself this elegance of love,
This fair-inspir'd delight: her temper'd pow'rs
Refine at length, and every passion wears
A chaster, milder, more attractive mien.
But if to ampler prospects, if to gaze
On nature's form where negligent of all
These lesser graces, she assumes the port
Of that eternal majesty that weigh'd
The world's foundations, if to these the mind
Exalt her daring eye; then mightier far
Will be the change, and nobler. Would the forms
Of servile custom cramp her generous pow'rs?
Would sordid policies, the barb'rous growth
Of ignorance and rapine, bow her down
To tame pursuits, to indolence and fear?
Lo! she appeals to nature, to the winds
And rowling waves, the sun's unwearied course,
The elements and seasons: all declare
For what th' eternal maker has ordain'd
The pow'rs of man: we feel within ourselves
His energy divine: he tells the heart,
He meant, he made us to behold and love
What he beholds and loves, the general orb
Of life and being; to be great like him,
Beneficent and active. Thus the men

Whom nature's works can charm, with GOD himself
Hold converse; grow familiar, day by day,
With his conceptions; act upon his plan;
And form to his, the relish of their souls.

The Pleasures of Imagination, Bk. iii, 1774

227   *Benevolence*

THRON'D in the sun's descending car,
    What power unseen diffuseth far
        This tenderness of mind?
What genius smiles on yonder flood?
What god, in whispers from the wood,
        Bids every thought be kind?

O thou, whate'er thy awful name,
Whose wisdom our untoward frame
        With social love restrains;
Thou, who by fair affection's ties
Giv'st us to double all our joys
        And half disarm our pains;

Let universal candor still,
Clear as yon heaven-reflecting rill,
        Preserve my open mind;
Nor this nor that man's crooked ways
One sordid doubt within me raise
        To injure human kind.

Against Suspicion—Odes, 1745

228 *Ode to the Evening Star*

TO-NIGHT retir'd the queen of heaven
  With young Endymion stays:
And now to Hesper is it given
Awhile to rule the vacant sky,
Till she shall to her lamp supply
  A stream of brighter rays.

O Hesper, while the starry throng
  With awe thy path surrounds,
Oh listen to my suppliant song,
If haply now the vocal sphere
Can suffer thy delighted ear
  To stoop to mortal sounds.

So may the bridegroom's genial strain
  Thee still invoke to shine:
So may the bride's unmarried train
To Hymen chaunt their flattering vow,
Still that his lucky torch may glow
  With lustre pure as thine.

Far other vows must I prefer
  To thy indulgent power.
Alas, but now I paid my tear
On fair Olympia's virgin tomb:
And lo, from thence, in quest I roam
  Of Philomela's bower.

335

Propitious send thy golden ray,
   Thou purest light above:
Let no false flame seduce to stray
Where gulph or steep lie hid for harm:
But lead where music's healing charm
   May sooth afflicted love.

To them, by many a grateful song
   In happier seasons vow'd,
These lawns, Olympia's haunt, belong:
Oft by yon silver stream we walk'd,
Or fix'd, while Philomela talk'd,
   Beneath yon copses stood.

Nor seldom, where the beachen boughs
   That roofless tower invade,
We came while her inchanting Muse
The radiant moon above us held:
Till by a clamorous owl compell'd
   She fled the solemn shade.

But hark; I hear her liquid tone.
   Now, Hesper, guide my feet
Down the red marle with moss o'ergrown,
Through yon wild thicket next the plain,
Whose hawthorns choke the winding lane
   Which leads to her retreat.

See the green space: on either hand
   Inlarg'd it spreads around:
See, in the midst she takes her stand,
Where one old oak his awful shade
Extends o'er half the level mead
   Inclos'd in woods profound.

Hark, how through many a melting note
 She now prolongs her lays:
How sweetly down the void they float!
The breeze their magic path attends:
The stars shine out: the forest bends:
 The wakeful heifers gaze.

Whoe'er thou art whom chance may bring
 To this sequester'd spot,
If then the plaintive Syren sing,
Oh softly tread beneath her bower,
And think of heaven's disposing power,
 Of man's uncertain lot.

Oh think, o'er all this mortal stage,
 What mournful scenes arise:
What ruin waits on kingly rage:
How often virtue dwells with woe:
How many griefs from knowledge flow:
 How swiftly pleasure flies.

O sacred bird, let me at eve,
 Thus wandering all alone,
Thy tender counsel oft receive,
Bear witness to thy pensive airs,
And pity nature's common cares
 Till I forget my own.

      To the Evening-Star—Poems, 1772

229 *England, Unprepared for War*

THOU, heedless Albion, what, alas, the while
 Dost thou presume? O inexpert in arms,
Yet vain of freedom, how dost thou beguile,
With dreams of hope, these near and loud alarms?

Thy splendid home, thy plan of laws renown'd,
The praise and envy of the nations round,
What care hast thou to guard from fortune's sway?
Amid the storms of war, how soon may all
The lofty pile from its foundations fall,
Of ages the proud toil, the ruin of a day!

No: thou art rich, thy streams and fertile vales
Add industry's wise gifts to nature's store:
And every port is crouded with thy sails,
And every wave throws treasure on thy shore.
What boots it? If luxurious plenty charm
Thy selfish heart from glory, if thy arm
Shrink at the frowns of danger and of pain,
Those gifts, that treasure is no longer thine.
Oh rather far be poor. Thy gold will shine
Tempting the eye of force, and deck thee to thy bane.

But what hath force or war to do with thee?
Girt by the azure tide and thron'd sublime
Amid thy floating bulwarks, thou canst see,
With scorn, the fury of each hostile clime
Dash'd ere it reach thee. Sacred from the foe
Are thy fair fields: athwart thy guardian prow
No bold invader's foot shall tempt the strand—
Yet say, my country, will the waves and wind
Obey thee? Hast thou all thy hopes resign'd
To the sky's fickle faith? the pilot's wavering hand?

. . . .

Nor yet be aw'd, nor yet your task disown,
Though war's proud votaries look on severe;
Though secrets, taught erewhile to them alone,
They deem profan'd by your intruding ear.

Let them in vain, your martial hope to quell,
Of new refinements, fiercer weapons tell,
And mock the old simplicity, in vain:
To the time's warfare, simple or refin'd,
The time itself adapts the warrior's mind;
And equal prowess still shall equal palms obtain.

An Ode to the Country Gentlemen of England, 1758

230 *Inscription*

For a Grotto

TO me, whom in their lays the shepherds call
Actæa, daughter of the neighbouring stream,
This cave belongs. The fig-tree and the vine,
Which o'er the rocky entrance downward shoot,
Were plac'd by Glycon. He with cowslips pale,
Primrose, and purple lychnis, deck'd the green
Before my threshold, and my shelving walls
With honeysuckle cover'd. Here at noon,
Lull'd by the murmur of my rising fount,
I slumber: here my clustering fruits I tend:
Or from the humid flowers, at break of day,
Fresh garlands weave, and chace from all my bounds
Each thing impure or noxious. Enter-in,
O stranger, undismay'd. Nor bat, nor toad
Here lurks: and if thy breast of blameless thoughts
Approve thee, not unwelcome shalt thou tread
My quiet mansion: chiefly, if thy name
Wise Pallas and the immortal muses own.

Dodsley's *Collection*, vi, 1758

Inscription

YE powers unseen, to whom the bards of Greece
   Erected altars; ye who to the mind
More lofty views unfold, and prompt the heart
With more divine emotions; if erewhile
Not quite unpleasing have my votive rites
Of you been deem'd when oft this lonely seat
To you I consecrated; then vouchsafe
Here with your instant energy to crown
My happy solitude. It is the hour
When most I love to invoke you, and have felt
Most frequent your glad ministry divine.
The air is calm: the sun's unveiled orb
Shines in the middle heaven: the harvest round
Stands quiet, and among the golden sheaves
The reapers lie reclin'd. The neighbouring groves
Are mute; nor even a linnet's random strain
Echoeth amid the silence. Let me feel
Your influence, ye kind powers. Aloft in heaven
Abide ye? or on those transparent clouds
Pass ye from hill to hill? or on the shades
Which yonder elms cast o'er the lake below
Do you converse retir'd? From what lov'd haunt
Shall I expect you? Let me once more feel
Your influence, O ye kind inspiring powers:
And I will guard it well, nor shall a thought
Rise in my mind, nor shall a passion move
Across my bosom unobserv'd, unstor'd
By faithful memory: and then at some

More active moment, will I call them forth
Anew; and join them in majestic forms,
And give them utterance in harmonious strains;
That all mankind shall wonder at your sway.

Poems, 1772

232 *Early Influences*

O YE Northumbrian shades, which overlook
The rocky pavement and the mossy falls
Of solitary Wensbeck's limpid stream;
How gladly I recall your well-known seats
Belov'd of old, and that delightful time
When all alone, for many a summer's day,
I wander'd through your calm recesses, led
In silence by some powerful hand unseen.
    Nor will I e'er forget you: nor shall e'er
The graver tasks of manhood, or the advice
Of vulgar wisdom, move me to disclaim
Those studies which possess'd me in the dawn
Of life, and fix'd the color of my mind
For every future year.

The Pleasures of Imagination, iv—*Poems,* 1772

233 *Poets*

BUT the chief
Are poets; eloquent men, who dwell on earth
To clothe whate'er the soul admires or loves
With language and with numbers. Hence to these
A field is open'd wide as nature's sphere;
Nay, wider: various as the sudden acts

Of human wit, and vast as the demands
Of human will. The bard nor length, nor depth,
Nor place, nor form controuls. To eyes, to ears,
To every organ of the copious mind,
He offereth all its treasures. Him the hours,
The seasons him obey: and changeful Time
Sees him at will keep measure with his flight,
At will outstrip it.

The Pleasures of Imagination, iv—*Poems*, 1772

WILLIAM COLLINS

1721-1759

234   *Ode to Simplicity*

O THOU by *Nature* taught,
  To breathe her genuine Thought,
In Numbers warmly pure, and sweetly strong:
  Who first on Mountains wild,
  In *Fancy* loveliest Child,
Thy Babe, or *Pleasure*'s, nurs'd the Pow'rs of Song!

  Thou, who with Hermit Heart
  Disdain'st the Wealth of Art,
And Gauds, and pageant Weeds, and trailing Pall:
  But com'st a decent Maid
  In *Attic* Robe array'd,
O chaste unboastful Nymph, to Thee I call!

  By all the honey'd Store
  On *Hybla*'s Thymy Shore,
By all her Blooms, and mingled Murmurs dear,
  By Her, whose Love-lorn Woe
  In Ev'ning Musings slow
Sooth'd sweetly sad *Electra*'s Poet's Ear!

WILLIAM COLLINS

By old *Cephisus* deep,
Who spread his wavy Sweep
In warbled Wand'rings round thy green Retreat,
    On whose enamel'd Side
    When holy *Freedom* died
No equal Haunt allur'd thy future Feet.

    O Sister meek of Truth,
    To my admiring Youth,
Thy sober Aid and native Charms infuse!
    The Flow'rs that sweetest breathe,
    Tho' Beauty cull'd the Wreath,
Still ask thy Hand to range their order'd Hues.

    While *Rome* could none esteem
    But Virtue's Patriot Theme,
You lov'd her Hills, and led her Laureate Band:
    But staid to sing alone
    To one distinguish'd Throne,
And turn'd thy Face, and fled her alter'd Land.

    No more, in Hall or Bow'r,
    The Passions own thy Pow'r,
Love, only Love her forceless Numbers mean:
    For Thou hast left her Shrine,
    Nor Olive more, nor Vine,
Shall gain thy Feet to bless the servile Scene.

    Tho' Taste, tho' Genius bless,
    To some divine Excess,
Faints the cold Work till Thou inspire the whole;
    What each, what all supply,
    May court, may charm, our Eye,
Thou, only Thou can'st raise the meeting Soul!

Of These let others ask,
To aid some mighty Task,
I only seek to find thy temp'rate Vale:
Where oft my Reed might sound
To Maids and Shepherds round,
And all thy Sons, O *Nature*, learn my Tale.

Odes on Several Subjects, 1747

235 ## Ode

Written in the beginning of the Year 1746

HOW sleep the Brave, who sink to Rest,
By all their Country's Wishes blest!
When *Spring*, with dewy Fingers cold,
Returns to deck their hallow'd Mold,
She there shall dress a sweeter Sod,
Than *Fancy*'s Feet have ever trod.

By Fairy Hands their Knell is rung,
By Forms unseen their Dirge is sung;
There *Honour* comes, a Pilgrim grey,
To bless the Turf that wraps their Clay,
And *Freedom* shall a-while repair,
To dwell a weeping Hermit there!

Odes on Several Subjects, 1747

236 ## Ode to Evening

IF ought of oaten stop, or pastoral song,
May hope, chaste EVE, to sooth thy modest ear,
Like thy own solemn springs,
Thy springs, and dying gales,

O Nymph reserv'd, while now the bright-hair'd sun
Sits in yon western tent, whose cloudy skirts,
    With brede ethereal wove,
    O'erhang his wavy bed :
Now air is hush'd, save where the weak-ey'd bat,
With short shrill shriek flits by on leathern wing,
    Or where the Beetle winds
    His small but sullen horn,
As oft he rises 'midst the twilight path,
Against the pilgrim born in heedless hum :
    Now teach me, Maid compos'd,
    To breathe some soften'd strain,
Whose numbers stealing thro' thy darkning vale,
May not unseemly with its stillness suit,
    As musing slow, I hail
    Thy genial lov'd return !
For when thy folding star arising shews
His paly circlet, at his warning lamp
    The fragrant Hours, and Elves
    Who slept in flow'rs the day,
And many a Nymph who wreaths her brows with sedge,
And sheds the fresh'ning dew, and lovelier still,
    The Pensive Pleasures sweet
    Prepare thy shadowy car.
Then lead, calm Vot'ress, where some sheety lake
Cheers the lone heath, or some time-hallow'd pile,
    Or up-land fallows grey
    Reflect it's last cool gleam.
But when chill blust'ring winds, or driving rain,
Forbid my willing feet, be mine the hut,
    That from the mountain's side,
    Views wilds, and swelling floods,

And hamlets brown, and dim-discover'd spires,
And hears their simple bell, and marks o'er all
    Thy dewy fingers draw
    The gradual dusky veil.
While Spring shall pour his show'rs, as oft he wont,
And bathe thy breathing tresses, meekest Eve !
    While Summer loves to sport
    Beneath thy ling'ring light ;
While sallow Autumn fills thy lap with leaves ;
Or Winter yelling thro' the troublous air,
    Affrights thy shrinking train,
    And rudely rends thy robes ;
So long, sure-found beneath the Sylvan shed,
Shall FANCY, FRIENDSHIP, SCIENCE, rose-lip'd HEALTH,
    Thy gentlest influence own,
    And hymn thy fav'rite name !

Odes on Several Subjects, 1747
Dodsley's *Collection*, i, 1748

237 *The Passions, An Ode for Music*

WHEN Music, Heav'nly Maid, was young,
    While yet in early *Greece* she sung,
The Passions oft to hear her Shell,
Throng'd around her magic Cell,
Exulting, trembling, raging, fainting,
Possest beyond the Muse's Painting;
By turns they felt the glowing Mind,
Disturb'd, delighted, rais'd, refin'd.
Till once, 'tis said, when all were fir'd,
Fill'd with Fury, rapt, inspir'd,
From the supporting Myrtles round,
They snatch'd her Instruments of Sound,

And as they oft had heard a-part
Sweet Lessons of her forceful Art,
Each, for Madness rul'd the Hour,
Would prove his own expressive Pow'r.

First *Fear* his Hand, its Skill to try,
    Amid the Chords bewilder'd laid,
And back recoil'd he knew not why,
    Ev'n at the Sound himself had made.

Next *Anger* rush'd, his Eyes on fire,
    In Lightnings own'd his secret Stings,
In one rude Clash he struck the Lyre,
    And swept with hurried Hand the Strings.

With woful Measures wan *Despair*,
    Low sullen Sounds, his Grief beguil'd,
A solemn, strange, and mingled Air,
    'Twas sad by Fits, by Starts 'twas wild.

But thou, O *Hope*, with Eyes so fair,
    What was thy delightful Measure?
Still it whisper'd promis'd Pleasure,
    And bad the lovely Scenes at distance hail!
Still would Her Touch the Strain prolong
    And from the Rocks, the Woods, the Vale,
She call'd on Echo still thro' all the Song;
    And, where Her sweetest Theme She chose,
    A soft responsive Voice was heard at ev'ry Close,
And *Hope* enchanted smil'd, and wav'd Her golden Hair.

And longer had She sung,—but with a Frown,
    Revenge impatient rose,

He threw his blood-stain'd Sword in Thunder down,
 And with a with'ring Look,
 The War-denouncing Trumpet took,
 And blew a Blast so loud and dread,
Were ne'er Prophetic Sounds so full of Woe.
  And ever and anon he beat
  The doubling Drum with furious Heat;
And tho' sometimes each dreary Pause between,
  Dejected *Pity* at his Side,
  Her Soul-subduing Voice applied,
 Yet still He kept his wild unalter'd Mien,
While each strain'd Ball of Sight seem'd bursting from his
   Head.

Thy Numbers, *Jealousy*, to nought were fix'd,
 Sad Proof of thy distressful State,
Of diff'ring Themes the veering Song was mix'd,
 And now it courted *Love*, now raving call'd on *Hate*.

With Eyes up-rais'd, as one inspir'd,
Pale *Melancholy* sate retir'd,
And from her wild sequester'd Seat,
In Notes by Distance made more sweet,
Pour'd thro' the mellow *Horn* her pensive Soul:
 And dashing soft from Rocks around,
 Bubbling Runnels join'd the Sound;
Thro' Glades and Glooms the mingled Measure stole,
Or o'er some haunted Stream with fond Delay,
  Round an holy Calm diffusing,
  Love of Peace, and lonely Musing,
 In hollow Murmurs died away.

But O how alter'd was its sprightlier Tone:
When *Chearfulness*, a Nymph of healthiest Hue,
  Her Bow a-cross her Shoulder flung,
  Her Buskins gem'd with Morning Dew,
Blew an inspiring Air, that Dale and Thicket rung,
  The Hunter's Call to *Faun* and *Dryad* known!
  The Oak-crown'd *Sisters*, and their chast-eye'd *Queen*,
  Satyrs and sylvan Boys were seen,
  Peeping from forth their Alleys green;
Brown *Exercise* rejoic'd to hear,
  And *Sport* leapt up, and seiz'd his Beechen Spear.

Last came *Joy*'s Ecstatic Trial,
He with viny Crown advancing,
  First to the lively Pipe his Hand addrest,
But soon he saw the brisk awak'ning Viol,
  Whose sweet entrancing Voice he lov'd the best.
    They would have thought who heard the Strain,
    They saw in *Tempe*'s Vale her native Maids,
    Amidst the festal sounding Shades,
To some unwearied Minstrel dancing,
  While as his flying Fingers kiss'd the Strings,
  LOVE fram'd with *Mirth*, a gay fantastic Round,
  Loose were Her Tresses seen, her Zone unbound,
  And HE amidst his frolic Play,
As if he would the charming Air repay,
Shook thousand Odours from his dewy Wings.

  O *Music*, Sphere-descended Maid,
  Friend of Pleasure, *Wisdom*'s Aid,
  Why, Goddess, why to us deny'd?
  Lay'st Thou thy antient Lyre aside?

349

As in that lov'd *Athenian* Bow'r,
You learn'd an all-commanding Pow'r,
Thy mimic Soul, O Nymph endear'd,
Can well recall what then it heard.
Where is thy native simple Heart,
Devote to Virtue, Fancy, Art?
Arise as in that elder Time,
Warm, Energic, Chaste, Sublime!
Thy Wonders in that God-like Age,
Fill thy recording *Sister*'s Page—
'Tis said, and I believe the Tale,
Thy humblest *Reed* could more prevail,
Had more of Strength, diviner Rage,
Than all which charms this laggard Age,
Ev'n all at once together found,
Cæcilia's mingled World of Sound—
O bid our vain Endeavors cease,
Revive the just Designs of *Greece*,
Return in all thy simple State!
Confirm the Tales Her Sons relate!

Odes on Several Subjects, 1747

238   *Ode on the Death of Thomson*

IN yonder Grave a DRUID lies
    Where slowly winds the stealing Wave!
The *Year*'s best Sweets shall duteous rise
    To deck *it's* POET'S sylvan Grave!

In yon deep Bed of whisp'ring Reeds
    His airy Harp shall now be laid,
That He, whose Heart in Sorrow bleeds,
    May love thro' Life the soothing Shade.

Then Maids and Youths shall linger here,
　　And while it's Sounds at distance swell,
Shall sadly seem in Pity's Ear
　　To hear the WOODLAND PILGRIM's Knell.

REMEMBRANCE oft shall haunt the Shore
　　When THAMES in Summer-wreaths is drest,
And oft suspend the dashing Oar
　　To bid his gentle Spirit rest!

And oft as EASE and HEALTH retire
　　To breezy Lawn, or Forest deep,
The Friend shall view yon whit'ning Spire,
　　And 'mid the varied Landschape weep.

But Thou, who own'st that Earthly Bed,
　　Ah! what will ev'ry Dirge avail?
Or Tears, which LOVE and PITY shed,
　　That mourn beneath the gliding Sail!

Yet lives there one, whose heedless Eye
　　Shall scorn thy pale Shrine glimm'ring near?
With Him, Sweet Bard, may FANCY die,
　　And Joy desert the blooming Year.

But thou, lorn STREAM, whose sullen Tide
　　No sedge-crown'd SISTERS now attend,
Now waft me from the green Hill's Side
　　Whose cold Turf hides the buried FRIEND!

And see, the Fairy Valleys fade,
　　Dun *Night* has veil'd the solemn View!
—Yet once again, Dear parted SHADE,
　　Meek NATURE's CHILD, again adieu!

The genial Meads assign'd to bless
   Thy Life, shall mourn thy early Doom;
Their Hinds, and Shepherd-Girls shall dress
   With simple Hands thy rural Tomb.

Long, long, thy Stone and pointed Clay
   Shall melt the musing BRITON's Eyes,
O! VALES, and WILD WOODS, shall HE say
   In yonder Grave YOUR DRUID lies!

    Ode Occasion'd by the Death of Mr. Thomson, 1749

239   *Dirge in Cymbeline*

TO fair FIDELE's grassy Tomb
   Soft Maids, and Village Hinds shall bring
Each op'ning Sweet, of earliest Bloom,
   And rifle all the breathing Spring.

No wailing Ghost shall dare appear
   To vex with Shrieks this quiet Grove:
But Shepherd Lads assemble here,
   And melting Virgins own their Love.

No wither'd Witch shall here be seen,
   No Goblins lead their Nightly crew:
The Female Fays shall haunt the Green,
   And dress thy Grave with pearly Dew!

The Redbreast oft at Ev'ning Hours
   Shall kindly lend his little Aid,
With hoary Moss, and gather'd Flow'rs,
   To deck the Ground where thou art laid.

When howling Winds, and beating Rain,
In Tempests shake the sylvan Cell:
Or midst the Chace on ev'ry Plain,
The tender Thought on thee shall dwell.

Each lonely Scene shall thee restore,
For thee the Tear be duly shed:
Belov'd, till Life could charm no more;
And mourn'd, till Pity's self be dead.

An Epistle Addrest to Sir Thomas Hanmer
(second edition), 1744

240 *Ode*

*On the Popular Superstitions of the
Highlands of Scotland*

H——, thou return'st from Thames, whose Naiads long
Have seen thee ling'ring, with a fond delay,
Mid those soft friends, whose hearts, some future day,
Shall melt, perhaps, to hear thy tragic song.
Go, not unmindful of that cordial youth,
Whom, long endear'd, thou leav'st by Lavant's side;
Together let us wish him lasting truth,
And joy untainted with his destin'd bride.
Go! nor regardless, while these numbers boast
My short-liv'd bliss, forget my social name;
But think far off how, on the southern coast,
I met thy friendship with an equal flame!
Fresh to that soil thou turn'st, whose ev'ry vale
Shall prompt the poet, and his song demand:
To thee thy copious subjects ne'er shall fail:
Thou need'st but take the pencil to thy hand,
And paint what all believe who own thy genial land.

There must thou wake perforce thy Doric quill,
    'Tis Fancy's land to which thou sett'st thy feet;
Where still, 'tis said, the fairy people meet
    Beneath each birken shade on mead or hill.
There each trim lass that skims the milky store
    To the swart tribes their creamy bowl allots;
By night they sip it round the cottage-door,
    While airy minstrels warble jocund notes.
There every herd, by sad experience, knows
    How, wing'd with fate, their elf-shot arrows fly;
When the sick ewe her summer food foregoes,
    Or, stretch'd on earth, the heart-smit heifers lie.
Such airy beings awe th' untutor'd swain:
    Nor thou, though learn'd, his homelier thoughts neglect;
Let thy sweet muse the rural faith sustain:
    These are the themes of simple, sure effect,
That add new conquests to her boundless reign,
And fill, with double force, her heart-commanding strain.

Ev'n yet preserv'd, how often may'st thou hear,
    Where to the pole the Boreal mountains run,
Taught by the father to his list'ning son
    Strange lays, whose power had charm'd a SPENCER's ear.
At ev'ry pause, before thy mind possest,
    Old RUNIC bards shall seem to rise around,
With uncouth lyres, in many-coloured vest,
    Their matted hair with boughs fantastic crown'd:
Whether thou bid'st the well-taught hind repeat
    The choral dirge that mourns some chieftain brave,
When ev'ry shrieking maid her bosom beat,
    And strew'd with choicest herbs his scented grave;
Or whether, sitting in the shepherd's shiel,

Thou hear'st some sounding tale of war's alarms;
When, at the bugle's call, with fire and steel,
    The sturdy clans pour'd forth their bony swarms,
And hostile brothers met to prove each other's arms.

'Tis thine to sing, how framing hideous spells
    In SKY's lone isle the gifted wizzard seer,
Lodged in the wintry cave with ————,
    Or in the depth of Uist's dark forests dwells:
How they, whose sight such dreary dreams engross,
    With their own visions oft astonish'd droop,
When o'er the wat'ry strath or quaggy moss
    They see the gliding ghosts unbodied troop.
Or if in sports, or on the festive green,
    Their ———— glance some fated youth descry,
Who, now perhaps in lusty vigour seen
    And rosy health, shall soon lamented die.
For them the viewless forms of air obey,
    Their bidding heed, and at their beck repair.
They know what spirit brews the stormful day,
    And heartless, oft like moody madness stare
To see the phantom train their secret work prepare.
           [25 (or 17 ?) lines lost.]

What though far off, from some dark dell espied,
    His glimm'ring mazes cheer th' excursive sight,
Yet turn, ye wand'rers, turn your steps aside,
    Nor trust the guidance of that faithless light;
For watchful, lurking 'mid th' unrustling reed,
    At those mirk hours the wily monster lies,
And listens oft to hear the passing steed,
    And frequent round him rolls his sullen eyes,
If chance his savage wrath may some weak wretch surprise.

Ah, luckless swain, o'er all unblest indeed!
 Whom late bewilder'd in the dank, dark fen,
Far from his flocks and smoking hamlet then!
 To that sad spot ——————————————:
On him enrag'd, the fiend, in angry mood,
 Shall never look with pity's kind concern,
But instant, furious, raise the whelming flood
 O'er its drown'd bank, forbidding all return.
Or, if he meditate his wish'd escape
 To some dim hill that seems uprising near,
To his faint eye the grim and grisly shape,
 In all its terrors clad, shall wild appear.
Meantime, the wat'ry surge shall around him rise,
 Pour'd sudden forth from ev'ry swelling source.
What now remains but tears and hopeless sighs?
 His fear-shook limbs have lost their youthly force,
And down the waves he floats, a pale and breathless corse.

For him, in vain, his anxious wife shall wait,
 Or wander forth to meet him on his way;
For him, in vain, at to-fall of the day,
 His babes shall linger at th' unclosing gate!
Ah, ne'er shall he return! Alone, if night
 Her travell'd limbs in broken slumbers steep,
With dropping willows drest, his mournful sprite
 Shall visit sad, perchance, her silent sleep:
Then he, perhaps, with moist and wat'ry hand,
 Shall fondly seem to press her shudd'ring cheek
And with his blue swoln face before her stand,
 And, shiv'ring cold, these piteous accents speak:
Pursue, dear wife, thy daily toils pursue
 At dawn or dusk, industrious as before;

Nor e'er of me one hapless thought renew,
   While I lie welt'ring on the ozier'd shore,
Drown'd by the KAELPIE's wrath, nor e'er shall aid thee
     more!

Unbounded is thy range; with varied stile
   Thy muse may, like those feath'ry tribes which spring
From their rude rocks, extend her skirting wing
   Round the moist marge of each cold Hebrid isle,
To that hoar pile which still its ruin shows:
   In whose small vaults a pigmy-folk is found,
Whose bones the delver with his spade upthrows,
   And culls them, wond'ring, from the hallow'd ground!
Or thither where beneath the show'ry west
   The mighty kings of three fair realms are laid:
Once foes, perhaps, together now they rest.
   No slaves revere them, and no wars invade:
Yet frequent now, at midnight's solemn hour,
   The rifted mounds their yawning cells unfold,
And forth the monarchs stalk with sov'reign pow'r
   In pageant robes, and wreath'd with sheeny gold,
And on their twilight tombs aerial council hold.

But O! o'er all, forget not KILDA's race,
   On whose bleak rocks, which brave the wasting tides,
Fair Nature's daughter, Virtue, yet abides.
   Go, just, as they, their blameless manners trace!
Then to my ear transmit some gentle song
   Of those whose lives are yet sincere and plain,
Their bounded walks the rugged cliffs along,
   And all their prospect but the wintry main.

With sparing temp'rance, at the needful time,
　They drain the sainted spring, or, hunger-prest,
Along th' Atlantic rock undreading climb,
　And of its eggs despoil the Solan's nest.
Thus blest in primal innocence they live,
　Suffic'd and happy with that frugal fare
Which tasteful toil and hourly danger give.
　Hard is their shallow soil, and bleak and bare:
Nor ever vernal bee was heard to murmur there!

Nor need'st thou blush, that such false themes engage
　Thy gentle mind, of fairer stores possest;
For not alone they touch the village breast,
　But fill'd in elder time th' historic page,
There SHAKESPEARE's self, with ev'ry garland crown'd,
In musing hour, his wayward sisters found,
　And with their terrors drest the magic scene.
From them he sung, when mid his bold design,
　Before the Scot afflicted and aghast,
The shadowy kings of BANQUO's fated line,
　Through the dark cave in gleamy pageant past.
Proceed, nor quit the tales which, simply told,
　Could once so well my answ'ring bosom pierce;
Proceed, in forceful sounds and colours bold
　The native legends of thy land rehearse;
To such adapt thy lyre and suit thy powerful verse.

In scenes like these, which, daring to depart
　From sober truth, are still to nature true,
And call forth fresh delight to fancy's view,
　Th' heroic muse employ'd her TASSO's art!

358

WILLIAM COLLINS

How have I trembled, when at TANCRED's stroke,
   Its gushing blood the gaping cypress pour'd;
When each live plant with mortal accents spoke,
   And the wild blast up-heav'd the vanish'd sword!
How have I sat, when pip'd the pensive wind,
   To hear his harp, by British FAIRFAX strung.
Prevailing poet, whose undoubting mind
   Believ'd the magic wonders which he sung!
Hence at each sound imagination glows;
Hence his warm lay with softest sweetness flows;
   Melting it flows, pure, num'rous, strong and clear,
And fills th' impassion'd heart, and wins th' harmonious ear.

All hail, ye scenes that o'er my soul prevail,
   Ye ———— friths and lakes which, far away,
Are by smooth ANNAN fill'd, or past'ral TAY,
   Or DON's romantic springs, at distance, hail!
The time shall come when I, perhaps, may tread
   Your lowly glens, o'erhung with spreading broom,
Or o'er your stretching heaths by fancy led:
   Then will I dress once more the faded bow'r,
   Where JOHNSON sat in DRUMMOND's ———— shade;
Or crop from Tiviot's dale each ————,
   And mourn on Yarrow's banks ————
Meantime, ye Pow'rs, that on the plains which bore
   The cordial youth, on LOTHIAN's plains attend,
Where'er he dwell, on hill, or lowly muir,
   To him I lose, your kind protection lend,
And, touch'd with love like mine, preserve my absent friend.

Written about 1749 ; *Transactions of the Royal
Society of Edinburgh*, 1788

1722–1800

241   *The Charms of Nature*

RICH in her weeping country's spoils, Versailles
   May boast a thousand fountains, that can cast
The tortur'd waters to the distant heav'ns;
Yet let me choose some pine-top'd precipice
Abrupt and shaggy, whence a foamy stream,
Like Anio, tumbling roars; or some bleak heath,
Where straggling stand the mournful juniper,
Or yew-tree scath'd; while in clear prospect round,
From the grove's bosom spires emerge, and smoak
In bluish wreaths ascends, ripe harvests wave,
Low, lonely cottages, and ruin'd tops
Of Gothick battlements appear, and streams
Beneath the sun-beams twinkle. The shrill lark,
That wakes the wood-man to his early task,
Or love-sick Philomel, whose luscious lays
Sooth lone night-wanderers, the moaning dove
Pitied by listening milk-maid, far excell
The deep-mouth'd viol, the soul-lulling lute,
And battle-breathing trumpet. Artful sounds!
That please not like the choristers of air,
When first they hail th' approach of laughing May.

  · · · · · · ·

O taste corrupt! that luxury and pomp,
In specious names of polish'd manners veil'd,
Should proudly banish Nature's simple charms!
All-beauteous Nature! by thy boundless charms
Oppress'd, O where shall I begin thy praise,
Where turn th' ecstatick eye, how ease my breast
That pants with wild astonishment and love!

360

JOSEPH WARTON

Dark forests, and the opening lawn, refresh'd
With ever-gushing brooks, hill, meadow, dale,
The balmy bean-field, the gay-clover'd close,
So sweetly interchang'd, the lowing ox,
The playful lamb, the distant water-fall
Now faintly heard, now swelling with the breeze,
The sound of pastoral reed from hazel-bower,
The choral birds, the neighing steed, that snuffs
His dappled mate, stung with intense desire,
The ripen'd orchard when the ruddy orbs
Betwixt the green leaves blush, the azure skies,
The chearful sun that thro' earth's vitals pours
Delight and health and heat; all, all conspire
To raise, to sooth, to harmonize the mind,
To lift on wings of praise, to the great sire
Of being and of beauty, at whose nod
Creation started from the gloomy vault
Of dreary Chaos, while the griesly king
Murmur'd to feel his boisterous power confin'd.

　　What are the lays of artful Addison,
Coldly correct, to Shakespear's warblings wild?
Whom on the winding Avon's willow'd banks
Fair fancy found, and bore the smiling babe
To a close cavern: (still the shepherds shew
The sacred place, whence with religious awe
They hear, returning from the field at eve,
Strange whisp'ring of sweet musick thro' the air)
Here, as with honey gather'd from the rock,
She fed the little prattler, and with songs
Oft' sooth'd his wondering ears, with deep delight
On her soft lap he sat, and caught the sounds.

　　　　　The Enthusiast : or the Lover of Nature, 1744

242   *Invocation to Fancy*

WHEN young-ey'd SPRING profusely throws
    From her green lap the pink and rose,
When the soft turtle of the dale
To SUMMER tells her tender tale,
When AUTUMN cooling caverns seeks,
And stains with wine his jolly cheeks.
When WINTER, like poor pilgrim old,
Shakes his silver beard with cold,
At every season let my ear
Thy solemn whispers, FANCY, hear.
O warm, enthusiastic maid,
Without thy powerful, vital aid,
That breathes an energy divine,
That gives a soul to every line,
Ne'er may I strive with lips profane
To utter an unhallow'd strain,
Nor dare to touch the sacred string,
Save when with smiles thou bid'st me sing.
O hear our prayer, O hither come
From thy lamented SHAKSPEAR's tomb,
On which thou lov'st to sit at eve,
Musing o'er thy darling's grave;
O queen of numbers, once again
Animate some chosen swain,
Who fill'd with unexhausted fire,
May boldly smite the sounding lyre,
Who with some new, unequall'd song,
May rise above the rhyming throng,
O'er all our list'ning passions reign,
O'erwhelm our souls with joy and pain,

With terror shake, and pity move,
Rouse with revenge, or melt with love.
O deign t' attend his evening walk,
With him in groves and grottos talk;
Teach him to scorn with frigid art
Feebly to touch th' unraptur'd heart;
Like light'ning, let his mighty verse
The bosom's inmost foldings pierce;
With native beauties win applause,
Beyond cold critics' studied laws:
O let each Muse's fame encrease,
O bid BRITANNIA rival GREECE!

Ode to Fancy—Odes, 1746

GILBERT WEST

1703–1756

243 *The Island of the Blest*

THE happy Mortal, who these Treasures shares,
  Well knows what Fate attends his gen'rous Cares;
Knows, that beyond the Verge of Life and Light,
In the sad Regions of infernal Night,
The fierce, impracticable, churlish Mind
Avenging Gods and penal Woes shall find;
Where strict inquiring Justice shall bewray
The Crimes committed in the Realms of Day.
The impartial Judge the rigid Law declares,
No more to be revers'd by Penitence or Pray'rs.

But in the happy Fields of Light,
Where *Phœbus* with an equal Ray
Illuminates the balmy Night,
  And gilds the cloudless Day,

GILBERT WEST

In peaceful, unmolested Joy,
The Good their smiling Hours employ.
Them no uneasy Wants constrain
      To vex th' ungrateful Soil,
To tempt the Dangers of the billowy Main,
And break their Strength with unabating Toil,
A frail disastrous Being to maintain.
      But in their joyous calm Abodes,
The Recompence of Justice they receive;
      And in the Fellowship of Gods
Without a Tear eternal Ages live.
While banish'd by the Fates from Joy and Rest,
Intolerable Woes the impious Soul infest.

      But they who, in true Virtue strong,
      The third Purgation can endure,
      And keep their Minds from fraudful Wrong
            And Guilt's Contagion pure;
      They through the starry Paths of *Jove*
      To *Saturn's* blissful Seat remove;
      Where fragrant Breezes, vernal Airs,
            Sweet Children of the Main,
Purge the blest Island from corroding Cares,
And fan the Bosom of each verdant Plain:
Whose fertile Soil immortal Fruitage bears;
      Trees, from whose flaming Branches flow
Array'd in golden Bloom refulgent Beams;
      And Flow'rs of golden Hue, that blow
On the fresh Borders of their Parent Streams.
These by the Blest in solemn Triumph worn,
Their unpolluted Hands and clust'ring Locks adorn.

Such is the righteous Will, the high Behest
Of *Rhadamanthus*, Ruler of the Blest;
The just Assessor of the Throne divine,
On which, high rais'd above all Gods, recline,
Link'd in the Golden Bands of wedded Love,
The great Progenitors of Thund'ring *Jove*
There, in the Number of the Blest enroll'd,
Live *Cadmus*, *Peleus*, Heroes fam'd of old;
And young *Achilles*, to those Isles remov'd,
Soon as, by *Thetis* won, relenting *Jove* approv'd:

   Achilles, whose resistless Might
   Troy's stable Pillar overthrew,
   The valiant *Hector*, firm in Fight,
     And hardy *Cygnus* slew,
   And *Memnon*, Offspring of the Morn,
   In torrid *Æthiopia* born—
   Yet in my well-stor'd Breast remain
     Materials to supply
With copious Argument my Moral Strain,
Whose mystick Sense the Wise alone descry,
Still to the Vulgar sounding harsh and vain.
   He only, in whose ample Breast
Nature hath true inherent Genius pour'd,
   The Praise of Wisdom may contest;
Not they who, with loquacious Learning stor'd,
Like Crows and chatt'ring Jays, with clam'rous Cries
Pursue the Bird of *Jove*, that sails along the Skies.

                 The Second Olympick Ode—
                  The Odes of Pindar, 1749

THOMAS GRAY

1716–1771

244

Ode

On a Distant Prospect of Eton College

YE distant spires, ye antique towers,
   That crown the watry glade,
Where grateful Science still adores
Her HENRY's holy Shade;
And ye, that from the stately brow
Of WINDSOR's heights th' expanse below
Of grove, of lawn, of mead survey,
Whose turf, whose shade, whose flowers among
Wanders the hoary Thames along
His silver-winding way.

  Ah happy hills, ah pleasing shade,
Ah fields belov'd in vain,
Where once my careless childhood stray'd,
A stranger yet to pain!
I feel the gales, that from ye blow,
A momentary bliss bestow,
As waving fresh their gladsome wing,
My weary soul they seem to sooth,
And, redolent of joy and youth,
To breathe a second spring.

  Say, Father THAMES, for thou hast seen
Full many a sprightly race
Disporting on thy margent green
The paths of pleasure trace,
Who foremost now delight to cleave
With pliant arm thy glassy wave?

The captive linnet which enthrall?
What idle progeny succeed
To chase the rolling circle's speed,
Or urge the flying ball?

While some on earnest business bent
Their murm'ring labours ply
'Gainst graver hours, that bring constraint
To sweeten liberty:
Some bold adventurers disdain
The limits of their little reign,
And unknown regions dare descry:
Still as they run they look behind,
They hear a voice in every wind,
And snatch a fearful joy.

Gay hope is theirs by fancy fed,
Less pleasing when possest;
The tear forgot as soon as shed,
The sunshine of the breast:
Theirs buxom health of rosy hue,
Wild wit, invention ever-new,
And lively chear of vigour born;
The thoughtless day, the easy night,
The spirits pure, the slumbers light,
That fly th' approach of morn.

Alas, regardless of their doom,
The little victims play!
No sense have they of ills to come,
Nor care beyond to-day:
Yet see how all around 'em wait
The Ministers of human fate,

And black Misfortune's baleful train!
Ah, shew them where in ambush stand
To seize their prey the murth'rous band
Ah, tell them, they are men!

These shall the fury Passions tear,
The vulturs of the mind,
Disdainful Anger, pallid Fear,
And Shame that sculks behind;
Or pineing Love shall waste their youth,
Or Jealousy with rankling tooth,
That inly gnaws the secret heart,
And Envy wan, and faded Care,
Grim-visag'd comfortless Despair,
And Sorrow's piercing dart.

Ambition this shall tempt to rise,
Then whirl the wretch from high,
To bitter Scorn a sacrifice,
And grinning Infamy.
The stings of Falsehood those shall try
And hard Unkindness' alter'd eye,
That mocks the tear it forc'd to flow;
And keen Remorse with blood defil'd,
And moody Madness laughing wild
Amid severest woe.

Lo, in the vale of years beneath
A griesly troop are seen,
The painful family of Death,
More hideous than their Queen:
This racks the joints, this fires the veins,
That every labouring sinew strains,

Those in the deeper vitals rage:
Lo, Poverty, to fill the band,
That numbs the soul with icy hand,
And slow-consuming Age.

To each his suff'rings: all are men,
Condemn'd alike to groan;
The tender for another's pain,
Th' unfeeling for his own.
Yet ah! why should they know their fate?
Since sorrow never comes too late,
And happiness too swiftly flies.
Thought would destroy their paradise.
No more; where ignorance is bliss,
'Tis folly to be wise.

> Written 1742 ; *An Ode on a Distant*
> *Prospect, &c.,* 1747

245   *Hymn to Adversity*

DAUGHTER of Jove, relentless Power,
    Thou Tamer of the human breast,
Whose iron scourge and tort'ring hour,
The Bad affright, afflict the Best!
Bound in thy adamantine chain
The Proud are taught to taste of pain,
And purple Tyrants vainly groan
With pangs unfelt before, unpitied and alone.

When first thy Sire to send on earth
Virtue, his darling Child, design'd,
To thee he gave the heav'nly Birth,
And bad to form her infant mind.

369

Stern rugged Nurse! thy rigid lore
With patience many a year she bore:
What sorrow was, thou bad'st her know,
And from her own she learn'd to melt at others' woe.

Scared at thy frown terrific, fly
Self-pleasing Folly's idle brood,
Wild Laughter, Noise, and thoughtless Joy,
And leave us leisure to be good.
Light they disperse, and with them go
The summer Friend, the flatt'ring Foe;
By vain Prosperity received,
To her they vow their truth, and are again believed.

Wisdom in sable garb array'd
Immers'd in rapt'rous thought profound,
And Melancholy, silent maid
With leaden eye, that loves the ground,
Still on thy solemn steps attend:
Warm Charity, the gen'ral Friend,
With Justice to herself severe,
And Pity, dropping soft the sadly-pleasing tear.

Oh, gently on thy Suppliant's head,
Dread Goddess, lay thy chast'ning hand!
Not in thy Gorgon terrors clad,
Nor circled with the vengeful Band
(As by the Impious thou art seen)
With thund'ring voice, and threat'ning mien,
With screaming Horror's funeral cry,
Despair, and fell Disease, and ghastly Poverty

THOMAS GRAY

Thy form benign, oh Goddess, wear,
Thy milder influence impart,
Thy philosophic Train be there
To soften, not to wound my heart.
The gen'rous spark extinct revive,
Teach me to love and to forgive,
Exact my own defects to scan,
What others are, to feel, and know myself a Man.

Written 1742 ; Six Poems, 1753

246   *Sonnet*

On the Death of Richard West

IN vain to me the smileing Mornings shine,
  And redning Phœbus lifts his golden Fire:
The Birds in vain their amorous Descant joyn;
  Or chearful Fields resume their green Attire:
These Ears, alas! for other Notes repine,
  A different Object do these Eyes require.
My lonely Anguish melts no Heart, but mine;
  And in my Breast the imperfect Joys expire.
Yet Morning smiles the busy Race to chear,
  And new-born Pleasure brings to happier Men:
The Fields to all their wonted Tribute bear:
  To warm their little Loves the Birds complain:
I fruitless mourn to him, that cannot hear,
  And weep the more because I weep in vain.

Written 1742 ; Poems (ed. Mason), 1775

247 *Ode*

On the Death of a Favourite Cat
Drowned in a Tub of Gold Fishes

'TWAS on a lofty vase's side,
  Where China's gayest art had dy'd
The azure flowers, that blow;
Demurest of the tabby kind,
The pensive Selima reclin'd,
  Gazed on the lake below.

Her conscious tail her joy declar'd;
The fair round face, the snowy beard,
  The velvet of her paws,
Her coat, that with the tortoise vies,
Her ears of jet, and emerald eyes,
  She saw; and purr'd applause.

Still had she gaz'd; but 'midst the tide
Two angel forms were seen to glide,
  The Genii of the stream:
Their scaly armour's Tyrian hue
Thro' richest purple to the view
  Betray'd a golden gleam.

The hapless Nymph with wonder saw:
A whisker first and then a claw,
  With many an ardent wish,
She stretch'd in vain to reach the prize.
What female heart can gold despise?
  What Cat's averse to fish?

Presumptuous Maid! with looks intent
Again she stretch'd, again she bent,
   Nor knew the gulf between.
(Malignant Fate sat by, and smil'd)
The slipp'ry verge her feet beguil'd,
   She tumbled headlong in.

Eight times emerging from the flood
She mew'd to ev'ry watry God,
   Some speedy aid to send.
No Dolphin came, no Nereid stirr'd:
Nor cruel *Tom*, nor *Susan* heard.
   A Fav'rite has no friend!

From hence, ye Beauties, undeceiv'd,
Know, one false step is ne'er retriev'd,
   And be with caution bold.
Not all that tempts your wand'ring eyes
And heedless hearts, is lawful prize;
   Nor all, that glisters, gold.

          Written 1747 ; Dodsley's *Collection*, ii, 1748

248   *Elegy*

Written in a Country Church-yard

THE Curfew tolls the knell of parting day,
  The lowing herd wind slowly o'er the lea,
The plowman homeward plods his weary way,
And leaves the world to darkness and to me.

Now fades the glimmering landscape on the sight,
And all the air a solemn stillness holds,
Save where the beetle wheels his droning flight,
And drowsy tinklings lull the distant folds;

373

THOMAS GRAY

Save that from yonder ivy-mantled tow'r
The mopeing owl does to the moon complain
Of such, as wand'ring near her secret bow'r,
Molest her ancient solitary reign.

Beneath those rugged elms, that yew-tree's shade,
Where heaves the turf in many a mould'ring heap,
Each in his narrow cell for ever laid,
The rude Forefathers of the hamlet sleep.

The breezy call of incense-breathing Morn,
The swallow twitt'ring from the straw-built shed,
The cock's shrill clarion, or the echoing horn,
No more shall rouse them from their lowly bed.

For them no more the blazing hearth shall burn,
Or busy housewife ply her evening care:
No children run to lisp their sire's return,
Or climb his knees the envied kiss to share.

Oft did the harvest to their sickle yield,
Their furrow oft the stubborn glebe has broke;
How jocund did they drive their team afield!
How bow'd the woods beneath their sturdy stroke!

Let not Ambition mock their useful toil,
Their homely joys, and destiny obscure;
Nor Grandeur hear with a disdainful smile,
The short and simple annals of the poor.

The boast of heraldry, the pomp of pow'r,
And all that beauty, all that wealth e'er gave,
Awaits alike th' inevitable hour.
The paths of glory lead but to the grave.

Nor you, ye Proud, impute to These the fault,
If Mem'ry o'er their Tomb no Trophies raise,
Where thro' the long-drawn isle and fretted vault
The pealing anthem swells the note of praise.

Can storied urn or animated bust
Back to its mansion call the fleeting breath?
Can Honour's voice provoke the silent dust,
Or Flatt'ry sooth the dull cold ear of Death?

Perhaps in this neglected spot is laid
Some heart once pregnant with celestial fire;
Hands, that the rod of empire might have sway'd,
Or wak'd to extasy the living lyre.

But Knowledge to their eyes her ample page
Rich with the spoils of time did ne'er unroll:
Chill Penury repress'd their noble rage,
And froze the genial current of the soul.

Full many a gem of purest ray serene,
The dark unfathom'd caves of ocean bear:
Full many a flower is born to blush unseen,
And waste its sweetness on the desert air.

Some village-Hampden, that with dauntless breast
The little Tyrant of his fields withstood;
Some mute inglorious Milton here may rest,
Some Cromwell guiltless of his country's blood

Th' applause of list'ning senates to command,
The threats of pain and ruin to despise,
To scatter plenty o'er a smiling land,
And read their hist'ry in a nation's eyes,

Their lot forbad: nor circumscrib'd alone
Their growing virtues, but their crimes confin'd;
Forbad to wade through slaughter to a throne,
And shut the gates of mercy on mankind,

The struggling pangs of conscious truth to hide,
To quench the blushes of ingenuous shame,
Or heap the shrine of Luxury and Pride
With incense kindled at the Muse's flame.

Far from the madding crowd's ignoble strife,
Their sober wishes never learn'd to stray;
Along the cool sequester'd vale of life
They kept the noiseless tenor of their way.

Yet ev'n these bones from insult to protect
Some frail memorial still erected nigh,
With uncouth rhimes and shapeless sculpture deck'd,
Implores the passing tribute of a sigh.

Their name, their years, spelt by th' unletter'd muse,
The place of fame and elegy supply:
And many a holy text around she strews,
That teach the rustic moralist to die.

For who to dumb Forgetfulness a prey,
This pleasing anxious being e'er resign'd,
Left the warm precincts of the chearful day,
Nor cast one longing ling'ring look behind?

On some fond breast the parting soul relies,
Some pious drops the closing eye requires;
Ev'n from the tomb the voice of Nature cries,
Ev'n in our Ashes live their wonted Fires.

For thee, who mindful of th' unhonour'd Dead
Dost in these lines their artless tale relate;
If chance, by lonely contemplation led,
Some kindred Spirit shall inquire thy fate,

Haply some hoary-headed Swain may say,
' Oft have we seen him at the peep of dawn
' Brushing with hasty steps the dews away
' To meet the sun upon the upland lawn.

' There at the foot of yonder nodding beech
' That wreathes its old fantastic roots so high,
' His listless length at noontide would he stretch,
' And pore upon the brook that babbles by.

' Hard by yon wood, now smiling as in scorn,
' Mutt'ring his wayward fancies he would rove,
' Now drooping, woeful wan, like one forlorn,
' Or craz'd with care, or cross'd in hopeless love.

' One morn I miss'd him on the custom'd hill,
' Along the heath and near his fav'rite tree;
' Another came; nor yet beside the rill,
' Nor up the lawn, nor at the wood was he;

' The next with dirges due in sad array
' Slow thro' the church-way path we saw him born.
' Approach and read (for thou can'st read) the lay,
' Grav'd on the stone beneath yon aged thorn.'

(' There scatter'd oft, the earliest of the Year,
' By Hands unseen, are show'rs of Violets found;
' The Red-breast loves to build and warble there,
' And little Footsteps lightly print the Ground.)

THOMAS GRAY

The EPITAPH

Here rests his head upon the lap of Earth
A Youth to Fortune and to Fame unknown.
Fair Science frown'd not on his humble birth,
And Melancholy mark'd him for her own.

Large was his bounty, and his soul sincere,
Heav'n did a recompence as largely send :
He gave to Mis'ry all he had, a tear,
He gain'd from Heav'n ('twas all he wish'd) a friend.

No farther seek his merits to disclose,
Or draw his frailties from their dread abode,
(There they alike in trembling hope repose,)
The bosom of his Father and his God.

Finished 1750 ; *An Elegy*, &c., 1751

249   *The Progress of Poesy*
A Pindaric Ode

I. 1.

AWAKE, Æolian lyre, awake,
  And give to rapture all thy trembling strings.
From Helicon's harmonious springs
A thousand rills their mazy progress take:
The laughing flowers, that round them blow,
Drink life and fragrance as they flow.
Now the rich stream of music winds along
Deep, majestic, smooth, and strong,
Thro' verdant vales, and Ceres' golden reign:
Now rowling down the steep amain,
Headlong, impetuous, see it pour:
The rocks, and nodding groves rebellow to the roar.

THOMAS GRAY

I. 2.

Oh! Sovereign of the willing soul,
Parent of sweet and solemn-breathing airs,
Enchanting shell! the sullen Cares,
And frantic Passions hear thy soft controul.
On Thracia's hills the Lord of War,
Has curb'd the fury of his car,
And drop'd his thirsty lance at thy command.
Perching on the scept'red hand
Of Jove, thy magic lulls the feather'd king
With ruffled plumes, and flagging wing:
Quench'd in dark clouds of slumber lie
The terror of his beak, and light'nings of his eye.

I. 3.

Thee the voice, the dance, obey,
Temper'd to thy warbled lay.
O'er Idalia's velvet-green
The rosy-crowned Loves are seen
On Cytherea's day
With antic Sports, and blue-eyed Pleasures,
Frisking light in frolic measures;
Now pursuing, now retreating,
Now in circling troops they meet:
To brisk notes in cadence beating
Glance their many-twinkling feet.
Slow melting strains their Queen's approach declare:
Where'er she turns the Graces homage pay.
With arms sublime, that float upon the air,
In gliding state she wins her easy way:
O'er her warm cheek, and rising bosom, move
The bloom of young Desire, and purple light of Love.

II. 1.

Man's feeble race what Ills await,
Labour, and Penury, the racks of Pain,
Disease, and Sorrow's weeping train,
And Death, sad refuge from the storms of Fate!
The fond complaint, my Song, disprove,
And justify the laws of Jove.
Say, has he giv'n in vain the heav'nly Muse?
Night, and all her sickly dews,
Her Spectres wan, and Birds of boding cry,
He gives to range the dreary sky:
Till down the eastern cliffs afar
Hyperion's march they spy, and glitt'ring shafts of war.

II. 2.

In climes beyond the solar road,
Where shaggy forms o'er ice-built mountains roam,
The Muse has broke the twilight-gloom
To chear the shiv'ring Native's dull abode.
And oft, beneath the od'rous shade
Of Chili's boundless forests laid,
She deigns to hear the savage Youth repeat
In loose numbers wildly sweet
Their feather-cinctured Chiefs, and dusky Loves.
Her track, where'er the Goddess roves,
Glory pursue, and generous Shame,
Th' unconquerable Mind, and Freedom's holy flame.

II. 3.

Woods, that wave o'er Delphi's steep
Isles, that crown th' Egæan deep,
Fields, that cool Ilissus laves,
Or where Mæander's amber waves

In lingering Lab'rinths creep,
How do your tuneful Echos languish.
Mute, but to the voice of Anguish?
Where each old poetic Mountain
Inspiration breath'd around:
Ev'ry shade and hallow'd Fountain
Murmur'd deep a solemn sound:
Till the sad Nine in Greece's evil hour
Left their Parnassus for the Latian plains.
Alike they scorn the pomp of tyrant-Power,
And coward Vice, that revels in her chains.
When Latium had her lofty spirit lost,
They sought, oh Albion! next thy sea-encircled coast

III. 1.

Far from the sun and summer-gale,
In thy green lap was Nature's Darling laid,
What time, where lucid Avon stray'd,
To Him the mighty Mother did unveil
Her aweful face: The dauntless Child
Stretch'd forth his little arms, and smiled.
This pencil take (she said) whose colours clear
Richly paint the vernal year:
Thine too these golden keys, immortal Boy!
This can unlock the gates of Joy;
Of Horrour that, and thrilling Fears,
Or ope the sacred source of sympathetic Tears.

III. 2.

Nor second He, that rode sublime
Upon the seraph-wings of Extasy,
The secrets of th' Abyss to spy.
He pass'd the flaming bounds of Place and Time:

The living Throne, the saphire-blaze,
Where Angels tremble, while they gaze.
He saw; but blasted with excess of light,
Closed his eyes in endless night.
Behold, where Dryden's less presumptuous car,
Wide o'er the fields of Glory bear
Two Coursers of ethereal race,
With necks in thunder cloath'd, and long-resounding
    pace.

III. 3.

  Hark, his hands the lyre explore!
Bright-eyed Fancy hovering o'er
Scatters from her pictured urn
Thoughts, that breath, and words, that burn.
But ah! 'tis heard no more——
Oh! Lyre divine, what daring Spirit
Wakes thee now? tho' he inherit
Nor the pride, nor ample pinion,
That the Theban Eagle bear,
Sailing with supreme dominion
Thro' the azure deep of air:
Yet oft before his infant eyes would run
Such forms, as glitter in the Muse's ray
With orient hues, unborrow'd of the Sun:
Yet shall he mount, and keep his distant way
Beyond the limits of a vulgar fate,
Beneath the Good how far—but far above the Great.

Written 1754 ; Odes by Mr. Gray, 1757

250   *The Bard*

A Pindaric Ode

I. I.

' **R**UIN seize thee, ruthless King!
    ' Confusion on thy banners wait,
' Tho' fann'd by Conquest's crimson wing
' They mock the air with idle state.
' Helm, nor Hauberk's twisted mail,
' Nor even thy virtues, Tyrant, shall avail
' To save thy secret soul from nightly fears,
' From Cambria's curse, from Cambria's tears!'
Such were the sounds, that o'er the crested pride
Of the first Edward scatter'd wild dismay,
As down the steep of Snowdon's shaggy side
He wound with toilsome march his long array.
Stout Glo'ster stood aghast in speechless trance:
To arms! cried Mortimer, and couch'd his quiv'ring
    lance.

I. 2.

  On a rock, whose haughty brow
Frowns o'er old Conway's foaming flood,
Robed in the sable garb of woe,
With haggard eyes the Poet stood;
(Loose his beard, and hoary hair
Stream'd, like a meteor, to the troubled air)
And with a Master's hand, and Prophet's fire,
Struck the deep sorrows of his lyre.

383

' Hark, how each giant-oak, and desert cave,
' Sighs to the torrent's aweful voice beneath!
' O'er thee, oh King! their hundred arms they wave,
' Revenge on thee in hoarser murmurs breath;
' Vocal no more, since Cambria's fatal day,
' To high-born Hoel's harp, or soft Llewellyn's lay.

I. 3.

' Cold is Cadwallo's tongue,
' That hush'd the stormy main:
' Brave Urien sleeps upon his craggy bed:
' Mountains, ye mourn in vain
' Modred, whose magic song
' Made huge Plinlimmon bow his cloud-top'd head.
' On dreary Arvon's shore they lie,
' Smear'd with gore, and ghastly pale:
' Far, far aloof th' affrighted ravens sail;
' The famish'd Eagle screams, and passes by.
' Dear lost companions of my tuneful art,
' Dear, as the light that visits these sad eyes,
' Dear, as the ruddy drops that warm my heart,
' Ye died amidst your dying country's cries—
' No more I weep. They do not sleep.
' On yonder cliffs, a griesly band,
' I see them sit, they linger yet,
' Avengers of their native land:
' With me in dreadful harmony they join,
' And weave with bloody hands the tissue of thy line.'

II. 1.

" Weave the warp, and weave the woof,
" The winding-sheet of Edward's race.
" Give ample room, and verge enough
" The characters of hell to trace.
" Mark the year, and mark the night,
" When Severn shall re-eccho with affright
" The shrieks of death, thro' Berkley's roofs that ring,
" Shrieks of an agonizing King!
" She-Wolf of France, with unrelenting fangs,
" That tear'st the bowels of thy mangled Mate,
" From thee be born, who o'er thy country hangs
" The scourge of Heav'n. What Terrors round him wait!
" Amazement in his van, with Flight combined,
" And Sorrow's faded form, and Solitude behind.

II. 2.

" Mighty Victor, mighty Lord,
" Low on his funeral couch he lies!
" No pitying heart, no eye, afford
" A tear to grace his obsequies.
" Is the sable Warriour fled?
" Thy son is gone. He rests among the Dead.
" The Swarm, that in thy noon-tide beam were born?
" Gone to salute the rising Morn.
" Fair laughs the Morn, and soft the Zephyr blows,
" While proudly riding o'er the azure realm
" In gallant trim the gilded Vessel goes;
" Youth on the prow, and Pleasure at the helm;
" Regardless of the sweeping Whirlwind's sway,
" That, hush'd in grim repose, expects his evening-prey.

II. 3.

" Fill high the sparkling bowl,
" The rich repast prepare,
" Reft of a crown, he yet may share the feast:
" Close by the regal chair
" Fell Thirst and Famine scowl
" A baleful smile upon their baffled Guest.
" Heard ye the din of battle bray,
" Lance to lance, and horse to horse?
" Long Years of havock urge their destined course,
" And thro' the kindred squadrons mow their way.
" Ye Towers of Julius, London's lasting shame,
" With many a foul and midnight murther fed,
" Revere his Consort's faith, his Father's fame,
" And spare the meek Usurper's holy head.
" Above, below, the rose of snow,
" Twined with her blushing foe, we spread:
" The bristled Boar in infant-gore
" Wallows beneath the thorny shade.
" Now, Brothers, bending o'er th' accursed loom
" Stamp we our vengeance deep, and ratify his doom.

III. 1.

" Edward, lo! to sudden fate
" (Weave we the woof. The thread is spun)
" Half of thy heart we consecrate.
" (The web is wove. The work is done.) "
' Stay, oh stay! nor thus forlorn
' Leave me unbless'd, unpitied, here to mourn:
' In yon bright track, that fires the western skies,
' They melt, they vanish from my eyes.

' But oh! what solemn scenes on Snowdon's height
' Descending slow their glitt'ring skirts unroll?
' Visions of glory, spare my aching sight,
' Ye unborn Ages, crowd not on my soul!
' No more our long-lost Arthur we bewail.
' All-hail, ye genuine Kings, Britannia's Issue, hail!

III. 2.

' Girt with many a Baron bold
' Sublime their starry fronts they rear;
' And gorgeous Dames, and Statesmen old
' In bearded majesty, appear.
' In the midst a Form divine!
' Her eye proclaims her of the Briton-Line;
' Her lyon-port, her awe-commanding face,
' Attemper'd sweet to virgin-grace.
' What strings symphonious tremble in the air,
' What strains of vocal transport round her play!
' Hear from the grave, great Taliessin, hear;
' They breathe a soul to animate thy clay.
' Bright Rapture calls, and soaring, as she sings,
' Waves in the eye of Heav'n her many-colour'd wings.

III. 3.

' The verse adorn again
' Fierce War, and faithful Love,
' And Truth severe, by fairy Fiction drest.
' In buskin'd measures move
' Pale Grief, and pleasing Pain,
' With Horrour, Tyrant of the throbbing breast.

' A Voice, as of the Cherub-Choir,
' Gales from blooming Eden bear;
' And distant warblings lessen on my ear,
' That lost in long futurity expire.
' Fond impious Man, think'st thou, yon sanguine cloud,
' Rais'd by thy breath, has quench'd the Orb of day?
' To-morrow he repairs the golden flood,
' And warms the nations with redoubled ray.
' Enough for me: With joy I see
' The different doom our Fates assign.
' Be thine Despair, and scept'red Care,
' To triumph, and to die, are mine.'
He spoke, and headlong from the mountain's height
Deep in the roaring tide he plung'd to endless night.

Written 1754-7 ; Odes by Mr. Gray, 1757

251   *Ode on the Pleasure arising*
from Vicissitude

A Fragment

NOW the golden Morn aloft
    Waves her dew-bespangled wing;
With vermeil cheek and whisper soft
    She woo's the tardy spring:
Till April starts, and calls around
The sleeping fragrance from the ground;
And lightly o'er the living scene
Scatters his freshest, tenderest green.

New-born flocks in rustic dance
    Frisking ply their feeble feet.
Forgetful of their wintry trance
    The Birds his presence greet.

But chief the Sky-lark warbles high
His trembling thrilling ecstasy
And, less'ning from the dazzled sight,
Melts into air and liquid light.

Yesterday the sullen year
   Saw the snowy whirlwind fly;
Mute was the musick of the air,
   The Herd stood drooping by:
Their raptures now that wildly flow,
No yesterday, nor morrow know;
'Tis Man alone that Joy descries
With forward and reverted eyes.

Smiles on past Misfortune's brow
   Soft Reflection's hand can trace;
And o'er the cheek of Sorrow throw
   A melancholy grace;
While Hope prolongs our happier hour,
Or deepest shades, that dimly lour
And blacken round our weary way,
Gilds with a gleam of distant day.

Still, where rosy Pleasure leads,
   See a kindred Grief pursue;
Behind the steps that Misery treads,
   Approaching Comfort view:
The hues of Bliss more brightly glow,
Chastised by sabler tints of woe;
And blended form, with artful strife,
The strength and harmony of Life.

THOMAS GRAY

See the Wretch, that long has tost
   On the thorny bed of Pain,
At length repair his vigour lost,
   And breathe and walk again:
The meanest flowret of the vale,
The simplest note that swells the gale,
The common Sun, the air, and skies,
To him are opening Paradise.

Written about 1754–5 ; Mason's
Memoirs of Gray, 1775

PHILIP DODDRIDGE

1702–1751

252   *Hymn*

YE golden Lamps of Heav'n, farewel
   With all your feeble Light:
Farewel, thou ever-changing Moon,
   Pale Empress of the Night.

And thou refulgent Orb of Day
   In brighter Flames array'd,
My Soul, that springs beyond thy Sphere,
   No more demands thine Aid.

Ye Stars are but the shining Dust
   Of my divine Abode,
The Pavement of those heav'nly Courts,
   Where I shall reign with GOD.

The Father of eternal Light
   Shall there his Beams display;
Nor shall one Moment's Darkness mix
   With that unvaried Day.

PHILIP DODDRIDGE

No more the Drops of piercing Grief
    Shall swell into mine Eyes;
Nor the Meridian Sun decline
    Amidst those brighter Skies.

There all the Millions of his Saints
    Shall in one Song unite,
And Each the Bliss of all shall view
    With infinite Delight.

Hymns, 1755

253   *Dum vivimus, vivamus*

LIVE while you live, the *Epicure* would say,
   And seize the pleasures of the present day.
Live while you live, the sacred *Preacher* cries,
And give to GOD each moment as it flies.
Lord, in *my* view, let both united be,
I live in pleasure if I live to Thee.

Miscellaneous Pieces of Poetry (Edinburgh), 1765 ;
Memoirs of Doddridge, 1766

JOHN WESLEY

1703–1791

254   *Hymn*

THOU hidden love of God, whose height,
   Whose depth unfathom'd no man knows,
I see from far thy beauteous light,
    Inly I sigh for thy repose;
My heart is pain'd, nor can it be
At rest, till it finds rest in thee.

JOHN WESLEY

Thy secret voice invites me still,
  The sweetness of thy yoke to prove:
And fain I would: but tho' my will
  Seem fix'd, yet wide my passions rove;
Yet hindrances strew all the way;
I aim at Thee, yet from Thee stray.

'Tis mercy all, that thou hast brought
  My mind to seek her peace in thee;
Yet while I seek, but find thee not,
  No peace my wand'ring soul shall see;
O when shall all my wand'rings end,
And all my steps to thee-ward tend!

Is there a thing beneath the sun
  That strives with thee my heart to share?
Ah! tear it thence, and reign alone,
  The Lord of ev'ry motion there;
Then shall my heart from earth be free,
When it hath found repose in thee.

O hide this self from me, that I
  No more, but Christ in me may live;
My vile affections crucify,
  Nor let one darling lust survive;
In all things nothing may I see,
Nothing desire or seek but thee.

O Love, thy sov'reign aid impart,
  To save me from low-thoughted care:
Chase this self-will thro' all my heart,
  Thro' all its latent mazes there:
Make me thy duteous child, that I
Ceaseless may Abba, Father, cry!

Ah no! ne'er will I backward turn:
 Thine wholly, thine alone I am!
Thrice happy he who views with scorn
 Earth's toys, for thee his constant flame;
O help that I may never move
From the blest footsteps of thy love!

Each moment draw from earth away
 My heart that lowly waits thy call:
Speak to my inmost soul, and say,
 I am thy love, thy God, thy all!
To feel thy power, to hear thy voice,
To taste thy love, be all my choice.

Psalms and Hymns, 1738

CHARLES WESLEY

1707-1788

A Morning Hymn

255

CHRIST, whose Glory fills the Skies,
 CHRIST, the true, the only Light,
Sun of Righteousness, arise,
 Triumph o'er the Shades of Night:
Day-spring from on High, be near:
Day-star, in my Heart appear.

Dark and Chearless is the Morn
 Unaccompanied by Thee,
Joyless is the Day's Return,
 Till thy Mercy's Beams I see;
Till they Inward Light impart,
Glad my Eyes, and warm my Heart.

Visit then this Soul of mine,
   Pierce the Gloom of Sin, and **Grief**,
Fill me, Radiancy Divine,
   Scatter all my Unbelief,
More and more Thyself display,
Shining to the Perfect Day.

Psalms and Hymns, 1740

256   *Wrestling Jacob*

COME, O Thou Traveller unknown,
   Whom still I hold, but cannot see,
My Company before is gone,
   And I am left alone with Thee,
With Thee all Night I mean to stay,
And wrestle till the Break of Day.

I need not tell Thee who I am,
   My Misery, or Sin declare,
Thyself hast call'd me by my Name,
   Look on thy Hands, and read it there,
But who, I ask Thee, who art Thou,
Tell me thy Name, and tell me now?

In vain Thou strugglest to get free,
   I never will unloose my Hold:
Art Thou the Man that died for me?
   The Secret of thy Love unfold;
Wrestling I will not let Thee go,
Till I thy Name, thy Nature know.

CHARLES WESLEY

Wilt Thou not yet to me reveal
   Thy new, unutterable Name?
Tell me, I still beseech Thee, tell,
   To know it Now resolv'd I am;
Wrestling I will not let Thee go,
Till I thy Name, thy Nature know.

'Tis all in vain to hold thy Tongue,
   Or touch the Hollow of my Thigh:
Though every Sinew be unstrung,
   Out of my Arms Thou shalt not fly;
Wrestling I will not let Thee go,
Till I thy Name, thy Nature know.

What tho' my shrinking Flesh complain,
   And murmur to contend so long,
I rise superior to my Pain,
   When I am weak then I am strong,
And when my All of Strength shall fail,
I shall with the GOD-man prevail.

My Strength is gone, my Nature dies,
   I sink beneath thy weighty Hand,
Faint to revive, and fall to rise;
   I fall, and yet by Faith I stand,
I stand, and will not let Thee go,
Till I thy Name, thy Nature know.

Yield to me Now——for I am weak;
   But confident in Self-despair:
Speak to my Heart, in Blessings speak,
   Be conquer'd by my Instant Prayer,
Speak, or Thou never hence shalt move,
And tell me, if thy Name is LOVE.

CHARLES WESLEY

'Tis Love, 'tis Love! Thou diedst for Me,
　I hear thy Whisper in my Heart.
The Morning breaks, the Shadows flee:
　Pure UNIVERSAL LOVE Thou art,
To me, to All thy Bowels move,
Thy Nature, and thy Name is LOVE.

My Prayer hath Power with GOD; the Grace
　Unspeakable I now receive,
Thro' Faith I see Thee Face to Face,
　I see Thee Face to Face, and live:
In vain I have not wept, and strove,
Thy Nature, and thy Name is LOVE.

I know Thee, Saviour, who Thou art,
　JESUS the feeble Sinner's Friend;
Nor wilt Thou with the Night depart,
　But stay, and love me to the End;
Thy Mercies never shall remove,
Thy Nature, and thy Name is LOVE.

The Sun of Righteousness on Me
　Hath rose with Healing in his Wings,
Wither'd my Nature's Strength; from Thee
　My Soul its Life and Succour brings,
My Help is all laid up above;
Thy Nature, and thy Name is LOVE.

Contented now upon my Thigh
　I halt, till Life's short Journey end;
All Helplessness, all Weakness I,
　On Thee alone for Strength depend,
Nor have I Power, from Thee, to move;
Thy Nature, and thy Name is LOVE.

Lame as I am, I take the Prey,
    Hell, Earth, and Sin with Ease o'ercome;
I leap for Joy, pursue my Way,
    And as a bounding Hart fly home,
Thro' all Eternity to prove
Thy Nature, and thy Name is Love.

Hymns and Sacred Poems, 1742

257   *Hymn*

O THOU who camest from above,
    The pure, celestial fire t' impart,
Kindle a flame of sacred love
    On the mean altar of my heart,
There let it for thy glory burn
    With inextinguishable blaze,
And trembling to it's Source return,
    In humble prayer, and fervent praise.

Jesus, confirm my heart's desire
    To work, and speak, and think for thee,
Still let me guard the holy fire,
    And still stir up thy gift in me,
Ready for all thy perfect will
    My acts of faith and love repeat,
'Till death thy endless mercies seal,
    And make my sacrifice compleat.

Short Hymns, 1762

THOMAS EDWARDS

1699–1757

258 *Sonnet*

On a Family Picture

WHEN pensive on that Portraiture I gaze,
   Where my four Brothers round about me stand,
And four fair Sisters smile with graces bland,
The goodly monument of happier days;
And think how soon insatiate Death, who preys
   On all, has cropp'd the rest with ruthless hand;
   While only I survive of all that band,
Which one chaste bed did to my Father raise;
It seems that like a Column left alone,
   The tottering remnant of some splendid Fane,
      Scape'd from the fury of the barbarous Gaul,
And wasting Time, which has the rest o'erthrown;
   Amidst our House's ruins I remain
      Single, unpropp'd, and nodding to my fall.

Dodsley's *Collection*, ii, 1748

BENJAMIN STILLINGFLEET

1702–1771

259 *Sonnet*

True Ambition

WHEN I behold thee, blameless Williamson,
   Wreck'd like an infant on a savage shore,
   While others round on borrow'd pinions soar,
My busy fancy calls thy thread misspun;
Till Faith instructs me the deceit to shun,
   While thus she speaks: ' Those wings that from the store
   Of virtue were not lent, howe'er they bore
In this gross air, will melt when near the sun.

BENJAMIN STILLINGFLEET

The truly ambitious wait for Nature's time,
    Content by certain though by slow degrees
        To mount above the reach of vulgar flight:
Nor is that man confin'd to this low clime,
    Who but the extremest skirts of glory sees,
        And hears celestial echoes with delight.'

                          Written 1746 ; Todd's *Milton*, v, 1801

ELIZABETH CARTER

1717–1806

260   *Ode to Wisdom*

THE solitary bird of night
    Thro' the thick shades now wings his flight,
    And quits his time-shook tow'r;
Where, shelter'd from the blaze of day,
In philosophick gloom he lay,
    Beneath his ivy bow'r.

With joy I hear the solemn sound,
Which midnight echoes waft around,
    And sighing gales repeat.
Fav'rite of PALLAS! I attend,
And, faithful to thy summons, bend
    At WISDOM's aweful seat.

She loves the cool, the silent eve,
Where no false shows of life deceive,
    Beneath the lunar ray.
Here folly drops each vain disguise,
Nor sport her gaily-colour'd dyes,
    As in the beam of day.

ELIZABETH CARTER

O PALLAS! queen of ev'ry art,
That glads the sense, and mends the heart,
   Blest source of purer joys:
In every form of beauty bright,
That captivates the mental sight
   With pleasure and surprize:

At thy unspotted shrine I bow:
Attend thy modest suppliant's vow,
   That breathes no wild desires:
But taught by thy unerring rules,
To shun the fruitless wish of fools,
   To nobler views aspires.

Not FORTUNE's gem, AMBITION's plume,
Nor CYTHEREA's fading bloom,
   Be objects of my pray'r:
Let AV'RICE, VANITY, and PRIDE,
Those envy'd glitt'ring toys, divide
   The dull rewards of care,

To me thy better gifts impart,
Each moral beauty of the heart,
   By studious thoughts refin'd;
For WEALTH, the smiles of glad content,
For POW'R, its amplest, best extent,
   An empire o'er the mind.

When FORTUNE drops her gay parade,
When PLEASURE's transient roses fade,
   And wither in the tomb,
Unchang'd is thy immortal prize;
Thy ever-verdant laurels rise
   In undecaying bloom.

By thee protected, I defy
The coxcomb's sneer, the stupid lye
   Of ignorance and spite:
Alike contemn the leaden fool,
And all the pointed ridicule
   Of undiscerning Wit.

From envy, hurry, noise, and strife,
The dull impertinence of life,
   In thy retreat I rest:
Pursue thee to the peaceful groves,
Where PLATO's sacred spirit roves,
   In all thy beauties dress'd.

He bade Ilissus' tuneful stream
Convey thy philosophick theme,
   Of Perfect, Fair, and Good:
Attentive Athens caught the sound,
And all her list'ning sons around,
   In aweful silence stood:

Reclaim'd, her wild licentious youth
Confess'd the potent voice of TRUTH,
   And felt its just controul.
The passions ceas'd their loud alarms,
And Virtue's soft persuasive charms
   O'er all their senses stole.

Thy breath inspires the POET's song,
The PATRIOT's free, unbiass'd tongue,
   The Hero's gen'rous strife;
Thine are Retirement's silent joys,
And all the sweet engaging ties
   Of still, domestick life.

ELIZABETH CARTER

No more to fabled Names confin'd,
To the supreme all-perfect Mind
   My thoughts direct their flight:
Wisdom's thy gift, and all her force
From thee deriv'd, eternal source
   Of intellectual light.

O send her sure, her steady ray,
To regulate my doubtful way,
   Thro' life's perplexing road:
The mists of error to controul,
And thro' its gloom direct my soul
   To happiness and good.

Beneath her clear discerning eye
The visionary shadows fly
   Of folly's painted show:
She sees thro' ev'ry fair disguise,
That all but VIRTUE's solid joys,
   Are vanity and woe.

The Gentleman's Magazine, December 1747

HESTER MULSO, MRS. CHAPONE
1727-1801

261   *To Stella*

NO more, my Stella, to the sighing shades,
   Of blasted hope and luckless love complain;
But join the sports of Dian's careless maids,
   And laughing Liberty's triumphant train.

And see, with these is holy Friendship found,
   With chrystal bosom open to the sight;
Her gentle hand shall close the recent wound,
   And fill the vacant heart with calm delight.

HESTER MULSO, MRS. CHAPONE

Nor Prudence slow, that ever comes too late,
    Nor stern-brow'd Duty, check her gen'rous flame;
On all her footsteps Peace and Honour wait,
    And Slander's ready tongue reveres her name.

Say, Stella, what is Love, whose tyrant pow'r
    Robs Virtue of content and Youth of joy?
What nymph or goddess in a fatal hour
    Gave to the world this mischief-making boy?

By lying bards in forms so various shewn,
    Deck'd with false charms or arm'd with terrors vain,
Who shall his real properties make known,
    Declare his nature, and his birth explain?

Some say, of Idleness and Pleasure bred,
    The smiling babe on beds of roses lay,
There, with sweet honey-dews by Fancy fed,
    His blooming beauties open'd to the day.

His wanton head with fading chaplets bound,
    Dancing, he leads his silly vot'ries on
To precipices deep o'er faithless ground,
    Then laughing flies, nor hears their fruitless moan.

Some say from Etna's burning entrails torn,
    More fierce than tygers on the Libyan plain,
Begot in tempests, and in thunders born,
    Love wildly rages like the foaming main.

With darts and flames some arm his feeble hands,
    His infant brow with regal honours crown;
Whilst vanquish'd Reason, bound with silken bands,
    Meanly submissive, falls below his throne.

HESTER MULSO, MRS. CHAPONE

Each fabling poet sure alike mistakes
  The gentle pow'r that reigns o'er tender hearts!
Soft Love no tempest hurls, nor thunder shakes,
  Nor lifts the flaming torch, nor poison'd darts.

Heav'n-born, the brightest seraph of the sky,
  For Eden's bow'r he left his blissful seat,
When Adam's blameless suit was heard on high,
  And beauteous Eve first chear'd his lone retreat.

At Love's approach all earth rejoic'd, each hill,
  Each grove that learnt it from the whisp'ring gale;
Joyous the birds their liveliest chorus fill,
  And richer fragrance breathes in ev'ry vale.

Well pleased in Paradise awhile he roves,
  With Innocence and Friendship, hand in hand;
Till Sin found entrance in the with'ring groves,
  And frighted Innocence forsook the land.

But Love, still faithful to the guilty pair,
  With them was driv'n amidst a world of woes,
Where oft he mourns his lost companion dear,
  And trembling flies before his rigid foes.

Honour, in burnish'd steel completely clad,
  And hoary Wisdom, oft against him arm;
Suspicion pale, and Disappointment sad,
  Vain Hopes and frantic Fears his heart alarm.

Fly then, dear Stella, fly th' unequal strife,
  Since Fate forbids that Peace should dwell with Love!
Friendship's calm joys shall glad thy future life,
  And Virtue lead to endless bliss above.

Written by 1755; *Miscellanies*, 1775

1721–1766

Solitude

O SOLITUDE, romantic maid,
   Whether by nodding towers you tread,
Or haunt the desart's trackless gloom,
Or hover o'er the yawning tomb,
Or climb the Andes' clifted side,
Or by the Nile's coy source abide,
Or starting from your half-year's sleep
From Hecla view the thawing deep,
Or Tadmor's marble wastes survey,
Or in yon roofless cloyster stray;
   You, Recluse, again I woo,
   And again your steps pursue.

Plum'd Conceit himself surveying,
Folly with her shadow playing,
Purse-proud, elbowing Insolence,
Bloated empirick, puff'd Pretence,
Noise that thro' a trumpet speaks,
Laughter in loud peals that breaks,
Intrusion with a sopling's face,
(Ignorant of time and place)
Sparks of fire Dissention blowing,
Ductile, court-bred Flattery, bowing,
Restraint's stiff neck, Grimace's leer,
Squint-ey'd Censure's artful sneer,
Ambition's buskins steep'd in blood,
Fly thy presence, Solitude.

Sage Reflection bent with years,
Conscious Virtue void of fears,

JAMES GRAINGER

Muffled Silence, wood-nymph shy,
Meditation's piercing eye,
Halcyon Peace on moss reclin'd,
Retrospect that scans the mind,
Rapt earth-gazing Resvery,
Blushing artless Modesty,
Health that snuffs the morning air,
Full-ey'd Truth with bosom bare,
Inspiration, Nature's child,
Seek the solitary wild.

.   .   .   .   .   .

When all Nature's hush'd asleep,
Nor Love nor Guilt their vigils keep,
Soft you leave your cavern'd den,
And wander o'er the works of men.
But when Phosphor brings the dawn
By her dappled coursers drawn,
Again you to the wild retreat
And the early huntsman meet,
Where as you pensive pace along,
You catch the distant shepherd's song,
Or brush from herbs the pearly dew,
Or the rising primrose view.
Devotion lends her heaven-plum'd wings,
You mount, and Nature with you sings.
But when mid-day fervors glow
To upland airy shades you go,
Where never sunburnt woodman came,
Nor sportsman chas'd the timid game ;
And there beneath an oak reclin'd,
With drowsy waterfalls behind,
You sink to rest.

JAMES GRAINGER

Till the tuneful bird of night
From the neighb'ring poplars height
Wake you with her solemn strain,
And teach pleas'd Echo to complain.

Ode to Solitude—Dodsley's *Collection*, iv, 1755

JOHN BROWN

1715–1766

263 *Night*

NOW sunk the Sun, now Twilight sunk, and Night
Rode in her zenith; nor a passing breeze
Sigh'd to the groves, which in the midnight air
Stood motionless, and in the peaceful floods
Inverted hung: For now the billow slept
Along the shore, nor heav'd the deep, but spread
A shining mirror to the Moon's pale orb,
Which, dim and waining, o'er the shadowy clifts,
The solemn woods and spiry mountain-tops,
Her glimmering faintness threw: Now every eye,
Oppress'd with toil, was drown'd in deep repose;
Save that the unseen shepherd in his watch,
Propt on his crook, stood list'ning to the fold,
And gaz'd the starry vault and pendant moon;
Nor voice nor sound broke on the deep serene,
But the soft murmur of swift-gushing rills,
Forth-issuing from the mountain's distant steep,
(Unheard till now, and now scarce heard) proclaim'd
All things at rest, and imag'd the still voice
Of quiet whispering in the ear of Night.

Odes by Richard Cumberland, Dedication, 1776

DAVID GARRICK

264   *To Mr. Gray*
          On the Publication of his Odes

REPINE not, Gray, that our weak dazzled eyes
    Thy daring heights and brightness shun;
How few can track the eagle to the skies,
    Or like him gaze upon the sun!

The gentle reader loves the gentle Muse,
    That little dares, and little means,
Who humbly sips her learning from *Reviews*,
    Or flutters in the *Magazines*.

                    The London Chronicle, October 1, 1757

265   *Heart of Oak*

COME, cheer up, my Lads! 'tis to Glory we stear,
    To add something more to this wonderfull Year;
To Honour we call you, not press you like slaves,
For who are so free as we Sons of the Waves.
              Heart of Oak are our ships,
              Heart of Oak are our Men,
              We always are ready,
              Steady! Boys! steady!
We'll fight and we'll conquer again and again.

We ne'er see our Foes but we wish them to stay,
They never see us but they wish us away;
If they run, why we follow and run them ashore,
For if they won't fight us, we cannot do more.
              Heart of Oak, &c.

They swear they'll invade us, these terrible Foes;
They frighten our Women, our Children, and Beaus;
But shou'd their Flat-Bottoms in Darkness get o'er,
Still Britons they'll find to receive them on Shore.
        Heart of Oak, &c.

We'll still make them run, and we'll still make them sweat,
In spite of the Devil and Brussels Gazette,
Then cheer up, my Lads, with one Heart let us sing,
Our Soldiers, our Sailors, our Statesmen, and King.
        Heart of Oak, &c.

        Sung in *Harlequin's Invasion*, 1759

GEORGE BUBB DODINGTON,
LORD MELCOMBE

1691–1762

266   *Ode*

LOVE thy Country, wish it well,
    Not with too intense a care,
'Tis enough, that when it fell,
    Thou, it's ruin, didst not share.

Envy's censure, Flattery's praise,
    With unmov'd Indifference, view;
Learn to tread Life's dangerous maze,
    With unerring Virtue's clue.

Void of strong Desires, and Fear,
    Life's wide Ocean trust no more;
Strive thy little Bark to steer,
    With the tide, but near the shore.

GEORGE BUBB DODINGTON

Thus prepar'd, thy shorten'd sail
   Shall, whene'er the winds encrease,
Seizing each propitious gale,
   Waft thee to the Port of Peace.

Keep thy conscience from offence,
   And tempestuous passions, free,
So, when thou art call'd from hence,
   Easy shall thy passage be;

Easy shall thy passage be,
   Chearfull, thy allotted stay;
Short th' account twixt God and thee;
   Hope shall meet thee, on the way;

Truth shall lead thee to the gate,
   Mercy's self shall let thee in;
Where it's never-changing state
   Full perfection shall begin.

Written 1761 ; Spence's *Anecdotes*
(ed. Singer), 1820

ROBERT LLOYD

1733-1764

267   *The Critic's Rules*

WHEN Shakespeare leads the mind a dance,
   From France to England, hence to France,
Talk not to me of time and place;
I own I'm happy in the chace.
Whether the drama 's here or there,
'Tis nature, Shakespeare, every where.
The poet's fancy can create,
Contract, enlarge, annihilate,

Bring past and present close together,
In spite of distance, seas, or weather;
And shut up in a single action,
What cost whole years in its transaction.
So, ladies at a play, or rout,
Can flirt the universe about,
Whose geographical account
Is drawn and pictur'd on the mount.
Yet, when they please, contract the plan,
And shut the world up in a fan.

True Genius, like Armida's wand,
Can raise the spring from barren land:
While all the art of Imitation,
Is pilf'ring from the first creation;
Transplanting flowers, with useless toil,
Which wither in a foreign soil.
As conscience often sets us right
By its interior active light,
Without th' assistance of the laws
To combat in the moral cause;
So Genius, of itself discerning,
Without the mystic rules of learning,
Can, from its present intuition,
Strike at the truth of composition.

Yet those who breathe the classic vein,
Enlisted in the mimic train,
Who ride their steed with double bit,
Ne'er run away with by their wit,
Delighted with the pomp of rules,
The specious pedantry of schools,
(Which rules, like crutches, ne'er became
Of any use but to the lame)

Pursue the method set before 'em;
Talk much of order, and decorum,
Of probability of fiction,
Of manners, ornament, and diction,
And with a jargon of hard names,
(A privilege which dulness claims,
And merely us'd by way of fence,
To keep out plain and common sense)
Extol the wit of antient days,
The simple fabric of their plays;
Then from the fable, all so chaste,
Trick'd up in antient-modern taste,
So mighty gentle all the while,
In such a sweet descriptive stile,
While Chorus marks the servile mode
With fine reflection, in an ode,
Present you with a perfect piece,
Form'd on the model of old Greece.

Shakespeare: An Epistle to Mr. Garrick, 1760

CHARLES CHURCHILL

1731–1764

268 *A Critical Fribble*

WITH that *low* CUNNING, which in fools supplies,
And amply too, the place of being wise,
Which Nature, kind indulgent parent, gave
To qualify the Blockhead for a Knave;
With that *smooth* FALSHOOD, whose appearance charms,
And reason of each wholsome doubt disarms,
Which to the lowest depths of guile descends,
By vilest means pursues the vilest ends,

Wears Friendship's mask for purposes of spite,
Fawns in the day, and Butchers in the night;
With that *malignant* ENVY, which turns pale,
And sickens, even if a friend prevail,
Which merit and success pursues with hate,
And damns the worth it cannot imitate;
With the *cold* CAUTION of a coward's spleen,
Which fears not guilt, but always seeks a screen,
Which keeps this maxim ever in her view—
What's *basely* done, should be done *safely* too;
With that *dull, rooted, callous* IMPUDENCE,
Which, dead to shame, and ev'ry nicer sense,
Ne'er blush'd, unless, in spreading VICE's snares,
She blunder'd on some Virtue *unawares*;
With all these blessings, which we seldom find
Lavish'd by Nature on *one* happy mind,
A Motley Figure, of the FRIBBLE Tribe,
Which Heart can scarce conceive, or pen describe,
Came *simp'ring* on; to ascertain whose sex
Twelve, sage, *impanell'd* Matrons would perplex.
Nor *Male*, nor *Female*; *Neither*, and yet both;
Of *Neuter* Gender, tho' of *Irish* growth;
A six-foot suckling, mincing in *Its* gait;
Affected, peevish, prim, and delicate;
Fearful *It* seem'd, tho' of Athletic make,
Lest *brutal breezes* should too roughly shake
Its tender form, and *savage* motion spread,
O'er *Its* pale cheeks, the horrid manly red.

Much did *It* talk, in *Its* own *pretty* phrase,
Of Genius and of Taste, of Play'rs and Plays;
Much too of writings, which *Itself* had wrote,
Of special merit, tho' of little note;

413

For Fate, in a strange humour, had decreed
That what *It* wrote, none but *Itself* should read;
Much too *It* chatter'd of *Dramatic* Laws,
Misjudging Critics, and misplac'd applause,
Then, with a self-complacent jutting air,
It smil'd, It smirk'd, It wriggled to the chair;
And, with an aukward briskness not its own,
Looking around, and *perking* on the throne,
Triumphant seem'd, when that strange savage Dame,
Known but to few, or only known by name,
Plain COMMON SENSE appear'd, by Nature there
Appointed, with plain TRUTH, to guard the Chair.
The Pageant saw, and blasted with her frown,
To *Its* first state of Nothing melted down.

Nor shall the MUSE (for even there the pride
Of this *vain Nothing* shall be mortified)
Nor shall the MUSE (should Fate ordain her rhimes,
Fond, pleasing thought! to live in after-times)
With such a Trifler's name her pages blot;
Known be the Character, the *Thing* forgot;
Let *It*, to disappoint each future aim,
Live without Sex, and die without a name!

Cold-blooded critics, by enervate sires
Scarce hammer'd out, when Nature's feeble fires
Glimmer'd their last; whose sluggish blood, half froze,
Creeps lab'ring thro' the veins; whose heart ne'er glows
With fancy-kindled heat:—A servile race,
Who, in mere want of fault, all merit place;
Who blind obedience pay to ancient schools,
Bigots to Greece, and slaves to musty rules;
With solemn consequence declar'd that none
Could judge that cause but SOPHOCLES alone.

Dupes to their fancied excellence, the crowd,
Obsequious to the sacred dictate, bow'd.

When, from amidst the throng, a Youth stood forth,
Unknown his person, not unknown his worth;
His looks bespoke applause; alone he stood,
Alone he stemm'd the mighty critic flood.
He talk'd of ancients, as the man became
Who priz'd our own, but envied not their fame;
With noble rev'rence spoke of Greece and Rome,
And scorn'd to tear the laurel from the tomb.

' But more than just to other countries grown,
' Must we turn base apostates to our own?
' Where do these words of Greece and Rome excel,
' That England may not please the ear as well?
' What mighty magic 's in the place or air,
' That all perfection needs must centre there?
' In states, let strangers blindly be preferr'd;
' In state of letters, Merit should be heard.
' Genius is of no country, her pure ray
' Spreads all abroad, as gen'ral as the day;
' Foe to restraint, from place to place she flies,
' And may hereafter e'en in Holland rise.
' May not (to give a pleasing fancy scope,
' And chear a patriot heart with patriot hope)
' May not some great extensive genius raise
' The name of Britain 'bove Athenian praise;
' And, whilst brave thirst of fame his bosom warms,
' Make England great in Letters as in Arms?
' There may—there hath—and SHAKESPEARE's muse aspires
' Beyond the reach of Greece; with native fires
' Mounting aloft, he wings his daring flight,
' Whilst SOPHOCLES below stands trembling at his height.

' Why should we then abroad for judges roam,
' When abler judges we may find at home?
' Happy in tragic and in comic pow'rs,
' Have we not SHAKESPEARE?—Is not JOHNSON ours?
' For them, your nat'ral judges, Britons, vote;
' They'll judge like Britons, who like Britons wrote.'
    He said, and conquer'd—Sense resum'd her sway,
And disappointed pedants stalk'd away.

The Rosciad, 1761

269   *On Himself*

ME, whom no muse of heav'nly birth inspires,
   No judgment tempers when rash genius fires;
Who boast no merit but mere knack of rhime,
Short gleams of sense, and satire out of time,
Who cannot follow where *trim* fancy leads
By *prattling* streams o'er *flow'r-empurpled* meads;
Who often, but without success, have pray'd
For *apt* ALLITERATION's *artful aid*;
Who would, but cannot, with a master's skill,
Coin fine new epithets, *which mean no ill*,
Me, thus uncouth, thus ev'ry way unfit
For *pacing* poesy, and *ambling* wit,
TASTE with contempt beholds, nor deigns to place
Amongst the lowest of her favour'd race.

The Prophecy of Famine, 1763

270   *Conscience*

'*T*IS not the babbling of a busy world,
   Where praise and censure are at random hurl'd,
Which can the meanest of my thoughts controul,
Or shake one settled purpose of my soul.

CHARLES CHURCHILL

Free and at large might their wild curses roam,
If All, if All alas! were well at home.
No—'tis the tale which angry Conscience tells,
When She with more than tragic horror swells
Each circumstance of guilt; when stern, but true,
She brings bad actions forth into review;
And, like the dread hand-writing on the wall,
Bids late Remorse awake at Reason's call,
Arm'd at all points bids Scorpion Vengeance pass,
And to the mind holds up Reflection's glass,
The mind, which starting, heaves the heart-felt groan,
And hates that form She knows to be her own.

The Conference, 1763

ISAAC BICKERSTAFFE

1735–1812

271   *Song*

THERE was a jolly miller once,
    Liv'd on the river Dee;
He work'd, and sung, from morn till night,
    No lark more blyth than he.
And this the burthen of his song
    For ever us'd to be,
I care for nobody, not I,
    If no one cares for me.

Love in a Village, Act i, 1762

272   *Song*

HOW happy were my days, till now
    I ne'er did sorrow feel;
I rose with joy to milk my cow,
    Or take my spinning wheel.

ISAAC BICKERSTAFFE

My heart was lighter than a fly,
    Like any bird I sung,
Till he pretended love, and I
    Believ'd his flatt'ring tongue.

Oh the fool, the silly, silly fool,
    Who trusts what man may be;
I wish I was a maid again,
    And in my own country.

                 Love in a Village, Act i, 1762

WILLIAM WHITEHEAD

1715–1785

273   *The* Je ne sçay quoi. *A Song*

YES, I'm in love, I feel it now,
    And *Cælia* has undone me;
And yet I'll swear I can't tell how
    The pleasing Plague stole on me.

'Tis not her Face that Love creates,
    For there no Graces revel;
'Tis not her Shape, for there the Fates
    Have rather been uncivil.

'Tis not her Air, for sure in that
    There's nothing more than common;
And all her Sense is only Chat,
    Like any other Woman.

Her Voice, her Touch might give th' Alarm—
    'Tis both perhaps, or neither;
In short, 'tis that provoking Charm
    Of *Cælia* all together.

                 The Museum, May 10, 1746

The Enthusiast : an Ode

ONCE, I remember well the day,
  'Twas ere the blooming sweets of May
    Had lost their freshest hues,
When every flower on every hill,
In every vale, had drank its fill
    Of sunshine, and of dews.

In short, 'twas that sweet season's prime
When Spring gives up the reins of Time
    To Summer's glowing hand,
And doubting mortals hardly know
By whose command the breezes blow
    Which fan the smiling land.

'Twas then, beside a green-wood shade,
Which cloath'd a lawn's aspiring head
    I urg'd my devious way,
With loitering steps regardless where,
So soft, so genial was the air,
    So wond'rous bright the day.

And now my eyes with transport rove
O'er all the blue expanse above,
    Unbroken by a cloud!
And now beneath delighted pass,
Where winding thro' the deep green-grass
    A full-brim'd river flow'd.

I stop, I gaze; in accents rude,
To thee, serenest Solitude,
    Burst forth th' unbidden lay;
' Begone, vile world, the learn'd, the wise,
The great, the busy I despise,
    And pity e'en the gay.

These, these are joys alone, I cry;
'Tis here, divine Philosophy,
    Thou deign'st to fix thy throne!
Here Contemplation points the road
Thro' Nature's charms to Nature's God!
    These, these are joys alone!

Adieu, ye vain low-thoughted cares,
Ye human hopes, and human fears,
    Ye pleasures and ye pains!'—
While thus I spake, o'er all my soul
A philosophic calmness stole,
    A Stoic stillness reigns.

The tyrant passions all subside,
Fear, anger, pity, shame, and pride
    No more my bosom move;
Yet still I felt, or seem'd to feel
A kind of visionary zeal
    Of universal love.

When lo! a voice! a voice I hear!
'Twas Reason whisper'd in my ear
    These monitory strains:
'What mean'st thou, man? would'st thou unbind
The ties which constitute thy kind,
    The pleasures and the pains?

The same Almighty Power unseen,
Who spreads the gay or solemn scene
    To Contemplation's eye,
Fix'd every movement of the soul,
Taught every wish its destin'd goal,
    And quicken'd every joy.

He bids the tyrant passions rage,
He bids them war eternal wage,
    And combat each his foe:
Till from dissensions concords rise,
And beauties from deformities,
    And happiness from woe.

Art thou not man, and dar'st thou find
A bliss which leans not to mankind?
    Presumptuous thought and vain!
Each bliss unshar'd is unenjoy'd,
Each power is weak unless employ'd
    Some social good to gain.

Shall light, and shade, and warmth, and air,
With those exalted joys compare
    Which active Virtue feels,
When on she drags, as lawful prize,
Contempt, and Indolence, and Vice,
    At her triumphant wheels?

As rest to labour still succeeds,
To man, whilst Virtue's glorious deeds
    Employ his toilsome day,
This fair variety of things
Are merely Life's refreshing springs,
    To sooth him on his way.

Enthusiast, go, unstring thy lyre,
In vain thou sing'st if none admire,
    How sweet soe'er the strain.
And is not thy o'erflowing mind,
Unless thou mixest with thy kind,
    Benevolent in vain?

Enthusiast, go, try every sense,
If not thy bliss, thy excellence,
   Thou yet hast learn'd to scan;
At least thy wants, thy weakness know,
And see them all uniting show
   That man was made for man.'

              Poems on Several Occasions, 1754

275   *On Friendship*

MUCH have we heard the peevish world complain
  Of friends neglected, and of friends forgot:
Another's frailties blindly we arraign,
  And blame, as partial ills, the common lot:
For what is Friendship?—'Tis the sacred tie
  Of souls unbodied, and of love refin'd;
Beyond, Benevolence, thy social sigh,
  Beyond the duties graven on our kind.
And ah how seldom, in this vale of tears,
  This frail existence, by ourselves debas'd,
In hopes bewilder'd, or subdued by fears,
  The joys unmix'd of mutual good we taste!
Proclaim, ye reverend Sires, whom Fate has spar'd
  As life's example, and as virtue's test,
How few, how very few, your hearts have shar'd,
  How much those hearts have pardon'd in the best.
Vain is their claim whom heedless pleasure joins
  In bands of riot, or in leagues of vice;
They meet, they revel, as the day declines,
  But, spectre like, they shudder at its rise.
For 'tis not Friendship, tho' the raptures run,
  Led by the mad'ning God, thro' every vein;

Like the warm flower, which drinks the noon-tide sun,
   Their bosoms open but to close again.
Yet there are hours of mirth, which Friendship loves,
   When Prudence sleeps, and Wisdom grows more kind,
Sallies of sense, which Reason scarce approves,
   When all unguarded glows the naked mind.
But far from those be each profaner eye
   With glance malignant withering fancy's bloom;
Far the vile ear, where whispers never die;
   Far the rank heart, which teems with ills to come.
Full oft, by fortune near each other plac'd,
   Ill-suited souls, nor studious much to please,
Whole fruitless years in awkward union waste,
   'Till chance divides, whom chance had join'd, with ease.
And yet, should either oddly soar on high,
   And shine distinguish'd in some sphere remov'd,
The friend observes him with a jealous eye,
   And calls ungrateful whom he never lov'd.
But leave we such for those of happier clay
   On whose emerging stars the Graces smile,
And search for truth, where Virtue's sacred ray
   Wakes the glad seed in Friendship's genuine soil.
In youth's soft season, when the vacant mind
   To each kind impulse of affection yields,
When Nature charms, and love of humankind
   With its own brightness every object gilds,
Should two congenial bosoms haply meet,
   Or on the banks of Camus, hoary stream,
Or where smooth Isis glides on silver feet,
   Nurse of the Muses each, and each their theme,
How blith the mutual morning task they ply!
   How sweet the saunt'ring walk at close of day!

How steal, secluded from the world's broad eye,
   The midnight hours insensibly away!
While glows the social bosom to impart
   Each young idea dawning science lends,
Or big with sorrow beats th' unpractis'd heart
   For suff'ring virtue, and disastrous friends.
Deep in the volumes of the mighty dead
   They feast on joys to vulgar minds unknown;
The hero's, sage's, patriot's path they tread,
   Adore *each* worth, and make it half their own.
Sublime and pure as Thebes or Sparta taught
   Eternal union from their souls they swear,
Each added converse swells the generous thought,
   And each short absence makes it more sincere—
—' And can—(I hear some eager voice exclaim,
   Whose bliss now blossoms, and whose hopes beat high)
Can Virtue's basis fail th' incumbent frame?
   And *may* such friendships *ever ever* die?'
Ah, gentle youth, they may. Nor thou complain
   If chance the sad experience should be thine.
What can not change where all is light and vain?
   —Ask of the Fates who twist life's varying line.
Ambition, vanity, suspense, surmise,
   On the wide world's tempestuous ocean roll;
New loves, new friendships, new desires arise.
   New joys elate, new griefs depress the soul.
Some, in the bustling mart of business, lose
   The still small voice retirement loves to hear;
Some at the noisy bar enlarge their views,
   And some in senates court a people's ear.
While others, led by glory's meteors, run
   To distant wars for laurels stain'd with blood.

WILLIAM WHITEHEAD

Meanwhile the stream of time glides calmly on,
   And ends its silent course in Lethe's flood.
Unhappy only he of Friendship's train
   Who never knew what change or fortune meant,
With whom th' ideas of his youth remain
   Too firmly fix'd, and rob him of content.
Condemn'd perhaps to some obscure retreat,
   Where pale reflection wears a sickly bloom,
Still to the past he turns with pilgrim feet,
   And ghosts of pleasure haunt him to his tomb.
O—but I will not name you—ye kind few,
   With whom the morning of my life I pass'd,
May every bliss, your generous bosoms knew
   In earlier days, attend you to the last.
I too, alas, am chang'd.—And yet there are
   Who still with partial love my friendship own,
Forgive the frailties which they could not share,
   Or find my heart unchang'd to them alone.
To them this votive tablet of the Muse
   Pleas'd I suspend.—Nor let th' unfeeling mind
From these loose hints its own vile ways excuse,
   Or start a thought to injure human-kind.
Who knows not Friendship, knows not bliss sincere.
   Court it, ye young; ye aged, bind it fast;
Earn it, ye proud; nor think the purchase dear,
   Whate'er the labour, if 'tis gain'd at last.
Compar'd with all th' admiring world calls great,
   Fame's loudest blast, ambition's noblest ends,
Ev'n the last pang of social life is sweet:
   The pang which parts us from our weeping friends.

Written before 1762 ; Poems, 1774

276 *A Prayer for Indifference*

OFT I've implor'd the Gods in vain,
   And pray'd till I've been weary;
For once I'll try my wish to gain
   Of Oberon, the fairy.

Sweet airy being, wanton sprite,
   That lurk'st in woods unseen,
And oft by Cynthia's silver light
   Tripst gaily o'er the green;

If e'er thy pitying heart was mov'd,
   As ancient stories tell,
And for th' Athenian maid, who lov'd,
   Thou sought'st a wondrous spell,

Oh! deign once more t' exert thy power;
   Haply some herb or tree,
Sov'reign as juice from western flower,
   Conceals a balm for me.

I ask no kind return in love,
   No tempting charm to please;
Far from the heart such gifts remove,
   That sighs for peace and ease.

Nor ease nor peace that heart can know,
   Which, like the needle true,
Turns at the touch of joy or woe,
   But, turning, trembles too.

426

FRANCES MACARTNEY, MRS. GREVILLE

Far as distress the soul can wound,
    'Tis pain in each degree;
Bliss goes but to a certain bound,
    Beyond is agony

Take then this treacherous sense of mine,
    Which dooms me still to smart;
Which pleasure can to pain refine,
    To pain new pangs impart.

Oh! haste to shed the sovereign balm
    My shatter'd nerves new string;
And for my guest, serenely calm,
    The nymph, Indifference, bring.

At her approach, see Hope, see Fear,
    See Expectation fly;
With Disappointment, in the rear,
    That blasts the promis'd joy.

The tears which pity taught to flow,
    My eyes shall then disown;
The heart which throbb'd at other's woe,
    Shall then scarce feel its own.

The wounds which now each moment bleed,
    Each moment then shall close,
And peaceful days shall still succeed
    To nights of sweet repose.

Oh, fairy elf! but grant me this,
    This one kind comfort send;
And so may never-fading bliss
    Thy flowery paths attend!

FRANCES MACARTNEY, MRS. GREVILLE

So may the glow-worm's glimmering light
    Thy tiny footsteps lead
To some new region of delight,
    Unknown to mortal tread.

And be thy acorn goblets fill'd
    With heaven's ambrosial dew,
From sweetest, freshest flowers distill'd,
    That shed fresh sweets for you.

And what of life remains for me
    I'll pass in sober ease,
Half-pleas'd, contented will I be,
    Contented, half to please.

The Edinburgh Chronicle, 19 April 1759; Fawkes and
    Woty's *Poetical Calendar*, June 1763

WILLIAM FALCONER

1732–1769

277   *Shipwreck*

IN vain the cords and axes were prepared,
  For every wave now smites the quivering yard;
High o'er the ship they throw a dreadful shade,
Then on her burst in terrible cascade;
Across the founder'd deck o'erwhelming roar,
And foaming, swelling, bound upon the shore.
Swift up the mounting billow now she flies,
Her shatter'd top half buried in the skies;
Borne o'er a latent reef the hull impends,
Then thundering on the marble crags descends:
Her ponderous bulk the dire concussion feels,
And o'er upheaving surges wounded reels—

428

WILLIAM FALCONER

Again she plunges! hark! a second shock
Bilges the splitting vessel on the rock.—
Down on the vale of death, with dismal cries,
The fated victims shuddering cast their eyes
In wild despair; while yet another stroke
With strong convulsion rends the solid oak:
Ah Heaven!—behold her crashing ribs divide!
She loosens, parts, and spreads in ruin o'er the tide.

The Shipwreck, Canto iii, 1762 (revised)

TOBIAS GEORGE SMOLLETT

1721–1771

278 *The Tears of Scotland*

Written in the Year MDCCXLVI

MOURN, hapless Caledonia, mourn
Thy banish'd peace, thy laurels torn!
Thy sons, for valour long renown'd,
Lie slaughter'd on their native ground;
Thy hospitable roofs no more
Invite the stranger to the door;
In smoaky ruins sunk they lie,
The monuments of cruelty.

The wretched owner sees, afar,
His all become the prey of war;
Bethinks him of his babes and wife,
Then smites his breast, and curses life.
Thy swains are famish'd on the rocks,
Where once they fed their wanton flocks:
Thy ravish'd virgins shriek in vain;
Thy infants perish on the plain.

TOBIAS GEORGE SMOLLETT

What boots it, then, in ev'ry clime,
Thro' the wide-spreading waste of time,
Thy martial glory, crown'd with praise,
Still shone with undiminish'd blaze?
Thy tow'ring spirit now is broke,
Thy neck is bended to the yoke:
What foreign arms could never quell,
By civil rage and rancour fell.

The rural pipe and merry lay
No more shall chear the happy day:
No social scenes of gay delight
Beguile the dreary winter night:
No strains, but those of sorrow, flow,
And nought be heard but sounds of woe,
While the pale phantoms of the slain
Glide nightly o'er the silent plain.

O baneful cause, oh, fatal morn,
Accurs'd to ages yet unborn!
The sons against their fathers stood;
The parent shed his children's blood.
Yet, when the rage of battle ceas'd,
The victor's soul was not appeas'd:
The naked and forlorn must feel
Devouring flames, and murd'ring steel!

The pious mother doom'd to death,
Forsaken, wanders o'er the heath,
The bleak wind whistles round her head,
Her helpless orphans cry for bread,

Bereft of shelter, food, and friend,
She views the shades of night descend,
And, stretch'd beneath th' inclement skies,
Weeps o'er her tender babes, and dies.

Whilst the warm blood bedews my veins,
And unimpair'd remembrance reigns,
Resentment of my country's fate
Within my filial breast shall beat;
And, spite of her insulting foe,
My sympathizing verse shall flow,
' Mourn, hapless Caledonia, mourn
' Thy banish'd peace, thy laurels torn.'

The Thrush, 1749; *The Union*, 1753

279   *Ode to Leven-Water*

O N Leven's banks, while free to rove,
  And tune the rural pipe to love;
I envied not the happiest swain
That ever trod the Arcadian plain.
  Pure stream! in whose transparent wave
My youthful limbs I wont to lave;
No torrents stain thy limpid source;
No rocks impede thy dimpling course,
That sweetly warbles o'er its bed,
With white, round, polish'd pebbles spread;
While, lightly pois'd, the scaly brood
In myriads cleave thy crystal flood;
The springing trout in speckled pride;
The salmon, monarch of the tide;
The ruthless pike, intent on war;
The silver eel, and mottled par.

Devolving from thy parent lake,
A charming maze thy waters make,
By bowers of birch, and groves of pine,
And hedges flower'd with eglantine.

  Still on thy banks so gayly green,
May num'rous herds and flocks be seen,
And lasses chanting o'er the pail,
And shepherds piping in the dale,
And ancient faith that knows no guile,
And industry imbrown'd with toil,
And hearts resolv'd, and hands prepar'd,
The blessings they enjoy to guard.

Town and Country Magazine, June 1771

280 *Independence*

THY spirit, INDEPENDENCE, let me share!
  Lord of the lion-heart and eagle-eye,
Thy steps I follow with my bosom bare,
Nor heed the storm that howls along the sky.
Deep in the frozen regions of the north,
A goddess violated brought thee forth,
Immortal Liberty, whose look sublime
Hath bleached the tyrant's cheek in every varying clime.

Ode to Independence, 1773

THOMAS OSBERT MORDAUNT

1730–1809

281   *Verses written during the War*
1756–1763

GO, lovely boy! to yonder tow'r,
    The fane of Janus, ruthless King!
And shut, O! shut the brazen door,
    And here the keys in triumph bring.

Full many a tender heart hath bled,
    Its joys in Belgia's soil entomb'd:
Which thou to Hymen's smiling bed,
    And length of sweetest hours, had doom'd.

Oh glory! you to ruin owe
    The fairest plume the hero wears:
Raise the bright helmet from his brow:
    You'll mock, beneath, the manly tears.

Who does not burn to place the crown
    Of conquest on his Albion's head?
Who weeps not at her plaintive moan,
    To give her hapless orphans bread?

Forgive, ye brave, the generous fault,
    If thus my virtue fails; alone
My Delia stole my earliest thought,
    And fram'd its feelings by her own.

Her mind so pure, her face so fair;
    Her breast the seat of softest love;
It seem'd her words an angel's were,
    Her gentle precepts from above.

THOMAS OSBERT MORDAUNT

My mind thus form'd, to misery gave
  The tender tribute of a tear:
O! Belgia, open thy vast grave,
  For I could pour an ocean there.

When first you show'd me at your feet
  Pale liberty, religion tied,
I flew to shut the glorious gate
  Of freedom on a tyrant's pride.

Tho' great the cause, so wore with woes,
  I cannot but lament the deed:
My youth to melancholy bows,
  And *Clotho* trifles with my thread.

But stop, my Clio, wanton muse,
  Indulge not this unmanly strain:
Beat, beat the drums, my ardour rouse,
  And call the soldier back again.

Sound, sound the clarion, fill the fife,
  Throughout the sensual world proclaim,
One crouded hour of glorious life
  Is worth an age without a name.

Go then, thou little lovely boy,
  I cannot, must not, hear thee now;
And all thy soothing arts employ
  To cheat my Delia of her woe.

If the gay flow'r, in all its youth,
  The scythe of glory here must meet;
Go, bear my laurel, pledge of truth,
  And lay it at my Delia's feet.

Her tears shall keep it ever green,
    To crown the image in her breast;
Till death doth close the hapless scene,
    And calls its angel home to rest.

The Bee, or Literary Weekly Intelligencer
(Edinburgh), October 12, 1791

CHRISTOPHER SMART

1722-1771

282   *A Song to David*

O THOU, that sit'st upon a throne,
    With harp of high majestic tone,
    To praise the King of kings;
And voice of heav'n-ascending swell,
Which, while its deeper notes excell,
    Clear, as a clarion, rings:

To bless each valley, grove and coast,
And charm the cherubs to the post
    Of gratitude in throngs;
To keep the days on Zion's mount,
And send the year to his account,
    With dances and with songs:

O Servant of God's holiest charge,
The minister of praise at large,
    Which thou may'st now receive;
From thy blest mansion hail and hear,
From topmost eminence appear
    To this the wreath I weave.

Great, valiant, pious, good, and clean,
Sublime, contemplative, serene,
   Strong, constant, pleasant, wise!
Bright effluence of exceeding grace;
Best man!—the swiftness and the race,
   The peril, and the prize!

Great—from the lustre of his crown,
From Samuel's horn and God's renown,
   Which is the people's voice;
For all the host, from rear to van,
Applauded and embrac'd the man—
   The man of God's own choice.

Valiant—the word, and up he rose—
The fight—he triumph'd o'er the foes,
   Whom God's just laws abhor;
And arm'd in gallant faith he took
Against the boaster, from the brook,
   The weapons of the war.

Pious—magnificent and grand;
'Twas he the famous temple plan'd:
   (The seraph in his soul)
Foremost to give his Lord his dues,
Foremost to bless the welcome news,
   And foremost to condole.

Good—from Jehudah's genuine vein,
From God's best nature good in grain,
   His aspect and his heart;
To pity, to forgive, to save,
Witness En-gedi's conscious cave,
   And Shimei's blunted dart.

CHRISTOPHER SMART

Clean—if perpetual prayer be pure,
And love, which could itself innure
   To fasting and to fear—
Clean in his gestures, hands, and feet,
To smite the lyre, the dance compleat,
   To play the sword and spear.

Sublime—invention ever young,
Of vast conception, tow'ring tongue,
   To God th' eternal theme;
Notes from yon exaltations caught,
Unrival'd royalty of thought,
   O'er meaner strains supreme.

Contemplative—on God to fix
His musings, and above the six
   The sabbath-day he blest;
'Twas then his thoughts self-conquest prun'd,
And heavenly melancholy tun'd,
   To bless and bear the rest.

Serene—to sow the seeds of peace,
Rememb'ring, when he watch'd the fleece,
   How sweetly Kidron purl'd—
To further knowledge, silence vice,
And plant perpetual paradise
   When God had calm'd the world.

Strong—in the Lord, who could defy
Satan, and all his powers that lie
   In sempiternal night;
And hell, and horror, and despair
Were as the lion and the bear
   To his undaunted might.

Constant—in love to God THE TRUTH,
Age, manhood, infancy, and youth—
   To Jonathan his friend
Constant, beyond the verge of death;
And Ziba, and Mephibosheth,
   His endless fame attend.

Pleasant—and various as the year;
Man, soul, and angel, without peer,
   Priest, champion, sage and boy;
In armour, or in ephod clad,
His pomp, his piety was glad;
   Majestic was his joy.

Wise—in recovery from his fall,
Whence rose his eminence o'er all,
   Of all the most revil'd;
The light of Israel in his ways,
Wise are his precepts, prayer and praise,
   And counsel to his child.

His muse, bright angel of his verse,
Gives balm for all the thorns that pierce,
   For all the pangs that rage;
Blest light, still gaining on the gloom,
The more than Michal of his bloom,
   Th' Abishag of his age.

He sung of God—the mighty source
Of all things—the stupendous force
   On which all strength depends;
From whose right arm, beneath whose eyes,
All period, pow'r, and enterprize
   Commences, reigns, and ends.

CHRISTOPHER SMART

Angels—their ministry and meed,
Which to and fro with blessings speed,
  Or with their citterns wait;
Where Michael with his millions bows,
Where dwells the seraph and his spouse,
  The cherub and her mate.

Of man—the semblance and effect
Of God and Love—the Saint elect
  For infinite applause—
To rule the land, and briny broad,
To be laborious in his laud,
  And heroes in his cause.

The world—the clustring spheres he made,
The glorious light, the soothing shade,
  Dale, champaign, grove, and hill;
The multitudinous abyss,
Where secrecy remains in bliss,
  And wisdom hides her skill.

Trees, plants, and flow'rs—of virtuous root;
Gem yielding blossom, yielding fruit,
  Choice gums and precious balm;
Bless ye the nosegay in the vale,
And with the sweetners of the gale
  Enrich the thankful psalm.

Of fowl—e'en ev'ry beak and wing
Which chear the winter, hail the spring,
  That live in peace or prey;
They that make music, or that mock,
The quail, the brave domestic cock,
  The raven, swan, and jay.

Of fishes—ev'ry size and shape,
Which nature frames of light escape,
   Devouring man to shun:
The shells are in the wealthy deep,
The shoals upon the surface leap,
   And love the glancing sun.

Of beasts—the beaver plods his task;
While the sleek tygers roll and bask,
   Nor yet the shades arouse:
Her cave the mining coney scoops;
Where o'er the mead the mountain stoops,
   The kids exult and brouse.

Of gems—their virtue and their price,
Which hid in earth from man's device,
   Their darts of lustre sheathe;
The jasper of the master's stamp,
The topaz blazing like a lamp
   Among the mines beneath.

Blest was the tenderness he felt
When to his graceful harp he knelt,
   And did for audience call;
When satan with his hand he quell'd,
And in serene suspence he held
   The frantic throes of Saul.

His furious foes no more malign'd
As he such melody divin'd,
   And sense and soul detain'd;
Now striking strong, now soothing soft,
He sent the godly sounds aloft,
   Or in delight refrain'd.

When up to heav'n his thoughts he pil'd,
From fervent lips fair Michal smil'd,
   As blush to blush she stood;
And chose herself the queen, and gave
Her utmost from her heart, ' so brave,
   ' And plays his hymns so good.'

The pillars of the Lord are seven,
Which stand from earth to topmost heav'n;
   His wisdom drew the plan;
His WORD accomplish'd the design,
From brightest gem to deepest mine,
   From CHRIST enthron'd to man.

Alpha, the cause of causes, first
In station, fountain, whence the burst
   Of light, and blaze of day;
Whence bold attempt, and brave advance,
Have motion, life, and ordinance,
   And heav'n itself its stay.

Gamma supports the glorious arch
On which angelic legions march,
   And is with sapphires pav'd;
Thence the fleet clouds are sent adrift,
And thence the painted folds, that lift
   The crimson veil, are wav'd.

Eta with living sculpture breathes,
With verdant carvings, flow'ry wreathes
   Of never-wasting bloom;
In strong relief his goodly base
All instruments of labour grace,
   The trowel, spade, and loom.

Next Theta stands to the Supreme—
Who form'd, in number, sign, and scheme,
   Th' illustrious lights that are;
And one address'd his saffron robe,
And one, clad in a silver globe,
   Held rule with ev'ry star.

Iota's tun'd to choral hymns
Of those that fly, while he that swims
   In thankful safety lurks;
And foot, and chapitre, and niche,
The various histories enrich
   Of God's recorded works.

Sigma presents the social droves,
With him that solitary roves,
   And man of all the chief;
Fair on whose face, and stately frame,
Did God impress his hallow'd name,
   For ocular belief.

OMEGA! GREATEST and the BEST,
Stands sacred to the day of rest,
   For gratitude and thought;
Which bless'd the world upon his pole,
And gave the universe his goal,
   And clos'd th' infernal draught.

O DAVID, scholar of the Lord!
Such is thy science, whence reward
   And infinite degree;
O strength, O sweetness, lasting ripe!
God's harp thy symbol, and thy type
   The lion and the bee!

There is but One who ne'er rebell'd,
But One by passion unimpell'd,
   By pleasures unintice't;
He from himself his semblance sent,
Grand object of his own content,
   And saw the God in CHRIST.

Tell them I am, JEHOVA said
To MOSES; while earth heard in dread,
   And smitten to the heart,
At once above, beneath, around,
All nature, without voice or sound,
   Replied, O Lord, THOU ART.

Thou art—to give and to confirm,
For each his talent and his term;
   All flesh thy bounties share:
Thou shalt not call thy brother fool:
The porches of the Christian school
   Are meekness, peace, and pray'r.

Open, and naked of offence,
Man's made of mercy, soul, and sense;
   God arm'd the snail and wilk;
Be good to him that pulls thy plough;
Due food and care, due rest, allow
   For her that yields thee milk.

Rise up before the hoary head,
And God's benign commandment dread,
   Which says thou shalt not die:
' Not as I will, but as thou wilt,'
Pray'd He whose conscience knew no guilt;
   With whose bless'd pattern vie.

Use all thy passions!—love is thine,
And joy, and jealousy divine;
   Thine hope's eternal fort,
And care thy leisure to disturb,
With fear concupiscence to curb,
   And rapture to transport.

Act simply, as occasion asks;
Put mellow wine in season'd casks;
   Till not with ass and bull:
Remember thy baptismal bond;
Keep from commixtures foul and fond,
   Nor work thy flax with wool.

Distribute: pay the Lord his tithe,
And make the widow's heart-strings blithe;
   Resort with those that weep:
As you from all and each expect,
For all and each thy love direct,
   And render as you reap.

The slander and its bearer spurn,
And propagating praise sojourn
   To make thy welcome last;
Turn from old Adam to the New;
By hope futurity pursue;
   Look upwards to the past.

Controul thine eye, salute success,
Honour the wiser, happier bless,
   And for thy neighbour feel;
Grutch not of mammon and his leaven,
Work emulation up to heaven
   By knowledge and by zeal.

CHRISTOPHER SMART

O DAVID, highest in the list
Of worthies, on God's ways insist,
  * The genuine word repeat:
Vain are the documents of men,
And vain the flourish of the pen
  That keeps the fool's conceit.

PRAISE above all—for praise prevails;
Heap up the measure, load the scales,
  And good to goodness add:
The gen'rous soul her Saviour aids,
But peevish obloquy degrades;
  The Lord is great and glad.

For ADORATION all the ranks
Of angels yield eternal thanks,
  And DAVID in the midst;
With God's good poor, which, last and least
In man's esteem, thou to thy feast,
  O blessed bride-groom, bidst.

For ADORATION seasons change,
And order, truth, and beauty range,
  Adjust, attract, and fill:
The grass the polyanthus cheques;
And polish'd porphyry reflects,
  By the descending rill.

Rich almonds colour to the prime
For ADORATION; tendrils climb,
  And fruit-trees pledge their gems;
And † Ivis with her gorgeous vest
Builds for her eggs her cunning nest,
  And bell-flowers bow their stems.

  * Ps. 119.   † Humming-bird.

445

With vinous syrup cedars spout;
From rocks pure honey gushing out,
    For ADORATION springs:
All scenes of painting croud the map
Of nature; to the mermaid's pap
    The scaled infant clings.

The spotted ounce and playsome cubs
Run rustling 'mongst the flow'ring shrubs,
    And lizards feed the moss;
For ADORATION * beasts embark,
While waves upholding halcyon's ark
    No longer roar and toss.

While Israel sits beneath his fig,
With coral root and amber sprig
    The wean'd advent'rer sports;
Where to the palm the jasmin cleaves,
For ADORATION 'mongst the leaves
    The gale his peace reports.

Increasing days their reign exalt,
Nor in the pink and mottled vault
    Th' opposing spirits tilt;
And, by the coasting reader spied,
The silverlings and crusions glide
    For ADORATION gilt.

For ADORATION rip'ning canes
And cocoa's purest milk detains

* There is a large quadruped that preys upon fish, and provides
himself with a species of timber for that purpose, with which he
is very handy (ed. 1765).

CHRISTOPHER SMART

The western pilgrim's staff;
Where rain in clasping boughs inclos'd,
And vines with oranges dispos'd,
    Embow'r the social laugh.

Now labour his reward receives,
For ADORATION counts his sheaves
    To peace, her bounteous prince;
The nectarine his strong tint imbibes,
And apples of ten thousand tribes,
    And quick peculiar quince.

The wealthy crops of whit'ning rice,
'Mongst thyine woods and groves of spice,
    For ADORATION grow;
And, marshall'd in the fenced land,
The peaches and pomegranates stand,
    Where wild carnations blow.

The laurels with the winter strive:
The crocus burnishes alive
    Upon the snow-clad earth:
For ADORATION myrtles stay
To keep the garden from dismay,
    And bless the sight from dearth.

The pheasant shows his pompous neck;
And ermine, jealous of a speck,
    With fear eludes offence:
The sable, with his glossy pride,
For ADORATION is descried,
    Where frosts the wave condense.

The chearful holly, pensive yew,
And holy thorn, their trim renew;
   The squirrel hoards his nuts:
All creatures batten o'er their stores,
And careful nature all her doors
   For ADORATION shuts.

For ADORATION, DAVID's psalms
Lift up the heart to deeds of alms;
   And he, who kneels and chants,
Prevails his passions to controul,
Finds meat and med'cine to the soul,
   Which for translation pants.

For ADORATION, beyond match,
The scholar bulfinch aims to catch
   The soft flute's iv'ry touch;
And, careless on the hazle spray,
The daring redbreast keeps at bay
   The damsel's greedy clutch.

For ADORATION, in the skies,
The Lord's philosopher espies
   The Dog, the Ram, and Rose;
The planets ring, Orion's sword;
Nor is his greatness less ador'd
   In the vile worm that glows.

For ADORATION * on the strings
The western breezes work their wings,
   The captive ear to sooth.—
Hark! 'tis a voice—how still, and small—
That makes the cataracts to fall,
   Or bids the sea be smooth.

            * Æolian harp.

For ADORATION, incense comes
From bezoar, and Arabian gums;
   And on the civet's furr.
But as for prayer, or e're it faints,
Far better is the breath of saints
   Than galbanum and myrrh.

For ADORATION from the down,
Of dam'sins to th' anana's crown,
   God sends to tempt the taste;
And while the luscious zest invites,
The sense, that in the scene delights,
   Commands desire be chaste.

For ADORATION, all the paths
Of grace are open, all the baths
   Of purity refresh;
And all the rays of glory beam
To deck the man of God's esteem,
   Who triumphs o'er the flesh.

For ADORATION, in the dome
Of Christ the sparrows find an home;
   And on his olives perch:
The swallow also dwells with thee,
O man of God's humility,
   Within his Saviour's CHURCH.

Sweet is the dew that falls betimes,
And drops upon the leafy limes;
   Sweet Hermon's fragrant air:
Sweet is the lilly's silver bell,
And sweet the wakeful tapers smell
   That watch for early pray'r.

CHRISTOPHER SMART

Sweet the young nurse with love intense,
Which smiles o'er sleeping innocence;
    Sweet when the lost arrive:
Sweet the musician's ardour beats,
While his vague mind's in quest of sweets
    The choicest flow'rs to hive.

Sweeter in all the strains of love,
The language of thy turtle dove,
    Pair'd to thy swelling chord;
Sweeter with ev'ry grace endu'd,
The glory of thy gratitude,
    Respir'd unto the Lord.

Strong is the horse upon his speed;
Strong in pursuit the rapid glede,
    Which makes at once his game:
Strong the tall ostrich on the ground;
Strong thro' the turbulent profound
    Shoots * xiphias to his aim.

Strong is the lion—like a coal
His eye-ball—like a bastion's mole
    His chest against the foes:
Strong, the gier-eagle on his sail,
Strong against tide, th' enormous whale
    Emerges as he goes.

But stronger still, in earth and air,
And in the sea, the man of pray'r;
    And far beneath the tide;
And in the seat to faith assign'd,
Where ask is have, where seek is find,
    Where knock is open wide.
                * The sword-fish.

CHRISTOPHER SMART

Beauteous the fleet before the gale;
Beauteous the multitudes in mail,
 Rank'd arms and crested heads:
Beauteous the garden's umbrage mild,
Walk, water, meditated wild,
 And all the bloomy beds.

Beauteous the moon full on the lawn;
And beauteous, when the veil's withdrawn,
 The virgin to her spouse:
Beauteous the temple deck'd and fill'd,
When to the heav'n of heav'ns they build
 Their heart-directed vows.

Beauteous, yea beauteous more than these,
The shepherd king upon his knees,
 For his momentous trust;
With wish of infinite conceit,
For man, beast, mute, the small and great,
 And prostrate dust to dust.

Precious the bounteous widow's mite;
And precious, for extream delight,
 * The largess from the churl:
Precious the ruby's blushing blaze,
And † alba's blest imperial rays,
 And pure cerulean pearl.

Precious the penitential tear;
And precious is the sigh sincere,
 Acceptable to God:
And precious are the winning flow'rs,
In gladsome Israel's feast of bow'rs,
 Bound on the hallow'd sod.

 * Sam. xxv. 18.   † Rev. xi. 17.

CHRISTOPHER SMART

More precious that diviner part
Of David, ev'n the Lord's own heart,
   Great, beautiful, and new:
In all things where it was intent,
In all extreams, in each event,
   Proof—answ'ring true to true.

Glorious the sun in mid career;
Glorious th' assembled fires appear;
   Glorious the comet's train:
Glorious the trumpet and alarm;
Glorious th' almighty stretch'd-out arm;
   Glorious th' enraptur'd main:

Glorious the northern lights astream;
Glorious the song, when God's the theme
   Glorious the thunder's roar:
Glorious hosanna from the den;
Glorious the catholic amen;
   Glorious the martyr's gore:

Glorious—more glorious is the crown
Of Him that brought salvation down
   By meekness, call'd thy Son;
Thou that stupendous truth believ'd,
And now the matchless deed's atchiev'd,
   DETERMINED, DARED, and DONE.

A Song to David, 1763

452

CHRISTOPHER SMART

283   *On a Bed of Guernsey Lilies*

Written in September 1763

YE beauties! O how great the sum
    Of sweetness that ye bring;
On what a charity ye come
    To bless the latter spring!
How kind the visit that ye pay,
Like strangers on a rainy day,
    When heartiness despair'd of guests:
No neighbour's praise your pride alarms,
No rival flow'r surveys your charms,
    Or heightens, or contests!

Lo, thro' her works gay nature grieves
    How brief she is and frail,
As ever o'er the falling leaves
    Autumnal winds prevail.
Yet still the philosophic mind
Consolatory food can find,
    And hope her anchorage maintain:
We never are deserted quite;
'Tis by succession of delight
    That love supports his reign.
                    Ode to the Earl of Northumberland, &c., 1764

284   *Spring*

NOW the winds are all composure,
    But the breath upon the bloom,
Blowing sweet o'er each inclosure
    Grateful off'rings of perfume.

Tansy, calaminth and daisies
  On the river's margin thrive;
And accompany the mazes
  Of the stream that leaps alive.

Muse, accordant to the season,
  Give the numbers life and air;
When the sounds and objects reason
  In behalf of praise and pray'r.

All the scenes of nature quicken,
  By the genial spirit fann'd;
And the painted beauties thicken,
  Colour'd by the master's hand.

Earth her vigour repossessing
  As the blasts are held in ward,
Blessing heap'd and press'd on blessing,
  Yield the measure of the Lord.

Beeches, without order seemly,
  Shade the flow'rs of annual birth,
And the lily smiles supremely,
  Mention'd by the Lord on earth.

Couslips seize upon the fallow,
  And the cardamine in white,
Where the corn-flow'rs join the mallow,
  Joy and health, and thrift unite.

Study sits beneath her arbour,
  By the bason's glossy side;
While the boat from out its harbour
  Exercise and pleasure guide.

CHRISTOPHER SMART

Pray'r and praise be mine employment,
  Without grudging or regret;
Lasting life, and long enjoyment
  Are not here, and are not yet.

Hark! aloud, the black-bird whistles,
  With surrounding fragrance blest,
And the goldfinch in the thistles
  Makes provision for her nest.

Ev'n the hornet hives his honey,
  Bluecap builds his stately dome,
And the rocks supply the coney
  With a fortress and an home.

Hymn xiii—The Psalms of David, 1765

JOHN CUNNINGHAM

285   *Day: A Pastoral*

Morning

IN the barn the tenant Cock,
  Close to partlet perch'd on high,
Briskly crows, (the shepherd's clock!)
  Jocund that the morning 's nigh.

Swiftly from the mountain's brow,
  Shadows, nurs'd by night, retire:
And the peeping sun-beam, now,
  Paints with gold the village spire.

Philomel forsakes the thorn,
  Plaintive where she prates at night;
And the Lark, to meet the morn,
  Soars beyond the shepherd's sight.

JOHN CUNNINGHAM

From the low-roof'd cottage ridge,
  See the chatt'ring Swallow spring;
Darting through the one-arch'd bridge,
  Quick she dips her dappled wing.

Now the pine-tree's waving top
  Gently greets the morning gale:
Kidlings, now, begin to crop
  Daisies, on the dewey dale.

From the balmy sweets, uncloy'd,
  (Restless till her task be done)
Now the busy Bee 's employ'd
  Sipping dew before the sun.

Trickling through the crevic'd rock,
  Where the limpid stream distills,
Sweet refreshment waits the flock
  When 'tis sun-drove from the hills.

COLIN 's for the promis'd corn
  (E're the harvest hopes are ripe)
Anxious;—whilst the huntsman's horn,
  Boldly sounding, drowns his pipe.

Sweet,—O sweet, the warbling throng,
  On the white emblossom'd spray!
Nature's universal song
  Echos to the rising day.

Noon

Fervid on the glitt'ring flood,
  Now the noontide radiance glows:
Drooping o'er its infant bud,
  Not a dew-drop 's left the rose.

JOHN CUNNINGHAM

By the brook the shepherd dines,
    From the fierce meridian heat
Shelter'd, by the branching pines,
    Pendant o'er his grassy seat.

Now the flock forsakes the glade,
    Where uncheck'd the sun-beams fall;
Sure to find a pleasing shade
    By the ivy'd abbey wall.

Echo in her airy round,
    O'er the river, rock and hill,
Cannot catch a single sound,
    Save the clack of yonder mill.

Cattle court the zephirs bland,
    Where the streamlet wanders cool;
Or with languid silence stand
    Midway in the marshy pool.

But from mountain, dell, or stream,
    Not a flutt'ring zephir springs
Fearful lest the noontide beam
    Scorch its soft, its silken wings.

Not a leaf has leave to stir,
    Nature 's lull'd—serene—and still!
Quiet e'en the shepherd's cur,
    Sleeping on the heath-clad hill.

Languid is the landscape round,
    Till the fresh descending shower,
Grateful to the thirsty ground,
    Raises ev'ry fainting flower.

JOHN CUNNINGHAM

Now the hill—the hedge—is green,
  Now the warblers' throats in tune;
Blithsome is the verdant scene,
  Brighten'd by the beams of Noon!

Evening

O'er the heath the heifer strays
  Free;—(the furrow'd task is done)
Now the village windows blaze,
  Burnish'd by the setting sun.

Now he sets behind the hill,
  Sinking from a golden sky:
Can the pencil's mimic skill
  Copy the refulgent dye?

Trudging as the plowmen go,
  (To the smoaking hamlet bound)
Giant-like their shadows grow,
  Lengthen'd o'er the level ground.

Where the rising forest spreads,
  Shelter, for the lordly dome!
To their high-built airy beds,
  See the rooks returning home!

As the Lark, with vary'd tune,
  Carrols to the evening loud,
Mark the mild resplendent moon
  Breaking through a parted cloud!

Now the hermit Howlet peeps
  From the barn, or twisted brake;
And the blue mist slowly creeps,
  Curling on the silver lake.

As the Trout, in speckled pride,
   Playful from its bosom springs,
To the banks a ruffled tide
   Verges in successive rings.

Tripping through the silken grass,
   O'er the path-divided dale,
Mark the rose-complexion'd lass
   With her well-pois'd milking pail.

Linnets with unnumber'd notes,
   And the Cuckow bird with two,
Tuning sweet their mellow throats,
   Bid the setting sun adieu.

The Scots Magazine, April and June 1761; Fawkes and
Woty's *Poetical Calendar*, April 1763

286   *The Miller*

IN a plain pleasant cottage, conveniently neat,
  With a mill and some meadows—a freehold estate,
A well-meaning miller by labour supplies
Those blessings that grandeur to great ones denies:

No passions to plague him, no cares to torment,
His constant companions are health and content;
Their lordships in lace may remark if they will,
He 's honest tho' daub'd with the dust of his mill.

Ere the lark's early carrols salute the new day
He springs from his cottage as jocund as May;
He chearfully whistles, regardless of care,
Or sings the last ballad he bought at the fair:

JOHN CUNNINGHAM

While courtiers are toil'd in the cobwebs of state,
Or bribing elections in hopes to be great,
No fraud, or ambition his bosom does fill,
Contented he works, if there's grist for his mill.

On Sunday bedeck'd in his homespun array,
At church he's the loudest, to chaunt or to pray:
He sits to a dinner of plain English food,
Tho' simple the pudding, his appetite's good;

At night, when the priest and exciseman are gone,
He quaffs at the alehouse with Roger and John,
Then reels to his pillow, and dreams of no ill;
No monarch more blest than the man of the mill.

The Universal Magazine, March 1760

OLIVER GOLDSMITH

1728–1774

287   *An Elegy on that Glory of her Sex,*
        Mrs. Mary Blaize

GOOD people all, with one accord,
     Lament for Madam BLAIZE,
Who never wanted a good word—
     From those who spoke her praise.

The needy seldom pass'd her door,
     And always found her kind;
She freely lent to all the poor,—
     Who left a pledge behind.

She strove the neighbourhood to please,
     With manners wond'rous winning,
And never follow'd wicked ways,—
     Unless when she was sinning.

460

At church, in silks and sattins new,
    With hoop of monstrous size,
She never slumber'd in her pew,—
    But when she shut her eyes.

Her love was sought, I do aver,
    By twenty beaus and more;
The king himself has follow'd her,—
    When she has walk'd before.

But now her wealth and finery fled,
    Her hangers-on cut short all;
The doctors found, when she was dead,—
    Her last disorder mortal.

Let us lament, in sorrow sore,
    For Kent-street well may say,
That had she liv'd a twelve-month more,
    She had not dy'd to-day.

              The Bee, October 27, 1759

288   *Memory*

O MEMORY, thou fond deceiver,
    Still importunate and vain;
To former joys recurring ever,
    And turning all the past to pain;
Hence, intruder, most distressing,
    Seek the happy and the free:
The wretch who wants each other blessing,
    Ever wants a friend in thee.

The Captivity, written 1764, published 1820; other version,
        The Haunch of Venison, 1776

289 *Hope*

TO the last moment of his breath
   On Hope the wretch relies,
And even the pang preceding death
   Bids Expectation rise.

Hope like the gleaming taper's light
   Adorns and cheers our way,
And still as darker grows the night
   Emits a brighter ray.

      The Captivity, 1764; *The Haunch of Venison*, 1776

290 *Real Happiness*

AS some lone miser visiting his store,
   Bends at his treasure, counts, recounts it o'er;
Hoards after hoards his rising raptures fill,
Yet still he sighs, for hoards are wanting still:
Thus to my breast alternate passions rise,
Pleas'd with each good that heaven to man supplies:
Yet oft a sigh prevails, and sorrows fall,
To see the sum of human bliss so small;
And oft I wish, amidst the scene, to find
Some spot to real happiness consign'd,
Where my worn soul, each wand'ring hope at rest,
May gather bliss to see my fellows blest.

  But where to find that happiest spot below,
Who can direct, when all pretend to know?
The shudd'ring tenant of the frigid zone
Boldly proclaims that happiest spot his own,
Extols the treasures of his stormy seas,
And his long nights of revelry and ease;

The naked negroe, panting at the line,
Boasts of his golden sands and palmy wine,
Basks in the glare, or stems the tepid wave,
And thanks his Gods for all the good they gave.
Such is the patriot's boast, where'er we roam,
His first, best country ever is, at home.

And yet, perhaps, if countries we compare,
And estimate the blessings which they share,
Tho' patriots flatter, still shall wisdom find
An equal portion dealt to all mankind,
As different good, by Art or Nature given,
To different nations makes their blessings even.

The Traveller, 1764

291 *France*

TO kinder skies, where gentler manners reign,
I turn; and France displays her bright domain.
Gay sprightly land of mirth and social ease,
Pleas'd with thyself, whom all the world can please,
How often have I led thy sportive choir,
With tuneless pipe, beside the murmuring Loire?
Where shading elms along the margin grew,
And freshen'd from the wave the Zephyr flew;
And haply, though my harsh touch faltering still,
But mock'd all tune, and marr'd the dancer's skill;
Yet would the village praise my wonderous pow'r,
And dance, forgetful of the noon-tide hour.
Alike all ages.   Dames of ancient days
Have led their children through the mirthful maze,
And the gay grandsire, skill'd in gestic lore,
Has frisk'd beneath the burthen of threescore.

463

So blest a life these thoughtless realms display,
Thus idly busy rolls their world away:
Theirs are those arts that mind to mind endear,
For honour forms the social temper here.
Honour, that praise which real merit gains,
Or even imaginary worth obtains,
Here passes current; paid from hand to hand,
It shifts in splendid traffic round the land:
From courts to camps, to cottages it strays,
And all are taught an avarice of praise;
They please, are pleas'd, they give to get esteem,
Till, seeming blest, they grow to what they seem.

The Traveller, 1764

292 *Happiness dependent on Ourselves*
(*Mainly by Johnson*)

VAIN, very vain, my weary search to find
  That bliss which only centers in the mind:
Why have I stray'd, from pleasure and repose,
To seek a good each government bestows?
In every government, though terrors reign,
Though tyrant kings, or tyrant laws restrain,
How small of all that human hearts endure,
That part which laws or kings can cause or cure.
Still to ourselves in every place consign'd,
Our own felicity we make or find:
With secret course, which no loud storms annoy,
Glides the smooth current of domestic joy.
The lifted ax, the agonizing wheel,
Luke's iron crown, and Damien's bed of steel,
To men remote from power but rarely known,
Leave reason, faith, and conscience, all our own.

The Traveller, 1764

293 *Elegy on the Death of a Mad Dog*

GOOD people all, of every sort,
  Give ear unto my Song;
And if you find it wond'rous short,
  It cannot hold you long.

In Isling town there was a man,
  Of whom the world might say,
That still a godly race he ran,
  Whene'er he went to pray.

A kind and gentle heart he had,
  To comfort friends and foes;
The naked every day he clad,
  When he put on his cloths.

And in that town a dog was found,
  As many dogs there be,
Both mungrel, puppy, whelp, and hound,
  And curs of low degree.

The dog and man at first were friends;
  But when a pique began,
The dog, to gain his private ends,
  Went mad and bit the man.

Around from all the neighbouring streets,
  The wondering neighbours ran,
And swore the dog had lost his wits,
  To bite so good a man.

The wound it seem'd both sore and sad,
  To every christian eye;
And while they swore the dog was mad,
  They swore the man would die.

But soon a wonder came to light,
    That shew'd the rogues they lied,
The man recovered of the bite,
    The dog it was that dy'd.
              The Vicar of Wakefield, 1766

294   *Song*

WHEN lovely woman stoops to folly,
    And finds too late that men betray,
What charm can sooth her melancholy,
    What art can wash her guilt away?

The only art her guilt to cover,
    To hide her shame from every eye,
To give repentance to her lover,
    And wring his bosom—is to die.
              The Vicar of Wakefield, 1766

295   *Auburn*

SWEET Auburn, loveliest village of the plain,
  Where health and plenty cheared the labouring swain,
Where smiling spring its earliest visit paid,
And parting summer's lingering blooms delayed,
Dear lovely bowers of innocence and ease,
Seats of my youth, when every sport could please,
How often have I loitered o'er thy green,
Where humble happiness endeared each scene!
How often have I paused on every charm,
The sheltered cot, the cultivated farm,
The never failing brook, the busy mill,
The decent church that topt the neighbouring hill,

The hawthorn bush, with seats beneath the shade,
For talking age and whispering lovers made!
How often have I blest the coming day,
When toil remitting lent its turn to play,
And all the village train from labour free
Led up their sports beneath the spreading tree,
While many a pastime circled in the shade,
The young contending as the old surveyed;
And many a gambol frolicked o'er the ground,
And slights of art and feats of strength went round;
And still as each repeated pleasure tired,
Succeeding sports the mirthful band inspired;
The dancing pair that simply sought renown
By holding out to tire each other down;
The swain mistrustless of his smutted face,
While secret laughter tittered round the place;
The bashful virgin's side-long looks of love,
The matron's glance that would those looks reprove!
These were thy charms, sweet village; sports like these,
With sweet succession taught even toil to please;
These round thy bowers their chearful influence shed,
These were thy charms—But all these charms are fled.

Sweet smiling village, loveliest of the lawn,
Thy sports are fled, and all thy charms withdrawn;
Amidst thy bowers the tyrant's hand is seen,
And desolation saddens all the green:
One only master grasps the whole domain,
And half a tillage stints thy smiling plain;
No more thy glassy brook reflects the day,
But choaked with sedges, works its weedy way;
Along thy glades, a solitary guest,
The hollow sounding bittern guards its nest;

Amidst thy desert walks the lapwing flies,
And tires their ecchoes with unvaried cries.
Sunk are thy bowers, in shapeless ruin all,
And the long grass o'ertops the mouldering wall;
And trembling, shrinking from the spoiler's hand,
Far, far away thy children leave the land.

Ill fares the land, to hastening ills a prey,
Where wealth accumulates, and men decay:
Princes and lords may flourish, or may fade;
A breath can make them, as a breath has made;
But a bold peasantry, their country's pride,
When once destroyed, can never be supplied.

The Deserted Village, 1770

296 *Blest Retirement*

SWEET Auburn! parent of the blissful hour,
Thy glades forlorn confess the tyrant's power.
Here as I take my solitary rounds,
Amidst thy tangling walks, and ruined grounds,
And, many a year elapsed, return to view
Where once the cottage stood, the hawthorn grew,
Remembrance wakes with all her busy train,
Swells at my breast, and turns the past to pain.

In all my wanderings round this world of care,
In all my griefs—and God has given my share—
I still had hopes, my latest hours to crown,
Amidst these humble bowers to lay me down;
To husband out life's taper at the close,
And keep the flame from wasting by repose:
I still had hopes, for pride attends us still,
Amidst the swains to shew my book-learned skill,

Around my fire an evening groupe to draw,
And tell of all I felt, and all I saw;
And, as an hare whom hounds and horns pursue,
Pants to the place from whence at first she flew,
I still had hopes, my long vexations past,
Here to return—and die at home at last.

O blest retirement, friend to life's decline,
Retreats from care that never must be mine,
How happy he who crowns in shades like these,
A youth of labour with an age of ease;
Who quits a world where strong temptations try,
And, since 'tis hard to combat, learns to fly!
For him no wretches, born to work and weep,
Explore the mine, or tempt the dangerous deep;
No surly porter stands in guilty state
To spurn imploring famine from the gate;
But on he moves to meet his latter end,
Angels around befriending virtue's friend;
Bends to the grave with unperceived decay,
While resignation gently slopes the way;
And all his prospects brightening to the last,
His Heaven commences ere the world be past!

The Deserted Village, 1770

297 *The Village Parson*

NEAR yonder copse, where once the garden smiled,
And still where many a garden flower grows wild;
There, where a few torn shrubs the place disclose,
The village preacher's modest mansion rose.
A man he was, to all the country dear,
And passing rich with forty pounds a year;

Remote from towns he ran his godly race,
Nor e'er had changed, nor wished to change his place;
Unpractised he to fawn, or seek for power,
By doctrines fashioned to the varying hour;
Far other aims his heart had learned to prize,
More skilled to raise the wretched than to rise.
His house was known to all the vagrant train,
He chid their wanderings, but relieved their pain;
The long remembered beggar was his guest,
Whose beard descending swept his aged breast;
The ruined spendthrift, now no longer proud,
Claimed kindred there, and had his claims allowed;
The broken soldier, kindly bade to stay,
Sate by his fire, and talked the night away;
Wept o'er his wounds, or tales of sorrow done,
Shouldered his crutch, and shewed how fields were won.
Pleased with his guests, the good man learned to glow,
And quite forgot their vices in their woe;
Careless their merits, or their faults to scan,
His pity gave ere charity began.

Thus to relieve the wretched was his pride,
And even his failings leaned to Virtue's side;
But in his duty prompt at every call,
He watched and wept, he prayed and felt, for all.
And, as a bird each fond endearment tries,
To tempt its new fledged offspring to the skies;
He tried each art, reproved each dull delay,
Allured to brighter worlds, and led the way.

Beside the bed where parting life was layed,
And sorrow, guilt, and pain, by turns dismayed
The reverend champion stood. At his control,
Despair and anguish fled the struggling soul

Comfort came down the trembling wretch to raise,
And his last faultering accents whispered praise.
   At church, with meek and unaffected grace,
His looks adorned the venerable place;
Truth from his lips prevailed with double sway,
And fools, who came to scoff, remained to pray.
The service past, around the pious man,
With steady zeal each honest rustic ran;
Even children followed with endearing wile,
And plucked his gown, to share the good man's smile.
His ready smile a parent's warmth exprest,
Their welfare pleased him, and their cares distrest;
To them his heart, his love, his griefs were given,
But all his serious thoughts had rest in Heaven.
As some tall cliff that lifts its awful form,
Swells from the vale, and midway leaves the storm,
Tho' round its breast the rolling clouds are spread,
Eternal sunshine settles on its head.

The Deserted Village, 1770

298   *The Village Schoolmaster*

BESIDE yon straggling fence that skirts the way,
   With blossomed furze unprofitably gay,
There, in his noisy mansion, skill'd to rule,
The village master taught his little school;
A man severe he was, and stern to view,
I knew him well, and every truant knew;
Well had the boding tremblers learned to trace
The day's disasters in his morning face;
Full well they laughed with counterfeited glee,
At all his jokes, for many a joke had he:

Full well the busy whisper circling round,
Conveyed the dismal tidings when he frowned;
Yet he was kind, or if severe in aught,
The love he bore to learning was in fault;
The village all declared how much he knew;
'Twas certain he could write, and cypher too;
Lands he could measure, terms and tides presage,
And even the story ran that he could gauge.
In arguing too, the parson owned his skill,
For even tho' vanquished, he could argue still;
While words of learned length, and thundering sound,
Amazed the gazing rustics ranged around;
And still they gazed, and still the wonder grew,
That one small head could carry all he knew.

The Deserted Village, 1770

299 *Farewell to Poetry*

DEAR charming nymph, neglected and decried,
My shame in crowds, my solitary pride;
Thou source of all my bliss, and all my woe,
That found'st me poor at first, and keep'st me so;
Thou guide by which the nobler arts excell,
Thou nurse of every virtue, fare thee well.
Farewell, and O where'er thy voice be tried,
On Torno's cliffs, or Pambamarca's side,
Whether where equinoctial fervours glow,
Or winter wraps the polar world in snow,
Still let thy voice, prevailing over time,
Redress the rigours of the inclement clime;
Aid slighted truth with thy persuasive strain,
Teach erring man to spurn the rage of gain;

472

Teach him, that states of native strength possest,
Tho' very poor, may still be very blest;
That trade's proud empire hastes to swift decay,
As ocean sweeps the labour'd mole away;
While self-dependent power can time defy,
As rocks resist the billows and the sky.

The Deserted Village, 1770

300 *Edmund Burke*

HERE lies our good Edmund, whose genius was such,
We scarcely can praise it, or blame it too much;
Who, born for the Universe, narrow'd his mind,
And to party gave up, what was meant for mankind.
Tho' fraught with all learning, yet straining his throat,
To persuade Tommy Townsend to lend him a vote;
Who, too deep for his hearers, still went on refining,
And thought of convincing, while they thought of dining;
Tho' equal to all things, for all things unfit,
Too nice for a statesman, too proud for a wit:
For a patriot too cool; for a drudge, disobedient,
And too fond of the *right* to pursue the *expedient*.
In short, 'twas his fate, unemploy'd, or in play, Sir,
To eat mutton cold, and cut blocks with a razor.

Retaliation, 1774

301 *David Garrick*

HERE lies David Garrick, describe me who can,
An abridgment of all that was pleasant in man;
As an actor, confest without rival to shine,
As a wit, if not first, in the very first line,

Yet with talents like these, and an excellent heart.
The man had his failings, a dupe to his art;
Like an ill judging beauty, his colours he spread,
And beplaister'd, with rouge, his own natural red.
On the stage he was natural, simple, affecting,
'Twas only that, when he was off, he was acting:
With no reason on earth to go out of his way,
He turn'd and he varied full ten times a day;
Tho' secure of our hearts, yet confoundedly sick,
If they were not his own by finessing and trick,
He cast off his friends, as a huntsman his pack,
For he knew when he pleased he could whistle them back.
Of praise, a mere glutton, he swallowed what came,
And the puff of a dunce, he mistook it for fame;
'Till his relish grown callous, almost to disease,
Who pepper'd the highest, was surest to please.
But let us be candid, and speak out our mind,
If dunces applauded, he paid them in kind.
Ye Kenricks, ye Kellys, and Woodfalls so grave,
What a commerce was yours, while you got and you gave?
How did Grub-street re-echo the shouts that you rais'd,
While he was beroscius'd, and you were beprais'd?
But peace to his spirit, wherever it flies,
To act as an angel, and mix with the skies:
Those poets, who owe their best fame to his skill,
Shall still be his flatterers, go where he will.
Old Shakespeare, receive him, with praise and with love,
And Beaumonts and Bens be his Kellys above.

Retaliation, 1774

OLIVER GOLDSMITH

302   *Sir Joshua Reynolds*

HERE Reynolds is laid, and to tell you my mind,
 He has not left a better or wiser behind;
His pencil was striking, resistless and grand,
His manners were gentle, complying and bland;
Still born to improve us in every part,
His pencil our faces, his manners our heart:
To coxcombs averse, yet most civilly steering,
When they judged without skill he was still hard of hearing·
When they talk'd of their Raphaels, Corregios and stuff,
He shifted his trumpet, and only took snuff.

Retaliation, 1774

THOMAS PERCY

1729–1811

303   *The Friar of Orders Gray*

*Dispersed thro' Shakespeare's plays are innumerable little frag-
ments of ancient ballads, the intire copies of which, could not be
recovered. Many of these being of the most beautiful and pathetic
simplicity, the Editor was tempted to select some of them, and with
a few supplemental stanzas to connect them together and form them
into a litile* TALE, *which is here submitted to the Reader's candour.
One small fragment was taken from Beaumont and Fletcher.*

> IT was a friar of orders gray,
> Walkt forth to tell his beades;
> And he met with a lady faire,
> Clad in a pilgrime's weedes.
>
> Now Christ thee save, thou reverend friar,
> I pray thee tell to me,
> If ever at yon holy shrine
> My true love thou didst see.

And how should I know your true love,
From many another one?
O by his cockle hat, and staff,
And by his sandal shoone *.

But chiefly by his face and mien,
That were so fair to view;
His flaxen locks that sweetly curl'd,
And eyne of lovely blue.

O lady, he is dead and gone!
Lady, he 's dead and gone!
And at his head a green grass turfe,
And at his heels a stone.

Within these holy cloysters long
He languisht, and he dyed,
Lamenting of a ladyes love,
And 'playning of her pride.

Here bore him barefac'd on his bier
Six proper youths and tall,
And many a tear bedew'd his grave
Within yon kirk-yard wall.

And art thou dead, thou gentle youth!
And art thou dead and gone!
And didst thou dye for love of me!
Break, cruel heart of stone!

O weep not, lady, weep not soe;
Some ghostly comfort seek:
Let not vain sorrow rive thy heart
Ne teares bedew thy cheek.

* *These are the distinguishing marks of a pilgrim. The chief places of devotion being beyond sea, the pilgrims were wont to put cockle shells in their hats to denote the intention or performance of their pilgrimage. Warburton, Shakespear. Vol. 8. p. 224.*

THOMAS PERCY

O do not, do not, holy friar,
    My sorrow now reprove;
For I have lost the sweetest youth,
    That e'er wan ladyes love.

And nowe, alas! for thy sad losse,
    I'll evermore weep and sigh;
For thee I only wisht to live,
    For thee I wish to dye.

Weep no more, lady, weep no more,
    Thy sorrowe is in vaine:
For, violets pluckt the sweetest showers
    Will ne'er make grow againe.

Our joys as winged dreams doe flye,
    Why then should sorrow last?
Since grief but aggravates thy losse,
    Grieve not for what is past.

O say not soe, thou holy friar;
    I pray thee, say not soe:
For since my true-love dyed for mee,
    'Tis meet my tears should flow.

And will he ne'er come again!
    Will he ne'er come again?
Ah! no, he is dead and laid in his grave,
    For ever to remain.

His cheek was redder than the rose,
    The comliest youth was he:—
But he is dead and laid in his grave:
    Alas, and woe is me!

THOMAS PERCY

Sigh no more, lady, sigh no more,
   Men were deceivers ever:
One foot on sea and one on land,
   To one thing constant never.

Hadst thou been fond, he had been false,
   And left thee sad and heavy;
For young men ever were fickle found,
   Since summer trees were leafy.

Now say not so, thou holy friar,
   I pray thee say not soe:
My love he had the truest heart:
   O he was ever true!

And art thou dead, thou much-lov'd youth,
   And didst thou dye for mee?
Then farewell home; for, ever-more
   A pilgrim I will bee.

But first upon my true-love's grave
   My weary limbs I'll lay,
And thrice I'll kiss the green-grass turf,
   That wraps his breathless clay.

Yet stay, fair lady; rest awhile
   Beneath this cloyster wall:
See through the hawthorn blows the cold wind,
   And drizzly rain doth fall.

O stay me not, thou holy friar;
   O stay me not I pray:
No drizzly rain that falls on me,
   Can wash my fault away.

THOMAS PERCY

Yet stay, fair lady, turn again,
  And dry those pearly tears;
For see beneath this gown of gray
  Thy owne true-love appears.

Here forc'd by grief, and hopeless love,
  These holy weeds I sought;
And here amid these lonely walls
  To end my days I thought.

But haply for my year of grace *
  Is not yet past away,
Might I still hope to win thy love,
  No longer would I stay.

Now farewell grief, and welcome joy
  Once more unto my heart:
For since I have found thee, lovely youth,
  We never more will part.

Percy's Reliques, i, 1765.

CHRISTOPHER ANSTEY

1724–1805

304   *Letter containing a Panegyric on Bath*

OF all the gay Places the World can afford,
  By Gentle and Simple for Pastime ador'd,
Fine Balls, and fine Concerts, fine Buildings, and Springs,
Fine Walks, and fine Views, and a Thousand fine Things,
Not to mention the sweet Situation and Air,
What Place, my dear Mother, with *Bath* can compare?

* *The year of probation, or noviciate.*

CHRISTOPHER ANSTEY

Let *Bristol* for Commerce and Dirt be renown'd,
At *Sal'sbury* Pen Knives and Scissars be ground;
The Towns of *Devizes*, of *Bradford*, and *Frome*,
May boast that they better can manage the Loom;
I believe that they may;—but the World to refine,
In Manners, in Dress, in Politeness to shine,
O *Bath!*—let the Art, let the Glory be thine.
I'm sure I have travell'd our Country all o'er
And ne'er was so civilly treated before;
Would you think, my dear Mother, (without the least Hint
That we all should be glad of appearing in Print)
The News-Writers here were so kind as to give all
The World an Account of our happy Arrival?—
You scarce can imagine what Numbers I've met,
(Tho' to me they are perfectly Strangers as yet)
Who all with Address and Civility came,
And seem'd vastly proud of SUBSCRIBING our Name.
Young TIMOTHY CANVASS is charm'd with the Place
Who, I hear, is come hither his Fibres to brace;
Poor Man! at th' Election he threw, t' other Day,
All his Victuals, and Liquor, and Money away;
And some People think with such Haste he began,
That soon he the Constable greatly outran,
And is qualify'd now for a Parliament Man:
Goes every Day to the Coffee-House, where
The Wits and the great Politicians repair;
Harangues on the Funds, and the State of the Nation,
And plans a good Speech for an Administration,
In Hopes of a Place, which he thinks he deserves,
As the Love of his Country has ruin'd his Nerves.—
Our Neighbour Sir EASTERLIN WIDGEON has swore
He ne'er will return to his Bogs any more:

CHRISTOPHER ANSTEY

The *Thicksculls* are settled; we've had Invitations
With a great many more on the Score of Relations:
The *Loungers* are come too.—Old STUCCO has just sent
His Plan for a House to be built in the *Crescent*;
'Twill soon be complete, and they say all their Work
Is as strong as *St. Paul's*, or the Minster at *York*.
Don't you think 'twould be better to lease our Estate,
And buy a good House here before 'tis too late?
You never can go, my dear Mother, where you
So much have to see, and so little to do.

I write this in Haste, for the Captain is come,
And so kind as to go with us all to the Room;
But be sure by the very next Post you shall hear
Of all I've the pleasure of meeting with there;
For I scribble my Verse with a great deal of Ease,
And can send you a Letter whenever I please;
And while at this Place I've the Honour to stay,
I think I can never want something to say.

But now, my dear Mother, &c. &c.

BATH, 1766.   *S—— B—N—R—D.*

POSTSCRIPT

I'm sorry to find at the City of *Bath*,
Many Folk are uneasy concerning their Faith:
NICODEMUS, the Preacher, strives all he can do
To quiet the Conscience of good Sister PRUE;
But TABBY from Scruples of Mind is releas'd,
Since she met with a learned MORAVIAN Priest,
Who says, *There is neither Transgression nor Sin*;
A Doctrine that brings many Customers in.

The New Bath Guide, Letter vii, 1766

HORACE WALPOLE, EARL OF ORFORD

1717–1797

305   *Anne Grenville, Countess Temple, appointed Poet Laureate to the King of the Fairies*

Written at the desire of Lady Suffolk, January 3, 1763

BY these presents be it known,
  To all who bend before our throne,
Fays and fairies, elves and sprites,
Beauteous dames and gallant knights,
That we, Oberon the grand,
Emperor of Fairyland,
King of moonshine, prince of dreams,
Lord of Aganippe's streams,
Baron of the dimpl'd isles
That lie in pretty maiden's smiles,
Arch-treasurer of all the graces
Dispers'd through fifty lovely faces,
Sovereign of the Slipper's order,
With all the rites thereon that border,
Defender of the sylphic faith,
Declare—and thus your monarch saith:
Whereas there is a noble dame,
Whom mortals Countess Temple name,
To whom ourself did erst impart
The choicest secrets of our art,
Taught her to tune th' harmonious line
To our own melody divine,
Taught her the graceful negligence,
Which, scorning art and veiling sense,

Achieves that conquest o'er the heart
Sense seldom gains, and never art:
This lady, 'tis our royal will
Our laureate's vacant seat should fill:
A chaplet of immortal bays
Shall crown her brow and guard her lays;
Of nectar sack an acorn cup
Be at her board each year fill'd up;
And as each quarter feast comes round
A silver penny shall be found
Within the compass of her shoe—
And so we bid you all adieu!

Given at our palace of Cowslip Castle, the shortest night
of the year.   OBERON.

Works, iv, 1798

306 *To Lady Anne Fitzpatrick, when about
Five Years old, with a Present of Shells.*
1772

O NYMPH, compar'd with whose young bloom
   Hebe's herself an ancient fright;
May these gay shells find grace and room
   Both in your baby-house and sight!
Shells! What are shells? you ask, admiring
   With stare half pleasure half surprise;
And fly with nature's art, enquiring
   In dear mamma's all-speaking eyes.
Shells, fairest Anne, are playthings, made
   By a brave god call'd Father Ocean,
Whose frown from pole to pole's obey'd,
   Commands the waves, and stills their motion.

483

HORACE WALPOLE, EARL OF ORFORD

From that old sire a daughter came,
   As like mamma, as blue to blue;
And, like mamma, the sea-born dame
   An urchin bore, not unlike you.
For him fond grand-papa compels
   The floods to furnish such a state
Of corals and of cockleshells,
   Would turn a little lady's pate.
The chit has tons of bawbles more;
   His nurs'ry 's stuff'd with doves and sparrows;
And litter'd is its azure floor
   With painted quivers, bows, and arrows.
Spread, spread your frock; you must be friends;
   His toys shall fill your lap and breast:
To-day the boy this sample sends,
   —And some years hence he'll send the rest.

Works, iv, 1798

WILLIAM MASON

1724–1797

307   *Ode*

To a Friend

AH! cease this kind persuasive strain,
   Which, when it flows from Friendship's tongue,
However weak, however vain,
   O'erpowers beyond the Siren's song:
Leave me, my friend, indulgent go,
And let me muse upon my woe.
Why lure me from these pale retreats?
Why rob me of these pensive sweets?
Can Musick's voice, can Beauty's eye,
Can Painting's glowing hand supply

484

WILLIAM MASON

A charm so suited to my mind,
As blows this hollow gust of wind,
As drops this little weeping rill
Soft tinkling down the moss-grown hill,
While thro' the west, where sinks the crimson Day,
Meek Twilight slowly sails, and waves her banners grey?

Say, from affliction's various source
Do none but turbid waters flow?
And cannot Fancy clear their course?
For Fancy is the friend of Woe.
Say, mid that grove, in love-lorn state,
While yon poor Ringdove mourns her mate,
Is all, that meets the shepherd's ear,
Inspir'd by anguish, and despair?
Ah! no; fair Fancy rules the Song:
She swells her throat; she guides her tongue;
She bids the waving Aspin spray
Quiver in cadence to her lay;
She bids the fringed Osiers bow,
And rustle round the lake below,
To suit the tenor of her gurgling sighs,
And sooth her throbbing breast with solemn sympathies.

To thee, whose young and polish'd brow
The wrinkling hand of Sorrow spares;
Whose cheeks, bestrew'd with roses, know
No channel for the tide of tears;
To thee yon Abbey dank, and lone,
Where ivy chains each mould'ring stone
That nods o'er many a Martyr's tomb,
May cast a formidable gloom.

Yet Some there are, who, free from fear,
Could wander thro' the cloysters drear,
Could rove each desolated Isle,
Tho' midnight thunders shook the pile:
And dauntless view, or seem to view,
(As faintly flash the lightnings blue)
Thin shiv'ring Ghosts from yawning charnels throng,
And glance with silent sweep the shaggy vaults along.

But such terrific charms as these,
I ask not yet: My sober mind
The fainter forms of sadness please;
My sorrows are of softer kind.
Thro' this still valley let me stray,
Rapt in some strain of pensive GRAY:
Whose lofty Genius bears along
The conscious dignity of Song;
And, scorning from the sacred store
To waste a note on Pride or Power,
Roves thro' the glimmering, twilight gloom,
And warbles round each rustic tomb:
He, too, perchance (for well I know,
His heart can melt with friendly woe)
He, too, perchance, when these poor limbs are laid,
Will heave one tuneful sigh, and sooth my hov'ring Shade.

Poems, 1746

308 *Landscape*

IN THY fair domain,
Yes, my lov'd Albion! many a glade is found,
The haunt of Wood-gods only: where if Art
E'er dar'd to tread, 'twas with unsandal'd foot,

WILLIAM MASON

Printless, as if the place were holy ground.
And there are scenes, where, tho' she whilom trod,
Led by the worst of guides, fell Tyranny,
And ruthless Superstition, we now trace
Her footsteps with delight; and pleas'd revere
What once we should have hated. But to Time,
Not her, the praise is due: his gradual touch
Has moulder'd into beauty many a tower,
Which, when it frown'd with all its battlements,
Was only terrible; and many a fane
Monastic, which, when deck'd with all its spires,
Serv'd but to feed some pamper'd Abbot's pride,
And awe th' unletter'd vulgar. Generous Youth,
Whoe'er thou art, that listen'st to my lay,
And feel'st thy soul assent to what I sing,
Happy art thou if thou can'st call thine own
Such scenes as these: where Nature and where Time
Have work'd congenial; where a scatter'd host
Of antique oaks darken thy sidelong hills;
While, rushing thro' their branches, rifted cliffs
Dart their white heads, and glitter thro' the gloom.
More happy still, if one superior rock
Bear on its brow the shiver'd fragment huge
Of some old Norman fortress; happier far,
Ah, then most happy, if thy vale below
Wash, with the crystal coolness of its rills,
Some mouldring abbey's ivy-vested wall.

The English Garden, i, 1772

WILLIAM MASON

Sonnet

Anniversary, February 23, 1795

A PLAINTIVE Sonnet flow'd from MILTON's pen,
  When Time had stol'n his three and twentieth year:
Say, shall not I then shed one tuneful tear,
Robb'd by the thief of threescore years and ten?
No! for the foes of all life-lengthen'd men
  Trouble and toil, approach not yet too near;
  Reason, meanwhile, and health, and memory dear
Hold unimpair'd their weak, yet wonted reign:
  Still round my shelter'd lawn I pleas'd can stray;
Still trace my sylvan blessings to their spring:
  BEING OF BEINGS! Yes, that silent lay,
Which musing Gratitude delights to sing,
  Still to thy sapphire Throne shall Faith convey,
And Hope, the Cherub of unwearied wing.

Poems, 1797

THOMAS WARTON

1728–1790

The Solemn Noon of Night

BENEATH yon' ruin'd Abbey's moss-grown piles
  Oft let me sit, at twilight hour of Eve,
Where thro' some western window the pale moon
Pours her long-levell'd rule of streaming light;
While sullen sacred silence reigns around,
Save the lone Screech-owl's note, who builds his bow'r
Amid the mould'ring caverns dark and damp,
Or the calm breeze, that rustles in the leaves
Of flaunting Ivy, that with mantle green
Invests some wasted tow'r. Or let me tread
It's neighb'ring walk of pines, where mus'd of old

THOMAS WARTON

The cloyster'd brothers: thro' the gloomy void
That far extends beneath their ample arch
As on I pace, religious horror wraps
My soul in dread repose. But when the world
Is clad in Midnight's raven-colour'd robe,
'Mid hollow charnel let me watch the flame
Of taper dim, shedding a livid glare
O'er the wan heaps; while airy voices talk
Along the glimm'ring walls, or ghostly shape
At distance seen, invites with beck'ning hand
My lonesome steps, thro' the far-winding vaults.
Nor undelightful is the solemn noon
Of night, when haply wakeful from my couch
I start: lo, all is motionless around!
Roars not the rushing wind; the sons of men
And every beast in mute oblivion lie;
All Nature's hush'd in silence and in sleep.
O then how fearful is it to reflect,
That thro' the still globe's aweful solitude
No Being wakes but me! 'till stealing sleep
My drooping temples bathes in opiate dews.
Nor then let dreams, of wanton Folly born,
My senses lead thro' flowery paths of joy;
But let the sacred Genius of the night
Such mystic visions send, as SPENSER saw,
When thro' bewild'ring Fancy's magic maze,
To the fell house of Busyrane, he led
Th' unshaken Britomart; or MILTON knew,
When in abstracted thought he first conceiv'd
All heav'n in tumult, and the Seraphim
Come tow'ring, arm'd in adamant and gold.

The Pleasures of Melancholy, 1747

311   *Sonnet*

Written in a blank leaf of Dugdale's Monasticon

DEEM not, devoid of elegance, the sage,
  By Fancy's genuine feelings unbeguil'd,
  Of painful Pedantry the poring child,
  Who turns, of these proud domes, th' historic page,
Now sunk by Time, and Henry's fiercer rage.
  Thinkst thou the warbling Muses never smil'd
  On his lone hours? Ingenuous views engage
  His thought, on themes, unclassic falsely stil'd,
Intent. While cloyster'd Piety displays
  Her mouldering roll, the piercing eye explores
  New manners, and the pomp of elder days,
Whence culls the pensive bard his pictur'd stores.
  Nor rough, nor barren, are the winding ways
  Of hoar Antiquity, but strown with flowers.   *Poems,* 1777

312   *Sonnet. Written after seeing Wilton-House*

FROM Pembroke's princely dome, where mimic Art
  Decks with a magic hand the dazzling bow'rs,
  Its living hues where the warm pencil pours,
  And breathing forms from the rude marble start,
How to life's humbler scene can I depart?
  My breast all glowing from those gorgeous tow'rs,
  In my low cell how cheat the sullen hours!
  Vain the complaint: for FANCY can impart
(To Fate superiour, and to Fortune's doom)
  Whate'er adorns the stately-storied hall:
  She, mid the dungeon's solitary gloom,
Can dress the Graces in their Attic pall:
  Bid the green landskip's vernal beauty bloom;
  And in bright trophies cloath the twilight wall.

  49c   *Poems,* 1777

313   *Sonnet*

To the River Lodon

AH! what a weary race my feet have run,
  Since first I trod thy banks with alders crown'd,
  And thought my way was all through fairy ground,
  Beneath thy azure sky, and golden sun:
Where first my muse to lisp her notes begun!
  While pensive memory traces back the round,
  Which fills the varied interval between;
  Much pleasure, more of sorrow, marks the scene.
Sweet native stream! those skies and suns so pure
  No more return, to chear my evening road!
  Yet still one joy remains, that not obscure,
Nor useless, all my vacant days have flow'd,
  From youth's gay dawn to manhood's prime mature;
  Nor with the Muse's laurel unbestow'd.   *Poems, 1777*

314 *Verses on Sir Joshua Reynolds's Painted
Window at New College, Oxford*

AH, stay thy treacherous hand, forbear to trace
  Those faultless forms of elegance and grace!
Ah, cease to spread the bright transparent mass,
With Titian's pencil, o'er the speaking glass!
Nor steal, by strokes of art with truth combin'd,
The fond illusions of my wayward mind!
For long, enamour'd of a barbarous age,
A faithless truant to the classic page;
Long have I lov'd to catch the simple chime
Of minstrel-harps, and spell the fabling rime;
To view the festive rites, the knightly play,
That deck'd heroic Albion's elder day;

To mark the mouldering halls of Barons bold,
And the rough castle, cast in giant mould;
With Gothic manners Gothic arts explore,
And muse on the magnificence of yore.

But chief, enraptur'd have I lov'd to roam,
A lingering votary, the vaulted dome,
Where the tall shafts, that mount in massy pride,
Their mingling branches shoot from side to side;
Where elfin sculptors, with fantastic clew,
Oer the long roof their wild embroidery drew;
Where SUPERSTITION, with capricious hand
In many a maze the wreathed window plann'd,
With hues romantic ting'd the gorgeous pane,
To fill with holy light the wondrous fane;
To aid the builder's model, richly rude,
By no Vitruvian symmetry subdued;
To suit the genius of the mystic pile:
Whilst as around the far-retiring ile,
And fretted shrines with hoary trophies hung,
Her dark illumination wide she flung,
With new solemnity, the nooks profound,
The caves of death, and the dim arches frown'd.
From bliss long felt unwillingly we part:
Ah, spare the weakness of a lover's heart!
Chase not the phantoms of my fairy dream,
Phantoms that shrink at Reason's painful gleam!
That softer touch, insidious artist, stay,
Nor to new joys my struggling breast betray!

Such was a pensive bard's mistaken strain.—
But, oh, of ravish'd pleasures why complain?
No more the matchless skill I call unkind
That strives to disenchant my cheated mind.

For when again I view thy chaste Design,
The just proportion, and the genuin line;
Those native pourtraitures of Attic art,
That from the lucid surface seem to start;
Those tints, that steal no glories from the day,
Nor ask the sun to lend his streaming ray;
The doubtful radiance of contending dies,
That faintly mingle, yet distinctly rise;
'Twixt light and shade the transitory strife;
The feature blooming with immortal life:
The stole in casual foldings taught to flow,
Not with ambitious ornaments to glow;
The tread majestic, and the beaming eye
That lifted speaks its commerce with the sky;
Heaven's golden emanation, gleaming mild
Oer the mean cradle of the virgin's child:
Sudden, the sombrous imagery is fled,
Which late my visionary rapture fed:
Thy powerful hand has broke the Gothic chain,
And brought my bosom back to truth again:
To truth, by no peculiar taste confin'd,
Whose universal pattern strikes mankind;
To truth, whose bold and unresisted aim
Checks frail caprice, and fashion's fickle claim;
To truth, whose Charms deception's magic quell,
And bind coy Fancy in a stronger spell.

Ye brawny Prophets, that in robes so rich,
At distance due, possess the crisped nich;
Ye Rows of Patriarchs, that sublimely rear'd
Diffuse a proud primeval length of beard:
Ye Saints, who clad in crimson's bright array,
More pride than humble poverty display:

493

THOMAS WARTON

Ye Virgins meek, that wear the palmy crown
Of patient faith, and yet so fiercely frown:
Ye Angels, that from clouds of gold recline,
But boast no semblance to a race divine:
Ye tragic Tales of legendary lore,
That draw devotion's ready tear no more:
Ye Martyrdoms of unenlighten'd days,
Ye Miracles, that now no wonder raise:
Shapes, that with one broad glare the gazer strike,
Kings, Bishops, Nuns, Apostles, all alike!
Ye Colours, that th' unwary sight amaze,
And only dazzle in the noontide blaze!
No more the Sacred Window's round disgrace,
But yield to Grecian groupes the shining space.
Lo, from the canvas Beauty shifts her throne,
Lo, Picture's powers a new formation own!
Behold she prints upon the crystal plain,
With her own energy, th' expressive stain!
The mighty Master spreads his mimic toil
More wide, nor only blends the breathing oil;
But calls the lineaments of life compleat
From genial alchymy's creative heat;
Obedient forms to the bright fusion gives,
While in the warm enamel Nature lives.

REYNOLDS, tis thine, from the broad window's height,
To add new lustre to religious light:
Not of it's pomp to strip this ancient shrine,
But bid that pomp with purer radiance shine:
With arts unknown before, to reconcile
The willing Graces to the Gothic pile.

Verses on Reynolds's Window, 1782

494

JAMES BEATTIE

1735-1803

315   *Solitude*

THY shades, thy silence, now be mine,
  Thy charms, my only theme:
My haunt, the hollow cliff, whose pine
Waves o'er the gloomy stream,
Whence the scared owl, on pinions grey,
Breaks from the rustling boughs,
And down the lone vale sails away,
To more profound repose.

   .   .   .   .

For me, no more the path invites
Ambition loves to tread;
No more I climb those toilsome heights,
By guileful Hope misled:
Leaps my fond fluttering heart no more
To Mirth's enlivening strain;
For present pleasure soon is o'er,
And all the past is vain.

           Retirement—Original Poems 1760 (revised)

316   *Nature's Charms*

O HOW canst thou renounce the boundless store
  Of charms which Nature to her votary yields!
The warbling woodland, the resounding shore,
The pomp of groves, and garniture of fields;
All that the genial ray of morning gilds,
And all that echoes to the song of even,
All that the mountain's sheltering bosom shields,
And all the dread magnificence of heaven,
O how canst thou renounce, and hope to be forgiven?

   .   .   .   .

JAMES BEATTIE

Lo! where the stripling, wrapt in wonder, roves
Beneath the precipice o'erhung with pine;
And sees, on high, amidst th' encircling groves,
From cliff to cliff the foaming torrents shine:
While waters, woods, and winds, in concert join,
And Echo swells the chorus to the skies.
Would Edwin this majestic scene resign
For aught the huntsman's puny craft supplies?
Ah! no: he better knows great Nature's charms to prize.

And oft he traced the uplands, to survey,
When o'er the sky advanced the kindling dawn,
The crimson cloud, blue main, and mountain grey,
And lake, dim-gleaming on the smoky lawn;
Far to the west the long long vale withdrawn,
Where twilight loves to linger for a while;
And now he faintly kens the bounding fawn,
And villager abroad at early toil.—
But, lo! the sun appears! and heaven, earth, ocean, smile.

And oft the craggy cliff he lov'd to climb,
When all in mist the world below was lost.
What dreadful pleasure! there to stand sublime,
Like shipwreck'd mariner on desert coast,
And view th' enormous waste of vapour, tost
In billows, lengthening to th' horizon round,
Now scoop'd in gulfs, with mountains now emboss'd!
And hear the voice of mirth and song rebound,
Flocks, herds, and waterfalls, along the hoar profound!

The Minstrel, 1771

JAMES BEATTIE

Nature and the Poets

BUT who the melodies of morn can tell?
  The wild brook babbling down the mountain side;
The lowing herd; the sheepfold's simple bell;
The pipe of early shepherd dim descried
In the lone valley; echoing far and wide
The clamorous horn along the cliffs above;
The hollow murmur of the ocean-tide;
The hum of bees, the linnet's lay of love,
And the full choir that wakes the universal grove.

The cottage-curs at early pilgrim bark;
Crown'd with her pail the tripping milkmaid sings;
The whistling plowman stalks afield; and, hark!
Down the rough slope the ponderous waggon rings;
Through rustling corn the hare astonish'd springs;
Slow tolls the village-clock the drowsy hour;
The partridge bursts away on whirring wings;
Deep mourns the turtle in sequester'd bower,
And shrill lark carols clear from her aereal tour.

O Nature, how in every charm supreme!
Whose votaries feast on raptures ever new!
O for the voice and fire of seraphim,
To sing thy glories with devotion due!
Blest be the day I scap'd the wrangling crew,
From Pyrrho's maze, and Epicurus' sty;
And held high converse with the godlike few,
Who to th' enraptured heart, and ear, and eye,
Teach beauty, virtue, truth, and love, and melody.

JAMES BEATTIE

Hence! ye, who snare and stupefy the mind,
Sophists, of beauty, virtue, joy, the bane!
Greedy and fell, though impotent and blind,
Who spread your filthy nets in Truth's fair fane,
And ever ply your venom'd fangs amain!
Hence to dark Error's den, whose rankling slime
First gave you form! hence! lest the Muse should deign
(Though loth on theme so mean to waste a rhyme)
With vengeance to pursue your sacrilegious crime.

But hail, ye mighty masters of the lay,
Nature's true sons, the friends of man and truth!
Whose song, sublimely sweet, serenely gay,
Amused my childhood, and inform'd my youth.
O let your spirit still my bosom sooth,
Inspire my dreams, and my wild wanderings guide.
Your voice each rugged path of life can smooth;
For well I know, where-ever ye reside,
There harmony, and peace, and innocence, abide.

The Minstrel, 1771

ALISON RUTHERFORD, MRS. COCKBURN
1712–1794

318   *The Flowers of the Forest*

I'VE seen the smiling
  Of Fortune beguiling,
I've felt all its favours, and found its decay;
  Sweet was its blessing,
  Kind, its caressing,
But now 'tis fled—fled far away.

ALISON RUTHERFORD, MRS. COCKBURN

I've seen the forest
Adorn'd the foremost,
With flowers of the fairest, most pleasant and gay;
Sae bonny was their blooming,
Their scent the air perfuming;
But now they are wither'd and weeded away.

I've seen the morning,
With gold the hills adorning,
And loud tempest storming before the mid-day.
I've seen Tweed's silver streams
Shining in the sunny beams,
Grow drumbly and dark as he row'd on his way.

O fickle Fortune!
Why this cruel sporting?
O why still perplex us, poor sons of a day?
Nae mair your smiles can chear me,
Nae mair your frowns can fear me,
For the flowers of the forest are withered away.

The Lark (Edinburgh), 1765; Herd's
Scottish Songs, i, 1776

JEAN ELLIOT

1727–1805

319   *The Flowers of the Forest*

I'VE heard them lilting, at the ewe milking,
 Lasses a' lilting, before dawn of day;
But now they are moaning, on ilka green loaning;
 The flowers of the forest are a' wede away.

wede] weeded

JEAN ELLIOT

At bughts, in the morning, nae blithe lads are scorning;
   Lasses are lonely, and dowie, and wae;
Nae daffing, nae gabbing, but sighing and sabbing;
   Ilk ane lifts her leglin, and hies her away.

At har'st, at the shearing, nae youths now are jearing;
   Bandsters are runkled, and lyart or gray;
At fair, or at preaching, nae wooing, nae fleeching;
   The flowers of the forest are a' wede away.

At e'en, in the gloaming, nae younkers are roaming
   'Bout stacks, with the lasses at bogle to play;
But ilk maid sits dreary, lamenting her deary—
   The flowers of the forest are weded away.

Dool and wae for the order, sent our lads to the Border!
   The English, for ance, by guile wan the day;
The flowers of the forest, that fought aye the foremost,
   The prime of our land, are cauld in the clay.

We'll hear nae mair lilting, at the ewe milking;
   Women and bairns are heartless and wae:
Sighing and moaning, on ilka green loaning—
   The flowers of the forest are a' wede away.

Written about 1763 ; Herd's Scottish Songs, i, 1776

bughts] sheep-folds   daffing] making merry   leglin]
milk-pail   har'st] harvest   bandsters] binders   lyart]
grizzled   fleeching] beseeching

MICHAEL BRUCE

1746–1767

Ode : To the Cuckoo

HAIL, beauteous stranger of the wood,
  Attendant on the spring!
Now heav'n repairs thy rural seat,
  And woods thy welcome sing.

Soon as the daisie decks the green,
  Thy certain voice we hear:
Hast thou a star to guide thy path,
  Or mark the rolling year?

Delightful visitant! with thee
  I hail the time of flow'rs,
When heav'n is fill'd with music sweet
  Of birds among the bow'rs.

The schoolboy, wand'ring in the wood
  To pull the flow'rs so gay,
Starts, thy curious voice to hear,
  And imitates thy lay.

Soon as the pea puts on the bloom,
  Thou fly'st thy vocal vale,
An annual guest, in other lands,
  Another spring to hail.

Sweet bird! thy bow'r is ever green,
  Thy sky is ever clear;
Thou hast no sorrow in thy song,
  No winter in thy year!

MICHAEL BRUCE

Alas, sweet bird! not so my fate,
　　Dark scowling skies I see
Fast gathering round, and fraught with woe
　　And wintry years to me.

O could I fly, I'd fly with thee:
　　We'd make, with social wing,
Our annual visit o'er the globe,
　　Companions of the spring.

Poems on Several Occasions, 1770

JOHN LANGHORNE

1735–1779

321　　*The Evening Primrose*

THERE are that love the shades of life,
　　And shun the splendid walks of fame;
There are that hold it rueful strife
　　To risque AMBITION's losing game:

That far from ENVY's lurid eye
　　The fairest fruits of GENIUS rear,
Content to see them bloom and die
　　In Friendship's small but genial sphere.

Than vainer flowers tho' sweeter far,
　　The Evening Primrose shuns the day;
Blooms only to the western star,
　　And loves its solitary ray.

In EDEN's vale an aged hind,
　　At the dim twilight's closing hour,
On his time-smoothed staff reclin'd,
　　With wonder view'd the opening flower.

502

JOHN LANGHORNE

' Ill-fated flower, at eve to blow,'
   In pity's simple thought he cries,
' Thy bosom must not feel the glow
    ' Of splendid suns, or smiling skies.

' Nor thee, the vagrants of the field,
    ' The hamlet's little train behold ;
' Their eyes to sweet oppression yield,
    ' When thine the falling shades unfold.

' Nor thee the hasty shepherd heeds,
    ' When love has fill'd his heart with cares,
' For flowers he rifles all the meads,
    ' For waking flowers—but thine forbears.

' Ah ! waste no more that beauteous bloom
    ' On night's chill shade, that fragrant breath,
' Let smiling suns those gems illume !
    ' Fair flower, to live unseen is death.'

Soft as the voice of vernal gales
   That o'er the bending meadow blow,
Or streams that steal thro' even vales,
   And murmur that they move so slow :

Deep in her unfrequented bower,
   Sweet Philomela pour'd her strain ;
The bird of eve approv'd her flower,
   And answer'd thus the anxious swain.

Live unseen !
By moonlight shades, in valleys green,
   Lovely flower, we'll live unseen.
Of our pleasures deem not lightly,
Laughing day may look more sprightly,

But I love the modest mien,
Still I love the modest mien
Of gentle evening fair, and her star-trained queen.

Didst thou, shepherd, never find,
Pleasure is of pensive kind?
Has thy cottage never known
That she loves to live alone?
Dost thou not at evening hour
Feel some soft and secret power,
Gliding o'er thy yielding mind,
Leave sweet serenity behind;
While all disarm'd, the cares of day
Steal thro' the falling gloom away?
Love to think thy lot was laid
In this undistinguish'd shade.
Far from the world's infectious view,
Thy little virtues safely blew.
Go, and in day's more dangerous hour,
Guard thy emblematic flower.

Fables of Flora, 1771

322   *Apology for Vagrants*

FOR Him, who, lost to ev'ry Hope of Life,
Has long with Fortune held unequal strife,
Known to no human Love, no human Care,
The friendless, homeless Object of Despair;
For the poor Vagrant, feel, while He complains,
Nor from sad Freedom send to sadder Chains.
Alike, if Folly or Misfortune brought
Those last of Woes his evil Days have wrought;
Believe with social Mercy and with Me,
Folly's Misfortune in the first Degree.

JOHN LANGHORNE

Perhaps on some inhospitable Shore
The houseless Wretch a widow'd parent bore;
Who, then, no more by golden Prospects led,
Of the poor Indian begg'd a Leafy bed.
Cold on Canadian Hills, or Minden's Plain,
Perhaps that Parent mourn'd her Soldier slain;
Bent o'er her Babe, her Eye dissolv'd in Dew,
The big Drops mingling with the Milk He drew,
Gave the sad Presage of his future Years,
The Child of Misery, baptiz'd in Tears!

The Country Justice, i, 1774

CUTHBERT SHAW
1738–1771

323   *Time's Balm*

THUS the poor bird, by some disast'rous fate
    Caught and imprison'd in a lonely cage,
Torn from its native fields, and dearer mate,
    Flutters awhile, and spends its little rage:
But, finding all its efforts weak and vain,
No more it pants and rages for the plain;
      Moping awhile, in sullen mood
        Droops the sweet mourner—but, ere long,
    Prunes its light wings, and pecks its food,
       And meditates the song:
Serenely sorrowing, breathes its piteous case,
And with its plaintive warblings saddens all the place.

． ． ． ． ． ． ． ． ．

But ah! th' unwelcome morn's obtruding light
    Will all my shadowy schemes of bliss depose,
Will tear the dear illusion from my sight,
    And wake me to the sense of all my woes:
      If to the verdant fields I stray,

CUTHBERT SHAW

Alas! what pleasures NOW can these convey?
Her lovely form pursues where e'er I go,
 And darkens all the scene with woe.
By Nature's lavish bounties chear'd no more,
  Sorrowing I rove
  Through valley, grot, and grove;
Nought can THEIR beauties or MY loss restore;
No herb, no plant, can med'cine my disease,
And my sad sighs are borne on ev'ry passing breeze.
   Monody to the Memory of a Young Lady, 1768

THOMAS CHATTERTON

1752–1770

324   *Bristowe Tragedie*

Or the Dethe of Syr Charles Bawdin

THE featherd songster chaunticleer
 Han wounde hys bugle horne,
And tolde the earlie villager
 The commynge of the morne:

Kynge EDWARDE sawe the ruddie streakes
 Of lyghte eclypse the greie;
And herde the raven's crokynge throte
 Proclayme the fated daie.

' Thou'rt ryght,' quod hee, ' for, by the Godde
 ' That syttes enthron'd on hyghe!
' CHARLES BAWDIN, and hys fellowes twaine,
 ' To-daie shall surelie die.'

Thenne wythe a jugge of nappy ale
 Hys Knyghtes dydd onne hymm waite;
' Goe tell the traytour, thatt to-daie
 ' Hee leaves thys mortall state.'

506

THOMAS CHATTERTON

Syr CANTERLONE thenne bendedd lowe,
 Wythe harte brymm-fulle of woe;
Hee journey'd to the castle-gate,
 And to Syr CHARLES dydd goe.

Butt whenne hee came, hys children twaine,
 And eke hys lovynge wyfe,
Wythe brinie tears dydd wett the floore,
 For goode Syr CHARLESES lyfe.

' O goode Syr CHARLES ! ' sayd CANTERLONE,
 ' Badde tydyngs I doe brynge.'
' Speke boldlie, manne,' sayd brave Syr CHARLES,
 ' Whatte says thie traytor kynge ? '

' I greeve to telle, before yonne sonne
 ' Does fromme the welkinn flye,
' Hee hath uponne hys honour sworne,
 ' Thatt thou shalt surelie die.'

' Wee all must die,' quod brave Syr CHARLES;
 ' Of thatte I'm not affearde;
' Whatte bootes to lyve a little space?
 ' Thanke JESU, I'm prepar'd:

' Butt telle thye kynge, for myne hee's not,
 ' I'de sooner die to-daie
' Thanne lyve hys slave, as manie are,
 ' Tho' I shoulde lyve for aie.'

Thenne CANTERLONE hee dydd goe out,
 To telle the maior straite
To gett all thynges ynne reddyness
 For goode Syr CHARLESES fate.

THOMAS CHATTERTON

Thenne Maisterr Canynge saughte the kynge,
    And felle down onne hys knee;
' I'm come,' quod hee, ' unto your grace
    ' To move your clemencye.'

Thenne quod the kynge, ' Youre tale speke out,
    ' You have been much oure friende;
' Whatever youre request may bee,
    ' Wee wylle to ytte attende.'

' My nobile leige! alle my request
    ' Ys for a nobile knyghte,
' Who, tho' may hap hee has donne wronge,
    ' He thoghte ytte stylle was ryghte:

' Hee has a spouse and children twaine,
    ' Alle rewyn'd are for aie;
' Yff thatt you are resolv'd to lett
    ' Charles Bawdin die to-daie.'

' Speke nott of such a traytour vile,'
    The kynge ynne furie sayde;
' Before the evening starre doth sheene,
    ' Bawdin shall loose hys hedde:

' Justice does loudlie for hym calle,
    ' And hee shalle have hys meede:
' Speke, Maister Canynge! Whatte thynge else
    ' Att present doe you neede?'

' My nobile leige!' goode Canynge sayde,
    ' Leave justice to our Godde,
' And laye the yronne rule asyde;
    ' Be thyne the olyve rodde.

THOMAS CHATTERTON

' Was Godde to serche our hertes and reines,
    ' The best were synners grete;
' CHRIST's vycarr only knowes ne synne,
    ' Ynne alle thys mortall state.

' Lett mercie rule thyne infante reigne,
    ' 'Twylle faste thye crowne fulle sure;
' From race to race thy familie
    ' Alle sov'reigns shall endure:

' But yff wythe bloode and slaughter thou
    ' Beginne thy infante reigne,
' Thy crowne uponne thy childrennes brows
    ' Wylle never long remayne.'

' CANYNGE, awaie! thys traytour vile
    ' Has scorn'd my power and mee;
' Howe canst thou thenne for such a manne
    ' Intreate my clemencye?'

' My nobile leige! the trulie brave
    ' Wylle val'rous actions prize,
' Respect a brave and nobile mynde,
    ' Altho' ynne enemies.'

' CANYNGE, awaie! By Godde ynne Heav'n
    ' Thatt dydd mee beinge gyve,
' I wylle nott taste a bitt of breade
    ' Whilst thys Syr CHARLES dothe lyve.

' By MARIE, and alle Seinctes ynne Heav'n,
    ' Thys sunne shall be hys laste.'
Thenne CANYNGE dropt a brinie teare,
    And from the presence paste.

THOMAS CHATTERTON

Wyth herte brymm-fulle of gnawynge grief,
    Hee to Syr CHARLES dydd goe,
And satt hymm downe uponne a stoole,
    And teares beganne to flowe.

' Wee all must die,' quod brave Syr CHARLES;
    ' Whatte bootes ytte howe or whenne;
' Dethe ys the sure, the certaine fate
    ' Of all wee mortall menne.

' Saye why, my friend, thie honest soul
    ' Runns overr att thyne eye;
' Is ytte for my most welcome doome
    ' Thatt thou dost child-lyke crye? '

Quod godlie CANYNGE, ' I doe weepe,
    ' Thatt thou so soone must dye,
' And leave thy sonnes and helpless wyfe;
    ' 'Tys thys thatt wettes myne eye.'

' Thenne drie the tears thatt out thyne eye
    ' From godlie fountaines sprynge;
' Dethe I despise, and alle the power
    ' Of EDWARDE, traytor kynge.

' Whan throgh the tyrant's welcom means
    ' I shall resigne my lyfe,
' The Godde I serve wylle soone provyde
    ' For bothe mye sonnes and wyfe.

' Before I sawe the lyghtsome sunne,
    ' Thys was appointed mee;
' Shall mortal manne repyne or grudge
    ' Whatt Godde ordeynes to bee?

' Howe oft ynne battaile have I stoode,
   ' Whan thousands dy'd arounde;
' Whan smokynge streemes of crimson bloode
   ' Imbrew'd the fatten'd grounde:

' How dydd I knowe thatt ev'ry darte,
   ' Thatt cutte the airie waie,
' Myghte nott fynde passage toe my harte,
   ' And close myne eyes for aie?

' And shall I nowe, forr feere of dethe,
   ' Looke wanne and bee dysmayde?
' Ne! fromm my herte flie childyshe feere,
   ' Bee alle the manne display'd.

' Ah, goddelyke HENRIE! Godde forefende,
   ' And guarde thee and thye sonne,
' Yff 'tis hys wylle; but yff 'tis nott,
   ' Why thenne hys wylle bee donne.

' My honest friende, my faulte has beene
   ' To serve Godde and mye prynce;
' And thatt I no tyme-server am,
   ' My dethe wylle soone convynce.

' Ynne Londonne citye was I borne,
   ' Of parents of grete note;
' My fadre dydd a nobile armes
   ' Emblazon onne hys cote:

' I make ne doubte butt hee ys gone
   ' Where soone I hope to goe;
' Where wee for ever shall bee blest,
   ' From oute the reech of woe:

' Hee taughte mee justice and the laws
    ' Wyth pitie to unite;
' And eke hee taughte mee howe to knowe
     ' The wronge cause fromm the ryghte:

' Hee taughte mee wythe a prudent hande
    ' To feede the hungrie poore,
' Ne lett mye sarvants dryve awaie
    ' The hungrie fromme my doore:

' And none can saye, butt alle mye lyfe
    ' I have hys wordyes kept;
' And summ'd the actyonns of the daie
    ' Eche nyghte before I slept.

' I have a spouse, goe aske of her,
    ' Yff I defyl'd her bedde?
' I have a kynge, and none can laie
    ' Blacke treason onne my hedde.

' Ynne Lent, and onne the holie eve,
    ' Fromm fleshe I dydd refrayne;
' Whie should I thenne appeare dismay'd
     ' To leave thys worlde of payne?

' Ne! hapless HENRIE! I rejoyce,
    ' I shalle ne see thye dethe;
' Moste willynglie ynne thye just cause
    ' Doe I resign my brethe.

' Oh, fickle people! rewyn'd londe!
    ' Thou wylt kenne peace ne moe;
' Whyle RICHARD's sonnes exalt themselves,
     ' Thye brookes wythe bloude wylle flowe.

' Saie, were ye tyr'd of godlie peace,
   ' And godlie HENRIE's reigne,
' Thatt you dydd choppe youre easie daies
    ' For those of bloude and peyne?

' Whatte tho' I onne a sledde bee drawne,
   ' And mangled by a hynde,
I doe defye the traytor's pow'r,
   ' Hee can ne harm my mynde;

' Whatte tho', uphoisted onne a pole,
   ' Mye lymbes shall rotte ynne ayre,
' And ne ryche monument of brasse
   ' CHARLES BAWDIN's name shall bear;

' Yett ynne the holie booke above,
   ' Whyche tyme can't eate awaie.
' There wythe the sarvants of the Lorde
   ' Mye name shall lyve for aie.

' Thenne welcome dethe! for lyfe eterne
   ' I leave thys mortall lyfe:
' Farewell, vayne worlde, and alle that's deare,
   ' Mye sonnes and lovynge wyfe!

' Nowe dethe as welcome to mee comes.
   ' As e'er the moneth of Maie;
' Nor woulde I even wyshe to lyve,
   ' Wyth my dere wyfe to staie.'

Quod CANYNGE, ' 'Tys a goodlie thynge
   ' To bee prepar'd to die;
' And from thys world of peyne and grefe
   ' To Godde ynne Heav'n to flie.'

And nowe the bell beganne to tolle,
    And claryonnes to sounde;
Syr CHARLES hee herde the horses feete
    A prauncyng onne the grounde:

And just before the officers,
    His lovynge wyfe came ynne,
Weepynge unfeigned teeres of woe,
    Wythe loude and dysmalle dynne.

' Sweet FLORENCE! nowe I praie forbere,
    ' Ynne quiet lett mee die;
' Praie Godde, thatt ev'ry Christian soule
    ' Maye looke onne dethe as I.

' Sweet FLORENCE! why these brinie teeres?
    ' Theye washe my soule awaie,
' And almost make mee wyshe for lyfe,
    ' Wyth thee, sweete dame, to staie.

' 'Tys butt a journie I shalle goe
    ' Untoe the lande of blysse;
' Nowe, as a proofe of husbande's love,
    ' Receive thys holie kysse.'

Thenne FLORENCE, fault'ring ynne her saie,
    Tremblynge these wordyes spoke,
' Ah, cruele EDWARDE! bloudie kynge!
    ' My herte ys welle nyghe broke:

' Ah, sweete Syr CHARLES! why wylt thou goe,
    ' Wythoute thye lovynge wyfe?
' The cruelle axe thatt cuttes thye necke,
    ' Ytte eke shall ende mye lyfe.'

And nowe the officers came ynne
    To brynge Syr CHARLES awaie,
Whoe turnedd toe his lovynge wyfe,
    And thus toe her dydd saie:

' I goe to lyfe, and nott to dethe,
    ' Truste thou ynne Godde above,
' And teache thye sonnes to feare the Lorde,
    ' And ynne theyre hertes hym love:

' Teache them to runne the nobile race
    ' Thatt I theyre fader runne:
' FLORENCE! shou'd dethe thee take—adieu!
    ' Yee officers, leade onne.'

Thenne FLORENCE rav'd as anie madde,
    And dydd her tresses tere;
' Oh! staie, mye husbande! lorde! and lyfe!'—
    Syr CHARLES thenne dropt a teare.

'Tyll tyredd oute wythe ravynge loud,
    Shee fellen onne the flore;
Syr CHARLES exerted alle hys myghte,
    And march'd fromm oute the dore.

Uponne a sledde hee mounted thenne,
    Wythe lookes fulle brave and swete;
Lookes, thatt enshone ne moe concern
    Thanne anie ynne the strete.

Before hym went the council-menne,
    Ynne scarlett robes and golde,
And tassils spanglynge ynne the sunne,
    Muche glorious to beholde:

THOMAS CHATTERTON

The Freers of Seincte AUGUSTYNE next
    Appeared to the syghte,
Alle cladd ynne homelie russett weedes,
    Of godlie monkysh plyghte:

Ynne diffraunt partes a godlie psaume
    Moste sweetlie theye dydd chaunt;
Behynde theyre backes syx mynstrelles came,
    Who tun'd the strunge bataunt.

Thenne fyve-and-twentye archers came;
    Echone the bowe dydd bende,
From rescue of kynge HENRIES friends
    Syr CHARLES forr to defend.

Bolde as a lyon came Syr CHARLES,
    Drawne onne a clothe-layde sledde,
Bye two blacke stedes ynne trappynges white,
    Wyth plumes uponne theyre hedde:

Behynde hym fyve-and-twentye moe
    Of archers stronge and stoute,
Wyth bended bowe echone ynne hande,
    Marched ynne goodlie route:

Seincte JAMESES Freers marched next,
    Echone hys parte dydd chaunt;
Behynde theyre backs syx mynstrelles came,
    Who tun'd the strunge bataunt:

Thenne came the maior and eldermenne,
    Ynne clothe of scarlett deck't;
And theyre attendyng menne echone,
    Lyke Easterne princes trickt:

THOMAS CHATTERTON

And after them, a multitude
    Of citizenns dydd thronge;
The wyndowes were alle fulle of heddes,
    As hee dydd passe alonge.

And whenne hee came to the hyghe crosse,
    Syr CHARLES dydd turne and saie,
' O Thou, thatt savest manne fromme synne,
    ' Washe mye soule clean thys daie ! '

Att the grete mynsterr wyndowe sat
    The kynge ynne myckle state,
To see CHARLES BAWDIN goe alonge
    To hys most welcom fate.

Soone as the sledde drewe nyghe enowe,
    Thatt EDWARDE hee myghte heare,
The brave Syr CHARLES hee dydd stande uppe,
    And thus hys wordes declare:

' Thou seest mee, EDWARDE ! traytour vile !
    ' Expos'd to infamie;
' Butt bee assur'd, disloyall manne !
    ' I'm greaterr nowe thanne thee.

' Bye foule proceedyngs, murdre, bloude,
    ' Thou wearest nowe a crowne;
' And hast appoynted mee to dye,
    ' By power nott thyne owne.

' Thou thynkest I shall dye to-daie;
    ' I have beene dede 'till nowe,
' And soone shall lyve to weare a crowne
    ' For aie uponne my browe:

' Whylst thou, perhapps, for som few yeares,
   ' Shalt rule thys fickle lande,
' To lett them knowe howe wyde the rule
    ' 'Twixt kynge and tyrant hande:

' Thye pow'r unjust, thou traytour slave!
   ' Shall falle onne thye owne hedde '—
Fromm out of hearyng of the kynge
   Departed thenne the sledde.

Kynge EDWARDE's soule rush'd to hys face,
   Hee turn'd hys hedde awaie,
And to hys broder GLOUCESTER
   Hee thus dydd speke and saie:

' To hym that soe-much-dreaded dethe
   ' Ne ghastlie terrors brynge,
' Beholde the manne! hee spake the truthe,
   ' Hee's greater thanne a kynge! '

' Soe lett hym die! ' Duke RICHARD sayde;
   ' And maye echone oure foes
' Bende downe theyre neckes to bloudie axe,
   ' And feede the carryon crowes.'

And nowe the horses gentlie drewe
   Syr CHARLES uppe the hyghe hylle;
The axe dydd glysterr ynne the sunne,
   Hys pretious bloude to spylle.

Syrr CHARLES dydd uppe the scaffold goe,
   As uppe a gilded carre
Of victorye, bye val'rous chiefs
   Gayn'd ynne the bloudie warre:

And to the people hee dydd saie,
   ' Beholde you see mee dye,
' For servynge loyally mye kynge,
    ' Mye kynge most rightfullie.

' As longe as EDWARDE rules thys lande,
   ' Ne quiet you wylle knowe;
' Youre sonnes and husbandes shalle bee slayne,
    ' And brookes wythe bloude shalle flowe.

' You leave youre goode and lawfulle kynge,
   ' Whenne ynne adversitye;
' Lyke mee, untoe the true cause stycke,
    ' And for the true cause dye.'

Thenne hee, wyth preestes, uponne hys knees,
   A pray'r to Godde dydd make,
Beseechynge hym unto hymselfe
    Hys partynge soule to take.

Thenne, kneelynge downe, hee layd hys hedde
   Most seemlie onne the blocke;
Whyche fromme hys bodie fayre at once
    The able heddes-manne stroke:

And oute the bloude beganne to flowe,
   And rounde the scaffolde twyne;
And teares, enow to washe't awaie,
    Dydd flowe fromme each mann's eyne.

The bloudie axe hys bodie fayre
   Ynnto foure parties cutte;
And ev'rye parte, and eke hys hedde,
    Uponne a pole was putte.

One parte dydd rotte onne Kynwulph-hylle,
    One onne the mynster-tower,
And one from off the castle-gate
    The crowen dydd devoure:

The other onne Seyncte Powle's goode gate,
    A dreery spectacle;
Hys hedde was plac'd onne the hyghe crosse,
    Ynne hyghe-streete most nobile.

Thus was the ende of BAWDIN's fate:
    Godde prosper longe oure kynge,
And grante hee maye, wyth BAWDIN's soule,
    Ynne heav'n Godd's mercie synge!

The Execution of Sir Charles Bawdin, 1772

325   *Mynstrelles Songe*

O! SYNGE untoe mie roundelaie,
    O! droppe the brynie teare wythe mee,
Daunce ne moe atte hallie daie,
Lycke a reynynge [1] ryver bee;
        Mie love ys dedde,
        Gon to hys death-bedde,
        Al under the wyllowe tree.

Blacke hys cryne [2] as the wyntere nyghte,
Whyte hys rode [3] as the sommer snowe,
Rodde hys face as the mornynge lyghte,
Cale he lyes ynne the grave belowe;
        Mie love ys dedde,
        Gon to hys deathe-bedde,
        Al under the wyllowe tree.

[1] running.   [2] hair.   [3] complexion.
                    cale] cold

THOMAS CHATTERTON

Swote hys tyngue as the throstles note,
Quycke ynn daunce as thoughte canne bee,
Defte hys taboure, codgelle stote,
O! hee lyes bie the wyllowe tree:
  Mie love ys dedde,
   Gonne to hys deathe-bedde,
   Alle underre the wyllowe tree.

Harke! the ravenne flappes hys wynge,
In the briered delle belowe;
Harke! the dethe-owle loude dothe synge,
To the nyghte-mares as heie goe;
  Mie love ys dedde,
   Gone to hys deathe-bedde,
   Al under the wyllowe tree.

See! the whyte moone sheenes onne hie;
Whyterre ys mie true loves shroude;
Whyterre yanne the mornynge skie,
Whyterre yanne the evenynge cloude;
  Mie love ys dedde,
   Gon to hys deathe-bedde,
   Al under the wyllowe tree.

Heere, uponne mie true loves grave,
Schalle the baren fleurs be layde,
Nee one hallie Seyncte to save
Al the celness of a mayde.
  Mie love ys dedde,
   Gonne to hys death-bedde,
   Alle under the wyllowe tree.

heie] they   celness] coldness

Wythe mie hondes I'lle dente the brieres
Rounde his hallie corse to gre,
Ouphante fairie, lyghte youre fyres,
Heere mie boddie stylle schalle bee.
>> Mie love ys dedde,
>> Gon to hys death-bedde,
>> Al under the wyllowe tree.

Comme, wythe acorne-coppe & thorne,
Drayne mie hartys blodde awaie;
Lyfe and all yttes goode I scorne,
Daunce bie nete, or feaste by daie.
>> Mie love ys dedde,
>> Gon to hys death-bedde,
>> Al under the wyllowe tree.

Waterre wytches, crownede wythe reytes,[1]
Bere mee to yer leathalle tyde.
I die; I comme; mie true love waytes.
Thos the damselle spake, and dyed.
>> *Ælla, a Tragycal Enterlude,* **1777**

326 *An Excelente Balade of Charitie*

IN Virgyne the sweltrie sun gan sheene,
  And hotte upon the mees[2] did caste his raie;
The apple rodded[3] from its palie greene,
And the mole[4] peare did bende the leafy spraie;
The peede chelandri[5] sunge the livelong daie;
'Twas nowe the pride, the manhode of the yeare,
And eke the grounde was dighte[6] in its mose defte[7] aumere.[8]

[1] water-flags.   [2] meads.   [3] reddened, ripened.   [4] soft.
[5] pied goldfinch.   [6] drest, arrayed.   [7] neat, ornamental.
[8] a loose robe or mantle.

Ouphante] elfin

522

THOMAS CHATTERTON

The sun was glemeing in the midde of daie,
Deadde still the aire, and eke the welken [1] blue,
When from the sea arist [2] in drear arraie
A hepe of cloudes of sable sullen hue,
The which full fast unto the woodlande drewe,
Hiltring [3] attenes [4] the sunnis fetive [5] face,
And the blacke tempeste swolne and gatherd up apace.

Beneathe an holme, faste by a pathwaie side,
Which dide unto Seyncte Godwine's covent [6] lede,
A hapless pilgrim moneynge did abide,
Pore in his viewe, ungentle [7] in his weede,
Longe bretful [8] of the miseries of neede,
Where from the hail-stone coulde the almer [9] flie?
He had no housen theere, ne anie covent nie.

Look in his glommed [10] face, his sprighte there scanne;
Howe woe-be-gone, how withered, forwynd [11], deade!
Haste to thie church-glebe-house [12], asshrewed [13] manne!
Haste to thie kiste [14], thie onlie dortoure [15] bedde.
Cale, as the claie whiche will gre on thie hedde,
Is Charitie and Love aminge highe elves;
Knightis and Barons live for pleasure and themselves.

[1] the sky, the atmosphere.   [2] arose.   [3] hiding, shrouding.   [4] at once.   [5] beauteous.   [6] It would have been *charitable*, if the author had not pointed at personal characters in this Ballad of Charity. The Abbot of St. Godwin's at the time of the writing of this was Ralph de Bellomont, a great stickler for the Lancastrian family. Rowley was a Yorkist.   [7] beggarly.   [8] filled with.   [9] beggar.   [10] clouded, dejected. A person of some note in the literary world is of opinion, that *glum* and *glom* are modern cant words ; and from this circumstance doubts the authenticity of Rowley's Manuscripts. Glum-mong in the Saxon signifies twilight, a dark or dubious light ; and the modern word *gloomy* is derived from the Saxon *glum*.   [11] dry, sapless.   [12] the grave.   [13] accursed, unfortunate.   [14] coffin   [15] a sleeping room.

The gatherd storme is rype; the bigge drops falle;
The forswat[1] meadowes smethe,[2] and drenche[3] the raine;
The comyng ghastness do the cattle pall,[4]
And the full flockes are drivynge ore the plaine;
Dashde from the cloudes the waters flott[5] againe;
The welkin opes; the yellow levynne[6] flies;
And the hot fierie smothe[7] in the wide lowings[8] dies.

Liste! now the thunder's rattling clymmynge[9] sound
Cheves[10] slowlie on, and then embollen[11] clangs,
Shakes the hie spyre, and losst, dispended, drown'd,
Still on the gallard[12] eare of terroure hanges;
The windes are up; the lofty elmen swanges;
Again the levynne and the thunder poures,
And the full cloudes are braste[13] attenes in stonen showers.

Spurreynge his palfrie oere the watrie plaine,
The Abbote of Seyncte Godwynes convente came;
His chapournette[14] was drented with the reine,
And his pencte[15] gyrdle met with mickle shame;
He aynewarde tolde his bederoll[16] at the same;
The storme encreasen, and he drew aside,
With the mist[17] almes craver neere to the holme to bide.

His cope[18] was all of Lyncolne clothe so fyne,
With a gold button fasten'd neere his chynne;
His autremete[19] was edged with golden twynne,

---

[1] sun-burnt. [2] smoke. [3] drink. [4] *pall*, a contraction from *appall*, to fright. [5] fly. [6] lightning.
[7] steam, or vapours. [8] flames. [9] noisy. [10] moves.
[11] swelled, strengthened. [12] frighted. [13] burst.
[14] a small round hat, not unlike the shapournette in heraldry, formerly worn by Ecclesiastics and Lawyers. [15] painted.
[16] He told his beads backwards; a figurative expression to signify cursing. [17] poor, needy. [18] a cloke.
[19] a loose white robe, worn by Priests.

And his shoone pyke a loverds [1] mighte have binne;
Full well it shewn he thoughten coste no sinne:
The trammels of the palfrye pleasde his sighte,
For the horse-millanare [2] his head with roses dighte.

An almes, sir prieste! the droppynge pilgrim saide,
O! let me waite within your covente dore,
Till the sunne sheneth hie above our heade,
And the loude tempeste of the aire is oer;
Helpless and ould am I alas! and poor;
No house, ne friend, ne moneie in my pouche;
All yatte I call my owne is this my silver crouche.

Varlet, replyd the Abbatte, cease your dinne;
This is no season almes and prayers to give;
Mie porter never lets a faitour [3] in;
None touch mie rynge who not in honour live.
And now the sonne with the blacke cloudes did stryve,
And shettynge on the grounde his glairie raie,
The Abbatte spurrde his steede, and eftsoones roadde awaie.

Once moe the skie was blacke, the thounder rolde;
Faste reyneynge oer the plaine a prieste was seen;
Ne dighte full proude, ne buttoned up in golde;
His cope and jape [4] were graie, and eke were clene;
A Limitoure he was of order seene;
And from the pathwaie side then turned hee,
Where the pore almer laie binethe the holmen tree.

---

[1] a lord's.   [2] I believe this trade is still in being, though
but seldom employed.   [3] a beggar, or vagabond.
[4] a short surplice, worn by Friars of an inferior class, and
secular priests.

THOMAS CHATTERTON

An almes, sir priest! the droppynge pilgrim sayde,
For sweete Seyncte Marie and your order sake.
The Limitoure then loosen'd his pouche threade,
And did thereoute a groate of silver take;
The mister pilgrim dyd for halline [1] shake.
 Here take this silver, it maie eathe [2] thie care;
We are Goddes stewards all, nete [3] of oure owne we bare.

But ah! unhailie [4] pilgrim, lerne of me,
Scathe anie give a rentrolle to their Lorde.
Here take my semecope [5], thou arte bare I see;
Tis thyne; the Seynctes will give me mie rewarde.
He left the pilgrim, and his waie aborde.
 Virgynne and hallie Seyncte, who sitte yn gloure [6],
Or give the mittee [7] will, or give the gode man power.

Poems, 1777

WILLIAM JULIUS MICKLE

1735-1788

327   *A Wild Romantic Dell*

SOOTHD by the murmurs of a plaintive streame,
 A wyld romantick dell its fragrance shed;
Safe from the thonder showre and scorching beame
  Their faerie charmes the summer bowres displaid;
  Wyld by the bancks the bashfull cowslips spread,
And from the rock above each ivied seat
  The spotted foxgloves hung the purple head,
And lowlie vilets kist the wanderers feet:
Sure never Hyblas bees rovd through a wilde so sweet.

---

 [1] joy.   [2] ease.   [3] nought.   [4] unhappy.
[5] a short under-cloke.   [6] glory.   [7] mighty, rich.

As winds the streamlett serpentine along,
   So leads a solemn walk its bowry way,
The pale-leaved palms and darker limes among,
   To where a grotto lone and secret lay;
   The yellow broome, where chirp the linnets gay,
Waves rownd the cave; and to the blue-streakd skyes
   A shatterd rock towres up in fragments gray:
The shee-goat from its height the lawnskepe eyes,
And calls her wanderd young, the call each banck replies.
                The Concubine, 1767

328   *Sunset*

STRAIGHT to Syr Martins hall the Hunters bend,
   The Knight perceives it from his oake-crownd hill,
Down the steep furzie height he slow gan wend,
   With troublous thoughts keen ruminating still;
   While grief and shame by turns his bosom fill.
And now, perchd prowdlie on the topmost spray,
   The sootie Blackbird chaunts his vespers shrill,
Whiles Twilight spreads his robe of sober grey,
And to their bowres the Rooks loud cawing wing their way.

And bright behind the Cambrian mountains hore
   Flames the red beam, while on the distant East
Led by her starre, the horned Moone looks o'er
   The bending forrest, and with rays increast
   Ascends, while trembling on the dappled West
The purple radiance shifts, and dies away;
   The willows with a deeper green imprest
Nod o'er the brooks; the brooks with gleamy ray
Glide on, and holy Peace assumes her woodland sway.
                The Concubine, 1767

329 *Cumnor Hall*

THE dews of summer nighte did falle,
   The moone (sweete regente of the skye)
Silver'd the walles of Cumnor Halle,
   And manye an oake that grewe therebye.

Nowe noughte was hearde beneath the skies.
   (The soundes of busye lyfe were stille,)
Save an unhappie ladie's sighes,
   That issued from that lonelye pile.

' Leicester,' shee cried, ' is thys thy love
   ' That thou so oft has sworne to mee,
' To leave mee in thys lonelye grove,
   ' Immurr'd in shameful privitie?

' No more thou com'st with lover's speede,
   ' Thy once-beloved bryde to see;
' But bee shee alive, or bee shee deade,
   ' I feare (sterne earle's) the same to thee.

' Not so the usage I receiv'd,
   ' When happye in my father's halle;
' No faithlesse husbande then me griev'd,
   ' No chilling feares did mee appall.

' I rose up with the chearful morne,
   ' No lark more blith, no flow'r more gaye;
' And, like the birde that hauntes the thorne,
   ' So merrylie sung the live-long daye.

' If that my beautye is but smalle,
   ' Among court ladies all despis'd;
' Why didst thou rend it from that halle,
   ' Where (scorneful earle) it well was priz'de?

' And when you first to mee made suite,
  ' How fayre I was you oft would saye!
' And, proude of conquest—pluck'd the fruite,
  ' Then lefte the blossom to decaye.

' Yes, nowe neglected and despis'd,
  ' The rose is pale—the lilly's deade—
' But hee that once their charmes so priz'd,
  ' Is sure the cause those charmes are fledde.

' For knowe, when sick'ning griefe doth preye
  ' And tender love's repay'd with scorne,
' The sweetest beautye will decaye—
  ' What flow'ret can endure the storme?

' At court I'm tolde is beauty's throne,
  ' Where everye lady's passing rare;
' That eastern flow'rs, that shame the sun,
  ' Are not so glowing, not soe fayre.

' Then, earle, why didst thou leave the bedds
  ' Where roses and where lillys vie,
' To seek a primrose, whose pale shades
  ' Must sicken—when those gaudes are bye?

' 'Mong rural beauties I was one,
  ' Among the fields wild flow'rs are faire;
' Some countrye swayne might mee have won,
  ' And thoughte my beautie passing rare.

But, Leicester, (or I much am wronge)
  ' Or tis not beautye lures thy vowes;
' Rather ambition's gilded crowne
  ' Makes thee forget thy humble spouse.

' Then, Leicester, why, again I pleade.
  ' (The injur'd surelye may repyne,)
' Why didst thou wed a countrye mayde,
  ' When some fayre princesse might be thyne?

' Why didst thou praise my humble charmes,
  ' And, oh! then leave them to decaye?
' Why didst thou win me to thy armes,
  ' Then leave me to mourne the live-long daye?

' The village maidens of the plaine
  ' Salute me lowly as they goe;
' Envious they marke my silken trayne,
  ' Nor thinke a countesse can have woe

' The simple nymphs! they little knowe,
  ' How farre more happy's their estate—
' —To smile for joye——than sigh for woe—
  ' —To be contente——than to be greate.

' Howe farre lesse bleste am I than them?
  ' Dailye to pyne and waste with care!
' Like the poore plante, that from its stem
  ' Divided—feeles the chilling ayre.

' Nor (cruel earl!) can I enjoye
  ' The humble charmes of solitude;
' Your minions proude my peace destroye,
  ' By sullen frownes or pratings rude.

' Laste nyghte, as sad I chanc'd to straye,
  ' The village deathe-bell smote my eare;
' They wink'd asyde, and seem'd to saye,
  ' Countesse, prepare—thy end is neare.

WILLIAM JULIUS MICKLE

' And nowe, while happye peasantes sleepe,
  ' Here I set lonelye and forlorne;
' No one to soothe mee as I weepe,
  ' Save phylomel on yonder thorne.

' My spirits flag—my hopes decaye—
  ' Still that dreade deathe-bell smites my eare,
' And many a boding seems to saye,
  ' Countess, prepare—thy end is neare.'

Thus sore and sad that ladie griev'd,
  In Cumnor Halle so lone and dreare;
And manye a heartefelte sighe shee heav'd,
  And let falle manye a bitter teare.

And ere the dawne of daye appear'd,
  In Cumnor Hall so lone and dreare,
Full manye a piercing screame was hearde,
  And manye a crye of mortal feare.

The death-belle thrice was hearde to ring,
  An aërial voyce was hearde to call,
And thrice the raven flapp'd its wyng
  Arounde the tow'rs of Cumnor Hall.

The mastiffe howl'd at village doore,
  The oaks were shatter'd on the greene;
Woe was the houre—for never more
  That haplesse countesse e'er was seene.

And in that manor now no more
  Is chearful feaste and sprightly balle;
For ever since that drearye houre
  Have spirits haunted Cumnor Hall.

The village maides, with fearful glance,
  Avoid the antient mossgrowne walle;
Nor ever leade the merrye dance,
  Among the groves of Cumnor Halle.

Full manye a travellor oft hath sigh'd,
  And pensive wepte the countess' falle,
As wand'ring onwards they've espied
  The haunted tow'rs of Cumnor Halle.

Evans's Old Ballads, iv, 1784

330 *There's nae Luck about the House*

AND are ye sure the news is true?
  And are ye sure he's weel?
Is this a time to think o' wark?
  Mak haste, lay by your wheel;
Is this the time to spin a thread
  When Colin's at the door?
Reach me my cloak, I'll to the quay
  And see him come ashore.
For there's nae luck about the house,
  There's nae luck at a',
There's little pleasure in the house
  When our gudeman's awa.

And gie to me my bigonet,
  My bishop's satin gown;
For I maun tell the bailie's wife
  That Colin's come to town.

bigonet] bonnet

WILLIAM JULIUS MICKLE

My Turkey slippers maun gae on,
    My stockings pearly blue;
It's a' to pleasure my gudeman,
    For he's baith leel and true.
            For there's nae luck, &c.

Rise, lass, and mak a clean fire side,
    Put on the muckle pot,
Gie little Kate her button gown,
    And Jock his Sunday coat;
And mak their shoon as black as slaes,
    Their hose as white as snaw,
It's a' to please my ain gudeman,
    For he's been lang awa.
            For there's nae, &c.

There's twa fat hens upo' the bauk,
    Been fed this month and mair,
Mak haste and thraw their necks about,
    That Colin weel may fare;
And mak the table neat and clean,
    Gar ilka thing look braw,
For wha can tell how Colin fared
    When he was far awa?
            Ah, there's nae, &c.

Sae true his heart, sae smooth his speech,
    His breath like cauler air,
His very foot has music in't
    As he comes up the stair!

            cauler] caller, fresh

And will I see his face again,
  And will I hear him speak?
I'm downright dizzy wi' the thought,
  In troth I'm like to greet.
    For there's nae, &c.

If Colin's weel, and weel content,
  I hae nae mair to crave—
And gin I live to keep him sae,
  I'm blest aboon the lave.
And will I see his face again,
  And will I hear him speak?
I'm downright dizzy wi' the thought,
  In troth I'm like to greet.
    For there's nae, &c.

Herd's Scots Songs, 1769

ROBERT FERGUSSON   1750–1774
Braid Claith

331

YE wha are fain to hae your name
  Wrote i' the bonny book o' Fame,
Let Merit nae pretension claim
      To laurel'd wreath,
But hap ye weel, baith back and wame,
      In gude Braid Claith

He that some ells o' this may fa',
An' slae-black hat on pow like snaw,
Bids bauld to bear the gree awa',
      Wi' a' this graith,
Whan beinly clad wi' shell fu' braw
      O' gude Braid Claith.

hap] wrap   wame] belly   fa'] obtain   pow] head
gree] prize   graith] gear, dress   beinly] comfortably

534

Waesuck for him wha has nae feck o't!
For he's a gowk they're sure to geck at,
A chiel that ne'er will be respekit,
      While he draws breath,
Till his four quarters are bedeckit
      Wi' gude Braid Claith.

On Sabbath-days the barber spark,
Whan he has done wi' scrapin wark,
Wi' siller broachie in his sark,
      Gangs trigly, faith!
Or to the Meadow, or the Park,
      In gude Braid Claith.

Weel might ye trow, to see them there,
That they to shave your haffits bare,
Or curl an' sleek a pickle hair,
      Would be right laith,
Whan pacing wi' a gawsy air
      In gude Braid Claith.

If ony mettl'd stirrah green
For favour frae a lady's een,
He maunna care for bein' seen
      Before he sheath
His body in a scabbard clean
      O' gude Braid Claith.

waesuck for] woe betide   feck] plenty   gowk] fool
geck] scoff   trigly] trimly   haffits] cheeks   a pickle]
a little, so much   gawsy] trim and portly   stirrah] young
fellow   green] yearn   maunna] must not

For, gin he come wi' coat thread-bare,
A feg for him she winna care,
But crook her bonny mou' fu' sair,
   And scald him baith:
Wooers shou'd ay their travel spare,
    Without Braid Claith.

Braid Claith lends fock an unco heese;
Makes mony kail-worms butterflies;
Gies mony a doctor his degrees
   For little skaith:
In short, you may be what you please
    Wi' gude Braid Claith.

For tho' ye had as wise a snout on
As Shakespeare or Sir Isaac Newton,
Your judgment fock would hae a doubt on,
   I'll tak my aith,
Till they cou'd see ye wi' a suit on
    O' gude Braid Claith.

The Weekly Magazine (Edinburgh), October 15, 1772

JOHN SKINNER

1721–1807

332   *Tullochgorum*

COME gie's a sang, Montgomery cry'd,
 And lay your disputes all aside,
What signifies't for folks to chide
   For what was done before them:

feg] fig fock] folk unco] uncouth, great heese] hoist, lift
skaith] pains   aith] oath

535

JOHN SKINNER

Let Whig and Tory all agree,
  Whig and Tory, Whig and Tory,
  Whig and Tory all agree,
   To drop their Whig-mig-morum;
Let Whig and Tory all agree
To spend the night wi' mirth and glee,
And cheerful sing alang wi' me
   The Reel o' Tullochgorum.

O' Tullochgorum's my delight,
It gars us a' in ane unite,
And ony sumph that keeps a spite,
   In conscience I abhor him:
For blythe and cheerie we'll be a',
  Blythe and cheerie, blythe and cheerie,
  Blythe and cheerie we'll be a',
   And make a happy quorum,
For blythe and cheerie we'll be a'
As lang as we hae breath to draw,
And dance till we be like to fa'
   The Reel o' Tullochgorum.

What needs there be sae great a fraise
Wi' dringing dull Italian lays,
I wadna gie our ain Strathspeys
   For half a hunder score o' them;
They're dowf and dowie at the best,
  Dowf and dowie, dowf and dowie,
  Dowf and dowie at the best,
   Wi' a' their variorum;

sumph] softy   fraise] fuss   dringing] drumming
dowf and dowie] dull and dismal

They're dowf and dowie at the best,
Their *allegros* and a' the rest,
They canna' please a Scottish taste
    Compar'd wi' Tullochgorum.

Let warldly worms their minds oppress
Wi' fears o' want and double cess,
And sullen sots themsells distress
    Wi' keeping up decorum:
Shall we sae sour and sulky sit,
    Sour and sulky, sour and sulky,
    Sour and sulky shall we sit
    Like old philosophorum!
Shall we sae sour and sulky sit,
Wi' neither sense, nor mirth, nor wit,
Nor ever try to shake a fit
    To th' Reel o' Tullochgorum?

May choicest blessings ay attend
Each honest, open hearted friend,
And calm and quiet be his end,
    And a' that's good watch o'er him;
May peace and plenty be his lot,
    Peace and plenty, peace and plenty,
    Peace and plenty be his lot,
    And dainties a great store o' them;
May peace and plenty be his lot,
Unstain'd by any vicious spot,
And may he never want a groat,
    That's fond o' Tullochgorum!

cess] assessment

But for the sullen frumpish fool,
That loves to be oppression's tool,
May envy gnaw his rotten soul,
  And discontent devour him;
May dool and sorrow be his chance,
  Dool and sorrow, dool and sorrow,
  Dool and sorrow be his chance,
  And nane say, wae's me for him!
May dool and sorrow be his chance,
Wi' a' the ills that come frae *France*,
Wha e'er he be that winna dance
  The Reel o' Tullochgorum.

   Two excellent new Songs (broadside), January 1776

JOHN LOGAN

1748–1788

333 *The Braes of Yarrow*

' THY braes were bonny, Yarrow stream!
  ' When first on them I met my lover;
' Thy braes how dreary, Yarrow stream!
  ' When now thy waves his body cover!
' For ever now, O Yarrow stream!
  ' Thou art to me a stream of sorrow;
' For never on thy banks shall I
  ' Behold my love, the flower of Yarrow.

' He promised me a milk-white steed,
  ' To bear me to his father's bowers;
' He promised me a little page,
  ' To 'squire me to his father's towers;

' He promised me a wedding-ring,—
  ' The wedding-day was fix'd to-morrow;—
' Now he is wedded to his grave,
  ' Alas, his watery grave, in Yarrow!

' Sweet were his words when last we met;
  ' My passion I as freely told him!
' Clasp'd in his arms, I little thought
  ' That I should never more behold him!
' Scarce was he gone, I saw his ghost;
  ' It vanish'd with a shriek of sorrow;
' Thrice did the water-wraith ascend,
  ' And gave a doleful groan thro' Yarrow.

' His mother from the window look'd,
  ' With all the longing of a mother;
' His little sister weeping walk'd
  ' The green-wood path to meet her brother:
' They sought him east, they sought him west,
  ' They sought him all the forest thorough;
' They only saw the cloud of night,
  ' They only heard the roar of Yarrow!

' No longer from thy window look,
  ' Thou hast no son, thou tender mother!
' No longer walk, thou lovely maid!
  ' Alas, thou hast no more a brother!
' No longer seek him east or west,
  ' And search no more the forest thorough;
' For, wandering in the night so dark,
  ' He fell a lifeless corse in Yarrow.

JOHN LOGAN

' The tear shall never leave my cheek,
    ' No other youth shall be my marrow;
' I'll seek thy body in the stream,
    ' And then with thee I'll sleep in Yarrow.'
The tear did never leave her cheek,
    No other youth became her marrow;
She found his body in the stream,
    And now with him she sleeps in Yarrow.

Poems, 1781

LADY ANNE LINDSAY
(LADY ANNE BARNARD)

1750–1825

334   *Auld Robin Gray*

WHEN the sheep are in the fauld, when the cows come
      hame,
When a' the weary world to quiet rest are gane,
The woes of my heart fa' in showers frae my ee,
Unken'd by my gudeman, who soundly sleeps by me.

Young Jamie loo'd me weel, and sought me for his bride;
But saving ae crown-piece, he'd naething else beside.
To make the crown a pound, my Jamie gaed to sea;
And the crown and the pound, oh! they were baith for me!

Before he had been gane a twelvemonth and a day,
My father brak his arm, our cow was stown away;
My mither she fell sick—my Jamie was at sea—
And auld Robin Gray, oh! he came a-courting me.

My father cou'dna work, my mother cou'dna spin;
I toil'd day and night, but their bread I cou'dna win;
And Rob maintain'd them baith, and, wi' tears in his ee,
Said, ' Jenny, oh! for their sakes, will you marry me?'

541

LADY ANNE LINDSAY

My heart it said na, and I look'd for Jamie back;
But hard blew the winds, and his ship was a wrack:
His ship it was a wrack! Why didna Jenny dee?
Or, wherefore am I spared to cry out, Woe is me!

My father argued sair—my mother didna speak,
But she look'd in my face till my heart was like to break:
They gied him my hand, but my heart was in the sea;
And so auld Robin Gray, he was gudeman to me.

I hadna been his wife, a week but only four,
When mournfu' as I sat on the stane at my door,
I saw my Jamie's ghaist—I cou'dna think it he,
Till he said, ' I'm come hame, my love, to marry thee! '

O sair, sair did we greet, and mickle say of a';
Ae kiss we took, nae mair—I bad him gang awa.
I wish that I were dead, but I'm no like to dee;
For O, I am but young to cry out, Woe is me!

I gang like a ghaist, and I carena much to spin;
I darena think o' Jamie, for that wad be a sin.
But I will do my best a gude wife aye to be,
For auld Robin Gray, oh! he is sae kind to me.

Herd's Scottish Songs, ii, 1776 ; ' the first authentic edition ',
Bannatyne Club, ed. Sir Walter Scott, 1825

SIR WILLIAM JONES

1746–1794

335   *A Persian Song of Hafiz*

SWEET maid, if thou wouldst charm my sight,
　And bid these arms thy neck infold;
That rosy cheek, that lily hand,
Would give thy poet more delight
Than all Bocara's vaunted gold,
Than all the gems of Samarcand.

Boy, let yon liquid ruby flow,
And bid thy pensive heart be glad,
Whate'er the frowning zealots say:
Tell them, their Eden cannot show
A stream so clear as Rocnabad,
A bow'r so sweet as Mosellay.

O! when these fair perfidious maids,
Whose eyes our secret haunts infest,
Their dear destructive charms display;
Each glance my tender breast invades,
And robs my wounded soul of rest,
As Tartars seize their destin'd prey.

In vain with love our bosoms glow:
Can all our tears, can all our sighs
New lustre to those charms impart?
Can cheeks, where living roses blow,
Where nature spreads her richest dies,
Require the borrow'd gloss of art?

SIR WILLIAM JONES

Speak not of fate:—ah! change the theme,
And talk of odours, talk of wine,
Talk of the flow'rs that round us bloom:
'Tis all a cloud, 'tis all a dream;
To love and joy thy thoughts confine,
Nor hope to pierce the sacred gloom.

Beauty has such resistless pow'r,
That ev'n the chaste Egyptian dame
Sigh'd for the blooming Hebrew boy;
For her how fatal was the hour,
When to the banks of Nilus came
A youth so lovely and so coy!

But ah! sweet maid, my counsel hear:
(Youth should attend when those advise
Whom long experience renders sage)
While musick charms the ravish'd ear,
While sparkling cups delight our eyes,
Be gay; and scorn the frowns of age.

What cruel answer have I heard!
And yet, by heav'n, I love thee still:
Can aught be cruel from thy lip?
Yet say, how fell that bitter word
From lips which streams of sweetness fill,
Which nought but drops of honey sip?

Go boldly forth, my simple lay,
Whose accents flow with artless ease
Like orient pearls at random strung;
Thy notes are sweet, the damsels say,
But O! far sweeter, if they please
Thy nymph for whom these notes are sung.

Poems, 1772

SIR WILLIAM JONES

336 *A Moral Tetrastich*

From the Persian

ON parent knees, a naked new-born child,
    Weeping thou satst, when all around thee smil'd:
So live, that, sinking in thy last long sleep,
Calm thou mayst smile, when all around thee weep.

The Asiatick Miscellany, ii, 1786

RICHARD BRINSLEY SHERIDAN

1751–1816

337 *Song*

HAD I a heart for falsehood fram'd,
    I ne'er could injure you:
For tho' your tongue no promise claim'd,
    Your charms would make me true.

To you no soul shall bear deceit,
    No stranger offer wrong;
For, friends in all the ag'd you'll meet,
    And lovers in the young.

But when they learn that you have blest
    Another with your heart,
They'll bid aspiring passions rest,
    And act a brother's part.

Then, lady, dread not here deceit,
    Nor fear to suffer wrong;
For friends in all the ag'd you'll meet,
    And brothers in the young.

The Duenna, Act i, 1775

338   *Song*

HERE'S to the maiden of bashful fifteen;
    Here's to the widow of fifty;
Here's to the flaunting extravagant quean,
    And here's to the housewife that's thrifty.
          Chorus.
    Let the toast pass,—
    Drink to the lass,
I'll warrant she'll prove an excuse for the glass.

Here's to the charmer whose dimples we prize;
    Now to the maid who has none, sir:
Here's to the girl with a pair of blue eyes,
    And here's to the nymph with but *one*, sir.
    Chorus. Let the toast pass, &c.

Here's to the maid with a bosom of snow;
    Now to her that's as brown as a berry:
Here's to the wife with a face full of woe,
    And now to the girl that is merry.
    Chorus. Let the toast pass, &c.

For let 'em be clumsy, or let 'em be slim,
    Young or ancient, I care not a feather;
So fill a pint bumper quite up to the brim,
    And let us e'en toast them together.
    Chorus. Let the toast pass, &c.
            The School for Scandal, Act iii, 1777

SIR JOHN HENRY MOORE

1756–1780

339   *Song*

INDEED, my Cælia, 'tis in vain;
  Away with this coquettish art,
These froward looks, this forced disdain,
    Believe me you mistake your part:
    'Tis kindness now alone can move,
    Can guide the wandering shaft of Love,
And fix it in the youthful heart.

Time was indeed, a scornful Beauty
  ('Twas then the mode, or History lies)
Was courted with obsequious duty,
    Was won with pray'rs, and tears, and sighs:
    Love now by other maxims rules;
    The God who made our Fathers fools
But serves to make their Offspring wise.

Yet though you've lost the power of teazing,
  Let no regrets perplex your mind,
You still retain the gift of pleasing,
    And that's a better art you'll find:
    Suppose then that I said and swore
    Whate'er each puppy vow'd before,
And own at once you will be kind.

Nor talk of constancy and truth,
  Eternal flames, and such droll fancies:
'Tis like perpetual health and youth,
    And only met with in Romances:
    While pleasure courts us, let's be gay,
    Nor think about a future day,
Care of itself too fast advances.

As the world changes we must change,
   'Tis all a farce, 'tis all a jest;
Then if 'tis now the mode to range,
    Why should the thought disturb our rest?
    Heroic love has flown away,
    Fine sentiments have had their day:
Who knows but all is for the best?

Poetical Trifles (third edition), 1783

340   *The Duke of Benevento*
            A Tale

I HATE a prologue to a story
   Worse than the tuning of a fiddle,
   Squeaking and dinning;
Hang order and connection,
   I love to dash into the middle;
    Exclusive of the fame and glory,
There is a comfort on reflection
    To think you've done with the beginning.

And so at supper one fine night,
   Hearing a cry of Alla, Alla,
The Prince was damnably confounded,
    And in a fright,
But more so when he saw himself surrounded
By fifty Turks; and at their head the fierce Abdalla.

And then he look'd a little grave
To find himself become a slave,
And thought the Corsair rather in a hurry,
    Out of all rules,
 To make the Duke of Benevento curry
    And take care of his mules:

But as 'twas vain to make a riot,
    Without grimace,
    Or a wry face,
He gave a shrug, and rubb'd his mules in quiet.

It would have been great sport
    To all the puppies of the court
To view these changes, and disasters;
    But their enjoyments
Were damp'd by certain slovenly employments,
Not more amusing than their master's.

But who can paint his grief,
Who can describe the transports of his sorrow
    When he beheld Almida's charms
    Conducted to Abdalla's arms,
    And saw no prospect of relief?
    But that the blooming Maid,
    By cruel destiny betray'd,
Must no more triumph in that name to-morrow.

Not understanding what he said,
    Seeing him caper like an antic,
And tear his hair, and beat his head,
The Eunuch wisely judg'd him to be frantic.

But she, the lovely cause of all his care,
Darting a look to his enraptur'd soul
Might soften e'en the madness of despair,
Bade him his weak, unmanly rage controul,
    Each favouring opportunity improve;
And bade him dare to hope, and bade him dare to love.

The Corsair in a transport of surprise,
When he beheld Almida's sparkling eyes,
    Her faultless figure, her majestic air,
The graceful ringlets of her auburn hair,
    That twin'd in many a fold to deck,
Not hide, the dazzling whiteness of her neck;
The various charms her flowing robe reveal'd,
While fancy whisper'd to his throbbing heart
    Each nameless beauty, that well-judging art,
To fix the roving mind, had carefully conceal'd.

' O Mahomet! I thank thee,' he exclaim'd,
    ' That to thy servant thou hast given
    ' This bright inhabitant of heaven,
' To gild the progress of his life below,
    ' For him this beauteous Houri fram'd;
' Enjoyment I have known, but never lov'd till now.'

        Then with a smile
    Might ev'n a Stoic's heart beguile,
        The fair one with a little flattery
    To his charm'd ears address'd her battery.

    ' Still may my Lord (said she) approve
    ' The happy object of his love,
        Then when Almida sues,
' Let not Abdalla's heart her first request refuse:
        ' Deign to suspend but for three days
        ' The progress of your amorous flame,
        ' And to console my heart for these delays,
        ' Grant me two small requests that I shall name.

' The first is to desire,
    ' If you incline,
' Five hundred lashes for two friends of mine,
    ' And just as many for a Fry'r;
    ' The next a litter, and two mules,
' The heavy hours of absence to amuse,
    ' Besides a Muleteer, that I shall chuse,
' At my disposal, subject to my rules.'

    So said, the culprit knaves appear,
    Upon each rascal's pamper'd hide
    The stripes are in due form applied,
        Which done, she chose,
        You may suppose,
    Her lover for her Muleteer.

Then with a voice sweet as an angel's song,
    While Tancred with attentive ear
    In silent rapture stoop'd to hear,
The beauteous Maid the silence broke,
    Conviction follow'd as she spoke,
And truth, and soft persuasion, dwelt on her enchanting
    tongue.

    ' With grief those scenes unwilling I disclose,
    ' Whence every error, each misfortune, rose;
    ' When pleasures, of the lowest, meanest kind,
    ' Unnerv'd your feeble frame, and checked the progress of
        your mind.
      ' In vain your people's curses, or their tears,
        ' Your heart assail'd,
    ' Two flattering knaves had charm'd your ears,
' And Raymond vainly counsel'd, or as vainly rail'd;

' He was your father's friend, wise, honest, brave,
    ' Him you displac'd,
' And listening to the malice of a slave,
' The Guardian of your Crown was banish'd, and disgrac'd.

' Me too you lov'd, and I approv'd the flame
    ' In hopes my counsels might have weight,
    ' To prompt you to redress the state,
' And save from infamy your sinking name.

' But soon your Confessor, the crafty Priest,
' Rage, hate, and malice, rankling in his breast,
' With timorous scruples fill'd your wavering mind;
    ' In vain each finer feeling strove
' To guard your heart, and court it to be kind,
' While haggard superstition triumph'd over love.

    ' But justice still pursues betimes,
    ' E'en now, for she directs the hour,
' The Priest, and the vile partners of his pow'r,
' Feel vengeance overtake their crimes.

' The Turks' unnotic'd march, last night's surprize,
' The foe unthought-of thundering at the gate,
    ' At length have clear'd your eyes,
Their treacherous negligence is found, is felt too late.

    ' No more of this unpleasing strain—
    ' If thinking, acting like a man,
    ' Reform'd by slavery's painful chain,
Virtue within your breast resume her reign,
Inspire your thoughts and guide your future plan,

' My heart will still be your's: e'en Raymond too
    ' Still loves his Prince, to him repair,
    ' Confess your faults, his aid demand,
The gallant veteran waits but your command
    ' To spread his conquering banners to the air,
     ' To sacrifice his life with you,
' Or rescue and relieve his native land.

    ' Abdalla claims my promise in three days.
      ' Think then on me,
      ' Danger and death attend delays,
    ' Be virtuous, be daring, and be free.'

The Lady's sermon was a little long,
Not but she talk'd both well and wittily,
    And then she look'd so prettily,
Her eyes excus'd the freedoms of her tongue.

For when a favourite mistress speaks,
    We always think her in the right,
E'en though she talks for days or weeks,
    Or in the middle of the night.

To say the truth, her speech was rather rough,
    But as she promis'd him her heart,
Upon the whole he took it in good part,
And as he lov'd her, lik'd it well enough.

So thank'd her for the good advice,
And took his leave; and ere he went,
    By way of compliment,
Call'd her his guardian angel, his sweet tutor,
    And kiss'd her fair hand, once, or twice,
And swore to be a good boy for the future.

553

In short, it was so settled; the third night,
  By good luck too 'twas dark as hell,
Tancred with Raymond and a chosen band
  Surprise the guards, who in their fright
    Make but a shabby stand,
And enter at the gates pell-mell.

Mean time Abdalla, snug in bed,
  Finding Almida staid away so long,
  Suspecting there was something wrong,
Look'd out; and found his troops were kill'd or gone,
  Himself a prisoner, and alone,
  And Tancred reigning in his stead.

And now the sore-back'd scoundrels in a trice
Came kindly with their counsels, and advice,
  Proposing as a pious work
    Just to impale
  Or stick a hedge-stake through the tail
    Of the poor Turk.

Indignant fury flash'd from Tancred's eye—
  ' Ye vile corruptors of my youth,
  ' Ye foes to honour, honesty, and truth,
    ' Hence from my sight, nor offer a reply:
    ' If the third day
    ' Within the limits of this state
    ' Disclose your stay,
' Not e'en Almida's self shall save you from your fate.

    ' Go, brave Abdalla, to your native shore;—
    ' From sloth, from vice, from infamy,
    ' Your kind instructions and assistance
      ' Have haply set me free:

'Thanks for your visit, pray return no more,
'Let us be always friends, but at a distance.

'And now, my better angel, whose kind care
    'The mists of error from my sight dispell'd,
'Burst the vile fetters that my reason held,
    'Restor'd fair wisdom's gentle sway,
'Guided my steps to her, and pointed out the way;
    'Now, while my people's eager voice,
    'And Raymond too confirms my choice,
        'O come, my heavenly fair!
    'Ascend, adorn, and bless my throne;
        'Still with that cheering influence preside,
        'My life, my future conduct, guide,
Inspire my raptur'd heart, and make it virtuous as your own.

Poetical Trifles, 1778

ANONYMOUS

341   *The British Grenadiers*

SOME talk of Alexander, and some of Hercules,
    Of Conon and Lysander, and some Miltiades;
But of all the World's brave Heroes, there's none that can
    compare,
With a tow, row, row, row, row, to the British Grenadiers.
    Chorus. But of all the World's brave Heroes, &c.

None of those ancient Heroes e'er saw a cannon ball,
Or knew the force of Powder to slay their foes with all;
But our brave Boys do know it, and banish all their fears,
With a tow, row, row, row, row, the British Grenadiers.
    Chorus. But our brave Boys, &c.

555

ANONYMOUS

When e'er we are commanded to storm the Palisades,
Our Leaders march with Fusees and we with hand Granades;
We throw them from the Glacis about our Enemies Ears,
With a tow, row, row, row, row, the British Grenadiers.
   Chorus. We throw them, &c.

The God of War was pleased and great Bellona smiles,
To see these noble Heroes of our British Isles;
And all the Gods celestial, descending from their spheres,
Beheld with admiration the British Grenadiers.
   Chorus. And all the Gods celestial, &c.

Then let us crown a Bumper, and drink a health to those
Who carry Caps and Pouches, that wear the louped Cloaths;
May they and their Commanders live happy all their Years,
With a tow, row, row, row, row, the British Grenadiers.
   Chorus. May they and their Commanders, &c.

First sung January 17, 1780 (text from
original broadside)

JOHN SCOTT (of Amwell)

1730–1783

342   *The Drum*

I HATE that drum's discordant sound,
  Parading round, and round, and round:
To thoughtless youth it pleasure yields,
And lures from cities and from fields,
To sell their liberty for charms
Of tawdry lace, and glittering arms;
And when Ambition's voice commands,
To march, and fight, and fall, in foreign lands.

JOHN SCOTT

I hate that drum's discordant sound,
Parading round, and round, and round:
To me it talks of ravag'd plains,
And burning towns, and ruin'd swains,
And mangled limbs, and dying groans,
And widows' tears, and orphans' moans;
And all that Misery's hand bestows,
To fill the catalogue of human woes.

Poetical Works, 1782

AUGUSTUS MONTAGUE TOPLADY
1740–1778

343   *A Prayer, living and dying*

ROCK of ages, cleft for me,
 Let me hide myself in Thee!
Let the Water and the Blood,
From thy riven Side which flow'd,
Be of sin the double cure;
Cleanse me from it's guilt and pow'r.

Not the labors of my hands
Can fulfill thy Law's demands:
Could my zeal no respite know,
Could my tears for ever flow,
All for sin could not atone:
Thou must save, and Thou alone.

Nothing in my hand I bring;
Simply to thy Cross I cling;
Naked, come to Thee for dress;
Helpless, look to Thee for grace;
Foul, I to the Fountain fly:
Wash me, SAVIOR, or I die!

While I draw this fleeting breath—
When my eye-strings break in death—
When I soar to worlds unknown—
See Thee on thy judgment-throne—
Rock of ages, cleft for me,
Let me hide myself in Thee.

Psalms and Hymns, 1776

JOHN NEWTON

1725–1807

344　　*The name of JESUS*

HOW sweet the name of JESUS sounds
   In a believer's ear?
It sooths his sorrows, heals his wounds,
   And drives away his fear.

It makes the wounded spirit whole,
   And calms the troubled breast;
'Tis Manna to the hungry soul,
   And to the weary rest.

Dear name! the rock on which I build,
   My shield and hiding place;
My never-failing treas'ry fill'd
   With boundless stores of grace.

By thee my pray'rs acceptance gain,
   Altho' with sin defil'd;
Satan accuses me in vain,
   And I am own'd a child.

JESUS! my Shepherd, Husband, Friend,
   My Prophet, Priest, and King;
My LORD, my Life, my Way, my End,
   Accept the praise I bring.

Weak is the effort of my heart,
 And cold my warmest thought
But when I see thee as thou art,
 I'll praise thee as I ought.

'Till then I would thy love proclaim
 With ev'ry fleeting breath;
And may the music of thy name
 Refresh my soul in death.

Olney Hymns, 1779

WILLIAM COWPER

1731–1800

345 *Walking with God*

OH! for a closer walk with GOD,
 A calm and heav'nly frame;
A light to shine upon the road
 That leads me to the Lamb!

Where is the blessedness I knew
 When first I saw the LORD?
Where is the soul-refreshing view
 Of JESUS, and his word?

What peaceful hours I once enjoy'd!
 How sweet their mem'ry still!
But they have left an aching void,
 The world can never fill.

Return, O holy Dove, return,
 Sweet messenger of rest;
I hate the sins that made thee mourn,
 And drove thee from my breast.

The dearest idol I have known,
　　Whate'er that idol be;
Help me to tear it from thy throne,
　　And worship only thee.

So shall my walk be close with GOD,
　　Calm and serene my frame;
So purer light shall mark the road
　　That leads me to the Lamb.

Olney Hymns, 1779

346　　　　　*Lovest thou me ?*

HARK, my soul! it is the LORD;
　　'Tis thy Saviour, hear his word;
JESUS speaks, and speaks to thee;
' Say, poor sinner, lov'st thou me?

I deliver'd thee when bound,
And, when wounded, heal'd thy wound;
Sought thee wand'ring, set thee right,
Turn'd thy darkness into light.

Can a woman's tender care
Cease, towards the child she bare?
Yes, she may forgetful be,
Yet will I remember thee.

Mine is an unchanging love,
Higher than the heights above;
Deeper than the depths beneath,
Free and faithful, strong as death.

Thou shalt see my glory soon,
When the work of grace is done;
Partner of my throne shalt be;
Say, poor sinner, lov'st thou me? '

Lord, it is my chief complaint,
That my love is weak and faint;
Yet I love thee and adore,
Oh for grace to love thee more!

Olney Hymns, 1779

347　　　*Light shining out of Darkness*

GOD moves in a mysterious way,
　His wonders to perform;
He plants his footsteps in the sea,
　And rides upon the storm.

Deep in unfathomable mines
　Of never failing skill,
He treasures up his bright designs,
　And works his sovereign will.

Ye fearful saints fresh courage take,
　The clouds ye so much dread
Are big with mercy, and shall break
　In blessings on your head.

Judge not the Lord by feeble sense,
　But trust him for his grace;
Behind a frowning providence,
　He hides a smiling face.

His purposes will ripen fast,
　Unfolding ev'ry hour;
The bud may have a bitter taste,
　But sweet will be the flow'r.

Blind unbelief is sure to err,
   And scan his work in vain;
God is his own interpreter,
   And he will make it plain.

Olney Hymns, 1779

348   *The Shrubbery*

Written in a Time of Affliction

OH happy shades! to me unblest,
   Friendly to peace, but not to me,
How ill the scene that offers rest,
   And heart that cannot rest, agree!

This glassy stream, that spreading pine,
   Those alders quiv'ring to the breeze,
Might sooth a soul less hurt than mine,
   And please, if any thing could please.

But fixt unalterable care
   Foregoes not what she feels within,
Shows the same sadness ev'ry where,
   And slights the season and the scene.

For all that pleas'd in wood or lawn,
   While peace possess'd these silent bow'rs,
Her animating smile withdrawn,
   Has lost its beauties and its pow'rs.

The saint or moralist should tread
   This moss-grown alley, musing, slow;
They seek, like me, the secret shade,
   But not, like me, to nourish woe.

Me fruitful scenes and prospects waste
    Alike admonish not to roam;
These tell me of enjoyments past,
    And those of sorrows yet to come.

Written 1773; *Poems,* 1782

349   *Simple Faith*

YON cottager who weaves at her own door,
  Pillow and bobbins all her little store,
Content though mean, and cheerful, if not gay,
Shuffling her threads about the live-long day,
Just earns a scanty pittance, and at night
Lies down secure, her heart and pocket light;
She, for her humble sphere by nature fit,
Has little understanding, and no wit,
Receives no praise, but (though her lot be such,
Toilsome and indigent) she renders much;
Just knows, and knows no more, her Bible true,
A truth the brilliant Frenchman never knew;
And in that charter reads, with sparkling eyes,
Her title to a treasure in the skies.
  Oh happy peasant! Oh unhappy bard!
His the mere tinsel, her's the rich reward;
He prais'd perhaps for ages yet to come,
She never heard of half a mile from home;
He lost in errors his vain heart prefers,
She safe in the simplicity of her's.

Truth—Poems, 1782

350   *The Statesman in Retirement*

YE groves (the statesman at his desk exclaims,
   Sick of a thousand disappointed aims)
My patrimonial treasure and my pride,
Beneath your shades your gray possessor hide,
Receive me languishing for that repose
The servant of the public never knows.
Ye saw me once (ah those regretted days
When boyish innocence was all my praise)
Hour after hour delightfully allot
To studies then familiar, since forgot,
And cultivate a taste for ancient song,
Catching its ardour as I mus'd along;
Nor seldom, as propitious heav'n might send,
What once I valued and could boast, a friend
Were witnesses how cordially I press'd
His undissembling virtue to my breast;
Receive me now, not uncorrupt as then,
Nor guiltless of corrupting other men,
But vers'd in arts that, while they seem to stay
A falling empire, hasten its decay.
To the fair haven of my native home,
The wreck of what I was, fatigu'd I come;
For once I can approve the patriot's voice,
And make the course he recommends, my choice:
We meet at last in one sincere desire,
His wish and mine both prompt me to retire.
'Tis done—he steps into the welcome chaise,
Lolls at his ease behind four handsome bays,
That whirl away from business and debate
The disincumber'd Atlas of the state.

WILLIAM COWPER

Ask not the boy, who when the breeze of morn
First shakes the glitt'ring drops from ev'ry thorn,
Unfolds his flock, then under bank or bush
Sits linking cherry stones or platting rush,
How fair is freedom?—he was always free:
To carve his rustic name upon a tree,
To snare the mole, or with ill-fashion'd hook
To draw th' incautious minnow from the brook,
Are life's prime pleasures in his simple view,
His flock the chief concern he ever knew:
She shines but little in his heedless eyes,
The good we never miss, we rarely prize:
But ask the noble drudge in state affairs,
Escap'd from office and its constant cares,
What charms he sees in freedom's smile express'd,
In freedom lost so long, now repossess'd,
The tongue whose strains were cogent as commands,
Rever'd at home, and felt in foreign lands,
Shall own itself a stamm'rer in that cause,
Or plead its silence as its best applause.
He knows indeed that, whether dress'd or rude,
Wild without art, or artfully subdu'd,
Nature in ev'ry form inspires delight,
But never mark'd her with so just a sight.
Her hedge-row shrubs, a variegated store,
With woodbine and wild roses mantled o'er,
Green baulks and furrow'd lands, the stream that spreads
Its cooling vapour o'er the dewy meads,
Downs that almost escape th' enquiring eye,
That melt and fade into the distant sky,
Beauties he lately slighted as he pass'd,
Seem all created since he travell'd last.

Master of all th' enjoyments he design'd,
No rough annoyance rankling in his mind,
What early philosophic hours he keeps,
How regular his meals, how sound he sleeps!
Not sounder he that on the mainmast head,
While morning kindles with a windy red,
Begins a long look-out for distant land,
Nor quits, till ev'ning watch, his giddy stand,
Then swift descending with a seaman's haste,
Slips to his hammock, and forgets the blast.
He chooses company, but not the squire's,
Whose wit is rudeness, whose good breeding tires;
Nor yet the parson's, who would gladly come,
Obsequious when abroad, though proud at home;
Nor can he much affect the neighb'ring peer,
Whose toe of emulation treads too near;
But wisely seeks a more convenient friend,
With whom, dismissing forms, he may unbend!
A man whom marks of condescending grace
Teach, while they flatter him, his proper place:
Who comes when call'd, and at a word withdraws,
Speaks with reserve, and listens with applause;
Some plain mechanic, who, without pretence
To birth or wit, nor gives nor takes offence;
On whom he rests well-pleas'd his weary pow'rs,
And talks and laughs away his vacant hours.
The tide of life, swift always in its course,
May run in cities with a brisker force,
But no where with a current so serene,
Or half so clear, as in the rural scene.
Yet how fallacious is all earthly bliss,
What obvious truths the wisest heads may miss;

Some pleasures live a month, and some a year,
But short the date of all we gather here;
No happiness is felt, except the true,
That does not charm the more for being new.
This observation, as it chanc'd, not made,
Or if the thought occurr'd, not duly weigh'd,
He sighs—for after all, by slow degrees,
The spot he lov'd has lost the pow'r to please;
To cross his ambling pony day by day,
Seems at the best but dreaming life away;
The prospect, such as might enchant despair,
He views it not, or sees no beauty there;
With aching heart, and discontented looks,
Returns at noon, to billiards or to books,
But feels, while grasping at his faded joys,
A secret thirst of his renounc'd employs.
He chides the tardiness of ev'ry post,
Pants to be told of battles won or lost,
Blames his own indolence, observes, though late.
'Tis criminal to leave a sinking state,
Flies to the levee, and, receiv'd with grace,
Kneels, kisses hands, and shines again in place.

Retirement—Poems, 1782

351   *Absence of Occupation*

LUCRATIVE offices are seldom lost
    For want of pow'rs proportion'd to the post:
Give ev'n a dunce th' employment he desires,
And he soon finds the talents it requires;
A business with an income at its heels
Furnishes always oil for its own wheels.

But in his arduous enterprize to close
His active years with indolent repose,
He finds the labours of that state exceed
His utmost faculties, severe indeed.
'Tis easy to resign a toilsome place,
But not to manage leisure with a grace
Absence of occupation is not rest,
A mind quite vacant is a mind distress'd.
The vet'ran steed excus'd his task at length,
In kind compassion of his failing strength,
And turn'd into the park or mead to graze,
Exempt from future service all his days,
There feels a pleasure perfect in its kind,
Ranges at liberty, and snuffs the wind.
But when his lord would quit the busy road,
To taste a joy like that he has bestow'd,
He proves, less happy than his favour'd brute,
A life of ease a difficult pursuit.

Retirement—Poems, 1782

352   *The Diverting History of*
          John Gilpin

JOHN GILPIN was a citizen
    Of credit and renown,
A train-band Captain eke was he
    Of famous London town.

John Gilpin's spouse said to her dear,
    —Though wedded we have been
These twice ten tedious years, yet we
    No holiday have seen.

WILLIAM COWPER

To-morrow is our wedding-day,
   And we will then repair
Unto the Bell at Edmonton
   All in a chaise and pair.

My sister, and my sister's child,
   Myself, and children three,
Will fill the chaise; so you must ride
   On horseback after we.

He soon replied—I do admire
   Of womankind but one,
And you are she, my dearest dear,
   Therefore it shall be done.

I am a linen-draper bold,
   As all the world doth know,
And my good friend the Callender
   Will lend his horse to go.

Quoth Mrs. Gilpin—That 's well said;
   And for that wine is dear,
We will be furnish'd with our own,
   Which is both bright and clear.

John Gilpin kiss'd his loving wife,
   O'erjoy'd was he to find
That though on pleasure she was bent,
   She had a frugal mind.

The morning came, the chaise was brought,
   But yet was not allow'd
To drive up to the door, lest all
   Should say that she was proud.

So three doors off the chaise was stay'd,
  Where they did all get in,
Six precious souls, and all agog
  To dash through thick and thin.

Smack went the whip, round went the wheels,
  Were never folk so glad,
The stones did rattle underneath
  As if Cheapside were mad.

John Gilpin at his horse's side
  Seiz'd fast the flowing mane,
And up he got, in haste to ride,
  But soon came down again.

For saddle-tree scarce reach'd had he,
  His journey to begin,
When, turning round his head, he saw
  Three customers come in.

So down he came; for loss of time,
  Although it griev'd him sore,
Yet loss of pence, full well he knew,
  Would trouble him much more.

'Twas long before the customers
  Were suited to their mind,
When Betty screaming came down stairs
  ' The wine is left behind.'

Good lack! quoth he, yet bring it me,
  My leathern belt likewise
In which I bear my trusty sword
  When I do exercise.

Now mistress Gilpin, careful soul,
   Had two stone bottles found,
To hold the liquor that she loved,
   And keep it safe and sound.

Each bottle had a curling ear,
   Through which the belt he drew,
And hung a bottle on each side,
   To make his balance true.

Then over all, that he might be
   Equipp'd from top to toe,
His long red cloak, well brush'd and neat,
   He manfully did throw.

Now see him mounted once again
   Upon his nimble steed,
Full slowly pacing o'er the stones
   With caution and good heed.

But finding soon a smoother road,
   Beneath his well-shod feet,
The snorting beast began to trot,
   Which gall'd him in his seat.

So, Fair and softly, John he cried,
   But John he cried in vain;
That trot became a gallop soon,
   In spite of curb and rein.

So stooping down, as needs he must
   Who cannot sit upright,
He grasp'd the mane with both his hands,
   And eke with all his might.

His horse, who never in that sort
    Had handled been before,
What thing upon his back had got
    Did wonder more and more.

Away went Gilpin neck or nought,
    Away went hat and wig,
He little dreamt when he set out
    Of running such a rig.

The wind did blow, the cloak did fly,
    Like streamer long and gay,
'Till, loop and button failing both,
    At last it flew away.

Then might all people well discern
    The bottles he had slung;
A bottle swinging at each side,
    As hath been said or sung.

The dogs did bark, the children scream'd,
    Up flew the windows all;
And ev'ry soul cried out, Well done!
    As loud as he could bawl.

Away went Gilpin—who but he?
    His fame soon spread around—
He carries weight, he rides a race,
    'Tis for a thousand pound.

And still as fast as he drew near,
    'Twas wonderful to view
How in a trice the turnpike-men
    Their gates wide open threw.

And now as he went bowing down
    His reeking head full low,
The bottles twain behind his back
    Were shatter'd at a blow.

Down ran the wine into the road,
    Most piteous to be seen,
Which made his horse's flanks to smoke
    As they had basted been.

But still he seem'd to carry weight,
    With leathern girdle brac'd;
For all might see the bottle-necks
    Still dangling at his waist.

Thus all through merry Islington
    These gambols he did play,
And till he came unto the Wash
    Of Edmonton so gay.

And there he threw the Wash about
    On both sides of the way,
Just like unto a trundling mop,
    Or a wild-goose at play.

At Edmonton his loving wife
    From the balcony spied
Her tender husband, wond'ring much
    To see how he did ride.

Stop, stop, John Gilpin!—Here 's the house—
    They all at once did cry,
The dinner waits and we are tir'd :
    Said Gilpin—So am I !

573

But yet his horse was not a whit
   Inclin'd to tarry there;
For why?—his owner had a house
   Full ten miles off, at Ware.

So like an arrow swift he flew,
   Shot by an archer strong;
So did he fly—which brings me to
   The middle of my song.

Away went Gilpin, out of breath,
   And sore against his will,
Till at his friend's the Callender's
   His horse at last stood still.

The Callender, amazed to see
   His neighbour in such trim,
Laid down his pipe, flew to the gate,
   And thus accosted him:—

What news? what news? your tidings tell,
   Tell me you must and shall—
Say why bare-headed you are come,
   Or why you come at all?

Now Gilpin had a pleasant wit
   And lov'd a timely joke,
And thus unto the Callender
   In merry guise he spoke:—

I came because your horse would come
   And if I well forebode,
My hat and wig will soon be here,
   They are upon the road.

The Callender, right glad to find
   His friend in merry pin,
Return'd him not a single word,
   But to the house went in.

Whence straight he came with hat and wig;
   A wig that flow'd behind,
A hat not much the worse for wear,
   Each comely in its kind.

He held them up, and in his turn
   Thus show'd his ready wit,
—My head is twice as big as yours,
   They therefore needs must fit.

But let me scrape the dirt away
   That hangs upon your face;
And stop and eat, for well you may
   Be in a hungry case.

Said John—It is my wedding-day,
   And all the world would stare,
If wife should dine at Edmonton
   And I should dine at Ware.

So turning to his horse, he said,
   I am in haste to dine;
'Twas for your pleasure you came here,
   You shall go back for mine.

Ah, luckless speech, and bootless boast!
   For which he paid full dear;
For, while he spake, a braying ass
   Did sing most loud and clear.

Whereat his horse did snort, as he
    Had heard a lion roar,
And gallop'd off with all his might,
    As he had done before.

Away went Gilpin, and away
    Went Gilpin's hat and wig;
He lost them sooner than at first,
    For why? they were too big.

Now mistress Gilpin, when she saw
    Her husband posting down
Into the country far away,
    She pull'd out half a crown;

And thus unto the youth she said
    That drove them to the Bell,
This shall be yours when you bring back
    My husband safe and well.

The youth did ride, and soon did meet
    John coming back amain;
Whom in a trice he tried to stop
    By catching at his rein;

But not performing what he meant,
    And gladly would have done,
The frighted steed he frighted more,
    And made him faster run.

Away went Gilpin, and away
    Went post-boy at his heels,
The post-boy's horse right glad to miss
    The lumb'ring of the wheels.

Six Gentlemen upon the road,
    Thus seeing Gilpin fly,
With post-boy scamp'ring in the rear,
    They rais'd the hue and cry:

Stop thief, stop thief—a highwayman!
    Not one of them was mute;
And all and each that pass'd that way
    Did join in the pursuit.

And now the turnpike gates again
    Flew open in short space,
The toll-men thinking as before
    That Gilpin rode a race.

And so he did, and won it too,
    For he got first to town,
Nor stopp'd till where he had got up
    He did again get down.

Now let us sing, Long live the king,
    And Gilpin long live he;
And when he next doth ride abroad,
    May I be there to see!

        The Public Advertiser, November 14, 1782

353   *On the Loss of the Royal George*

TOLL for the brave—
    The brave! that are no more:
    All sunk beneath the wave,
Fast by their native shore.
    Eight hundred of the brave,
Whose courage well was tried,
    Had made the vessel heel

And laid her on her side;
  A land-breeze shook the shrouds,
And she was overset;
  Down went the Royal George
With all her crew complete.

  Toll for the brave—
Brave Kempenfelt is gone,
  His last sea-fight is fought,
His work of glory done.
  It was not in the battle,
No tempest gave the shock,
  She sprang no fatal leak,
She ran upon no rock;
  His sword was in the sheath,
His fingers held the pen,
  When Kempenfelt went down
With twice four hundred men.

  Weigh the vessel up,
Once dreaded by our foes,
  And mingle with your cup
The tears that England owes;
  Her timbers yet are sound,
And she may float again,
  Full charg'd with England's thunder,
And plough the distant main;
  But Kempenfelt is gone,
His victories are o'er;
  And he and his Eight hundred
Must plough the wave no more.

Written 1782 ; *Life and Letters*
(W. Hayley), 1803

354 ## The Poplar-Field

THE poplars are fell'd, farewell to the shade
    And the whispering sound of the cool colonnade,
The winds play no longer, and sing in the leaves,
Nor Ouse on his bosom their image receives.

Twelve years have elaps'd since I first took a view
Of my favourite field and the bank where they grew,
And now in the grass behold they are laid,
And the tree is my seat that once lent me a shade.

The blackbird has fled to another retreat
Where the hazels afford him a screen from the heat,
And the scene where his melody charm'd me before,
Resounds with his sweet-flowing ditty no more.

My fugitive years are all hasting away,
And I must ere long lie as lowly as they,
With a turf on my breast, and a stone at my head,
Ere another such grove shall arise in its stead.

'Tis a sight to engage me, if any thing can,
To muse on the perishing pleasures of man;
Though his life be a dream, his enjoyments, I see,
Have a being less durable even than he.

The Gentleman's Magazine, January 1785

355 ## Slaves cannot breathe in England

SLAVES cannot breathe in England; if their lungs
    Receive our air, that moment they are free;
They touch our country, and their shackles fall.
That 's noble, and bespeaks a nation proud

And jealous of the blessing.   Spread it then,
And let it circulate through ev'ry vein
Of all your empire; that where Britain's pow'r
Is felt, mankind may feel her mercy too.

The Task, ii, 1785

356 *England*

ENGLAND, with all thy faults, I love thee still—
  My country! and, while yet a nook is left
Where English minds and manners may be found,
Shall be constrain'd to love thee.   Though thy clime
Be fickle, and thy year most part deform'd
With dripping rains, or wither'd by a frost,
I would not yet exchange thy sullen skies,
And fields without a flow'r, for warmer France
With all her vines; nor for Ausonia's groves
Of golden fruitage, and her myrtle bow'rs.
To shake thy senate, and from heights sublime
Of patriot eloquence to flash down fire
Upon thy foes, was never meant my task:
But I can feel thy fortunes, and partake
Thy joys and sorrows, with as true a heart
As any thund'rer there.   And I can feel
Thy follies, too; and with a just disdain
Frown at effeminates, whose very looks
Reflect dishonour on the land I love.
How, in the name of soldiership and sense,
Should England prosper, when such things, as smooth
And tender as a girl, all essenc'd o'er
With odours, and as profligate as sweet;
Who sell their laurel for a myrtle wreath,

580

And love when they should fight; when such as these
Presume to lay their hand upon the ark
Of her magnificent and awful cause?
Time was when it was praise and boast enough
In ev'ry clime, and travel where we might,
That we were born her children. Praise enough
To fill th' ambition of a private man,
That Chatham's language was his mother tongue,
And Wolfe's great name compatriot with his own.
Farewell those honours, and farewell with them
The hope of such hereafter! They have fall'n
Each in his field of glory; one in arms,
And one in council—Wolfe upon the lap
Of smiling victory that moment won,
And Chatham heart-sick of his country's shame!
They made us many soldiers. Chatham, still
Consulting England's happiness at home,
Secur'd it by an unforgiving frown,
If any wrong'd her. Wolfe, where'er he fought,
Put so much of his heart into his act,
That his example had a magnet's force,
And all were swift to follow whom all lov'd.
Those suns are set. Oh, rise some other such!
Or all that we have left is empty talk
Of old achievements, and despair of new.

The Task, ii, 1785

357   *Winter*

OH Winter, ruler of th' inverted year,
    Thy scatter'd hair with sleet like ashes fill'd,
Thy breath congeal'd upon thy lips, thy cheeks
Fring'd with a beard made white with other snows

Than those of age, thy forehead wrapt in clouds,
A leafless branch thy sceptre, and thy throne
A sliding car, indebted to no wheels,
But urg'd by storms along its slipp'ry way,
I love thee, all unlovely as thou seem'st,
And dreaded as thou art! Thou hold'st the sun
A pris'ner in the yet undawning east,
Short'ning his journey between morn and noon,
And hurrying him, impatient of his stay,
Down to the rosy west; but kindly still
Compensating his loss with added hours
Of social converse and instructive ease,
And gath'ring, at short notice, in one group
The family dispers'd, and fixing thought,
Not less dispers'd by day-light and its cares.
I crown thee king of intimate delights,
Fire-side enjoyments, home-born happiness,
And all the comforts that the lowly roof
Of undisturb'd retirement, and the hours
Of long uninterrupted ev'ning, know.

The Task, iv, 1785

358 *Evening*

COME, Ev'ning, once again, season of peace;
Return, sweet Ev'ning, and continue long!
Methinks I see thee in the streaky west,
With matron-step slow-moving, while the night
Treads on thy sweeping train; one hand employ'd
In letting fall the curtain of repose
On bird and beast, the other charg'd for man
With sweet oblivion of the cares of day:
Not sumptuously adorn'd, nor needing aid,
Like homely featur'd night, of clust'ring gems;

A star or two, just twinkling on thy brow,
Suffices thee; save that the moon is thine
No less than her's, not worn indeed on high
With ostentatious pageantry, but set
With modest grandeur in thy purple zone,
Resplendent less, but of an ampler round.
Come then, and thou shalt find thy vot'ry calm,
Or make me so. Composure is thy gift:
And whether I devote thy gentle hours
To books, to music, or the poet's toil;
To weaving nets for bird-alluring fruit;
Or turning silken threads round iv'ry reels,
When they command whom man was born to please;
I slight thee not, but make thee welcome still.

The Task, iv, 1785

359   *Winter Scene*

THE night was winter in his roughest mood;
    The morning sharp and clear. But now at noon
Upon the southern side of the slant hills,
And where the woods fence off the northern blast,
The season smiles, resigning all its rage,
And has the warmth of May. The vault is blue
Without a cloud, and white without a speck
The dazzling splendour of the scene below.
Again the harmony comes o'er the vale;
And through the trees I view th' embattled tow'r
Whence all the music. I again perceive
The soothing influence of the wafted strains,
And settle in soft musings as I tread
The walk, still verdant, under oaks and elms,
Whose outspread branches overarch the glade.
The roof, though moveable through all its length

As the wind sways it, has yet well suffic'd,
And, intercepting in their silent fall
The frequent flakes, has kept a path for me.
No noise is here, or none that hinders thought.
The redbreast warbles still, but is content
With slender notes, and more than half suppress'd:
Pleas'd with his solitude, and flitting light
From spray to spray, where'er he rests he shakes
From many a twig the pendent drops of ice,
That tinkle in the wither'd leaves below.
Stillness, accompanied with sounds so soft,
Charms more than silence.   Meditation here
May think down hours to moments.   Here the heart
May give an useful lesson to the head,
And learning wiser grow without his books.
Knowledge and wisdom, far from being one,
Have oft-times no connexion.   Knowledge dwells
In heads replete with thoughts of other men;
Wisdom in minds attentive to their own.
Knowledge, a rude unprofitable mass,
The mere materials with which wisdom builds,
Till smooth'd and squar'd and fitted to its place,
Does but encumber whom it seems t' enrich.
Knowledge is proud that he has learn'd so much;
Wisdom is humble that he knows no more.
Books are not seldom talismans and spells,
By which the magic art of shrewder wits
Holds an unthinking multitude enthrall'd.
Some to the fascination of a name
Surrender judgment, hood-wink'd.   Some the style
Infatuates, and through labyrinths and wilds
Of error leads them by a tune entranc'd.

While sloth seduces more, too weak to bear
The insupportable fatigue of thought,
And swallowing, therefore, without pause or choice,
The total grist unsifted, husks and all.
But trees, and rivulets whose rapid course
Defies the check of winter, haunts of deer,
And sheep-walks populous with bleating lambs,
And lanes in which the primrose ere her time
Peeps through the moss that clothes the hawthorn root,
Deceive no student. Wisdom there, and truth,
Not shy, as in the world, and to be won
By slow solicitation, seize at once
The roving thought, and fix it on themselves.

The Task, vi, 1785

360   *On the Receipt of my Mother's*
Picture out of Norfolk

OH that those lips had language! Life has pass'd
With me but roughly since I heard thee last.
Those lips are thine—thy own sweet smiles I see,
The same that oft in childhood solaced me;
Voice only fails, else how distinct they say,
' Grieve not, my child, chase all thy fears away!'
The meek intelligence of those dear eyes
(Blest be the art that can immortalize,
The art that baffles time's tyrannic claim
To quench it) here shines on me still the same.
    Faithful remembrancer of one so dear,
Oh welcome guest, though unexpected, here!
Who bidd'st me honour with an artless song,
Affectionate, a mother lost so long.
I will obey, not willingly alone,

But gladly, as the precept were her own;
And, while that face renews my filial grief,
Fancy shall weave a charm for my relief—
Shall steep me in Elysian reverie,
A momentary dream, that thou art she.

My mother! when I learn'd that thou wast dead,
Say, wast thou conscious of the tears I shed?
Hover'd thy spirit o'er thy sorrowing son,
Wretch even then, life's journey just begun?
Perhaps thou gav'st me, though unseen, a kiss;
Perhaps a tear, if souls can weep in bliss—
Ah that maternal smile! it answers—Yes.
I heard the bell toll'd on thy burial day,
I saw the hearse that bore thee slow away,
And, turning from my nurs'ry window, drew
A long, long sigh, and wept a last adieu!
But was it such?—It was.—Where thou art gone
Adieus and farewells are a sound unknown.
May I but meet thee on that peaceful shore,
The parting sound shall pass my lips no more!
Thy maidens griev'd themselves at my concern,
Oft gave me promise of a quick return.
What ardently I wish'd, I long believ'd,
And, disappointed still, was still deceiv'd;
By disappointment every day beguil'd,
Dupe of *to-morrow* even from a child.
Thus many a sad to-morrow came and went,
Till, all my stock of infant sorrow spent,
I learn'd at last submission to my lot,
But, though I less deplor'd thee, ne'er forgot.

Where once we dwelt our name is heard no more,
Children not thine have trod my nurs'ry floor

And where the gard'ner Robin, day by day,
Drew me to school along the public way,
Delighted with my bauble coach, and wrapt
In scarlet mantle warm, and velvet capt,
'Tis now become a history little known,
That once we call'd the past'ral house our own.
Short-liv'd possession! but the record fair,
That mem'ry keeps of all thy kindness there,
Still outlives many a storm that has effac'd
A thousand other themes less deeply trac'd.
Thy nightly visits to my chamber made,
That thou might'st know me safe and warmly laid;
Thy morning bounties ere I left my home,
The biscuit, or confectionary plum;
The fragrant waters on my cheeks bestow'd,
By thy own hand, till fresh they shone and glow'd:
All this, and, more endearing still than all,
Thy constant flow of love, that knew no fall,
Ne'er roughen'd by those cataracts and brakes
That humour interpos'd too often makes;
All this still legible in mem'ry's page,
And still to be so, to my latest age,
Adds joy to duty, makes me glad to pay
Such honours to thee as my numbers may;
Perhaps a frail memorial, but sincere,
Not scorn'd in heav'n, though little notic'd here.

Could time, his flight revers'd, restore the hours,
When, playing with thy vesture's tissued flow'rs,
The violet, the pink, and jassamine,
I prick'd them into paper with a pin,
(And thou wast happier than myself the while,
Would'st softly speak, and stroke my head and smile)

Could those few pleasant hours again appear,
Might one wish bring them, would I wish them here?
I would not trust my heart—the dear delight
Seems so to be desir'd, perhaps I might.—
But no—what here we call our life is such,
So little to be lov'd, and thou so much,
That I should ill requite thee to constrain
Thy unbound spirit into bonds again.

    Thou, as a gallant bark from Albion's coast
(The storms all weather'd and the ocean cross'd)
Shoots into port at some well-haven'd isle,
Where spices breathe and brighter seasons smile,
There sits quiescent on the floods that show
Her beauteous form reflected clear below,
While airs impregnated with incense play
Around her, fanning light her streamers gay;
So thou, with sails how swift! hast reach'd the shore
' Where tempests never beat nor billows roar,'
And thy lov'd consort on the dang'rous tide
Of life, long since, has anchor'd at thy side.
But me, scarce hoping to attain that rest,
Always from port withheld, always distress'd—
Me howling winds drive devious, tempest toss'd,
Sails ript, seams op'ning wide, and compass lost,
And day by day some current's thwarting force
Sets me more distant from a prosp'rous course.
But oh the thought, that thou art safe, and he!
That thought is joy, arrive what may to me.
My boast is not that I deduce my birth
From loins enthron'd, and rulers of the earth;
But higher far my proud pretensions rise—
The sons of parents pass'd into the skies.

And now, farewell—time, unrevok'd, has run
His wonted course, yet what I wish'd is done.
By contemplation's help, not sought in vain,
I seem t' have liv'd my childhood o'er again;
To have renew'd the joys that once were mine,
Without the sin of violating thine:
And, while the wings of fancy still are free,
And I can view this mimic shew of thee,
Time has but half succeeded in his theft—
Thyself removed, thy power to soothe me left.

Written 1790 ; Poems, 1798

361 *Sonnet to Mrs. Unwin*

MARY! I want a lyre with other strings;
 Such aid from Heaven as some have feign'd they
   drew!
An eloquence scarce given to mortals, new,
And undebas'd by praise of meaner things!
That, ere through age or woe I shed my wings,
I may record thy worth, with honour due,
In verse as musical as thou art true,—
Verse, that immortalizes whom it sings!
But thou hast little need: there is a book,
By seraphs writ with beams of heav'nly light,
On which the eyes of God not rarely look;
A chronicle of actions just and bright!
 There all thy deeds, my faithful Mary, shine,
 And since thou own'st that praise, I spare thee mine.

Written 1793 ; Life and Letters, 1803

362

To Mary

THE twentieth year is well-nigh past,
Since first our sky was overcast;
Ah would that this might be the last!
                    My Mary!

Thy spirits have a fainter flow,
I see thee daily weaker grow—
'Twas my distress that brought thee low,
                    My Mary!

Thy needles, once a shining store,
For my sake restless heretofore,
Now rust disus'd, and shine no more,
                    My Mary!

For though thou gladly wouldst fulfil
The same kind office for me still,
Thy sight now seconds not thy will,
                    My Mary!

But well thou play'd'st the housewife's part,
And all thy threads with magic art
Have wound themselves about this heart,
                    My Mary!

Thy indistinct expressions seem
Like language utter'd in a dream;
Yet me they charm, whate'er the theme,
                    My Mary!

Thy silver locks, once auburn bright,
Are still more lovely in my sight
Than golden beams of orient light,
                    My Mary!

For could I view nor them nor thee,
What sight worth seeing could I see?
The sun would rise in vain for me,
                    My Mary!

Partakers of thy sad decline,
Thy hands their little force resign;
Yet, gently prest, press gently mine,
                    My Mary!

And then I feel that still I hold
A richer store ten thousandfold
Than misers fancy in their gold,
                    My Mary!

Such feebleness of limbs thou prov'st,
That now at every step thou mov'st
Upheld by two; yet still thou lov'st,
                    My Mary!

And still to love, though prest with ill,
In wintry age to feel no chill,
With me is to be lovely still,
                    My Mary!

But ah! by constant heed I know,
How oft the sadness that I show
Transforms thy smiles to looks of woe,
                    My Mary!

And should my future lot be cast
With much resemblance of the past,
Thy worn-out heart will break at last,
                    My Mary!

Written 1793 ; *Life and Letters*, 1803

363

The Castaway

OBSCUREST night involv'd the sky,
   Th' Atlantic billows roar'd,
When such a destin'd wretch as I,
   Wash'd headlong from on board,
Of friends, of hope, of all bereft,
His floating home for ever left.

No braver chief could Albion boast
   Than he with whom he went,
Nor ever ship left Albion's coast,
   With warmer wishes sent.
He lov'd them both, but both in vain,
Nor him beheld, nor her again.

Not long beneath the whelming brine,
   Expert to swim, he lay;
Nor soon he felt his strength decline,
   Or courage die away;
But wag'd with death a lasting strife,
Supported by despair of life.

He shouted: nor his friends had fail'd
   To check the vessel's course,
But so the furious blast prevail'd,
   That, pitiless perforce,
They left their outcast mate behind,
And scudded still before the wind.

Some succour yet they could afford;
   And, such as storms allow,
The cask, the coop, the floated cord,
   Delay'd not to bestow.
But he (they knew) nor ship, nor shore,
Whate'er they gave, should visit more.

WILLIAM COWPER

Nor, cruel as it seem'd, could he
    Their haste himself condemn,
Aware that flight, in such a sea,
    Alone could rescue them;
Yet bitter felt it still to die
Deserted, and his friends so nigh.

He long survives, who lives an hour
    In ocean, self-upheld:
And so long he, with unspent pow'r,
    His destiny repell'd;
And ever, as the minutes flew,
Entreated help, or cried—Adieu!

At length, his transient respite past,
    His comrades, who before
Had heard his voice in ev'ry blast,
    Could catch the sound no more.
For then, by toil subdued, he drank
The stifling wave, and then he sank.

No poet wept him: but the page
    Of narrative sincere,
That tells his name, his worth, his age,
    Is wet with Anson's tear.
And tears by bards or heroes shed
Alike immortalize the dead.

I therefore purpose not, or dream,
    Descanting on his fate,
To give the melancholy theme
    A more enduring date:
But misery still delights to trace
Its 'semblance in another's case.

WILLIAM COWPER

No voice divine the storm allay'd,
  No light propitious shone;
When, snatch'd from all effectual aid,
  We perish'd, each alone:
But I beneath a rougher sea,
And whelm'd in deeper gulphs than he.

Written 1799 ; Life and Letters, 1803

GEORGE CRABBE

1754–1832

364   *Life*

THINK ye the joys that fill our early day,
  Are the poor prelude to some full repast?
Think you they *promise*?—ah! believe they *pay*;
  The purest ever, they are oft the last.
The jovial swain that yokes the morning team,
  And all the verdure of the field enjoys,
See him, how languid! when the noontide beam
  Plays on his brow, and all his force destroys.
So 'tis with us, when, love and pleasure fled,
  We at the summit of our hill arrive:
Lo! the gay lights of Youth are past—are dead,
  But what still deepening clouds of Care survive!

Written 1779 ; Poetical Works, 1834

365   *Books*

LO! all in Silence, all in Order stand,
  And mighty Folio's first, a lordly Band;
Then Quarto's their well-order'd Ranks maintain,
And light Octavo's fill a spacious Plain;
See yonder, rang'd in more frequented Rows,
An humbler band of Duodecimo's;

While undistinguish'd Trifles swell the Scene,
The last new Play and fritter'd Magazine:
Thus 'tis in Life, where first the Proud, the Great,
In leagu'd Assembly keep their cumbrous State;
Heavy and huge, they fill the World with dread,
Are much admir'd, and are but little read:
The Commons next, a middle Rank are found;
Professions fruitful pour their Offspring round;
Reasoners and Wits are next their place allow'd,
And last, of vulgar Tribes, a countless Crowd.

    First let us view the Form, the Size, the Dress;
For, these the Manners, nay the Mind express;
That Weight of Wood, with leathern Coat o'erlaid,
Those ample Clasps, of solid Metal made;
The close-prest Leaves, unclos'd for many an age,
The dull red Edging of the well-fill'd Page;
On the broad Back the stubborn Ridges roll'd,
Where yet the Title stands in tarnish'd Gold:
These all a sage and labour'd Work proclaim,
A painful candidate for lasting Fame:
No idle Wit, no trifling Verse can lurk
In the deep bosom of that weighty Work;
No playful Thoughts degrade the solemn Style,
Nor one light Sentence claims a transient Smile.

    Hence, in these Times, untouch'd the Pages lie,
And slumber out their Immortality;
They *had* their Day, when, after all his Toil,
His Morning Study, and his Midnight Oil,
At length an Author's ONE great Work appear'd,
By patient Hope and Length of Days, endear'd;
Expecting Nations hail'd it from the Press,
Poetic Friends prefix'd each kind Address;

Princes and Kings receiv'd the pondrous Gift,
And Ladies read the Work, they could not lift.
Fashion, though Folly's Child, and Guide of Fools,
Rules e'en the Wisest, and in Learning rules;
From Crowds and Courts to Wisdom's Seat she goes
And reigns triumphant o'er her Mother's Foes.
For lo! these Fav'rites of the ancient Mode
Lie all neglected like the *Birth-day Ode*;
Ah! needless now this weight of massy Chain,
Safe in themselves, the once-lov'd Works remain;
No Readers now invade their still Retreat,
None try to steal them from their Parent-Seat;
Like antient Beauties, they may now discard
Chains, Bolts, and Locks, and lie without a Guard.

Our patient Fathers trifling Themes laid by,
And roll'd, o'er labour'd Works, th' attentive Eye;
Page after Page, the much-enduring Men
Explor'd the Deeps and Shallows of the Pen;
Till, every former Note and Comment known,
They mark'd the spacious Margin with their own:
Minute Corrections prov'd their studious Care;
The little Index pointing, told us where;
And many an Emendation show'd, the Age
Look'd far beyond the Rubric Title-page.

Our nicer Palates lighter Labours seek,
Cloy'd with a Folio-*Number* once a Week;
Bibles with Cuts and Comments, thus go down;
Ev'n light Voltaire is *number'd* through the Town:
Thus Physic flies abroad and thus the Law,
From men of Study and from men of Straw;
Abstracts, Abridgements, please the fickle Times,
Pamphlets and Plays and Politics and Rhymes:

But though to write be now a Task of Ease,
The Task is hard by manly Arts to please;
When all our Weakness is expos'd to view,
And half our Judges are our Rivals too.

The Library, 1781

366 *Crusty Critics*

WHILE thus, of Power and fancy'd Empire vain,
   With various Thoughts my Mind I entertain;
While Books, my Slaves, with tyrant hand I seize,
Pleas'd with the Pride that will not let them please;
Sudden I find terrific Thoughts arise,
And sympathetic Sorrow fills my Eyes;
For, lo! while yet my Heart admits the Wound,
I see the CRITIC Army rang'd around.—
Foes to our Race! if ever ye have known
A Father's fears for Offspring of your own;—
If ever, smiling o'er a lucky Line,
Ye thought the sudden Sentiment divine,
Then paus'd and doubted, and then, tir'd of doubt,
With rage as sudden dash'd the Stanza out;—
If, after fearing much and pausing long,
Ye ventur'd on the World your labour'd Song,
And from the crusty Critics of those Days,
Implor'd the feeble Tribute of their Praise;
Remember now, the Fears that mov'd you then,
And, spite of Truth, let Mercy guide your Pen.

The Library, 1781

Truth in Poetry

FLED are those times, when, in harmonious strains,
The rustic Poet prais'd his native Plains;
No Shepherds now in smooth alternate verse,
Their Country's beauty or their Nymphs' rehearse;
Yet still for these we frame the tender strain,
Still in our lays fond CORYDONS complain,
And Shepherds boys their amorous pains reveal,
The only pains, alas! they never feel.

On MINCIO's banks, in CÆSAR's bounteous reign,
If TITYRUS found the Golden Age again,
Must sleepy bards the flattering dream prolong,
Mechanic echo's of the Mantuan song?
From truth and nature shall we widely stray,
Where VIRGIL, not where fancy, leads the way?

Yes, thus the Muses sing of happy Swains,
Because the Muses never knew their pains:
They boast their Peasants' pipes; but Peasants now
Resign their pipes and plod behind the plough;
And few amid the rural tribe have time,
To number syllables and play with rhyme;
Save honest DUCK, what son of verse could share
The Poet's rapture and the Peasant's care?
Or the great labours of the Field degrade,
With the new peril of a poorer trade?

From this chief cause these idle praises spring,
That, themes so easy, few forbear to sing;
For no deep thought the trifling subjects ask,
To sing of Shepherds is an easy task;
The happy youth assumes the common strain,
A nymph his mistress and himself a swain;

With no sad scenes he clouds his tuneful prayer,
But all, to look like her, is painted fair.

 I grant indeed that Fields and Flocks have charms,
For him that gazes or for him that farms;
But when amid such pleasing scenes I trace
The poor laborious natives of the place,
And see the mid-day sun, with fervid ray,
On their bare heads and dewy temples play;
While some, with feebler heads and fainter hearts,
Deplore their fortune, yet sustain their parts,
Then shall I dare these real ills to hide,
In tinsel trappings of poetic pride?

 No; cast by Fortune on a frowning coast,
Which neither groves nor happy valleys boast;
Where other cares than those the Muse relates,
And other Shepherds dwell with other mates;
By such examples taught, I paint the Cot,
As truth will paint it and as bards will not.
Nor you, ye Poor, of letter'd scorn complain,
To you the smoothest song is smooth in vain;
O'ercome by labour and bow'd down by time,
Feel you the barren flattery of a rhyme?
Can Poets sooth you, when you pine for bread,
By winding myrtles round your ruin'd shed?
Can their light tales your weighty griefs o'erpower,
Or glad with airy mirth the toilsome hour?

 Lo! where the heath, with withering brake grown o'er,
Lends the light turf that warms the neighbouring poor;
From thence a length of burning sand appears,
Where the thin harvest waves its wither'd ears;
Rank weeds, that every art and care defy,
Reign o'er the land and rob the blighted rye:

There Thistles stretch their prickly arms afar,
And to the ragged infant threaten war;
There Poppies nodding, mock the hope of toil,
There the blue Bugloss paints the sterile soil;
Hardy and high, above the slender sheaf,
The slimy Mallow waves her silky leaf;
O'er the young shoot the Charlock throws a shade,
And clasping Tares cling round the sickly blade;
With mingled tints the rocky coasts abound,
And a sad splendour vainly shines around.

So looks the Nymph whom wretched arts adorn,
Betray'd by Man, then left for Man to scorn;
Whose cheek in vain assumes the mimic rose,
While her sad eyes the troubled breast disclose;
Whose outward splendour is but folly's dress,
Exposing most, when most it gilds distress.

The Village, 1783

368 *The Parish Poor-house*

THEIR'S is yon House that holds the Parish Poor,
Whose walls of mud scarce bear the broken door;
There, where the putrid vapours flagging, play,
And the dull wheel hums doleful through the day;—
There Children dwell who know no Parents' care;
Parents, who know no Children's love, dwell there;
Heart-broken Matrons on their joyless bed,
Forsaken Wives and Mothers never wed;
Dejected Widows with unheeded tears,
And crippled Age with more than childhood-fears;
The Lame, the Blind, and, far the happiest they!
The moping Idiot and the Madman gay.

Here too the Sick their final doom receive,
Here brought amid the scenes of grief, to grieve;
Where the loud groans from some sad chamber flow,
Mixt with the clamours of the crowd below;
Here sorrowing, they each kindred sorrow scan,
And the cold charities of man to man:
Whose laws indeed for ruin'd Age provide,
And strong compulsion plucks the scrap from pride;
But still that scrap is bought with many a sigh,
And pride imbitters what it can't deny.

Say ye, opprest by some fantastic woes,
Some jarring nerve that baffles your repose;
Who press the downy couch, while slaves advance
With timid eye, to read the distant glance;
Who with sad prayers the weary Doctor tease,
To name the nameless ever-new disease;
Who with mock patience dire complaints endure,
Which real pain and that alone can cure;
How would ye bear in real pain to lie,
Despis'd, neglected, left alone to die?
How would ye bear to draw your latest breath,
Where all that's wretched paves the way for death?

Such is that room which one rude beam divides,
And naked rafters form the sloping sides;
Where the vile bands that bind the thatch are seen,
And lath and mud are all that lie between;
Save one dull pane, that, coarsely patch'd, gives way
To the rude tempest, yet excludes the day:
Here, on a matted flock, with dust o'erspread,
The drooping wretch reclines his languid head;
For him no hand the cordial cup applies,
Or wipes the tear that stagnates in his eyes;

No friends with soft discourse his pain beguile,
Or promise hope till sickness wears a smile.

But soon a loud and hasty summons calls,
Shakes the thin roof, and echoes round the walls;
Anon, a Figure enters, quaintly neat,
All pride and business, bustle and conceit;
With looks unalter'd by these scenes of woe,
With speed that, entering, speaks his haste to go;
He bids the gazing throng around him fly,
And carries Fate and Physic in his eye;
A potent Quack, long vers'd in human ills,
Who first insults the victim whom he kills;
Whose murd'rous hand a drowsy Bench protect,
And whose most tender mercy is neglect.

Paid by the Parish for attendance here,
He wears contempt upon his sapient sneer;
In haste he seeks the bed where Misery lies,
Impatience mark'd in his averted eyes;
And, some habitual queries hurried o'er,
Without reply, he rushes on the door;
His drooping Patient, long inur'd to pain,
And long unheeded, knows remonstrance vain;
He ceases now the feeble help to crave
Of Man; and silent sinks into the grave.

But ere his death some pious doubts arise,
Some simple fears which ' bold bad ' men despise;
Fain would he ask the Parish Priest to prove
His title certain to the Joys above;
For this he sends the murmuring Nurse, who calls
The holy Stranger to these dismal walls;
And doth not he, the pious man, appear,
He, ' passing rich with forty pounds a year? '

Ah! no, a Shepherd of a different stock,
And far unlike him, feeds this little flock;
A jovial youth, who thinks his Sunday's task,
As much as GOD or Man can fairly ask;
The rest he gives to loves and labours light,
To Fields the morning and to Feasts the night;
None better skill'd the noisy pack to guide,
To urge their chace, to cheer them or to chide;
A Sportsman keen, he shoots through half the day,
And skill'd at Whist, devotes the night to play;
Then, while such honours bloom around his head,
Shall he sit sadly by the Sick Man's bed
To raise the hope he feels not, or with zeal
To combat fears that ev'n the pious feel?
Now once again the gloomy scene explore,
Less gloomy now; the bitter hour is o'er,
The Man of many Sorrows sighs no more.—
Up yonder hill, behold how sadly slow
The Bier moves winding from the vale below;
There lie the happy Dead from trouble free,
And the glad Parish pays the frugal fee:
No more, O Death! thy victim starts to hear
Churchwarden stern, or kingly Overseer;
No more the Farmer claims his humble bow,
Thou art his lord, the best of tyrants thou!

Now to the Church behold the Mourners come,
Sedately torpid and devoutly dumb;
The Village Children now their games suspend,
To see the Bier that bears their antient Friend;
For he was one in all their idle sport,
And like a monarch rul'd their little court;
The pliant Bow he form'd, the flying Ball,

603

GEORGE CRABBE

The Bat, the Wicket, were his labours all;
Him now they follow to his grave, and stand
Silent and sad, and gazing, hand in hand;
While bending low, their eager eyes explore
The mingled relicks of the Parish Poor:
The bell tolls late, the moping owl flies round,
Fear marks the flight and magnifies the sound;
The busy Priest, detain'd by weightier care,
Defers his duty till the day of prayer;
And waiting long, the crowd retire distrest,
To think a Poor Man's bones should lie unblest.

The Village, 1783

WILLIAM HAYLEY

1745–1820

369 *A Card of Invitation to Mr. Gibbon,*
at Brighthelmstone. 1781

AN English Sparrow, pert and free,
Who chirps beneath his native tree,
Hearing the Roman Eagle's near,
And feeling more respect than fear,
Thus, with united love and awe,
Invites him to his shed of straw.
Tho' he is but a twittering Sparrow,
The field he hops in rather narrow,
When nobler plumes attract his view
He ever pays them homage due,
And looks with reverential wonder
On him whose talons bear the thunder;

WILLIAM HAYLEY

Nor could the Jack-daws e'er inveigle
His voice to vilify the Eagle,
Tho', issuing from those holy tow'rs
In which they build their warmest bow'rs,
Their Sovereign's haunt they slily search,
In hopes to find him on his perch
(For PINDAR says, beside his God
The thunder-bearing Bird will nod)
Then, peeping round his still retreat,
They pick from underneath his feet
Some molted feather he lets fall,
And swear he cannot fly at all.—
Lord of the sky! whose pounce can tear
These croakers, that infest the air,
Trust him, the Sparrow loves to sing
The praise of thy imperial wing!
He thinks thou'lt deem him, on his word,
An honest, tho' familiar Bird;
And hopes thou soon wilt condescend
To look upon thy little friend;
That he may boast around his grove
A visit from the BIRD OF JOVE.

Poems and Plays, 1785

1745-1833

370   *Conversation*

O'ER books the mind inactive lies,
  Books, the Mind's food, not exercise!
Her vigorous wing she scarcely feels,
'Till use the latent strength reveals;
Her slumbering energies call'd forth,
She springs, she mounts, she feels her worth;
And, at her new-found powers elated,
Thinks them not rous'd, but new created.

  Enlighten'd spirits! you, who know
What charms from polish'd converse flow,
Speak, for you can, the pure delight
When kindling sympathies unite;
When correspondent tastes impart
Communion sweet from heart to heart;
You ne'er the cold gradations need
Which vulgar souls to union lead;
No dry discussion to unfold
The meaning caught ere well 'tis told:
In taste, in learning, wit, or science,
Still kindled souls demand alliance;
Each in the other joys to find
The image answering to his mind.
But sparks electric only strike
On souls electrical alike;
The flash of Intellect expires,
Unless it meet congenial fires:
The language to th' Elect alone
Is, like the Mason's mystery, known;

HANNAH MORE

In vain th' unerring *sign* is made
To him who is not of the *Trade*.
What lively pleasure to divine,
The thought implied, the hinted line,
To feel Allusion's artful force,
And trace the image to it's source!
Quick Memory blends her scatter'd rays,
'Till Fancy kindles at the blaze;
The works of ages start to view,
And ancient Wit elicits new.

The Bas Bleu, written 1784 ; *Works*, i, 1801

CHARLOTTE SMITH

1749–1806

371   *Sonnet*

Written at the Close of Spring

THE garlands fade that Spring so lately wove,
    Each simple flower, which she had nurs'd in dew,
Anemonies that spangled every grove,
    The primrose wan, and hare-bell, mildly blue.
No more shall violets linger in the dell,
    Or purple orchis variegate the plain,
Till spring again shall call forth every bell,
    And dress with humid hands, her wreaths again.
Ah! poor humanity! so frail, so fair,
    Are the fond visions of thy early day,
Till tyrant passion, and corrosive care,
    Bid all thy fairy colours fade away!
Another May new buds and flowers shall bring;
Ah! why has happiness—no second spring?

The European Magazine, December 1782

1762–1788

372   *Sonnet*

To Oxford

OXFORD, since late I left thy peaceful shore,
　　Much I regret thy domes with turrets crown'd,
　Thy crested walls with twining ivy bound,
　Thy Gothic fanes, dim isles, and cloysters hoar,
And treasur'd rolls of Wisdom's ancient lore;
　　Nor less thy varying bells, which hourly sound
　　In pensive chime, or ring in lively round,
　　Or toll in the slow Curfeu's solemn roar;
Much too thy moonlight walks, and musings grave
　　Mid silent shades of high-embowering trees,
　　And much thy Sister-Streams, whose willows wave
In whispering cadence to the evening breeze;
　　But most those Friends, whose much-lov'd converse gave
　　Thy gentle charms a tenfold power to please.

Sonnets and Miscellaneous Poems, 1789

373   *Sonnet*

To Valclusa

WHAT tho', VALCLUSA, the fond Bard be fled,
　　That woo'd his Fair in thy sequester'd bowers,
Long lov'd her living, long bemoan'd her dead,
　　And hung her visionary shrine with flowers!
What tho' no more he teach thy shades to mourn
　　The hapless chances that to Love belong,
As erst, when drooping o'er her turf forlorn
　　He charm'd wild Echo with his plaintive song!
Yet still, enamour'd of the tender tale,
　　Pale PASSION haunts thy grove's romantic gloom,

Yet still soft Music breathes in every gale,
    Still undecay'd the Fairy-garlands bloom,
Still heavenly incense fills each fragrant vale,
Still PETRARCH's GENIUS weeps o'er LAURA's tomb.
Sonnets and Miscellaneous Poems, 1789

374   *Sonnet*

COULD then the Babes from yon unshelter'd cot
    Implore thy passing charity in vain?
Too thoughtless Youth! what tho' thy happier lot
    Insult their life of poverty and pain!
What tho' their Maker doom'd them thus forlorn
    To brook the mockery of the taunting throng,
Beneath th' Oppressor's iron scourge to mourn,
    To mourn, but not to murmur at his wrong!
Yet when their last late evening shall decline,
    Their evening chearful, tho' their day distrest,
A Hope perhaps more heavenly-bright than thine,
    A Grace by thee unsought, and unpossest,
A Faith more fix'd, a Rapture more divine
    Shall gild their passage to eternal Rest.
Sonnets and Miscellaneous Poems, 1789

375   *Sonnet*

Suppos'd to be written at Lemnos

ON this lone Isle, whose rugged rocks affright
    The cautious pilot, ten revolving years
Great Pæan's Son, unwonted erst to tears,
Wept o'er his wound: alike each rolling light
Of heaven he watch'd, and blam'd it's lingering flight,
    By day the sea-mew screaming round his cave
    Drove slumber from his eyes, the chiding wave,
And savage howlings chas'd his dreams by night.

HOPE still was his: in each low breeze, that sigh'd
  Thro' his rude grot, he heard a coming oar,
  In each white cloud a coming sail he spied;
Nor seldom listen'd to the fancied roar
  Of Oeta's torrents, or the hoarser tide
  That parts fam'd Trachis from th' Euboic shore.

Sonnets and Miscellaneous Poems, 1789

376   *The Maniac*

THO' Grief had nipp'd her early bloom,
  Young JULIA still was fair:
The rose indeed had left her cheek,
  The lily still was there.

Tho' of all other actions past
  Her memory bore no part,
The dear remembrance of her love
  Still linger'd in her heart.

Long in that heart had reign'd alone
  A swain of equal youth,
Of equal beauty too with her's,
  But not of equal truth.

Whole years her yielding breast he sooth'd
  With passion's tender tale;
Till Avarice call'd him from her arms
  O'er the wide seas to sail.

With many a vow of quick return
  He cross'd the briny tide,
But when a foreign shore he reach'd,
  Soon found a wealthier bride.

THOMAS RUSSELL

Poor JULIA sicken'd at the news,
    Yet never told her pain,
Long on her secret soul it prey'd,
    And turn'd at last her brain.

From Brethren, Parents, house, and home
    The mourning MANIAC fled;
The sky was all her roof by day,
    A bank by night her bed.

When thirst and hunger griev'd her most,
    If any food she took,
It was the berry from the thorn,
    The water from the brook.

Now hurrying o'er the heath she hied,
    Now wander'd thro' the wood,
Now o'er the precipice she peep'd,
    Now stood and eyed the flood.

From every hedge a flower she pluck'd,
    And moss from every stone,
To make a garland for her Love,
    Yet left it still undone.

Still, as she rambled, was she wont
    To trill a plaintive song,
'Twas wild, and full of fancies vain,
    Yet suited well her wrong.

All loose, yet lovely, to the wind
    Her golden tresses flew,
And now alas! with heat were scorch'd,
    And now were drench'd with dew.

THOMAS RUSSELL

No Friend was left the tears to wipe
  That dimm'd her radiant eyes,
Yet oft their beams like those would shine
  That gleam from watry skies.

Oft too a smile, but not of joy,
  Play'd on her brow o'ercast;
It was the faint cold smile of Spring,
  Ere Winter yet is past.

Those sorrows, which her tongue conceal'd,
  Her broken sighs confest;
Her cloak was too much torn to hide
  The throbbings of her breast.

From all, who near her chanc'd to stray,
  With wild affright she ran;
Each voice that reach'd her scar'd her breast,
  But most the voice of Man.

To me alone, when oft we met,
  Her ear she would incline,
And with me weep, for well she knew
  Her woes resembled mine.

One morn I sought her; but too late—
  Her wound had bled so sore—
God rest thy Spirit, gentle Maid!
  Thou'rt gone for evermore!

Sonnets and Miscellaneous Poems, 1789

WILLIAM LISLE BOWLES

1762-1850

377 Sonnet

July 18, 1787

O TIME! who know'st a lenient hand to lay
  Softest on sorrow's wounds, and slowly thence,
  (Lulling to sad repose the weary sense)
The faint pang stealest unperceiv'd away;
  On Thee I rest my only hope at last,
And think, when thou hast dried the bitter tear
That flows in vain o'er all my soul held dear,
  I may look back on many a sorrow past,
And meet life's peaceful evening with a smile—
  As some lone bird, at day's departing hour,
  Sings in the sunbeam of the transient shower,
Forgetful, tho' its wings are wet the while:—
  Yet ah! how much must that poor heart endure,
  Which hopes from thee, and thee alone, a cure!

Sonnets, 1789

378 Sonnet

At Dover Cliffs

July 20, 1787

ON these white cliffs, that calm above the flood
  Uplift their shadowing heads, and, at their feet,
  Scarce hear the surge that has for ages beat,
Sure many a lonely wanderer has stood;
  And, whilst the lifted murmur met his ear,
  And o'er the distant billows the still Eve

Sail'd slow, has thought of all his heart must leave
To-morrow,—of the friends he lov'd most dear,—
    Of social scenes, from which he wept to part:—
But if, like me, he knew how fruitless all
    · The thoughts that would full fain the past recall,
Soon would he quell the risings of his heart,
    And brave the wild winds and unhearing tide,
    The World his country, and his GOD his guide.

Sonnets, 1789

379   *Sonnet*

At Ostend

July 22, 1787

HOW sweet the tuneful bells' responsive peal!
    As when, at opening morn, the fragrant breeze
Breathes on the trembling sense of wan disease,
So piercing to my heart their force I feel!
    And hark! with lessening cadence now they fall,
And now, along the white and level tide,
They fling their melancholy musick wide;
    Bidding me many a tender thought recall
Of summer-days, and those delightful years
    When by my native streams, in life's fair prime,
    The mournful magic of their mingling chime
First wak'd my wond'ring childhood into tears!
    But seeming now, when all those days are o'er,
    The sounds of joy, once heard, and heard no more.

Sonnets, 1789

HELEN MARIA WILLIAMS

1762–1827

380 *To Hope*

OH, ever skill'd to wear the form we love!
To bid the shapes of fear and grief depart,
Come, gentle Hope! with one gay smile remove
The lasting sadness of an aching heart.
Thy voice, benign enchantress! let me hear;
Say that for me some pleasures yet shall bloom,
That fancy's radiance, friendship's precious tear,
Shall soften, or shall chase, misfortune's gloom.
But come not glowing in the dazzling ray
Which once with dear illusions charm'd my eye;
Oh, strew no more, sweet flatterer! on my way
The flowers I fondly thought too bright to die:
Visions less fair will sooth my pensive breast,
That asks not happiness, but longs for rest.

Julia, a Novel, 1790

WILLIAM BLAKE

1757–1827

381 *To Spring*

O THOU with dewy locks, who lookest down
Thro' the clear windows of the morning, turn
Thine angel eyes upon our western isle,
Which in full choir hails thy approach, O Spring!

The hills tell each other, and the list'ning
Vallies hear; all our longing eyes are turned
Up to thy bright pavillions: issue forth,
And let thy holy feet visit our clime.

615

Come o'er the eastern hills, and let our winds
Kiss thy perfumèd garments; let us taste
Thy morn and evening breath; scatter thy pearls
Upon our love-sick land that mourns for thee.

O deck her forth with thy fair fingers; pour
Thy soft kisses on her bosom; and put
Thy golden crown upon her languish'd head,
Whose modest tresses were bound up for thee!

Poetical Sketches, 1783

382 *Song*

HOW sweet I roam'd from field to field
And tasted all the summer's pride,
'Till I the prince of love beheld
Who in the sunny beams did glide!

He shew'd me lilies for my hair,
And blushing roses for my brow;
He led me through his gardens fair
Where all his golden pleasures grow.

With sweet May dews my wings were wet,
And Phoebus fir'd my vocal rage;
He caught me in his silken net,
And shut me in his golden cage.

He loves to sit and hear me sing,
Then, laughing, sports and plays with me;
Then stretches out my golden wing,
And mocks my loss of liberty.

Poetical Sketches, 1783

383 *Song*

MY silks and fine array,
 My smiles and languish'd air,
By love are driv'n away;
And mournful lean Despair
Brings me yew to deck my grave:
Such end true lovers have.

His face is fair as heav'n
When springing buds unfold
O why to him was 't giv'n
Whose heart is wintry cold?
His breast is love's all worship'd tomb,
Where all love's pilgrims come.

Bring me an axe and spade,
Bring me a winding sheet;
When I my grave have made
Let winds and tempests beat:
Then down I'll lie as cold as clay.
True love doth pass away!

Poetical Sketches, 1783

384 *To the Muses*

WHETHER on Ida's shady brow,
 Or in the chambers of the East,
The chambers of the sun, that now
From antient melody have ceas'd;

Whether in Heav'n ye wander fair,
Or the green corners of the earth,
Or the blue regions of the air
Where the melodious winds have birth

Whether on chrystal rocks ye rove,
Beneath the bosom of the sea
Wand'ring in many a coral grove,
Fair Nine, forsaking Poetry!

How have you left the antient love
That bards of old enjoy'd in you!
The languid strings do scarcely move!
The sound is forc'd, the notes are few!

Poetical Sketches, 1783

385   *Piping down the Valleys wild*

PIPING down the valleys wild,
  Piping songs of pleasant glee,
On a cloud I saw a child,
And he laughing said to me:

' Pipe a song about a Lamb! '
So I piped with merry chear.
' Piper, pipe that song again; '
So I piped: he wept to hear.

' Drop thy pipe, thy happy pipe;
Sing thy songs of happy chear: '
So I sang the same again,
While he wept with joy to hear.

' Piper, sit thee down and write
In a book, that all may read.'
So he vanish'd from my sight,
And I pluck'd a hollow reed,

And I made a rural pen,
And I stain'd the water clear,
And I wrote my happy songs
Every child may joy to hear.

Songs of Innocence, 1789

386   *The Echoing Green*

THE Sun does arise,
   And make happy the skies;
The merry bells ring
To welcome the Spring;
The sky lark and thrush,
The birds of the bush,
Sing louder around
To the bells' chearful sound,
While our sports shall be seen
On the Ecchoing Green.

Old John, with white hair,
Does laugh away care,
Sitting under the oak,
Among the old folk.
They laugh at our play,
And soon they all say:
' Such, such were the joys
When we all, girls and boys,
In our youth time were seen
On the Ecchoing Green.'

Till the little ones, weary,
No more can be merry;
The sun does descend,
And our sports have an end.

Round the laps of their mothers
Many sisters and brothers,
Like birds in their nest,
Are ready for rest,
And sport no more seen
On the darkening Green.

Songs of Innocence, 1789

387

The Lamb

LITTLE Lamb, who made thee?
  Dost thou know who made thee?
Gave thee life, and bid thee feed,
By the stream and o'er the mead;
Gave thee clothing of delight,
Softest clothing, woolly, bright;
Gave thee such a tender voice,
Making all the vales rejoice?
    Little Lamb, who made thee?
    Dost thou know who made thee?

    Little Lamb, I'll tell thee,
    Little Lamb, I'll tell thee:
He is callèd by thy name,
For he calls himself a Lamb.
He is meek, and he is mild;
He became a little child.
I a child, and thou a lamb,
We are callèd by his name.
    Little Lamb, God bless thee!
    Little Lamb, God bless thee!

Songs of Innocence, 1789

WILLIAM BLAKE

388 *The Shepherd*

HOW sweet is the Shepherd's sweet lot!
From the morn to the evening he strays;
He shall follow his sheep all the day,
And his tongue shall be fillèd with praise.

For he hears the lamb's innocent call,
And he hears the ewe's tender reply;
He is watchful while they are in peace,
For they know when their Shepherd is nigh.

Songs of Innocence, 1789

389 *The Little Black Boy*

MY mother bore me in the southern wild,
And I am black, but O my soul is white
White as an angel is the English child,
But I am black, as if bereav'd of light.

My mother taught me underneath a tree,
And, sitting down before the heat of day,
She took me on her lap and kissèd me,
And, pointing to the east, began to say:

' Look on the rising sun,—there God does live,
And gives his light, and gives his heat away;
And flowers and trees and beasts and men receive
Comfort in morning, joy in the noon day.

' And we are put on earth a little space,
That we may learn to bear the beams of love;
And these black bodies and this sun-burnt face
Is but a cloud, and like a shady grove.

621

' For when our souls have learn'd the heat to bear,
The cloud will vanish, we shall hear his voice,
Saying: " come out from the grove, my love and care,
And round my golden tent like lambs rejoice." '

Thus did my mother say, and kissèd me;
And thus I say to little English boy.
When I from black, and he from white cloud free,
And round the tent of God like lambs we joy,

I'll shade him from the heat, till he can bear
To lean in joy upon our father's knee;
And then I'll stand and stroke his silver hair,
And be like him, and he will then love me.

Songs of Innocence, 1789

390   Nurse's Song

WHEN the voices of children are heard on the green,
    And laughing is heard on the hill,
My heart is at rest within my breast,
And everything else is still.

' Then come home, my children, the sun is gone down,
And the dews of night arise;
Come, come, leave off play, and let us away
Till the morning appears in the skies.'

' No, no, let us play, for it is yet day,
And we cannot go to sleep;
Besides, in the sky the little birds fly,
And the hills are all cover'd with sheep.'

' Well, well, go and play till the light fades away,
And then go home to bed.'
The little ones leapèd and shoutèd and laugh'd
And all the hills ecchoèd.

Songs of Innocence, 1789

391 *Holy Thursday*

'TWAS on a Holy Thursday, their innocent faces clean,
The children walking two & two, in red & blue & green,
Grey headed beadles walk'd before, with wands as white as
snow,
Till into the high dome of Paul's they like Thames' waters
flow.

O what a multitude they seem'd, these flowers of London
town!
Seated in companies, they sit with radiance all their own.
The hum of multitudes was there, but multitudes of lambs,
Thousands of little boys & girls raising their innocent hands.

Now like a mighty wind they raise to heaven the voice of
song,
Or like harmonious thunderings the seats of heaven among.
Beneath them sit the agèd men, wise guardians of the poor;
Then cherish pity, lest you drive an angel from your door.

Songs of Innocence, 1789

392 *The Divine Image*

TO Mercy, Pity, Peace, and Love
All pray in their distress;
And to these virtues of delight
Return their thankfulness.

For Mercy, Pity, Peace, and Love
Is God, our father dear,
And Mercy, Pity, Peace, and Love
Is Man, his child and care.

For Mercy has a human heart,
Pity a human face,
And Love, the human form divine,
And Peace, the human dress.

Then every man, of every clime,
That prays in his distress,
Prays to the human form divine,
Love, Mercy, Pity, Peace.

And all must love the human form,
In heathen, turk, or jew;
Where Mercy, Love, and Pity dwell,
There God is dwelling too.

Songs of Innocence, 1789

393 *Night*

THE sun descending in the west,
  The evening star does shine;
The birds are silent in their nest,
  And I must seek for mine.
    The moon, like a flower,
    In heaven's high bower,
      With silent delight
      Sits and smiles on the night.

Farewell, green fields and happy groves,
  Where flocks have took delight.
Where lambs have nibbled, silent moves
  The feet of angels bright;

Unseen they pour blessing,
And joy without ceasing,
On each bud and blossom,
And each sleeping bosom.

They look in every thoughtless nest,
Where birds are cover'd warm;
They visit caves of every beast,
To keep them all from harm.
If they see any weeping
That should have been sleeping,
They pour sleep on their head,
And sit down by their bed.

When wolves and tygers howl for prey,
They pitying stand and weep;
Seeking to drive their thirst away,
And keep them from the sheep.
But if they rush dreadful,
The angels, most heedful,
Receive each mild spirit,
New worlds to inherit.

And there the lion's ruddy eyes
Shall flow with tears of gold,
And pitying the tender cries,
And walking round the fold,
Saying ' wrath, by his meekness,
And, by his health, sickness
Is driven away
From our immortal day.

' And now beside thee, bleating lamb,
I can lie down and sleep;
Or think on him who bore thy name,
Graze after thee and weep.
For, wash'd in life's river,
My bright mane for ever
Shall shine like the gold
As I guard o'er the fold.'

Songs of Innocence, 1789

394   *Hear the Voice of the Bard*

HEAR the voice of the Bard!
Who Present, Past, & Future, sees;
Whose ears have heard
The Holy Word
That walk'd among the ancient trees,

Calling the lapsèd Soul,
And weeping in the evening dew;
That might controll
The starry pole,
And fallen fallen light renew!

' O Earth, O Earth, return!
Arise from out the dewy grass;
Night is worn,
And the morn
Rises from the slumberous mass.

' Turn away no more;
Why wilt thou turn away?
The starry floor,
The wat'ry shore,
Is giv'n thee till the break of day.'

Songs of Experience, 1794

WILLIAM BLAKE

395 *The Tiger*

TYGER! Tyger! burning bright
  In the forests of the night,
What immortal hand or eye
Could frame thy fearful symmetry?

In what distant deeps or skies
Burnt the fire of thine eyes?
On what wings dare he aspire?
What the hand dare seize the fire,

And what shoulder, and what art,
Could twist the sinews of thy heart?
And when thy heart began to beat,
What dread hand? and what dread feet?

What the hammer? what the chain?
In what furnace was thy brain?
What the anvil? what dread grasp
Dare its deadly terrors clasp?

When the stars threw down their spears,
And water'd heaven with their tears,
Did he smile his work to see?
Did he who made the Lamb make thee?

Tyger! Tyger! burning bright
In the forests of the night,
What immortal hand or eye,
Dare frame thy fearful symmetry?

Songs of Experience, 1794

396 *The Clod and the Pebble*

' LOVE seeketh not Itself to please,
      Nor for itself hath any care,
But for another gives its ease,
And builds a Heaven in Hell's despair.

So sung a little Clod of Clay,
Trodden with the cattle's feet,
But a Pebble of the brook
Warbled out these metres meet:

' Love seeketh only Self to please,
To bind another to Its delight,
Joys in another's loss of ease,
And builds a Hell in Heaven's despite.'

Songs of Experience, 1794

397 *Ah! Sun-Flower*

AH, Sun-flower! weary of time,
      Who countest the steps of the Sun;
Seeking after that sweet golden clime,
Where the traveller's journey is done;

Where the Youth pined away with desire,
And the pale Virgin shrouded in snow,
Arise from their graves, and aspire
Where my Sun-flower wishes to go.

Songs of Experience, 1794

398 *Never seek to tell thy love*

NEVER seek to tell thy love,
      Love that never told can be;
For the gentle wind does move
Silently, invisibly.

I told my love, I told my love,
I told her all my heart;
Trembling, cold, in ghastly fears,
Ah! she doth depart.

Soon as she was gone from me,
A traveller came by,
Silently, invisibly:
He took her with a sigh.

Written about 1793

399 *A Cradle Song*

SLEEP! Sleep! beauty bright,
Dreaming o'er the joys of night;
Sleep! Sleep! in thy sleep
Little sorrows sit & weep.

Sweet Babe, in thy face
Soft desires I can trace,
Secret joys & secret smiles,
Little pretty infant wiles.

As thy softest limbs I feel,
Smiles as of the morning steal
O'er thy cheek, & o'er thy breast
Where thy little heart does rest.

O! the cunning wiles that creep
In thy little heart asleep.
When thy little heart does wake
Then the dreadful lightnings break,

From thy cheek & from thy eye,
O'er the youthful harvests nigh.
Infant wiles & infant smiles
Heaven & Earth of peace beguiles.

Written about 1793

ROBERT BURNS

1759–1796

400 *Epistle to James Smith*

DEAR Smith, the sleest, paukie thief,
  That e'er attempted stealth or rief,
Ye surely hae some warlock-breef
            Owre human hearts;
For ne'er a bosom yet was prief
            Against your arts.

For me, I swear by sun an' moon,
And ev'ry star that blinks aboon,
Ye've cost me twenty pair o' shoon
            Just gaun to see you;
And ev'ry ither pair that's done,
            Mair taen I'm wi' you.

That auld capricious carlin, Nature,
To mak amends for scrimpit stature,
She's turn'd you off, a human creature
            On her *first* plan,
And in her freaks, on ev'ry feature,
            She's wrote, *the Man.*

sleest] slyest   paukie] artful   rief] plunder   warlock]
wizard   prief] proof   gaun] going   taen] taken   carlin]
old woman   scrimpit] stinted

ROBERT BURNS

Just now I've taen the fit o' rhyme,
My barmie noddle's working prime,
My fancy yerkit up sublime
        Wi' hasty summon:
Hae ye a leisure-moment's time
          To hear what's comin?

Some rhyme a neebor's name to lash;
Some rhyme (vain thought!) for needfu' cash;
Some rhyme to court the countra clash,
        An' raise a din;
For me, an *aim* I never fash;
          I rhyme for fun.

The star that rules my luckless lot,
Has fated me the russet coat,
An' damn'd my fortune to the groat;
        But in requit,
Has blest me wi' a random shot
          O' countra wit.

This while my notion's taen a sklent,
To try my fate in guid, black *prent*;
But still the mair I'm that way bent,
        Something cries, ' Hoolie!
' I red you, honest man, tak tent!
          ' Ye'll shaw your folly.

There's ither poets, much your betters,
' Far seen in *Greek*, deep men o' letters,

barmie] fermenting   noddle] head   clash] talk
fash] trouble about   sklent] slant, turn   hoolie] gently
red] advise   tak tent] take care

' Hae thought they had ensur'd their debtors,
   ' A' future ages;
' Now moths deform in shapeless tatters,
   ' Their unknown pages.'

Then farewel hopes o' laurel-boughs,
To garland my poetic brows!
Henceforth I'll rove where busy ploughs
   Are whistling thrang,
An' teach the lanely heights an' howes
   My rustic sang,

I'll wander on with tentless heed
How never-halting moments speed,
Till fate shall snap the brittle thread;
   Then, all unknown,
I'll lay me with th' inglorious dead,
   Forgot and gone!

But why o' Death begin a tale?
Just now we're living sound and hale;
Then top and maintop croud the sail,
   Heave *Care* o'er-side
And large, before Enjoyment's gale,
   Let 's tak the tide.

This life, sae far's I understand,
Is a' enchanted fairy land,
Where Pleasure is the Magic Wand,
   That, wielded right,
Maks Hours like Minutes, hand in hand,
   Dance by fu' light.

thrang] thronged, in plenty   howes] hollows

ROBERT BURNS

The magic-wand then let us wield;
For, ance that five-an'-forty's speel'd,
See crazy, weary, joyless Eild,
                    Wi' wrinkl'd face,
Comes hostin, hirplin owre the field,
                    Wi' creepin pace.

When ance *life's day* draws near the gloamin,
Then fareweel vacant careless roamin;
An' fareweel chearfu' tankards foamin,
                    An' social noise;
An' fareweel dear, deluding *woman*,
                    The joy of joys!

O Life! how pleasant in thy morning,
Young Fancy's rays the hills adorning!
Cold-pausing Caution's lesson scorning,
                    We frisk away,
Like school-boys, at th' expected warning,
                    To joy and play.

We wander there, we wander here,
We eye the rose upon the brier,
Unmindful that the thorn is near,
                    Among the leaves;
And tho' the puny wound appear,
                    Short while it grieves.

Some, lucky, find a flow'ry spot,
For which they never toil'd nor swat;

speel'd] climbed   Eild] Old Age   hostin] coughing
hirplin] creeping   gloamin] twilight   swat] sweated

633

They drink the sweet and eat the fat,
            But care or pain;
And, haply, eye the barren hut
            With high disdain.

  With steady aim, some Fortune chase;
Keen hope does ev'ry sinew brace;
Thro' fair, thro' foul, they urge the race,
            And seize the prey:
Then canie, in some cozie place,
            They close the *day*.

  And others, like your humble servant,
Poor wights! nae rules nor roads observin;
To right or left, eternal swervin,
            They zig zag on;
Till curst with age, obscure an' starvin,
            They aften groan.

  Alas! what bitter toil an' straining—
But truce with peevish, poor complaining!
Is Fortune's fickle *Luna* waning?
            E'en let her gang!
Beneath what light she has remaining,
            Let's sing our sang.

  My pen I here fling to the door,
And kneel, ' Ye Pow'rs! ' and warm implore,
' Tho' I should wander *Terra* o'er,
            ' In all her climes,
' Grant me but this, I ask no more,
            ' Ay rowth o' rhymes.

        rowth] plenty

' Gie dreeping roasts to countra **Lairds,**
' Till icicles hing frae their beards;
' Gie fine braw claes to fine Life-guards,
    ' And Maids of Honor;
' And yill an' whisky gie to Cairds,
    ' Until they sconner.

 ' A Title, *Dempster* merits it;
' A Garter gie to *Willie Pitt*;
' Gie wealth to some be-ledger'd Cit,
    ' In cent. per cent.
' But give me real, sterling Wit,
    ' And I'm content.

 ' While Ye are pleas'd to keep me hale,
' I'll sit down o'er my scanty meal,
' Be't *water-brose,* or *muslin-kail,*
    ' Wi' chearfu' face,
' As lang's the Muses dinna fail
    ' To say the grace.'

An anxious e'e I never throws
Behint my lug, or by my nose;
I jouk beneath Misfortune's blows
    As weel's I may;
Sworn foe to Sorrow, Care, and Prose,
    I rhyme away.

O ye douce folk, that live by rule,
Grave, tideless-blooded, calm and cool,

claes] clothes yill] ale cairds] tinkers sconner] flinch,
feel disgust   muslin-kail] broth made of water, barley, and
greens lug] ear jouk] duck

Compar'd wi' you—O fool! fool! fool!
    How much unlike!
Your hearts are just a standing pool,
    Your lives, a dyke!

 Nae hair-brain'd, sentimental traces
In your unletter'd, nameless faces!
In *arioso* trills and graces
    Ye never stray,
But *gravissimo,* solemn basses
    Ye hum away.

 Ye are sae *grave,* nae doubt ye're *wise*;
Nae ferly tho' ye do despise
The hairum-scairum, ram-stam boys,
    The rattlin squad:
I see you upward cast your eyes—
    —Ye ken the road.—

 Whilst I—but I shall haud me there—
Wi' you I'll scarce gang *ony where*—
Then, *Jamie,* I shall say nae mair,
    But quat my sang.
Content wi' *You* to mak a pair,
    Whare'er I gang.

        Poems (Kilmarnock), 1786

ferly] wonder   haud] hold   quat] quit

401 *Halloween* *

UPON that night, when Fairies light,
　　On *Cassilis Downans*† dance,
Or owre the lays, in splendid blaze,
　　On sprightly coursers prance;
Or for *Colean* the rout is ta'en,
　　Beneath the moon's pale beams;
There, up the *Cove*,‡ to stray an' rove
　　Amang the rocks an' streams
　　　　　　To sport that night:

Amang the bony, winding banks,
　　Where *Doon* rins, wimplin, clear,
Where BRUCE § ance rul'd the martial ranks,
　　An' shook his *Carrick* spear,
Some merry, friendly, countra folks,
　　Together did convene,
To *burn* their nits, an' *pou* their stocks,
　　An' haud their *Halloween*
　　　　　　Fu' blythe that night.

---

* Is thought to be a night when Witches, Devils, and other mischief-making beings, are all abroad on their baneful, midnight errands : particularly, those aerial people, the Fairies, are said, on that night, to hold a grand Anniversary.

† Certain little, romantic, rocky, green hills, in the neighbourhood of the ancient seat of the Earls of Cassilis.

‡ A noted cavern near Colean-house, called the Cove of Colean ; which, as well as Cassilis Downans, is famed, in country story, for being a favourite haunt of Fairies.

§ The famous family of that name, the ancestors of Robert the great Deliverer of his country, the Earls of Carrick.

lays] leas	wimplin] meandering	nits] nuts
pou] pull	stocks] cabbage plants	haud] hold

ROBERT BURNS

The lasses feat, an' cleanly neat,
    Mair braw than when they're fine;
Their faces blythe fu' sweetly kythe
    Hearts leal, an' warm, an' kin':
The lads sae trig, wi' wooer-babs
    Weel knotted on their garten;
Some unco blate, an' some wi' gabs
    Gar lasses hearts gang startin
                Whiles fast at night.

.   .   .   .   .   .

The auld Guidwife's weel-hoordet *nits**
    Are round an' round divided,
An' monie lads and lasses fates
    Are there that night decided:
Some kindle, couthie, side by side,
    An' burn thegither trimly;
Some start awa, wi' saucy pride,
    And jump out-owre the chimlie
                Fu' high that night.

Jean slips in twa wi' tentie e'e;
    Wha 'twas, she wadna tell;
But this is *Jock*, an' this is *me*,
    She says in to hersel:

* Burning the nuts is a favourite charm. They name the lad and lass to each particular nut, as they lay them in the fire ; and according as they burn quietly together, or start from beside one another, the course and issue of the Courtship will be.

feat] spruce   braw] handsome   kythe] make known
leal] loyal   wooer-babs] love-knots   garten] garters
blate] shy   couthie] kindly   tentie] careful

He bleez'd owre her, an' she owre him,
   As they wad never mair part,
Till fuff! he started up the lum,
   An' Jean had e'en a sair heart
                To see't that night.

   .   .   .   .   .

A wanton widow Leezie was,
   As canty as a kittlen;
But, Och! that night, amang the shaws,
   She gat a fearfu' settlin!
She thro' the whins, an' by the cairn,
   An' owre the hill gaed scrievin,
Whare *three Lairds' lands met at a burn,**
   To dip her left sark-sleeve in,
                Was bent that night.

Whyles owre a linn the burnie plays,
   As thro' the glen it wimpl't;
Whyles round a rocky scar it strays;
   Whyles in a wiel it dimpl't;
Whyles glitter'd to the nightly rays,
   Wi' bickering, dancing dazzle;
Whyles cookit underneath the braes,
   Below the spreading hazle,
                Unseen that night.

* You go out, one or more, for this is a social spell, to a south-running spring, or rivulet, where ' three Lairds' lands meet ', and dip your left shirt-sleeve. Go to bed in sight of a fire, and hang your wet sleeve before it to dry. Lie awake ; and sometime near midnight, an apparition, having the exact figure of the grand object in question, will come and turn the sleeve, as if to dry the other side of it.

   lum] chimney   canty] lively   shaws] copses
scrievin] moving swiftly   whyles] at times   linn] water-fall
scar] crag   wiel] eddy   cookit] disappeared suddenly

Amang the brachens, on the brae,
  Between her an' the moon,
The Deil, or else an outler Quey,
  Gat up an' gae a croon:
Poor Leezie's heart maist lap the hool;
  Near lav'rock-height she jumpit,
But mist a fit, an' in the *pool*
  Out-owre the lugs she plumpit,
        Wi' a plunge that night.

In order, on the clean hearth-stane,
  The *Luggies** three are ranged,
And ev'ry time great care is ta'en
  To see them duly changed:
Auld uncle John, wha wedlock's joys
  Sin *Mar's-year* did desire,
Because he gat the toom dish thrice,
  He heav'd them on the fire
        In wrath that night.

Wi' merry sangs, an' friendly cracks,
  I wat they did na weary;
An' unco tales, an' funnie jokes,
  Their sports were cheap an' cheary:

* Take three dishes; put clean water in one, foul water in
another, and leave the third empty: blindfold a person, and lead
him to the hearth where the dishes are ranged; he (or she) dips
the left hand: if by chance in the clean water, the future husband
or wife will come to the bar of Matrimony, a Maid; if in the
foul, a widow; if in the empty dish, it foretells, with equal
certainty, no marriage at all. It is repeated three times; and
every time the arrangement of the dishes is altered.

outler] not housed   quey] young cow   maist] almost
lap] leapt   hool] outer skin   lav'rock-height] lark-high
fit] foot   lugs] ears   luggie] small wooden dish   Mar's-
year] 1715   toom] empty

Till *butter'd Son's,** wi' fragrant lunt,
   Set a' their gabs a-steerin;
Syne, wi' a social glass o' strunt,
   They parted aff careerin
           Fu' blythe that night.

Poems (Kilmarnock), 1786

402   *The Cotter's Saturday Night*

NOVEMBER chill blaws loud wi' angry sugh;
   The short'ning winter-day is near a close;
The miry beasts retreating frae the pleugh;
   The black'ning trains o' craws to their repose:
The toil-worn *Cotter* frae his labour goes,
   This night his weekly moil is at an end,
Collects his spades, his mattocks, and his hoes,
   Hoping the *morn* in ease and rest to spend,
And weary, o'er the moor, his course does hameward bend.

At length his lonely Cot appears in view,
   Beneath the shelter of an aged tree;
Th' expectant *wee-things*, toddlin, stacher through
   To meet their Dad, wi' flichterin noise an' glee.
His wee bit ingle, blinkin bonnily,
   His clean hearth-stane, his thriftie *Wifie's* smile,
The lisping infant prattling on his knee,
   Does a' his weary carking cares beguile,
An' makes him quite forget his labor an' his toil.

  * Sowens, with butter instead of milk to them, is always the *Halloween Supper*.

  Sowens] flummery of oats   lunt] smoke   a-steerin] stirring
syne] then   strunt] liquor   sugh] sough, noise of wind
stacher] stagger   flichterin] fluttering

Belyve the elder bairns come drapping in,
   At service out, amang the Farmers roun';
Some ca' the pleugh, some herd, some tentie rin
   A cannie errand to a neebor town:
Their eldest hope, their *Jenny*, woman grown,
   In youthfu' bloom, Love sparkling in her e'e,
Comes hame, perhaps, to shew a braw new gown,
   Or deposite her sair-won penny-fee,
To help her Parents dear, if they in hardship be.

Wi' joy unfeign'd brothers and sisters meet,
   An' each for other's weelfare kindly speirs:
The social hours, swift-wing'd, unnotic'd fleet;
   Each tells the uncos that he sees or hears;
The Parents, partial, eye their hopeful years;
   Anticipation forward points the view.
The *Mother*, wi' her needle an' her sheers,
   Gars auld claes look amaist as weel's the new;
The *Father* mixes a' wi' admonition due.

Their Master's an' their Mistress's command,
   The younkers a' are warned to obey;
An' mind their labours wi' an eydent hand,
   An' ne'er, tho' out o' sight, to jauk or play;
' An' O! be sure to fear the LORD alway!
   ' An' mind your *duty*, duely, morn an' night!
' Lest in temptation's path ye gang astray,
   ' Implore his counsel and assisting might:
' They never sought in vain that sought the LORD aright.'

belyve] by and by   ca'] drive   tentie] heedful
sair] sore, hard   speirs] asks   uncos] strange things
gars] makes   claes] clothes   eydent] diligent   jauk] trifle

But hark! a rap comes gently to the door;
   Jenny, wha kens the meaning o' the same,
Tells how a neebor lad cam o'er the moor,
   To do some errands, and convoy her hame.
The wily mother sees the conscious flame
   Sparkle in *Jenny's* e'e, and flush her cheek;
With heart-struck anxious care, enquires his name,
   While *Jenny* hafflins is afraid to speak;
Weel pleas'd the Mother hears, it's nae wild, worthless **Rake.**

Wi' kindly welcome *Jenny* brings him ben;
   A strappan youth; he takes the Mother's eye;
Blythe *Jenny* sees the visit's no ill ta'en;
   The Father cracks of horses, pleughs, and kye.
The Youngster's artless heart o'erflows wi' joy,
   But blate and laithfu', scarce can weel behave;
The Mother, wi' a woman's wiles, can spy
   What makes the youth sae bashfu' an' sae grave;
Weel pleas'd to think her *bairn's* respected like the lave.

O happy love! where love like this is found!
   O heart-felt raptures! bliss beyond compare!
I've paced much this weary, mortal round,
   And sage *Experience* bids me this declare—
' If Heav'n a draught of heav'nly pleasure spare,
   ' One cordial in this melancholy Vale,
' 'Tis when a youthful, loving, modest Pair,
   ' In other's arms breathe out the tender tale,
' Beneath the milk-white thorn that scents the ev'ning gale.'

.   .   .   .   *

hafflins] half   kye] cows, cattle   blate] shy, bashful
laithfu'] loathful   the lave] the rest

But now the Supper crowns their simple board,
   The healsome *Parritch*, chief o' *Scotia*'s food:
The soupe their only *Hawkie* does afford,
   That 'yont the hallan snugly chows her cood:
The dame brings forth in complimental mood,
   To grace the lad, her weel-hain'd kebbuck, fell,
An' aft he's prest, an' aft he ca's it guid;
   The frugal Wifie, garrulous, will tell,
How 'twas a towmond auld, sin' Lint was i' the bell.

The cheerfu' Supper done, wi' serious face,
   They, round the ingle, form a circle wide;
The sire turns-o'er, wi' patriarchal grace,
   The big *ha'-Bible*, ance his Father's pride:
His bonnet rev'rently is laid aside,
   His lyart haffets wearing thin an' bare;
Those strains that once did sweet in Zion glide,
   He wales a portion with judicious care;
And ' *Let us worship* God!' he says, with solemn air.

They chant their artless notes in simple guise;
   They tune their hearts, by far the noblest aim:
Perhaps *Dundee*'s wild warbling measures rise,
   Or plaintive *Martyrs*, worthy of the name;
Or noble *Elgin* beets the heav'n-ward flame,
   The sweetest far of *Scotia*'s holy lays:
Compar'd with these, Italian trills are tame;
   The tickl'd ears no heart-felt raptures raise;
Nae unison hae they with our Creator's praise.

.   .   .   .

healsome] wholesome   hawkie] a white-faced cow   'yont]
beyond   hallan] partition wall   hain'd] saved   kebbuck]
cheese   fell] sharp   towmond] twelve-month   lint i' the bell]
flax in flower   lyart] grey   haffets] temples, cheeks   wales]
chooses   beets] adds fuel to

Then homeward all take off their sev'ral way;
    The youngling Cottagers retire to rest:
The Parent pair their *secret homage* pay,
    And proffer up to Heav'n the warm request,
That *He* who stills the raven's clam'rous nest,
    And decks the lily fair in flow'ry pride,
Would in the way His Wisdom sees the best,
    For them and for their little ones provide;
But chiefly, in their hearts with *Grace divine* preside.

Poems (Kilmarnock), 1786

403   *To a Mouse*
On turning her up in her nest with the plough, November 1785

WEE, sleekit, cowrin, tim'rous beastie,
    O, what a panic's in thy breastie!
Thou need na start awa sae hasty,
                Wi' bickering brattle!
I wad be laith to rin an' chase thee,
                Wi' murd'ring *pattle !*

I'm truly sorry Man's dominion
Has broken Nature's social union,
An' justifies that ill opinion
                Which makes thee startle
At me, thy poor, earth-born companion,
                An' *fellow-mortal !*

I doubt na, whyles, but thou may thieve
What then? poor beastie, thou maun live!
A *daimen icker* in a *thrave*
                'S a sma' request.
I'll get a blessin wi' the lave,
                And never miss't !

brattle] scamper   pattle] plough-staff   daimen] odd
icker] ear of corn   thrave] twenty-four sheaves

Thy wee bit *housie*, too, in ruin!
Its silly wa's the win's are strewin!
An' naething, now, to big a new ane,
   O' foggage green!
An' bleak December's winds ensuin,
    Baith snell and keen!

Thou saw the fields laid bare an' waste,
An' weary Winter comin fast,
An' cozie here, beneath the blast,
   Thou thought to dwell,
Till crash! the cruel *coulter* past
    Out thro' thy cell.

That wee bit heap o' leaves an' stibble,
Has cost thee mony a weary nibble!
Now thou's turn'd out, for a' thy trouble,
   But house or hald,
To thole the Winter's sleety dribble,
    An' cranreuch cauld!

But, Mousie, thou art no thy lane,
In proving *foresight* may be vain:
The best-laid schemes o' *Mice* an' *Men*,
   Gang aft a-gley,
An' lea'e us nought but grief and pain,
    For promis'd joy.

big] build foggage] coarse grass snell] biting but] without
thole] endure   cranreuch] hoar-frost thy lane] by thyself
a-gley] askew

Still thou art blest, compar'd wi' *me !*
The present only toucheth thee·
But, Och! I backward cast my e'e,
　　　　　　On prospects drear!
An' forward, tho' I canna *see,*
　　　　　I guess an' *fear !*
　　　　　　　　Poems (Kilmarnock), 1786

404　　*Epistle to Davie, A Brother Poet*

WHILE winds frae aff *Ben-Lomond* blaw,
　　And bar the doors wi' driving snaw,
　　And hing us owre the ingle,
I set me down, to pass the time,
And spin a verse or twa o' rhyme,
　　In hamely westlin jingle.
While frosty winds blaw in the drift,
　　Ben to the chimla lug,
I grudge a wee the Great folk's gift,
　　That live sae bien an' snug:
　　　　I tent less, and want less
　　　　　Their roomy fire-side;
　　　　But hanker and canker,
　　　　　To see their cursed pride.

It's hardly in a body's pow'r,
To keep, at times, frae being sour,
　　To see how things are shar'd;
How best o' chiels are whiles in want,
While coofs on countless thousands rant,
　　And ken na how to wair't:

hing] hang　　　westlin] westland　　　ben . . . lug] in to the
chimney corner　　bien] comfortable　　tent] care for　　chiels]
fellows　　coofs] blockheads　　rant] roister　　wair] spend

647

But *Davie*, lad, ne'er fash your head,
   Tho' we hae little gear,
We're fit to win our daily bread,
   As lang's we're hale and fier:
      ' Mair spier na, nor fear na',
        Auld age ne'er mind a feg,
     The last o't, the warst o't,
       Is only but to beg.

To lie in kilns and barns at e'en,
When banes are craz'd, and bluid is thin,
   Is, doubtless, great distress!
Yet then content could make us blest;
Ev'n then, sometimes we'd snatch a taste
   Of truest happiness.
The honest heart that's free frae a'
   Intended fraud or guile,
However Fortune kick the ba',
   Has ay some cause to smile,
     And mind still, you'll find still,
      A comfort this nae sma';
     Nae mair then, we'll care then,
      Nae farther can we fa'.

What tho', like Commoners of air,
We wander out, we know not where,
   But either house or hal'?
Yet Nature's charms, the hills and woods,
The sweeping vales, and foaming floods,
   Are free alike to all.

fash] trouble   fier] healthy   mair spier na] more ask not
(quotation from Ramsay)   feg] fig

In days when Daisies deck the ground,
    And Blackbirds whistle clear,
With honest joy our hearts will bound,
    To see the coming year:
        On braes when we please, then,
            We'll sit and sowth a tune;
        Syne *rhyme* till't, we'll time till't,
            And sing't when we hae done.

It's no in titles nor in rank;
It's no in wealth like Lon'on Bank,
    To purchase peace and rest;
It's no in makin muckle *mair*:
It's no in books; it's no in lear,
    To make us truly blest:
If Happiness hae not her seat
    And centre in the breast,
We may be wise, or rich, or great,
    But never can be blest:
        Nae treasures, nor pleasures,
            Could make us happy lang;
        The *heart* ay's the part ay,
            That makes us right or wrang.

Poems (Kilmarnock), 1786

405   *Address to the Unco Guid*

O YE wha are sae guid yoursel,
    Sae pious and sae holy,
Ye've nought to do but mark and tell
    Your Neebour's fauts and folly!

sowth] hum, whistle softly   syne] then   till't] to it
muckle mair] much more   lear] lore, learning

Whase life is like a weel-gaun mill,
  Supply'd wi' store o' water,
The heapet happer's ebbing still,
  And still the clap plays clatter.

Hear me, ye venerable Core,
  As counsel for poor mortals,
That frequent pass douce Wisdom's door
  For glaikit Folly's portals;
I, for their thoughtless, careless sakes,
  Would here propone defences,
Their donsie tricks, their black mistakes,
  Their failings and mischances.

Ye see your state wi' their's compar'd,
  And shudder at the niffer;
But cast a moment's fair regard,
  What maks the mighty differ?
Discount what scant occasion gave,
  That purity ye pride in,
And (what's aft mair than a' the lave)
  Your better art o' hiding.

Think, when your castigated pulse
  Gies now and then a wallop,
What ragings must his veins convulse,
  That still eternal gallop:
Wi' wind and tide fair i' your tail,
  Right on ye scud your sea-way;
But in the teeth o' baith to sail,
  It maks an unco leeway.

weel-gaun] well-going   core] corps   douce] sober
glaikit] giddy   propone] put forward   donsie] unlucky
niffer] exchange

See Social-life and Glee sit down,
　　All joyous and unthinking,
Till, quite transmugrify'd, they're grown
　　Debauchery and Drinking:
O would they stay to calculate
　　Th' eternal consequences;
Or your more dreaded hell to state,
　　Damnation of expences!

Ye high, exalted, virtuous Dames,
　　Ty'd up in godly laces,
Before ye gie poor *Frailty* names,
　　Suppose a change o' cases;
A dear-lov'd lad, convenience snug,
　　A treacherous inclination——
But, let me whisper i' your lug,
　　Ye're aiblins nae temptation.

Then gently scan your brother Man,
　　Still gentler sister Woman;
Tho' they may gang a kennin wrang,
　　To step aside is human:
One point must still be greatly dark,
　　The moving *Why* they do it:
And just as lamely can ye mark,
　　How far perhaps they rue it.

Who made the heart, 'tis *He* alone
　　Decidedly can try us,
He knows each chord, its various tone,
　　Each spring, its various bias:

aiblins] perhaps　　a kennin] a little, enough to be ' kenned '

Then at the balance let's be mute,
   We never can adjust it;
What's *done* we partly may compute,
   But know not what's *resisted*.

Poems (Edinburgh), 1787

406   *Epistle to Dr. Blacklock*

ELLISLAND, 21*st Oct.* 1789

WOW, but your letter made me vauntie!
   And are ye hale, and weel, and cantie?
I kenn'd it still your wee bit jauntie
      Wad bring ye to:
Lord send you aye as weel 's I want ye,
      And then ye'll do.

   .   .   .   .

But what d'ye think, my trusty fier?
I'm turn'd a gauger—Peace be here!
Parnassian queans, I fear, I fear,
      Ye'll now disdain me!
And then my fifty pounds a year
      Will little gain me.

Ye glaikit, gleesome, dainty damies,
Wha by Castalia's wimplin' streamies
Lowp, sing, and lave your pretty limbies,
      Ye ken, ye ken,
That strang necessity supreme is
      'Mang sons o' men.

vauntie] proud   cantie] cheerful   wee bit jauntie] little
jaunt   fier] friend   glaikit] giddy   lowp] leap, dance

652

I hae a wife and twa wee laddies,
They maun hae brose and brats o' duddies;
Ye ken yoursels my heart right proud is—
            I need na vaunt—
But I'll sned besoms, thraw saugh woodies,
            Before they want.

Lord help me thro' this warld o' care!
I'm weary, sick o't, late and air!
Not but I hae a richer share
            Than mony ithers;
But why should ae man better fare,
            And a' men brithers?

Come, Firm Resolve, take thou the van,
Thou stalk o' carl-hemp in man!
And let us mind, faint heart ne'er wan
            A lady fair;
Wha does the utmost that he can,
            Will whyles do mair.

But to conclude my silly rhyme
(I'm scant o' verse, and scant o' time)—
To make a happy fire-side clime
            To weans and wife,
That's the true pathos and sublime
            Of human life.

Works (ed. Currie), 1800

brats] rags	duddies] clothes	sned] lop	thraw] twist
saugh] willow	woodies] withes	air] early	carl-hemp]
male hemp	weans] children		

ROBERT BURNS

Tam o' Shanter

WHEN chapman billies leave the street.
And drouthy neebors, neebors meet,
As market-days are wearing late,
An' folk begin to tak the gate;
While we sit bousing at the nappy,
An' getting fou and unco happy,
We think na on the lang Scots miles,
The mosses, waters, slaps, and styles,
That lie between us and our hame,
Whare sits our sulky sullen dame,
Gathering her brows like gathering storm,
Nursing her wrath to keep it warm.

    This truth fand honest *Tam o' Shanter*,
As he frae Ayr ae night did canter,
(Auld Ayr wham ne'er a town surpasses,
For honest men and bonny lasses.)

    O *Tam!* hadst thou but been sae wise,
As ta'en thy ain wife *Kate's* advice!
She tauld thee weel thou was a skellum,
A blethering, blustering, drunken blellum;
That frae November till October,
Ae market-day thou was nae sober;
That ilka melder, wi' the miller,
Thou sat as lang as thou had siller;
That ev'ry naig was ca'd a shoe on,
The smith and thee gat roaring fou on;
That at the L—d's house, ev'n on Sunday,

billies] fellows   drouthy] thirsty   gate] way, road
nappy] ale   mosses] bogs   slaps] gaps, passes   ta'en] to
have taken   skellum] rascal   blellum] babbler   melder]
meal-grinding   naig] nag   ca'd a shoe on] shod

Thou drank wi' Kirkton Jean till Monday.
She prophesy'd that late or soon,
Thou would be found deep drown'd in Doon;
Or catch'd wi' warlocks in the mirk,
By *Alloway's* auld haunted kirk.

Ah, gentle dames! it gars me greet,
To think how mony counsels sweet,
How mony lengthen'd sage advices,
The husband frae the wife despises!

But to our tale: Ae market night,
Tam had got planted unco right;
Fast by an ingle, bleezing finely,
Wi' reaming swats, that drank divinely;
And at his elbow, Souter *Johnny*,
His ancient, trusty, drouthy crony;
Tam lo'ed him like a vera brither;
They had been fou for weeks thegither.
The night drave on wi' sangs and clatter;
And ay the ale was growing better:
The landlady and *Tam* grew gracious,
Wi' favours, secret, sweet, and precious:
The Souter tauld his queerest stories;
The landlord's laugh was ready chorus:
The storm without might rair and rustle,
Tam did na mind the storm a whistle.

Care, mad to see a man sae happy,
E'en drown'd himself amang the nappy.
As bees flee hame wi' lades o' treasure,
The minutes wing'd their way wi' pleasure:
Kings may be blest, but *Tam* was glorious,

mirk] dark   greet] weep   reaming swats] frothing ale
Souter] shoemaker   rair] roar

655

O'er a' the ills o' life victorious!
　　But pleasures are like poppies spread,
You seize the flow'r, its bloom is shed;
Or like the snow falls in the river,
A moment white—then melts for ever;
Or like the borealis race,
That flit ere you can point their place;
Or like the rainbow's lovely form
Evanishing amid the storm.—
Nae man can tether time or tide;
The hour approaches Tam maun ride;
That hour, o' night's black arch the key-stane,
That dreary hour he mounts his beast in;
And sic a night he taks the road in,
As ne'er poor sinner was abroad in.

　　The wind blew as 'twad blawn its last;
The rattling show'rs rose on the blast;
The speedy gleams the darkness swallow'd;
Loud, deep, and lang, the thunder bellow'd:
That night, a child might understand,
The Deil had business on his hand.

　　Weel mounted on his gray mare, *Meg*,
A better never lifted leg,
Tam skelpit on thro' dub and mire,
Despising wind, and rain, and fire;
Whiles holding fast his gude blue bonnet;
Whiles crooning o'er some auld Scots sonnet;
Whiles glow'ring round wi' prudent cares,
Lest bogles catch him unawares:
Kirk-Alloway was drawing nigh,

falls] that falls　　maun] must　　　'twad] it would have
skelpit] hurried　　dub] puddle　　whiles] at times

Whare ghaists and houlets nightly cry.—
  By this time he was cross the ford,
Whare in the snaw, the chapman smoor'd;
And past the birks and meikle stane,
Whare drunken *Charlie* brak's neck-bane;
And thro' the whins, and by the cairn,
Whare hunters fand the murder'd bairn;
And near the thorn, aboon the well,
Whare *Mungo's* mither hang'd hersel.—
Before him *Doon* pours all his floods;
The doubling storm roars thro' the woods;
The lightnings flash from pole to pole;
Near and more near the thunders roll:
When, glimmering thro' the groaning trees,
Kirk-Alloway seem'd in a bleeze;
Thro' ilka bore the beams were glancing;
And loud resounded mirth and dancing.—
  Inspiring bold *John Barleycorn!*
What dangers thou canst make us scorn!
Wi' tippeny, we fear nae evil;
Wi' usquabae we'll face the devil!—
The swats sae ream'd in *Tammie's* noddle,
Fair play, he car'd na deils a boddle.
But *Maggie* stood right fair astonish'd,
Till, by the heel and hand admonish'd,
She ventur'd forward on the light;
And, vow! *Tam* saw an unco sight!
Warlocks and witches in a dance;
Nae cotillion brent new frae *France*,

houlets] owlets   smoor'd] was smothered   aboon] above
tippeny] twopenny ale   usquabae] whiskey   na deils a
boddle] not a farthing for devils   brent] brand

But hornpipes, jigs, strathspeys, and reels,
Put life and mettle in their heels.
A winnock-bunker in the east,
There sat auld Nick, in shape o' beast;
A towzie tyke, black, grim, and large,
To gie them music was his charge:
He screw'd the pipes and gart them skirl,
Till roof and rafters a' did dirl.—
Coffins stood round, like open presses,
That shaw'd the dead in their last dresses;
And by some devilish cantraip slight
Each in its cauld hand held a light.—
By which heroic *Tam* was able
To note upon the haly table,
A murderer's banes in gibbet airns;
Twa span-lang, wee, unchristen'd bairns;
A thief, new-cutted frae a rape,
Wi' his last gasp his gab did gape;
Five tomahawks, wi' blude red-rusted;
Five scymitars, wi' murder crusted;
A garter, which a babe had strangled;
A knife, a father's throat had mangled,
Whom his ain son o' life bereft,
The grey hairs yet stack to the heft;
Wi' mair o' horrible and awefu',
Which ev'n to name wad be unlawfu'.

As *Tammie* glowr'd, amaz'd, and curious,
The mirth and fun grew fast and furious:
The piper loud and louder blew;
The dancers quick and quicker flew;

winnock-bunker] window-seat   towzie] dishevelled, shaggy
dirl] vibrate   cantraip] magic   airns] irons   rape] rope

They reel'd, they set, they cross'd, they cleekit,
Till ilka carlin swat and reekit,
And coost her duddies to the wark,
And linket at it in her sark!

Now *Tam*, O *Tam!* had thae been queans,
A' plump and strapping in their teens,
Their sarks, instead o' creeshie flannen,
Been snaw-white seventeen hunder linnen!
Thir breeks o' mine, my only pair,
That ance were plush, o' gude blue hair,
I wad hae gi'en them off my hurdies,
For ae blink o' the bonie burdies!

But wither'd beldams, auld and droll,
Rigwoodie hags wad spean a foal,
Lowping and flinging on a crummock,
I wonder didna turn thy stomach.

But *Tam* kend what was what fu' brawlie,
There was ae winsome wench and wawlie,
That night enlisted in the core,
(Lang after kend on *Carrick* shore;
For mony a beast to dead she shot,
And perish'd mony a bony boat,
And shook baith meikle corn and bear,
And kept the country-side in fear.)
Her cutty sark, o' Paisley harn,
That while a lassie she had worn,
In longitude tho' sorely scanty,
It was her best, and she was vauntie.—

cleekit] joined arms   coost her duddies] cast off her clothes
linket] went quickly   creeshie flannen] greasy flannel   thir]
these   hurdies] buttocks   burdies] girls   rigwoodie] wretched(?)
spean] wean   crummock] crooked staff   brawlie] well   wawlie]
comely core] corps   bear] barley   cutty] short   harn] coarse cloth

Ah! little kend thy reverend grannie,
That sark she coft for her wee Nannie,
Wi' twa pund Scots, ('twas a' her riches),
Wad ever grac'd a dance of witches!

But here my Muse her wing maun cour;
Sic flights are far beyond her pow'r;
To sing how Nannie lap and flang,
(A souple jade she was, and strang),
And how *Tam* stood, like ane bewitch'd,
And thought his very een enrich'd;
Even Satan glowr'd, and fidg'd fu' fain,
And hotch'd and blew wi' might and main:
Till first ae caper, syne anither,
Tam tint his reason a' thegither,
And roars out, ' Weel done, Cutty-sark! '
And in an instant all was dark:
And scarcely had he Maggie rallied,
When out the hellish legion sallied.

As bees bizz out wi' angry fyke,
When plundering herds assail their byke;
As open pussie's mortal foes,
When, pop! she starts before their nose;
As eager runs the market-crowd,
When ' Catch the thief! ' resounds aloud;
So Maggie runs, the witches follow,
Wi' mony an eldritch skreech and hollow.

Ah, *Tam!* Ah, *Tam!* thou'll get thy fairin!
In hell they'll roast thee like a herrin!

coft] bought fidg'd] fidgeted hotch'd] jerked
tint] lost fyke] fuss herds] shepherd-boys byke]
hive pussie's] the hare's fairin] present from a fair,
deserts

In vain thy *Kate* awaits thy comin!
Kate soon will be a woefu' woman!
Now, do thy speedy utmost, Meg,
And win the key-stane of the brig;
There at them thou thy tail may toss,
A running stream they dare na cross.
But ere the key-stane she could make,
The fient a tail she had to shake!
For Nannie, far before the rest,
Hard upon noble Maggie prest,
And flew at Tam wi' furious ettle;
But little wist she Maggie's mettle——
Ae spring brought off her master hale,
But left behind her ain gray tail:
The carlin claught her by the rump,
And left poor Maggie scarce a stump.

Now, wha this tale o' truth shall read,
Ilk man and mother's son, take heed:
Whene'er to drink you are inclin'd,
Or cutty sarks run in your mind,
Think, ye may buy the joys o'er dear,
Remember Tam o' Shanter's mare.

The Edinburgh Magazine, March 1791

408   *Green grow the Rashes, O*

GREEN grow the rashes O,
Green grow the rashes O;
The sweetest hours that e'er I spend,
Are spent amang the lasses O!

fient] devil   ettle] purpose   hale] whole   claught]
clutched

There 's nought but care on ev'ry han',
    In ev'ry hour that passes O;
What signifies the life o' man,
    An' 'twere na for the lasses O.

The warly race may riches chase,
    An' riches still may fly them O;
An' tho' at last they catch them fast,
    Their hearts can ne'er enjoy them O.

But gie me a canny hour at e'en,
    My arms about my dearie O;
An' warly cares, an' warly men,
    May a' gae tapsalteerie O!

For you sae douce, ye sneer at this,
    Ye're nought but senseless asses O:
The wisest man the warl' saw,
    He dearly lov'd the lasses O.

Auld nature swears, the lovely dears
    Her noblest work she classes O;
Her prentice han' she tried on man,
    An' then she made the lasses O.

Poems (Edinburgh), 1787

409   *Mary Morison*

O MARY, at thy window be,
    It is the wish'd, the trysted hour!
Those smiles and glances let me see,
    That make the miser's treasure poor:

warly] worldly   tapsalteerie] topsy-turvy

How blythely wad I bide the stoure,
   A weary slave frae sun to sun,
Could I the rich reward secure,
   The lovely Mary Morison.

Yestreen, when to the trembling string
   The dance gaed thro' the lighted ha',
To thee my fancy took its wing,
   I sat, but neither heard nor saw:
Tho' this was fair, and that was braw,
   And yon the toast of a' the town,
I sigh'd, and said amang them a',
   ' Ye are na Mary Morison.'

O Mary, canst thou wreck his peace,
   Wha for thy sake wad gladly die?
Or canst thou break that heart of his,
   Whase only faut is loving thee?
If love for love thou wilt na gie,
   At least be pity to me shown!
A thought ungentle canna be
   The thought o' Mary Morison.

Works (ed. Currie), 1800

410 *Auld Lang Syne*

SHOULD auld acquaintance be forgot,
  And never brought to min'?
Should auld acquaintance be forgot,
   And auld lang syne?

     For auld lang syne, my dear.
      For auld lang syne,
     We'll tak a cup o' kindness yet,
      For auld lang syne.

      stoure] dust, turmoil

We twa hae run about the braes,
　　And pu'd the gowans fine;
But we've wander'd mony a weary foot
　　Sin' auld lang syne.

We twa hae paidled i' the burn,
　　From morning sun till dine;
But seas between us braid hae roar'd
　　Sin' auld lang syne.

And there 's a hand, my trusty fiere,
　　And gie 's a hand o' thine;
And we'll tak a right guid-willie waught,
　　For auld lang syne.

And surely ye'll be your pint-stowp,
　　And surely I'll be mine;
And we'll tak a cup o' kindness yet
　　For auld lang syne.

　　　　　　Written 1788 ; *The Scots Musical*
　　　　　　　　　Museum, v, 1797

411　　　　*John Anderson my Jo*

JOHN ANDERSON my jo, John,
　　When we were first acquent,
Your locks were like the raven,
　　Your bonnie brow was brent;
But now your brow is beld, John,
　　Your locks are like the snow;
But blessings on your frosty pow,
　　John Anderson, my jo.

　gowans] daisies　　paidled] paddled　　dine] dinner　　fiere]
companion　　guid-willie waught] hearty draught　　ye'll be]
you will be good for　　jo] sweetheart　　brent] unwrinkled
beld] bald　　pow] head

John Anderson my jo, John,
  We clamb the hill thegither;
And mony a canty day, John,
  We've had wi' ane anither:
Now we maun totter down, John,
  And hand in hand we'll go,
And sleep thegither at the foot,
  John Anderson, my jo.

The Scots Musical Museum, iii, 1790

412   *The Silver Tassie*

GO fetch to me a pint o' wine,
  An' fill it in a silver tassie;
That I may drink, before I go,
  A service to my bonnie lassie.
That boat rocks at the pier o' Leith,
  Fu' loud the wind blaws frae the ferry,
The ship rides by the Berwick-law,
  And I maun leave my bonnie Mary.

The trumpets sound, the banners fly,
  The glittering spears are rankèd ready;
The shouts o' war are heard afar,
  The battle closes thick and bloody;
But it 's no the roar o' sea or shore
  Wad mak me langer wish to tarry;
Nor shout o' war that 's heard afar,
  It 's leaving thee, my bonnie Mary.

The Scots Musical Museum, iii, 1790

canty] cheerful   tassie] cup

413 *Of a' the Airts*

OF a' the airts the wind can blaw,
　I dearly like the west,
For there the bonnie lassie lives,
　The lassie I lo'e best:
There 's wild woods grow, and rivers row,
　And mony a hill between;
But day and night my fancy's flight
　Is ever wi' my Jean.

I see her in the dewy flowers,
　I see her sweet and fair:
I hear her in the tunefu' birds,
　I hear her charm the air:
There 's not a bonnie flower that springs
　By fountain, shaw, or green;
There 's not a bonnie bird that sings,
　But minds me o' my Jean.

The Scots Musical Museum, iii, 1790

414 *Tam Glen*

MY heart is a-breaking, dear tittie,
　Some counsel unto me come len',
To anger them a' is a pity,
　But what will I do wi' Tam Glen?

I'm thinking, wi' sic a braw fellow
　In poortith I might mak a fen';
What care I in riches to wallow,
　If I maunna marry Tam Glen?

airts] points of the compass　　　row] roll　　　tittie] sister
poortith] poverty　　fen'] shift

666

ROBERT BURNS

There 's Lowrie the laird o' Dumeller,
    ' Guid-day to you ', brute! he comes ben;
He brags and he blaws o' his siller,
    But when will he dance like Tam Glen?

My minnie does constantly deave me,
    And bids me beware o' young men;
They flatter, she says, to deceive me;
    But wha can think sae o' Tam Glen?

My daddie says, gin I'll forsake him,
    He'll gie me guid hunder marks ten;
But, if it 's ordain'd I maun take him,
    O wha will I get but Tam Glen?

Yestreen at the Valentines' dealing,
    My heart to my mou gied a sten,
For thrice I drew ane without failing,
    And thrice it was written, Tam Glen.

The last Halloween I was waukin
    My droukit sark-sleeve, as ye ken,
His likeness cam up the house staukin,
    And the very grey breeks o' Tam Glen!

Come, counsel, dear tittie, don't tarry;
    I'll gie you my bonnie black hen,
Gif ye will advise me to marry
    The lad I lo'e dearly, Tam Glen.

The Scots Musical Museum, iii, 1790

minnie] mother   deave] deafen, bewilder   gied a sten] gave
a bound   waukin] watching (see foot-note, p. 639)   droukit]
soaked   staukin] stalking

Thou lingering star

THOU lingering star, with lessening ray,
  That lov'st to greet the early morn,
Again thou usherest in the day
  My Mary from my soul was torn.
O Mary! dear departed shade!
  Where is thy place of blissful rest?
Seest thou thy lover lowly laid?
  Hear'st thou the groans that rend his breast?

That sacred hour can I forget,
  Can I forget the hallow'd grove,
Where by the winding Ayr we met,
  To live one day of parting love?
Eternity will not efface
  Those records dear of transports past;
Thy image at our last embrace—
  Ah! little thought we 'twas our last!

Ayr gurgling kiss'd his pebbled shore;
  O'erhung with wild woods, thickening green;
The fragrant birch, and hawthorn hoar,
  Twin'd amorous round the raptur'd scene;
The flowers sprang wanton to be prest,
  The birds sang love on ev'ry spray,
Till too too soon, the glowing west
  Proclaim'd the speed of winged day.

Still o'er these scenes my memory wakes,
  And fondly broods with miser care!
Time but the impression deeper makes,
  As streams their channels deeper wear.

My Mary, dear departed shade!
  Where is thy blissful place of rest?
Seest thou thy lover lowly laid?
  Hear'st thou the groans that rend his breast?
                    The Scots Musical Museum, iii, 1790

416   *Highland Mary*

YE banks and braes and streams around
    The castle o' Montgomery,
Green be your woods, and fair your flowers,
  Your waters never drumlie!
There simmer first unfauld her robes,
  And there the langest tarry;
For there I took the last fareweel
  O' my sweet Highland Mary.

How sweetly bloom'd the gay green birk,
  How rich the hawthorn's blossom,
As underneath their fragrant shade
  I clasp'd her to my bosom!
The golden hours on angel wings
  Flew o'er me and my dearie;
For dear to me as light and life
  Was my sweet Highland Mary.

Wi' mony a vow and lock'd embrace
  Our parting was fu' tender;
And, pledging aft to meet again,
  We tore oursels asunder;
But oh! fell Death's untimely frost,
  That nipt my flower sae early!
Now green's the sod, and cauld's the clay,
  That wraps my Highland Mary!
                    drumlie] turbid

669

O pale, pale now, those rosy lips,
 I aft have kiss'd sae fondly!
And closed for aye the sparkling glance,
 That dwelt on me sae kindly!
And mould'ring now in silent dust,
 That heart that lo'ed me dearly!
But still within my bosom's core
 Shall live my Highland Mary.

Select Collection of Original Scotish Airs,
ii, 1799

417   *The Banks o' Doon*

YE banks and braes o' bonnie Doon,
 How can ye bloom sae fresh and fair?
How can ye chant, ye little birds,
 And I sae weary fu' o' care?
Thou'lt break my heart, thou warbling bird,
 That wantons thro' the flowering thorn:
Thou minds me o' departed joys,
 Departed never to return.

Aft hae I rov'd by bonnie Doon,
 To see the rose and woodbine twine;
And ilka bird sang o' its love,
 And fondly sae did I o' mine.
Wi' lightsome heart I pu'd a rose,
 Fu' sweet upon its thorny tree;
And my fause lover stole my rose,
 But ah! he left the thorn wi' me.

The Scots Musical Museum, iv, 1792

418 *Ye Flowery Banks*

YE flowery banks o' bonie Doon,
  How can ye blume sae fair?
How can ye chant, ye little birds,
  And I sae fu' o' care?

Thou'll break my heart, thou bonie bird,
  That sings upon the bough:
Thou minds me o' the happy days
  When my fause Luve was true.

Thou'll break my heart, thou bonie bird,
  That sings beside thy mate:
For sae I sat, and sae I sang,
  And wist na o' my fate

Aft hae I rov'd by bonie Doon
  To see the woodbine twine,
And ilka bird sang o' its luve,
  And sae did I o' mine.

Wi' lightsome heart I pu'd a rose
  Frae aff its thorny tree,
And my fause luver staw my rose,
  But left the thorn wi' me.

                    Reliques (ed. Cromek) 1808

419 *Ae fond Kiss*

AE fond kiss, and then we sever!
  Ae fareweel, and then for ever!
Deep in heart-wrung tears I'll pledge thee,
Warring sighs and groans I'll wage thee.

Who shall say that Fortune grieves him
While the star of hope she leaves him?
Me, nae cheerfu' twinkle lights me,
Dark despair around benights me.

I'll ne'er blame my partial fancy,
Naething could resist my Nancy;
But to see her was to love her,
Love but her, and love for ever.
Had we never lov'd sae kindly,
Had we never lov'd sae blindly,
Never met—or never parted,
We had ne'er been broken-hearted.

Fare thee weel, thou first and fairest!
Fare thee weel, thou best and dearest!
Thine be ilka joy and treasure,
Peace, Enjoyment, Love, and Pleasure.
Ae fond kiss, and then we sever;
Ae fareweel, alas, for ever!
Deep in heart-wrung tears I'll pledge thee,
Warring sighs and groans I'll wage thee.

The Scots Musical Museum, iv, 1792

420   *A Red, Red Rose*

MY love is like a red red rose
That 's newly sprung in June:
My love is like the melodie
That 's sweetly play'd in tune.

As fair art thou, my bonnie lass,
So deep in love am I:
And I will love thee still, my dear,
Till a' the seas gang dry.

Till a' the seas gang dry, my dear,
   And the rocks melt wi' the sun:
And I will love thee still, my dear,
   While the sands o' life shall run.

And fare thee weel, my only love,
   And fare thee weel a while!
And I will come again, my love,
   Tho' it were ten thousand mile.

              Urbani, *Selection of Scots Songs*, ii, 1794

421   *Bonnie Lesley*

O SAW ye bonnie Lesley
   As she gaed o'er the Border?
She 's gane, like Alexander,
   To spread her conquests farther.

To see her is to love her,
   And love but her for ever;
For Nature made her what she is,
   And never made anither!

Thou art a queen, fair Lesley,
   Thy subjects we, before thee:
Thou art divine, fair Lesley,
   The hearts o' men adore thee.

The Deil he could na skaith thee,
   Or aught that wad belang thee;
He'd look into thy bonnie face,
   And say, ' I canna wrang thee.'

The Powers aboon will tent thee:
    Misfortune sha'na steer thee;
Thou'rt like themsel' sae lovely,
    That ill they'll ne'er let near thee.

Return again, fair Lesley,
    Return to Caledonie!
That we may brag we hae a lass
    There 's nane again sae bonnie.

Written 1792 ; *Select Collection of Original*
Scotish Airs, i, 1798

422   *Duncan Gray*

DUNCAN GRAY came here to woo,
    Ha, ha, the wooing o't!
On blythe Yule-night when we were fou,
    Ha, ha, the wooing o't!
Maggie coost her head fu' high,
Look'd asklent and unco skeigh,
Gart poor Duncan stand abeigh—
    Ha, ha, the wooing o't!

Duncan fleech'd, and Duncan pray'd,
    Ha, ha, the wooing o't!
Meg was deaf as Ailsa Craig,
    Ha, ha, the wooing o't!
Duncan sigh'd baith out and in,
Grat his een baith bleer't and blin',
Spak o' lowpin o'er a linn—
    Ha, ha, the wooing o't!

tent] take care of   steer] molest   coost] cast   asklent]
aslant   skeigh] skittish   abeigh] aside   fleech'd] beseeched
grat] wept   een] eyes   lowpin] leaping   linn] waterfall

Time and chance are but a tide,
  Ha, ha, the wooing o't!
Slighted love is sair to bide,
  Ha, ha, the wooing o't!
' Shall I, like a fool,' quoth he,
' For a haughty hizzie die?
She may gae to—France for me!'—
  Ha, ha, the wooing o't!

How it comes let doctors tell,
  Ha, ha, the wooing o't!
Meg grew sick as he grew haill,
  Ha, ha, the wooing o't!
Something in her bosom wrings;
For relief a sigh she brings;
And O, her een they spak sic things!—
  Ha, ha, the wooing o't!

Duncan was a lad o' grace,
  Ha, ha, the wooing o't!
Maggie's was a piteous case,
  Ha, ha, the wooing o't!
Duncan couldna be her death,
Swelling pity smoor'd his wrath;
Now they're crouse and cantie baith—
  Ha, ha, the wooing o't!

    Written 1792 ; *Select Collection of Original*
           Scotish Airs, i, 1798

hizzie] hussy   smoor'd] smothered   crouse] lively
cantie] cheerful

423 *Scots wha hae*

SCOTS, wha hae wi' Wallace bled
Scots, wham Bruce has aften led,
Welcome to your gory bed,
    Or to victorie!

Now 's the day, and now 's the hour;
See the front o' battle lour,
See approach proud Edward's power—
    Chains and slaverie!

Wha will be a traitor knave?
Wha can fill a coward's grave?
Wha sae base as be a slave?—
    Let him turn, and flee!

Wha for Scotland's King and Law
Freedom's sword will strongly draw,
Freeman stand or freeman fa',
    Let him follow me!

By Oppression's woes and pains,
By your sons in servile chains,
We will drain our dearest veins,
    But they shall be free!

Lay the proud usurpers low!
Tyrants fall in every foe!
Liberty 's in every blow!
    Let us do, or die!

The Morning Chronicle, May 8, 1794

424 *Is there for honest Poverty*

IS there, for honest poverty,
  That hangs his head, and a' that?
The coward-slave, we pass him by,
  We dare be poor for a' that!
    For a' that, and a' that,
      Our toils obscure, and a' that,
     The rank is but the guinea's stamp,
      The man's the gowd for a' that,

What tho' on hamely fare we dine,
  Wear hodden-gray, and a' that?
Gie fools their silks, and knaves their wine,
  A man's a man for a' that.
    For a' that, and a' that,
      Their tinsel show, and a' that,
     The honest man, tho' e'er sae poor,
      Is king o' men for a' that.

Ye see yon birkie ca'd a lord,
  Wha struts, and stares, and a' that?
Tho' hundreds worship at his word,
  He's but a coof for a' that.
    For a' that, and a' that,
      His ribband, star, and a' that,
     The man of independent mind,
      He looks and laughs at a' that.

gowd] gold   hodden-gray] undyed homespun   birkie]
smart fellow   ca'd] called   coof] dolt

A prince can mak a belted knight,
  A marquis, duke, and a' that;
But an honest man 's aboon his might,
  Guid faith, he mauna fa' that!
    For a' that, and a' that,
      Their dignities, and a' that,
      The pith o' sense and pride o' worth
      Are higher rank than a' that.

Then let us pray that come it may,
  As come it will for a' that,
That Sense and Worth, o'er a' the earth,
  May bear the gree, and a' that.
    For a' that, and a' that,
      It 's coming yet for a' that,
      That man to man the warld o'er
      Shall brithers be for a' that.

The Glasgow Magazine, August 1795

425   *O, wert thou in the cauld blast*

O, WERT thou in the cauld blast,
  On yonder lea, on yonder lea,
My plaidie to the angry airt,
  I'd shelter thee, I'd shelter thee.
Or did Misfortune's bitter storms
  Around thee blaw, around thee blaw,
Thy bield should be my bosom,
  To share it a', to share it a'.

mauna fa'] must not lay claim to   bear the gree] have
the prize, first place   airt] quarter from which the wind
is blowing   bield] shelter

Or were I in the wildest waste,
    Sae black and bare, sae black and bare,
The desert were a Paradise,
    If thou wert there, if thou wert there.
Or were I monarch o' the globe,
    Wi' thee to reign, wi' thee to reign,
The brightest jewel in my crown
    Wad be my queen, wad be my queen.

            Written 1796 ; *Works* (ed. Currie), 1800

ANNE HOME, MRS. HUNTER
1742–1821

426 *My Mother bids me bind my Hair*

MY mother bids me bind my hair
    With bands of rosey hue,
Tye up my sleeves with ribbands rare,
    And lace my boddice blue.

' For why,' she cries, ' sit still and weep,
    While others dance and play ? '
Alas ! I scarce can go or creep
    While Lubin is away.

'Tis sad to think the days are gone
    When those we love were near ;
I sit upon this mossy stone,
    And sigh, when none can hear.

And while I spin my flaxen thread,
    And sing my simple lay,
The village seems asleep, or dead,
    Now Lubin is away.

          Haydn's VI Original Canzonettas, 1794

ROBERT GRAHAM, OF GARTMORE

1735-1797

427   *O tell me how to woo thee*

IF doughty deeds my ladye please,
     Right soon I'll mount my steed;
And strong his arm, and fast his seat,
     That bears frae me the meed.
I'll wear thy colours in my cap,
     Thy picture in my heart;
And he that bends not to thine eye,
     Shall rue it to his smart.
          Then tell me how to woo thee, love;
               O tell me how to woo thee!
          For thy dear sake, nae care I'll take,
               Tho' ne'er another trow me.

If gay attire delight thine eye,
     I'll dight me in array;
I'll tend thy chamber door all night,
     And squire thee all the day.
If sweetest sounds can win thy ear,
     These sounds I'll strive to catch;
Thy voice I'll steal to woo thysell,
     That voice that nane can match.
          Then tell me how to woo thee, love, &c.

But if fond love thy heart can gain,
     I never broke a vow;
Nae maiden lays her skaith to me,
     I never loved but you.
For you alone I ride the ring,
     For you I wear the blue;

ROBERT GRAHAM, OF GARTMORE

For you alone I strive to sing,
  O tell me how to woo!
    O tell me how to woo thee, love;
     O tell me how to woo thee!
    For thy dear sake, nae care I'll take,
     Tho' ne'er another trow me.

Minstrelsy of the Scottish Border, iii, 1803

ERASMUS DARWIN

1731–1802

428   *Vegetable Loves*

[Whereas P. Ovidius Naso, a great Necromancer in the famous
Court of Augustus Caesar, did by art poetic transmute Men,
Women, and even Gods and Goddesses, into Trees and Flowers;
I have undertaken by similar art to restore some of them to their
original animality, after having remained prisoners so long in
their respective vegetable mansions.]

FROM giant Oaks, that wave their branches dark,
To the dwarf Moss that clings upon their bark,
What Beaux and Beauties crowd the gaudy groves,
And woo and win their vegetable Loves.
How Snowdrops cold, and blue-eyed Harebels blend
Their tender tears, as o'er the stream they bend;
The love-sick Violet, and the Primrose pale,
Bow their sweet heads, and whisper to the gale;
With secret sighs the Virgin Lily droops,
And jealous Cowslips hang their tawny cups.
How the young Rose in beauty's damask pride
Drinks the warm blushes of his bashful bride;
With honey'd lips enamour'd Woodbines meet,
Clasp with fond arms, and mix their kisses sweet.—
  Stay thy soft murmuring waters, gentle Rill;
Hush, whispering Winds; ye rustling Leaves, be still;

681

Rest, silver Butterflies, your quivering wings;
Alight, ye Beetles, from your airy rings;
Ye painted Moths, your gold-eyed plumage furl,
Bow your wide horns, your spiral trunks uncurl;
Glitter, ye Glow-worms, on your mossy beds;
Descend, ye Spiders, on your lengthened threads;
Slide here, ye horned Snails, with varnish'd shells;
Ye Bee-nymphs, listen in your waxen cells!

 BOTANIC MUSE! who in this latter age
Led by your airy hand the Swedish sage,
Bade his keen eye your secret haunts explore
On dewy dell, high wood, and winding shore;
Say on each leaf how tiny Graces dwell;
How laugh the Pleasures in a blossom's bell;
How insect Loves arise on cobweb wings,
Aim their light shafts, and point their little stings.

The Loves of the Plants, i, 1789

429   *Steam Power*

SOON shall thy arm, UNCONQUER'D STEAM! afar
Drag the slow barge, or drive the rapid car;
Or on wide-waving wings expanded bear
The flying-chariot through the fields of air.
—Fair crews triumphant, leaning from above,
Shall wave their fluttering kerchiefs as they move;
Or warrior-bands alarm the gaping crowd,
And armies shrink beneath the shadowy cloud.

The Economy of Vegetation, i, 1792

430 *Immortal Nature*

ROLL on, YE STARS! exult in youthful prime,
Mark with bright curves the printless steps of Time;
Near and more near your beamy cars approach,
And lessening orbs on lessening orbs encroach;—
Flowers of the sky! ye too to age must yield,
Frail as your silken sisters of the field!
Star after star from Heaven's high arch shall rush,
Suns sink on suns, and systems systems crush,
Headlong, extinct, to one dark centre fall,
And Death and Night and Chaos mingle all!
—Till o'er the wreck, emerging from the storm,
Immortal NATURE lifts her changeful form,
Mounts from her funeral pyre on wings of flame,
And soars and shines, another and the same.

The Economy of Vegetation, iv, 1792

JOHN WOLCOT
(PETER PINDAR)

1738–1819

431 *Apple Dumplings and a King*

ONCE on a time, a Monarch, tir'd with whooping,
Whipping and spurring,
Happy in worrying
A poor, defenceless, harmless buck,
The horse and rider wet as muck,
From his high consequence and wisdom stooping,
Enter'd, through curiosity, a cot,
Where sat a poor old woman and her pot.

683

JOHN WOLCOT

The wrinkl'd, blear-ey'd, good old granny,
In this same cot illum'd by many a cranny,
 Had finish'd apple dumplings for her pot:
In tempting row the naked dumplings lay,
When, lo! the Monarch, in his usual way,
Like lightning spoke, ' What's this? what's this? what?
  what? '

Then taking up a dumpling in his hand,
His eyes with admiration did expand—
 And oft did Majesty the dumpling grapple:
' 'Tis monstrous, monstrous hard indeed,' he cried:
' What makes it, pray, so hard? '—The Dame replied,
 Low curtsying, ' Please Your Majesty, the apple.'

' Very astonishing indeed!—strange thing! '
Turning the dumpling round, rejoined the King.
 ' 'Tis most extraordinary then, all this is—
 ' It beats Pinetti's conjuring all to pieces—
' Strange I should never of a dumpling dream—
' But, Goody, tell me where, where, where's the seam? '

' Sir, there's no seam (quoth she); I never knew
' That folks did apple dumplings *sew*.'—
 ' No! (cried the staring Monarch with a grin)
 ' How, how the devil got the apple in? '

Reader, thou likest not my tale—look'st *blue*—
 Thou art a Courtier,—roarest ' Lies, Lies, Lies! '—
  Do, for a moment, stop thy cries—
  I tell thee, roaring infidel, 'tis *true*.

JOHN WOLCOT

Why should it not be true? The *greatest men*
May ask a foolish question now and then—
    This is the language of all ages:
Folly lays many a trap—we can't escape it:
Nemo (says some one) *omnibus horis sapit:*
    Then why not Kings, like *me* and *other* sages?

Far from despising Kings, I like the breed,
    Provided *King-like* they behave:
Kings are an instrument we need,
    Just as we razors want—to shave;
To keep the State's face smooth—give it an air—
Like my Lord North's, so jolly, round, and fair.

My sense of Kings tho' freely I impart—
I hate not royalty, Heav'n knows my heart:
Princes and Princesses I like, so loyal—
    Great GEORGE's children are my great delight;
The sweet Augusta, and sweet Princess Royal,
    Obtain my love by day, and pray'rs by night.

Yes! I like Kings—and oft look back with pride
    Upon the Edwards, Harrys of our isle—
Great souls! in virtue as in valour try'd,
    Whose actions bid the cheek of Britons smile.

      Muse! let us also *forward* look,
      And take a peep into Fate's book.

Behold! the sceptre young AUGUSTUS sways;
    I hear the mingled voice of millions rise;
    I see uprais'd to Heav'n their ardent eyes;
That for their Monarch ask a length of days.

Bright in the *brightest* annals of renown,
Behold fair Fame his youthful temples crown
    With laurels of unfading bloom;
Behold DOMINION swell beneath his care,
And GENIUS, rising from a dark despair,
    His long-extinguish'd fires relume.

Such are the Kings that suit my taste, I own—
    Not *those* where all the *littlenesses* join—
Whose souls should start to find their lot a *throne*,
    And blush to show their noses on a coin.
                    An Apologetic Postscript to Ode upon Ode, 1787

GEORGE ELLIS (?)

1753–1815

432   *Rondeau*

*Humbly inscribed to the Right Hon. William Eden,
Minister Plenipotentiary of Commercial Affairs
at the Court of Versailles* *

OF EDEN lost, in ancient days,
    If we believe what Moses says,
A paltry pippin was the price,
One crab was bribe enough to entice
Frail human kind from Virtue's ways.

But now, when PITT, the all-perfect, sways,
No such vain lures the tempter lays,
    Too poor to be the purchase twice
            Of EDEN lost.

* William Eden, afterwards Lord Auckland, had been sent by Pitt, at a salary of £6,000, to negotiate the commercial treaty with France signed in 1786.

GEORGE ELLIS

The Dev'l grown wiser, to the gaze
Six thousand pounds a year displays,
   And finds success from the device;
   Finds this fair fruit too well suffice
To pay the peace, and honest praise,
          Of EDEN lost.

The European Magazine, December 1785

CHARLES DIBDIN

1745–1814

433   *Poor Tom, or the Sailor's Epitaph*

HERE, a sheer hulk, lies poor Tom Bowling,
   The darling of our crew;
No more he'll hear the tempest howling,
   For death has broach'd him to.
His form was of the manliest beauty,
   His heart was kind and soft,
Faithful below he did his duty,
   And now he's gone aloft.

Tom never from his word departed,
   His virtues were so rare,
His friends were many, and true hearted,
   His Poll was kind and fair:
And then he'd sing so blithe and jolly,
   Ah many's the time and oft!
But mirth is turn'd to melancholy,
   For Tom is gone aloft.

Yet shall Poor Tom find pleasant weather,
   When he who all commands
Shall give, to call life's crew together,
   The word to pipe all hands.

Thus death, who Kings and Tars dispatches,
   In vain Tom's life has doffed,
For, though his body 's under hatches,
   His soul is gone aloft.

          Poor Tom (also *Selected Songs*), **1790**

SAMUEL ROGERS

1763–1855

434   *A Wish*

MINE be a cot beside the hill;
   A bee-hive's hum shall sooth my ear;
A willowy brook, that turns a mill,
With many a fall, shall linger near.

The swallow, oft, beneath my thatch,
   Shall twitter from her clay-built nest;
Oft shall the pilgrim lift the latch,
   And share my meal, a welcome guest.

Around my ivy'd porch shall spring
   Each fragrant flower that drinks the dew;
And Lucy, at her wheel, shall sing,
   In russet gown and apron blue.

The village church, among the trees,
   Where first our marriage-vows were giv'n,
With merry peals shall swell the breeze,
   And point with taper spire to heav'n.

        An Ode to Superstition with some other
                        Poems, 1786

SAMUEL ROGERS

435   *Inscription on a Grot*

HENCE away, nor dare intrude!
    In this secret, shadowy cell
Musing MEMORY loves to dwell,
    With her sister Solitude.
Far from the busy world she flies,
To taste that peace the world denies.
Entranced she sits; from youth to age,
Reviewing Life's eventful page;
And noting, ere they fade away,
The little lines of yesterday.

The Pleasures of Memory, Part ii, 1792

WILLIAM WORDSWORTH

1770–1850

436   *Lines*

Written near Richmond, upon the Thames,
at Evening

HOW rich the wave, in front, imprest
    With evening-twilight's summer hues,
While, facing thus the crimson west,
    The boat her silent path pursues!
And see how dark the backward stream!
A little moment past, so smiling!
And still, perhaps, with faithless gleam,
Some other loiterer beguiling.

Such views the youthful bard allure,
    But, heedless of the following gloom,
He deems their colours shall endure
    'Till peace go with him to the tomb.

—And let him nurse his fond deceit,
And what if he must die in sorrow!
Who would not cherish dreams so sweet,
Though grief and pain may come to-morrow?

Glide gently, thus for ever glide,
O Thames! that other bards may see
As lovely visions by thy side
As now, fair river! come to me.
Oh glide, fair stream! for ever so;
Thy quiet soul on all bestowing,
'Till all our minds for ever flow,
As thy deep waters now are flowing.

Vain thought! yet be as now thou art,
That in thy waters may be seen
The image of a poet's heart,
How bright, how solemn, how serene!
Such heart did once the poet bless,
Who, pouring here a *later* ditty,
Could find no refuge from distress,
But in the milder grief of pity.

Remembrance! as we glide along,
For him suspend the dashing oar,
And pray that never child of Song
May know his freezing sorrows more.
How calm! how still! the only sound,
The dripping of the oar suspended!
—The evening darkness gathers round
By virtue's holiest powers attended.

        Written 1789; *Lyrical Ballads*, 1798.

* Collins's Ode on the death of Thomson.

437   *Swans*

NOW while the solemn evening Shadows sail,
  On red slow-waving pinions down the vale,
And, fronting the bright west in stronger lines,
The oak its dark'ning boughs and foliage twines,
I love beside the flowing lake to stray,
Where winds the road along the secret bay;
By rills that tumble down the woody steeps,
And run in transport to the dimpling deeps;
Along the ' wild meand'ring ' shore to view,
Obsequious Grace the winding swan pursue.
He swells his lifted chest, and backward flings
His bridling neck between his tow'ring wings;
Stately, and burning in his pride, divides,
And glorying looks around, the silent tides:
On as he floats, the silver'd waters glow,
Proud of the varying arch and moveless form of snow.
While tender Cares and mild domestic Loves
With furtive watch pursue her as she moves,
The female with a meeker charm succeeds,
And her brown little ones around her leads,
Nibbling the water lilies as they pass,
Or playing wanton with the floating grass:
She in a mother's care, her beauty's pride
Forgets, unweary'd watching every side,
She calls them near, and with affection sweet
Alternately relieves their weary feet;
Alternately they mount her back, and rest
Close by her mantling wings' embraces prest.

                              An Evening Walk, **1793**

WILLIAM WORDSWORTH

438   *The Swiss Peasant*

ONCE Man entirely free, alone and wild,
   Was bless'd as free—for he was Nature's child.
He, all superior but his God disdain'd,
Walk'd none restraining, and by none restrain'd
Confess'd no law but what his reason taught,
Did all he wish'd, and wish'd but what he ought.
As Man in his primæval dower array'd
The image of his glorious sire display'd,
Ev'n so, by vestal Nature guarded, here
The traces of primæval Man appear.
The native dignity no forms debase,
The eye sublime, and surly lion-grace.
The slave of none, of beasts alone the lord,
He marches with his flute, his book, and sword,
Well taught by that to feel his rights, prepar'd
With this ' the blessings he enjoys to guard.'

Descriptive Sketches, 1793

WILLIAM GIFFORD

1756–1826

439   *The Della Cruscans*

OH for the good old times! When all was new,
   And every hour brought prodigies to view,
Our sires in unaffected language told
Of streams of amber, and of rocks of gold:
Full of their theme, they spurn'd all idle art,
And the plain tale was trusted to the heart.
Now all is changed! We fume and fret, poor elves,
Less to display our subject, than ourselves:
Whate'er we paint—a grot, a flow'r, a bird,
Heavens, how we sweat, laboriously absurd!

692

WILLIAM GIFFORD

Words of gigantic bulk, and uncouth sound,
In rattling triads the long sentence bound;
While points with points, with periods periods jar,
And the whole work seems one continued war!
Is not THIS sad?

   Friend. ' 'Tis pitiful, God knows,
' 'Tis wondrous pitiful.' E'en take the prose;
But for the poetry—oh, that, my friend,
I still aspire—nay, smile not—to defend.
You praise our sires, but, though they wrote with force,
Their rhymes were vicious, and their diction coarse;
We want their *strength*: agreed. But we atone
For that, and more, by *sweetness* all our own.
For instance—' * Hasten to the lawny vale,
' Where yellow morning breathes her saffron gale,
' And bathes the landscape—'

   Poet. Pshaw! I have it here:
' A voice seraphic grasps my listening ear:
' Wond'ring I gaze; when lo! methought afar,
' More bright than dauntless day's imperial star,
' A godlike form advances.'

   F. You suppose
These lines perhaps too turgid; what of those?
' THE MIGHTY MOTHER—'

   P. Now 'tis plain you sneer,
For † Weston's self could find no semblance here:

---

* Hasten, &c.—This and the following quotation are taken
from the ' Laurel of Liberty ', a work on which the great author
[Robert Merry] most justly rests his claims to immortality.

† Weston.—This indefatigable gentleman has been attacking
the moral character of Pope in the *Gentleman's Magazine*, with
all the virulence of Gildon, all the impudence of Smedley, and
all the ignorance of Curll and his associates.

Weston! who slunk from truth's imperious light,
Swells, like a filthy toad, with secret spite,
And, envying the fair fame he cannot hope,
Spits his black venom at the dust of Pope.
Reptile accurs'd!—O memorable long,
If there be force in virtue or in song,
O injur'd bard! accept the grateful strain,
That I, the humblest of the tuneful train,
With glowing heart, yet trembling hand, repay
For many a pensive, many a sprightly lay:
So may thy varied verse, from age to age,
Inform the simple, and delight the sage!
While canker'd Weston, and his loathsome rhymes,
Stink in the nose of all succeeding times!

   Enough. But where (for these, you seem to say,
Are samples of the high, heroic lay)
Where are the soft, the tender strains, that call
For the moist eye, bow'd head, and lengthen'd drawl?
Lo! here——' Canst thou, Matilda, urge my fate,
' And bid me mourn thee?—yes, and mourn too late!
  O rash, severe decree! my maddening brain
' Cannot the ponderous agony sustain;
' But forth I rush, from vale to mountain run,
' And with my mind's thick gloom obscure the sun.

   Heavens! if our ancient vigour were not fled,
Could VERSE like this be written, or be read?
VERSE! THAT's the mellow fruit of toil intense,
Inspir'd by genius, and inform'd by sense;
THIS, the abortive progeny of Pride
And Dulness, gentle pair, for aye allied;
Begotten without thought, born without pains,
The ropy drivel of rheumatic brains.

694   *The Baviad,* 1794

MATTHEW GREGORY LEWIS

1775–1818

440 *Alonzo the Brave and Fair Imogine*

A WARRIOR so bold and a virgin so bright
　　Conversed, as they sat on the green;
They gazed on each other with tender delight:
Alonzo the Brave was the name of the knight,
　　The maid's was the Fair Imogine.

—' And, oh!' said the youth, ' since to-morrow I go
　　' To fight in a far-distant land,
' Your tears for my absence soon leaving to flow,
' Some other will court you, and you will bestow
　　' On a wealthier suitor your hand.'—

—' Oh! hush these suspicions,' Fair Imogine said,
　　' Offensive to love and to me!
' For, if you be living, or if you be dead,
' I swear by the Virgin, that none in your stead
　　' Shall husband of Imogine be.

' And if e'er for another my heart should decide,
　　' Forgetting Alonzo the Brave,
' God grant, that, to punish my falsehood and pride,
' Your ghost at the marriage may sit by my side,
' May tax me with perjury, claim me as bride,
　　' And bear me away to the grave!'—

To Palestine hasten'd the hero so bold;
　　His love she lamented him sore:
But scarce had a twelvemonth elapsed, when behold,
A Baron all cover'd with jewels and gold
　　Arrived at Fair Imogine's door.

His treasure, his presents, his spacious domain,
   Soon made her untrue to her vows:
He dazzled her eyes; he bewilder'd her brain;
He caught her affections so light and so vain,
   And carried her home as his spouse.

And now had the marriage been bless'd by the priest;
   The revelry now was begun:
The tables they groan'd with the weight of the feast;
Nor yet had the laughter and merriment ceased,
   When the bell of the castle toll'd—' one!'

Then first with amazement Fair Imogine found
   That a stranger was placed by her side:
His air was terrific; he utter'd no sound;
He spoke not, he moved not, he look'd not around,
   But earnestly gazed on the bride.

His vizor was closed, and gigantic his height;
   His armour was sable to view:
All pleasure and laughter were hush'd at his sight;
The dogs, as they eyed him, drew back in affright;
   The lights in the chamber burnt blue!

His presence all bosoms appear'd to dismay;
   The guests sat in silence and fear:
At length spoke the bride, while she trembled:—' I pray,
' Sir Knight, that your helmet aside you would lay,
   ' And deign to partake of our cheer.'—

The lady is silent: the stranger complies,
   His vizor he slowly unclosed:
Oh! then what a sight met Fair Imogine's eyes!
What words can express her dismay and surprise,
   When a skeleton's head was exposed!

696

All present then utter'd a terrified shout;
    All turn'd with disgust from the scene.
The worms they crept in, and the worms they crept out,
And sported his eyes and his temples about,
    While the spectre address'd Imogine:

' Behold me, thou false one! behold me!' he cried;
    ' Remember Alonzo the Brave!
' God grants, that, to punish thy falsehood and pride,
' My ghost at thy marriage should sit by thy side,
' Should tax thee with perjury, claim thee as bride,
    ' And bear thee away to the grave!'

Thus saying, his arms round the lady he wound,
    While loudly she shriek'd in dismay;
Then sank with his prey through the wide-yawning ground:
Nor ever again was Fair Imogine found,
    Or the spectre who bore her away.

Not long lived the Baron: and none since that time
    To inhabit the castle presume;
For chronicles tell, that, by order sublime,
There Imogine suffers the pain of her crime,
    And mourns her deplorable doom.

At midnight four times in each year does her sprite,
    When mortals in slumber are bound,
Array'd in her bridal apparel of white,
Appear in the hall with the skeleton-knight,
    And shriek as he whirls her around.

While they drink out of skulls newly torn from the grave,
    Dancing round them pale spectres are seen:
Their liquor is blood, and this horrible stave
They howl:—' To the health of Alonzo the Brave,
    And his consort, the False Imogine!'   *The Monk*, 1795

441   *Songs of the Pixies*

WHOM the untaught Shepherds call
 Pixies in their madrigal,
Fancy's children, here we dwell:
 Welcome, Ladies! to our cell.
Here the wren of softest note
 Builds its nest and warbles well;
Here the blackbird strains his throat;
 Welcome, Ladies! to our cell.

When fades the moon to shadowy-pale,
And scuds the cloud before the gale,
Ere the Morn all gem-bedight
Hath streak'd the East with rosy light,
We sip the furze-flower's fragrant dews
Clad in robes of rainbow hues;
Or sport amid the shooting gleams
To the tune of distant-tinkling teams,
While lusty Labour scouting sorrow
Bids the Dame a glad good-morrow,
Who jogs the accustom'd road along,
And paces cheery to her cheering song.

 But not our filmy pinion
We scorch amid the blaze of day,
When Noontide's fiery-tressèd minion
  Flashes the fervid ray.
  Aye from the sultry heat
  We to the cave retreat

698

O'ercanopied by huge roots intertwin'd
With wildest texture, blacken'd o'er with age:
Round them their mantle green the ivies bind,
  Beneath whose foliage pale
  Fann'd by the unfrequent gale
We shield us from the Tyrant's mid-day rage.

  Thither, while the murmuring throng
  Of wild-bees hum their drowsy song,
  By Indolence and Fancy brought,
  A youthful Bard, ' unknown to Fame,'
  Wooes the Queen of Solemn Thought,
And heaves the gentle misery of a sigh
   Gazing with tearful eye,
  As round our sandy grot appear
  Many a rudely-sculptur'd name
   To pensive Memory dear!
Weaving gay dreams of sunny-tinctur'd hue,
  We glance before his view;
O'er his hush'd soul our soothing witcheries shed
And twine the future garland round his head.

  When Evening's dusky car
  Crown'd with her dewy star
Steals o'er the fading sky in shadowy flight;
  On leaves of aspen trees
  We tremble to the breeze
Veil'd from the grosser ken of mortal sight.
  Or, haply, at the visionary hour,
Along our wildly-bower'd sequester'd walk,
We listen to the enamour'd rustic's talk;

Heave with the heavings of the maiden's breast,
Where young-eyed Loves have hid their turtle nest;
   Or guide of soul-subduing power
The glance that from the half-confessing eye
Darts the fond question or the soft reply.

Or through the mystic ringlets of the vale
We flash our faery feet in gamesome prank;
Or, silent-sandal'd, pay our defter court,
Circling the Spirit of the Western Gale,
Where wearied with his flower-caressing sport,
Supine he slumbers on a violet bank;
Then with quaint music hymn the parting gleam
By lonely Otter's sleep-persuading stream;
Or where his wave with loud unquiet song
Dash'd o'er the rocky channel froths along;
Or where, his silver waters smooth'd to rest,
The tall tree's shadow sleeps upon his breast.

     Hence thou lingerer, Light!
     Eve saddens into Night.
Mother of wildly-working dreams! we view
    The sombre hours, that round thee stand
    With down-cast eyes (a duteous band!)
Their dark robes dripping with the heavy dew.
     Sorceress of the ebon throne!
     Thy power the Pixies own,
     When round thy raven brow
     Heaven's lucent roses glow,
  And clouds in watery colours drest
Float in light drapery o'er thy sable vest:

What time the pale moon sheds a softer day
Mellowing the woods beneath its pensive beam:
For mid the quivering light 'tis ours to play,
Aye dancing to the cadence of the stream.

Welcome, Ladies! to the cell
Where the blameless Pixies dwell:
But thou, Sweet Nymph! proclaim'd our Faery Queen,
With what obeisance meet
Thy presence shall we greet?
For lo! attendant on thy steps are seen
Graceful Ease in artless stole,
And white-robed Purity of soul,
With Honour's softer mien;
Mirth of the loosely-flowing hair,
And meek-eyed Pity eloquently fair,
Whose tearful cheeks are lovely to the view,
As snow-drop wet with dew.

Unboastful Maid! though now the Lily pale
Transparent grace thy beauties meek;
Yet ere again along the impurpling vale,
The purpling vale and elfin-haunted grove,
Young Zephyr his fresh flowers profusely throws,
We'll tinge with livelier hues thy cheek;
And, haply, from the nectar-breathing Rose
Extract a Blush for Love!

Poems on Various Subjects, 1796 (revised)

442

To a Young Ass

Its Mother being tethered near it

POOR little Foal of an oppressed race!
  I love the languid patience of thy face:
And oft with gentle hand I give thee bread,
And clap thy ragged coat, and pat thy head.
But what thy dulled spirits hath dismay'd,
That never thou dost sport along the glade?
And (most unlike the nature of things young)
That earthward still thy moveless head is hung?
Do thy prophetic fears anticipate,
Meek Child of Misery! thy future fate?
The starving meal, and all the thousand aches
' Which patient Merit of the Unworthy takes '?
Or is thy sad heart thrill'd with filial pain
To see thy wretched mother's shorten'd chain?
And truly, very piteous is *her* lot—
Chain'd to a log within a narrow spot,
Where the close-eaten grass is scarcely seen,
While sweet around her waves the tempting green!

  Poor Ass! thy master should have learnt to show
Pity—best taught by fellowship of Woe!
For much I fear me that *He* lives like thee,
Half famish'd in a land of Luxury!
How *askingly* its footsteps hither bend?
It seems to say, ' And have I then *one* friend?'
Innocent foal! thou poor despis'd forlorn!
I hail thee *Brother*—spite of the fool's scorn!
And fain would take thee with me, in the Dell
Of Peace and mild Equality to dwell,

702

Where Toil shall call the charmer Health his bride,
And Laughter tickle Plenty's ribless side!
How thou wouldst toss thy heels in gamesome play,
And frisk about, as lamb or kitten gay!
Yea! and more musically sweet to me
Thy dissonant harsh bray of joy would be,
Than warbled melodies that soothe to rest
The aching of pale Fashion's vacant breast!

The Morning Chronicle, December 30, 1794 (revised)

443 *Reflections*

On having left a Place of Retirement

LOW was our pretty Cot: our tallest Rose
Peep'd at the chamber-window. We could hear
At silent noon, and eve, and early morn,
The Sea's faint murmur. In the open air
Our Myrtles blossom'd; and across the porch
Thick Jasmins twined: the little landscape round
Was green and woody, and refresh'd the eye.
It was a spot which you might aptly call
The Valley of Seclusion! Once I saw
(Hallowing his Sabbath-day by quietness)
A wealthy son of Commerce saunter by,
Bristowa's citizen: methought, it calm'd
His thirst of idle gold, and made him muse
With wiser feelings: for he paus'd, and look'd
With a pleas'd sadness, and gaz'd all around,
Then eyed our Cottage, and gaz'd round again,
And sigh'd, and said, it was a Blessed Place.
And we *were* bless'd. Oft with patient ear
Long-listening to the viewless sky-lark's note
(Viewless, or haply for a moment seen

Gleaming on sunny wings) in whisper'd tones
I've said to my Beloved, ' Such, sweet Girl!
The inobtrusive song of Happiness,
Unearthly minstrelsy! then only heard
When the Soul seeks to hear; when all is hush'd,
And the Heart listens!'

But the time, when first
From that low Dell, steep up the stony Mount
I climb'd with perilous toil and reach'd the top,
Oh! what a goodly scene! *Here* the bleak mount,
The bare bleak mountain speckled thin with sheep;
Grey clouds, that shadowing spot the sunny fields;
And river, now with bushy rocks o'er-brow'd,
Now winding bright and full, with naked banks;
And seats, and lawns, the Abbey and the wood,
And cots, and hamlets, and faint city-spire;
The Channel *there*, the Islands and white sails,
Dim coasts, and cloud-like hills, and shoreless Ocean—·
It seem'd like Omnipresence! God, methought,
Had built him there a Temple: the whole World
Seem'd *imag'd* in its vast circumference:
No *wish* profan'd my overwhelmed heart.
Blest hour! It was a luxury,—to be!

Ah! quiet Dell! dear Cot, and Mount sublime!
I was constrain'd to quit you. Was it right,
While my unnumber'd brethren toil'd and bled,
That I should dream away the entrusted hours
On rose-leaf beds, pampering the coward heart
With feelings all too delicate for use?
Sweet is the tear that from some Howard's eye
Drops on the cheek of one he lifts from earth:
And he that works me good with unmov'd face,

Does it but half: he chills me while he aids,
My benefactor, not my brother man!
Yet even this, this cold beneficence
Praise, praise it, O my Soul! oft as thou scann'st
The sluggard Pity's vision-weaving tribe!
Who sigh for Wretchedness, yet shun the Wretched,
Nursing in some delicious solitude
Their slothful loves and dainty sympathies!
I therefore go, and join head, heart, and hand,
Active and firm, to fight the bloodless fight
Of Science, Freedom, and the Truth in Christ.

Yet oft when after honourable toil
Rests the tir'd mind, and waking loves to dream,
My spirit shall revisit thee, dear Cot!
Thy Jasmin and thy window-peeping Rose,
And Myrtles fearless of the mild sea-air.
And I shall sigh fond wishes—sweet Abode!
Ah!—had none greater! And that all had such!
It might be so—but the time is not yet.
Speed it, O Father! Let thy Kingdom come!

The Monthly Magazine, October 1796

ROBERT SOUTHEY

1774-1843

444   *Inscription*

For a Tablet on the Banks of a Stream

STRANGER! awhile upon this mossy bank
Recline thee. If the Sun rides high, the breeze,
That loves to ripple o'er the rivulet,
Will play around thy brow, and the cool sound
Of running waters soothe thee. Mark how clear
It sparkles o'er the shallows, and behold

Where o'er its surface wheels with restless speed
Yon glossy insect, on the sand below
How the swift shadow flies. The stream is pure
In solitude, and many a healthful herb
Bends o'er its course and drinks the vital wave:
But passing on amid the haunts of man,
It finds pollution there, and rolls from thence
A tainted tide. Seek'st thou for HAPPINESS?
Go Stranger, sojourn in the woodland cot
Of INNOCENCE, and thou shalt find her there.

Poems, 1797

445   *Written on a Sunday Morning*

GO thou and seek the House of Prayer!
   I to the Woodlands wend, and there
In lovely Nature see the GOD OF LOVE.
   The swelling organ's peal
   Wakes not my soul to zeal,
Like the wild music of the wind-swept grove.
The gorgeous altar and the mystic vest
Rouse not such ardor in my breast,
   As where the noon-tide beam,
   Flash'd from the broken stream,
Quick vibrates on the dazzled sight;
   Or where the cloud-suspended rain
   Sweeps in shadows o'er the plain;
Or when reclining on the clift's huge height
I mark the billows burst in silver light.

   Go thou and seek the House of Prayer!
   I to the Woodlands shall repair,
   Feed with all Nature's charms mine eyes,
   And hear all Nature's melodies.

The primrose bank shall there dispense
Faint fragrance to the awaken'd sense,
The morning beams that life and joy impart
Shall with their influence warm my heart,
And the full tear that down my cheek will steal,
Shall speak the prayer of praise I feel!

Go thou and seek the House of Prayer!
I to the woodlands bend my way
   And meet RELIGION there.
She needs not haunt the high-arch'd dome to pray
Where storied windows dim the doubtful day:
With LIBERTY she loves to rove,
   Wide o'er the heathy hill or cowslip'd dale;
Or seek the shelter of the embowering grove,
   Or with the streamlet wind along the vale.
Sweet are these scenes to her, and when the night
Pours in the north her silver streams of light,
She woos Reflection in the silent gloom,
And ponders on the world to come.

Poems, 1797

446   *The Soldier's Wife*

Dactylics

WEARY way-wanderer, languid and sick at heart,
   Travelling painfully over the rugged road,
Wild-visag'd Wanderer! ah for thy heavy chance!

Sorely thy little one drags by thee bare-footed,
Cold is the baby that hangs at thy bending back,
Meagre and livid and screaming its wretchedness.

* Woe-begone mother, half anger, half agony,
As over thy shoulder thou lookest to hush the babe,
Bleakly the blinding snow beats in thy hagged face.

Thy husband will never return from the war again,
Cold is thy hopeless heart even as Charity—
Cold as thy famish'd babes—God help thee, widow'd One!

Poems, 1797

447 *The Widow*

Sapphics

COLD was the night wind, drifting fast the snows fell,
  Wide were the downs and shelterless and naked,
When a poor Wanderer struggled on her journey
      Weary and way-sore.

Drear were the downs, more dreary her reflections;
Cold was the night wind, colder was her bosom!
She had no home, the world was all before her,
      She had no shelter.

Fast o'er the bleak heath rattling drove a chariot,
' Pity me!' feebly cried the poor night wanderer.
' Pity me Strangers! lest with cold and hunger
      Here I should perish.

' Once I had friends,—but they have all forsook me!
' Once I had parents,—they are now in Heaven!
' I had a home once—I had once a husband—
      ' Pity me Strangers!

  * This stanza was supplied by S. T. COLERIDGE.

ROBERT SOUTHEY

' I had a home once—I had once a husband—
' I am a Widow poor and broken-hearted ! '
Loud blew the wind, unheard was her complaining,
      On drove the chariot.

On the cold snows she laid her down to rest her ;
She heard a horseman, ' pity me ! ' she groan'd out ;
Loud blew the wind, unheard was her complaining,
      On went the horseman.

Worn out with anguish, toil and cold and hunger,
Down sunk the Wanderer, sleep had seiz'd her senses ;
There, did the Traveller find her in the morning,
      GOD had releast her.

Poems, 1797

GEORGE CANNING

1770–1827

448   *Sapphics*

The Friend of Humanity and the Knife-Grinder

FRIEND OF HUMANITY

' NEEDY Knife-grinder ! whither are you going ?
    Rough is the road, your Wheel is out of order—
Bleak blows the blast ;—your hat has got a hole in't,
      So have your breeches !

' Weary Knife-grinder ! little think the proud ones,
Who in their coaches roll along the turnpike-
-road, what hard work 'tis crying all day " Knives and
      Scissars to grind O ! "

' Tell me, Knife-grinder, how you came to grind knives ?
Did some rich man tyrannically use you ?
Was it the 'Squire ? or Parson of the Parish ?
      Or the Attorney ?

GEORGE CANNING

' Was it the 'Squire for killing of his Game? or
Covetous Parson for his Tythes distraining?
Or roguish Lawyer made you lose your little

All in a law-suit?

' (Have you not read the Rights of Man, by Tom Paine?)
Drops of compassion tremble on my eye-lids,
Ready to fall, as soon as you have told your

Pitiful story.'

KNIFE-GRINDER

' Story! God bless you! I have none to tell, Sir,
Only last night a-drinking at the Chequers,
This poor old hat and breeches, as you see, were

Torn in a scuffle.

' Constables came up for to take me into
Custody; they took me before the Justice;
Justice Oldmixon put me in the Parish-

-Stocks for a Vagrant.

' I should be glad to drink your Honour's health in
A Pot of Beer, if you would give me Sixpence;
But for my part, I never love to meddle

With Politics, Sir.'

FRIEND OF HUMANITY

' *I* give thee Sixpence! I will see thee damn'd first—
Wretch! whom no sense of wrongs can rouse to vengeance—
Sordid, unfeeling, reprobate, degraded,

Spiritless outcast!'

(*Kicks the Knife-grinder, overturns his Wheel, and exit in
a transport of republican enthusiasm and universal philan-
thropy.*)

The Anti-Jacobin, No. 2, November 27, 1797

449   *The Soldier's Friend*

Dactylics

COME, little Drummer Boy, lay down your knapsack
     here:
I am the Soldier's Friend—here are some Books for you;
Nice clever Books, by TOM PAINE the Philanthropist.

Here's Half-a-crown for you—here are some Handbills
     too—
Go to the Barracks, and give all the Soldiers some.
Tell them the Sailors are all in a Mutiny.

         [*Exit Drummer Boy, with Hand-bills and
           Half-a-crown.—Manet Soldier's Friend.*

Liberty's friends thus all learn to amalgamate,
Freedom's volcanic explosion prepares itself,
Despots shall bow to the Fasces of Liberty,
     Reason, Philosophy, ' fiddledum diddledum,'
     Peace and Fraternity, higgledy, piggledy,
     Higgledy, piggledy, ' fiddledum diddledum.'

         Et cætera, et cætera, et cætera.

     The Anti-Jacobin, No. 5, December 11, 1797

450   *Song*

                    By Rogero, in The Rovers

WHENE'ER with haggard eyes I view
       This Dungeon, that I'm rotting in,
I think of those Companions true
    Who studied with me at the U—
            —NIVERSITY of *Gottingen,*—
            —NIVERSITY of *Gottingen.*

                    (*Weeps, and pulls out a blue kerchief,
                    with which he wipes his eyes; gazing
                    tenderly at it, he proceeds—*

Sweet kerchief, check'd with heav'nly blue,
    Which once my love sat knotting in!—
Alas! MATILDA *then* was true!—
    At least I thought so at the U—
            —NIVERSITY of *Gottingen*—
            —NIVERSITY of *Gottingen.*

                    (*At the repetition of this Line* ROGERO
                    clanks his Chains in cadence.)

Barbs! Barbs! alas! how swift you flew
    Her neat Post-Waggon trotting in!
Ye bore MATILDA from my view.
    Forlorn I languish'd at the U—
            —NIVERSITY of *Gottingen*—
            —NIVERSITY of *Gottingen.*

GEORGE CANNING

This faded form! this pallid hue!
  This blood my veins is clotting in.
My years are many—They were few
  When first I entered at the U—
      —NIVERSITY of *Gottingen*—
      —NIVERSITY of *Gottingen*.

There first for thee my passion grew,
  Sweet! sweet MATILDA POTTINGEN!
Thou wast the daughter of my Tu-
  —TOR, *Law Professor* at the U—
      —NIVERSITY of *Gottingen*!—
      —NIVERSITY of *Gottingen*!—

Sun, moon, and thou vain world, adieu,
  That kings and priests are plotting in:
Here doom'd to starve on water-gru—
  —el, never shall I see the U—
      —NIVERSITY of *Gottingen*—
      —NIVERSITY of *Gottingen*.

           The Anti-Jacobin, No. 30, June 4, 1798

INDEX OF AUTHORS

The references are to the numbers of the poems.

INDEX OF AUTHORS

INDEX OF FIRST LINES

INDEX OF FIRST LINES

INDEX OF FIRST LINES

INDEX OF FIRST LINES

INDEX OF FIRST LINES

INDEX OF FIRST LINES

INDEX OF FIRST LINES

INDEX OF FIRST LINES

INDEX OF FIRST LINES

INDEX OF FIRST LINES

INDEX OF FIRST LINES

PRINTED IN GREAT BRITAIN
AT THE UNIVERSITY PRESS, OXFORD
BY VIVIAN RIDLER
PRINTER TO THE UNIVERSITY